The Making of South Africa
Culture and Politics

Aran S. MacKinnon
State University of West Georgia

PEARSON
Prentice Hall

Upper Saddle River, NJ 07458

Library of Congress Cataloging-in-Publication Data

MacKinnon, Aran S.
  The making of South Africa : culture and politics / Aran S. MacKinnon.—1st ed.
    p. cm.
  Includes bibliographical references (p.) and index.
  ISBN 0-13-040681-3
    1. South Africa—History. 2. South Africa—Politics and government. 1. Title.

DT1787.M33 2003
968—dc21

2003054903

VP, Editorial Director: Charlyce Jones Owen
Senior Acquisitions Editor: Charles Cavaliere
Associate Editor: Emsal Hasan
Editorial Assistant: Shannon Corliss
Executive Marketing Manager: Heather Shelstaad
Senior Marketing Assistant: Jennifer Bryant
Manager Editor: Joanne Riker
Production Editor: Jan H. Schwartz
Manufacturing Buyer: Tricia Kenny
Cover Design: Bruce Kenselaar
Composition: This book was set in AGaramond 11/13. Pine Tree Composition, Inc.
Printer: RR Donnelley and Sons
Cover Printer: Phoenix Color Corporation
Credits and acknowledgments borrowed from other sources and reproduced, with permission,
in this textbook appear on the appropriate page within the text.

Cover photo: Courtesy of the Library of Congress

Pearson Education LTD.
Pearson Education Australia PTY, Limited
Pearson Education Singapore, Pte. Ltd.
Pearson Education North Asia Ltd.
Pearson Education Canada, Ltd.
Pearson Educación de Mexico, S.A. de C.V.
Pearson Education—Japan
Pearson Education Malaysia, Pte. Ltd.

10 9 8 7 6 5 4 3 2 1

ISBN: 0-13-040681-3

Contents

Maps

The following list of maps covers the range of geographic, environmental, human, and historical information that supports and reflects the various developments covered in the text. The maps are intended to provide readers with a spatial and visual dimension to the history of South Africa.

Illustrations

The following list represents the range of photographs used in the text to illustrate particular people, historical events, or locations, which are either discussed directly in the text, or are the backdrop to a particular issue or event. The photographs were drawn from various collections in South Africa and overseas.

Abbreviations

The following list of abbreviations and acronyms represents the most common and standard uses of terms for various South African organizations, political parties, and government bodies that are found in this text. In cases where an abbreviation denotes more than one organization or body, such as SAP (South African Party and South African Police) this is noted in the list and in the text where the term is found. All other abbreviations and acronyms are noted and explained in the text.

AAC: All African Convention
ANC: African National Congress (formerly SANNC: South African Native National Congress)
CAD: Coloured Affairs Department
APO: African People's Organization
AWB: Afrikaner Weerstands Beweging (Afrikaner Resistance Movement)
AZAPO: Azanian People's Organization
BSA: Black Students Association
CCB: Civil Cooperation Bureau
CODESA: Convention for a Democratic South Africa
CONTRALESA: Congress of Traditional Leaders of South Africa
COSATU: Congress of South African Trade Unions
ESCOM: Electricity Supply Commission
FNLA: Front for the National Liberation of Angola
FOSATU: Federation of Trade Unions of South Africa
FRELIMO: Front for the Liberation of Mozambique
GEAR: Growth Employment and Redistribution Program
GNU: Government of National Unity
HNP: Herstigte Nasionale Party (Reformed National Party)
IFP: Inkatha Freedom Party
ISCOR: Iron and Steel Corporation of South Africa
LMS: London Missionary Society
MDM: Mass Democratic Movement
MK: Mkhonto we Sizwe (Spear of the Nation)
MPLA: Popular Movement for the Liberation of Angola
NCOP: National Council of Provinces
NEDLAC: National Economic Development and Labour Council
NIC: Natal Indian Congress
NP: National Party
NRC: Native Representative Council (also Native Recruiting Corporation)
NUM: National Union of Mineworkers

NUSAS: National Union of South African Students
OAU: Organization of African Unity
OFS: Orange Free State (Free State)
PAC: Pan African Congress
PUTCO: Public Utility Transport Company
RDP: Reconstruction and Development Programme
SACP: South African Communist Party
SADC: Southern African Development Community
SAFTU: South African Federation of Trade Unions
SAIC: South African Indian Congress
SANLAM: Suid-Afrikaanse Nasionale Lewensassuransie Maatskappy (South
         African National Afrikaner Insurance Company)
SANNC: South African Native National Congress
SAP: South African Party (also South African Police)
SASOL: South African Synthetic Oil Company
SWAPO: South West African People's Organization
TRC: Truth and Reconciliation Commission
UDF: United Democratic Front
UDM: United Democratic Movement
UNITA: National Union for the Total Independence of Angola
VOC: Vereenigde Oost-Indische Compagnie (Dutch East India Company)

Preface

In this text I have sought to provide readers with an overview and details of some of the major developments in South African history. It has been based upon my interpretation of most of the major recent works on South Africa. In rendering the narrative for the chapters, I have sought to provide a sense of what I see as the most recent consensus of historians on the major features and important trends in South African history. In places where there is no consensus, or where there is controversy, I have attempted to capture the nature of the current debate and to suggest what I see as the most compelling arguments. As with any text such as this, compromises had to be made. I do not pretend to have covered all aspects of the field, but I have emphasized what I feel is a judicious blend of social, economic, and political history. I remain an unabashed materialist historian, and so my interpretations of these features of South African history are grounded in an analysis of the country's political economy. While I have sought to emphasize the African story, I have attempted to show that South Africa's history was made by many people from different backgrounds who often had different experiences, but all of whom share points of historical convergence in this region.

The focus of the text, of necessity, is rigidly on South Africa, with only brief references to states beyond. This is not intended to convey a sense that these states are not important parts of the broader region, but rather that their stories are perhaps best told in their own rights, where more justice can be done to them. The major themes I have sought to highlight are the spatial dimensions of social, political, and economic interaction, and the black initiative in transforming the country. I will not comment here on the challenges posed for South African history by things such as terminology and orthography, save to say again, I have sought to employ what I see as the consensus of historians' views and practices.

It is both a curious and pleasant minor note about the current position of South Africa in our globalizing world that I completed this work while sipping rooibos tea imported to the U.S. from South Africa. Rooibos is an herbal tea credited with medicinal properties first used by the San people of the Cape region, but it has become widely popular in South Africa and now, perhaps it will become so in the rest of the world. This apparently trivial thing seems to me significant for two reasons. First, it shows off just one of the fine things about the country, and second, it shows that South Africa, since the transition from apartheid, is able to take its place on the world stage for very positive reasons. In the face of the current challenges for the health and welfare of South Africans, it is gratifying to see that the struggles of the people of the country have now provided great hope for a promising future.

Acknowledgments

This text emerged from an idea and an inspiration from two friends and colleagues. David Duncan first suggested I consider writing a text on South African history, and my wife and colleague, Elaine MacKinnon, inspired me to see it through to completion. It is to her that I owe my greatest thanks for her tireless patience, support, and understanding. I dedicate this book to her, to my son Kieran, and to my parents, Ruth Ann and Victor MacKinnon, who first introduced me to South Africa nearly twenty years ago.

This book has been shaped by my work and research in South Africa, the U.K., and the United States. I have benefitted from the enormous intellectual contributions of valued colleagues and mentors. First, I would like to thank William Beinart, Alan Jeeves, and Shula Marks for their support and mentoring over the years. To paraphrase, if I have seen further, it has been by standing on their shoulders. I would also like to thank friends and colleagues in South Africa, without whose support and hospitality this work could not have been undertaken. The Fenners, the Horlocks, Dumisani Hadebe, Ntombi Mkhize, and Mavis Mdhladhla were all helpful in various ways. My colleagues in South Africa Peter Alexander, Wessel Visser, Philip Warhurst, and Brown Maaba were also invaluable for my thinking about aspects of the book. I owe special thanks to my dear friends in South Africa, Simon and Tracy Howie and their family, Lesley-Anne Wilkinson and her family, as well as Sue Rolando and Rob Sansbury. Without their generosity and hospitality, I could not have done the final research needed for the book. Gregor and Wendy MacKinnon made it possible for me to survive my years in London, and Phyllis McClarnand's help made it possible for me to finish writing the text. Thanks are due to Charles Cavaliere, and Jan Schwartz, my editors at Prentice Hall, for their hard work and patience with the book. I would also like to thank the University of West Georgia for a Faculty Research Grant which enabled me to return to South Africa to conduct further research. I would also like to thank Anthony Q. Cheesboro, Earl Mulderink III, Wayne Ackerson, Gretchen Eick, Jonathan T. Reynolds, and John Mason, for their reviews and insightful commentary on various drafts of the manuscript. Finally, I want to thank my valued colleagues in the Department of History at the University of West Georgia, especially Jonathan Ablard and Steve Goodson for their insightful comments on the manuscript.

CHAPTER I

The Setting: Climate, Geography, and People in South Africa

The prehistory (i.e., the period before written material became the dominant part of the human record) and early history of South Africa show the remarkable and important role that indigenous people have played in African and world history. These periods also show that **"Africans"**, (those people of the Khoesan, Nguni, and Sotho-Tswana language groups, which are part of the continent-based Bantu language family, as well as some others such as the Venda and Lemba languages) developed their own social institutions and political economies long before the arrival of Europeans. Indeed, it was the extraordinary strength and resilience of these people and their institutions which allowed Africans to challenge and eventually throw off the imposition of white domination. It is important to note that throughout their history, the people and societies of South Africa were constantly changing.

There are no essential "types" of people based on rigid ethnicity or on physical characteristics to be found in this history. Groups and societies are fluid and change over time. Rather, this text argues that people are best understood on the basis of the human struggle to satisfy material needs and its related social activities. The constructs of "race" and "tribe" do not tell us the whole story about who the people really were, what their potential was, and what they did or why they did it. However, in South Africa labels came to be used to define and limit people. For our purposes, it is convenient to rely on some labels such as "white" (to refer to people of European descent and who define themselves as white) and "African" (as previously defined). Other labels used include "Coloured" (people of mixed African and white descent), "Indian" (people from the Indian subcontinent), and "Asian" (for people from China, Southeast Asia, and India). These labels and other labels used to refer

1

to tribes and ethnic groups were variously invented or manipulated, corrupted, and abused. They served largely as a way of defining and articulating ideas about differences in the systems of white domination. As we shall see, however, some labels were also used defensively by Africans who sought to define and protect their interests in the face of oppression based on race and class. Over time, people who were not defined as "white" came to refer to themselves as "black" as we shall see in Chapter 9, "Apartheid and South African Society."

There are other terms in the record of South African history which are derived from perceived racial stereotypes which were hateful and derogatory. Terms such as "Kaffir" (an Arabic term meaning "unbeliever," referring to Africans), "Bushman" for the San, who are described in this chapter, and "Hottentot" (a term for turkeys clucking based on what Europeans thought their language sounded like) for the Khoe (also described later in this chapter) were used by whites and were based on their inaccurate and racist views of these people.

THE ENVIRONMENT

As with all early human communities, the local South African environment shaped the ways in which people organized their lives socially, economically, and politically and it continues to do so. South Africa is a beautiful land of markedly varied geographic and climatic zones within a fairly small region. The interior is dominated by two major geographic features. The highveld plateau is an elevated region that has mild to cool, dry winters and hot summers with fairly regular rainfall each year along the eastern part, but comparatively little annual rainfall on average (less than twenty inches per year) inland to the west and north. The interior is also hemmed in by an escarpment and punctuated by mountain ranges. Some ranges, such as the Pilansburg and Magaliesburg, are small and concentrated but the largest and highest range, the Drakensberg, extends along the eastern interior through modern Lesotho and into the eastern Cape. The Drakensberg presented both formidable obstacles to those white settlers who wanted to traverse it and secure defensible mountain fortresses for the Sotho who sought refuge there. Rainfall tends to increase as one moves south and to the coast from the interior. Where there is sufficient rainfall in the eastern highveld, the land supports grain farming as well as cattle and small livestock pastoralism. To the north and west, including areas beyond what would become South Africa, are the massive arid regions of the Namib and Kalahari deserts where rainfall is extremely rare and light. In the deserts, water sources are few and far between, and people had to adapt to the climate and region with disciplined patterns of foraging and seasonal movements to maximize their access to water sources. Northern South Africa is defined by the mighty Limpopo River. There are three major rivers within the interior which cut across the highveld and flow south and west from the watershed line of the Drakensberg. The Orange, Vaal, and Caledon rivers all

TABLE MOUNTAIN AND CAPE TOWN A view of the port town and the European ships that linked South Africa to wider colonial commerce. *Source: National Archives of South Africa.*

provide a regular source of water within fertile valleys, which attracted humans from the earliest time. However, these rivers are not, navigable and so do not provide people with a ready means to reach the interior from the coast; easier access might have aided development and political control much sooner.

The western coastal region begins as a series of rocky points and sandy bays with a Mediterranean-type climate in the Cape of Good Hope and then gradually shades up to the wet sub-tropical belt along the Indian Ocean in the northeast. In the southwest and at the Cape, cool, wet winters and dry, warm summers provided later Dutch settlers with a good climate and fertile soils for grain and grape farming as well as stock-keeping. As we shall see, the earliest inhabitants did not have access to, or develop, these sorts of crops which could thrive at the Cape, and so they remained exclusively foragers and pastoralists.

Along the east coast, however, the climate is hot and provides for a high average rainfall, especially during the southern hemisphere's summer, which extends from December to March. The winters are warm and dry with no normal snowfall except in the interior on the highest peaks of the Drakensberg. There are, moreover, a great many rivers along the eastern coast beginning with the Breede River in the Cape and ranging all the way to the Pongola in northern Zululand and Swaziland. Although these rivers are not navigable from the coast, the river valleys and the well-watered lands between provided important zones for cultivation and livestock grazing. Indeed, pastoralists in this region required access to both coastal lands where sweet and mixed grasses

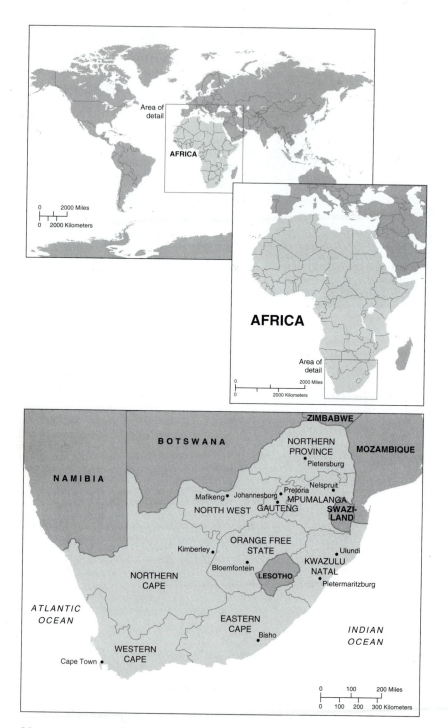

Map 1–1 South Africa: Overview in Global and Regional Contexts. *Adapted from F. J. Ramsay, Ed. Global Studies: Africa, 9/e. McGraw Hill/Dushkin. Guilford, CT. 2001.*

provided for summer grazing, and to upland areas that provided "sourveld," that is, grasses which retained nutritional value during the dry winter months. There are also in the Cape and along the east coast substantial forests, both inland and on the massive coastal sand dunes of Natal and Zululand. Between these forested zones, the land gives way to "thornveld," a grassy area punctuated by clumps of thorn and other indigenous trees, and then it shades up to the vast grassy plains of the inland highveld.

Southern Africa also contains substantial mineral deposits. Iron ore is commonly found throughout the region, and skilled Africans mined it to manufacture farm implements (principally iron hoes) and weapons from very early times. Africans also had easy access to luxury metal ores such as gold and copper, and they used them to fashion impressive ornaments and ritual art pieces of exceptional quality. More recently, deposits of diamonds and a vast reef of gold as well as platinum, uranium, and other minerals of military and technological importance have been found and have become the focus of capital-intensive industrial mining.

These geographic zones provide for a robust ecology that supports a vast array of plants, insects, and animals. South Africa once contained everything from aardvarks (an Afrikaans word meaning "earth pig") and antelopes to elephants, giraffes, lions and leopards, rhinos, water buffaloes, to zebras. Over time, with increased demands for elephant ivory and the arrival of whites who sought to hunt big game, Africans and whites decimated the game population to the extent that some species, such as the quagga (a zebra-like animal) became extinct, and others, such as the rhino, now require protection in limited game parks such as Kruger National Park, the largest game reserve in the country. The local environment also plays host to a range of insects and diseases which are pernicious to humans and their domesticated animals, although these are not as widespread or virulent as some diseases to the north in tropical Africa. Chief among these is the tsetse fly, which lives in the deep bush, feeds on large mammals, and is the carrier of *Nagana* (trypanosomiasis or sleeping sickness), which is deadly for cattle but not for people in South Africa. (A human form of the disease also exists in tropical Africa.) With the advent of white settlement, global trading links, and the implantation of a capitalist economy, other diseases of livestock such as scab, rinderpest, anthrax, and east coast fever also started to take a toll on cattle and sheep. Until the explosion of modern industrial diseases such as tuberculosis and sexually transmitted diseases such as syphilis and AIDS, malaria was (and remains) the major health concern for people. These mosquito-borne diseases are found primarily in the wet low-lying areas of the eastern Transvaal, Swaziland and, coastal Zululand where heavy rains provide ideal breeding sites for the carrier. Africans had learned well how and when to avoid the lower lying river and bush areas which harbored mosquitoes. Yet they faced epidemics of malaria once white conquest

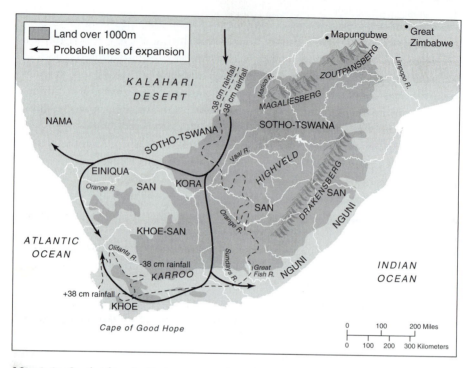

Map 1–2   South Africa: Its Environment and Peoples. *Adapted from J. Omer-Cooper, History of Southern Africa, 2/e. Reed Publishing Inc. Portsmouth, MA. 1994.*

and settlement forced them into these disease-ridden areas. Drought was probably the most devastating and recurrent environmental calamity for African farmers and herders, but crop blights and locust swarms could also wipe out food supplies. This resulted in severe famines in these societies which had no long-term storage capacity for food. While the climate and geography set many challenges for humans, they nonetheless, provided ample opportunities for the earliest people to thrive in the region (see Map 1–2).

HUMAN COMMUNITIES: THE SAN AND THE KHOE

The evidence suggests that South Africa (as well as East and Northeast Africa) is home to the direct ancestors of modern humans who were in turn linked to the earliest hominids (proto-humans or the probable precursors to us), and so it is quite probably the cradle of us all. Indeed, recent analyses of the skeletal remains which contain modern human genetic material show that our genetic ancestors, early *Homo sapiens,* originated in the region probably up to 200,000 years ago, though there may be other regions where early humans developed independently of our African ancestors. Regardless of what racial classification they would later carry, all of South Africa's modern inhabitants, whites included, have genetic material from these African ancestors. Yet it is the combined analyses of the material evidence and of later linguistic relationships which provide us with clues about who these early people were and how they lived. What we can surmise from the evidence is that modern humans emerged from and others moved into this region probably in slow, overlapping, and fluid phases of migration as they passed the traditions of pastoralism, tool-making, and farming from one group to another. Humans have thus continuously inhabited the region for over 200,000 years. About 50,000 years ago, stone-tool-making people established fluid societies that began to forage and hunt from caves and other types of shelters throughout the region. Following these hunters and gatherers, the first major social formations to emerge were those of the San, followed by the Khoe, and later by the various Nguni-speaking peoples (who are part of the larger family of Bantu languages which cover much of southern, central, and western Africa). These societies, respectively, engaged in hunting and gathering, herding or pastoralism, and mixed farming combining both agriculture and herding. As we shall see, over time these three traditions of pastoralism, tool-making, and farming were synthesized through interactions in the fluid social relations of the region. While hunting and gathering remained a viable alternative for the people of the southern and western Cape for a long time, mixed farming came to dominate the landscape and the livelihood of the majority until the arrival of whites.

The earliest people in South Africa with a direct link to our recent history were the ancestors of the Khoesan peoples of the Cape and the western interior. The Khoesan became an interrelated group that emerged from two different but linked traditions: San hunting and gathering (i.e., foraging for fruits, seeds, etc.) and Khoe pastoralism (i.e., herding of animals). The hunting and gathering San communities which emerged from the earlier stone-tool making group were decentralized, small in size and number. Each group probably contained no more than forty people, and there were likely fewer than 20,000 San when the first whites arrived in South Africa in the sixteenth century. The San organized their communities along fairly open, fluid lines; as with all these early societies, they were subject to significant change over time. There was no centralized authority and only a limited social hierarchy which was based on the loose organization of hunting bands and the predominance of men in consensus decision-making. In exceptional cases, the bands did follow a chief, probably based on the need for timely leadership decisions for raiding or seasonal hunting movements. There was no meaningful differentiation among group members on the basis of material wealth. Their few material possessions could easily be obtained by anyone as they were readily available with little added work from their surroundings and so did not constitute a means of accumulating wealth. Each family subunit was only as strong and well-off as its members, as was the larger community.

San communities relied upon the patriarchal leadership of male heads of family. Their way of living and their use of the abundant natural resources did not require the creation of an elaborate state structure. They lived across most of the interior and relied upon the profundity of their knowledge to exploit the bountiful natural environment. They adapted their mode of living and material needs to what they could readily find around them with a low expenditure of labor. Indeed, it is likely that, at most, they spent a mere two to three hours a day satisfying their material and food needs. Each San band claimed a set territory which extended over a large area with a wide range of bioclimatic zones. Within this range, they took advantage of naturally occurring plants, insects, and animals which could be trapped and hunted. They divided work along gender lines: Men hunted game and women gathered roots, nuts, insects, and fruits. Given that hunting was a dangerous activity which required considerable time and could fail to yield any food, it was probably the women who supplied the bulk of the family's daily nutritional requirements.

San activities were based upon seasonal patterns in the movement of animals and the appearance of plants. Since they could meet their needs relatively easily from nature, and because their pattern of foraging required that they move on a regular basis, they did not seek to burden themselves with material possessions. Each person carried all he or she needed in the way of tools: an ostrich shell for water, a few stone digging and cutting tools, bows and arrows and knives, and very little clothing. This uncomplicated life provided for considerable leisure time to pursue the arts, and over time, San people mastered the use of plant and mineral dyes and created many impressive rock paintings, as well as lyrical music. Their paintings reflected a deep spirituality based on shamanistic associations between people and nature and a belief in the transformation of human consciousness into that of the animals they hunted. Yet the San were also open to regional interaction and specialization to a degree. Different San groups had access to different resources such as iron ores or particular animals such as ostriches, and so they could exchange their locally developed goods for trade with others. These patterns of interaction may well have encouraged intermingling with other societies which were engaged in other activities such as herding, or with different societies which originated elsewhere, such as the Bantu-speakers.

The Khoe, or Khoekhoe, were herders of sheep and cattle. They emerged from earlier groups of San ancestors from the Tshu-Khwe-speaking people who probably coalesced in and then dispersed from an area of modern northwestern Botswana about 1,500 years ago. The Khoe had already started to acquire livestock—fat-tailed or Persian sheep and the "Africander" long-horned cattle—from herding peoples to the north as they slowly spread out from their primary areas in Botswana. It is not clear if the Khoe first moved west, then south or, more probably, south through the South African highveld and then east and west along the coast, but they did begin to make contact with the San hunters and gatherers at an early time. Moreover, they probably also settled in the central region of modern Zimbabwe and along coastal Natal. Although they were absorbed into the Bantu-speaking societies which came to dominate these areas, the presence of certain click sounds (made by imploding the tongue on the upper palate of the mouth, or by sharply drawing the tongue away from the inside of the front and side teeth) and similar or related terms for livestock in the local Zulu and Xhosa languages suggests definite interaction.

It is likely that the Khoe faced some tension and conflict with the early San bands since their two different lifestyles would have led to competition over local resources. The San probably retreated from the areas of Khoe herding expansion, although they remained in the general region. Moreover, Khoe livestock would have appeared (as did later white settler stock) as an easy and fitting target for San hunters, and there is evidence of San raiding against the herding communities. Nevertheless, the Khoe and the San did work out patterns of cooperation. As the Khoe herders spread out, first south, then west and east along the coast, they challenged and then absorbed many San clans. They then established the San as herding clients who, with their skills derived from hunting, could care for and protect the herds from predators. In time, these San clients adopted the Khoe lifestyle and undertook herding as part of the wider Khoe community. Such intermingling became so common that it is very difficult to distinguish between Khoe and San communities or lifestyles within this context; the term *Khoesan* reflects the cycles of interaction between the two. Indeed, as population pressures, environmental calamities, and the arrival of whites—first the Portuguese and then the Dutch—impinged on the Khoe (as discussed further in Chapter 2), some clans lost their livestock. In other cases, San raiding and theft reduced some Khoe family stock holdings. In such cases, the Khoe would reverse the process and undertake hunting and foraging strategies until they could recoup their cattle.

Although Khoe communities did sometimes lose their cattle and were obliged to undertake San strategies, their society was more organized and stable than the loose San clans. The Khoe organized themselves into chiefdoms with a leading senior male heading up the ruling clan. Each clan claimed descent through a patrilineal system of inheritance where the other families paid allegiance to him as chief, although decision making was through consultation. Chiefs did not exercise absolute power since they did not own the land, nor did they control a standing army. Indeed, they relied upon the support of all the clan heads. The chiefdoms were larger than San clans, up to two thousand members, and the overall Khoe population grew to possibly over 100,000 by the mid-seventeenth century. Yet, because of the decentralized nature of rule and the relative abundance of land, the chiefdoms were flexible. They frequently accommodated newcomers and they could—and often did—split up.

In a practice which was common among African herding societies, conflicts between clan leaders and the chief, or between younger men and their fathers, could lead to a clan separating from the main chiefdom and establishing its own community elsewhere. Communities also expanded by a natural increase in population and through intermarriage with neighboring Nguni-speaking communities.

The Khoe economy was driven by herding and some trade. Cattle and sheep herding provided an important, regular supply of nutritious food, principally milk and meat, although the Khoe (and also the San) hunted for wild game. Moreover, animal by-products such as skins, bones, and sinews were used for specialized tools and clothing. The Khoe also traded in cattle and *dagga* (mild marijuana) and small amounts of metals with neighboring Nguni-speaking communities. These material goods and the livestock represented real wealth which could be accumulated and so differentiated wealthier Khoe from those with few or no cattle at all. In such cases, the poor would become clients to a wealthier herd-owner, and could, over time, accumulate a beast or two in return for herding the patron's cattle. As we shall see, when whites arrived in the Cape, these patterns of differentiation and the loss of herds became more common and acute. Then, the Khoe were pressed to trade increasing numbers of their best cattle, and competition for resources drove more San to raid for cattle. Overall, the Khoe with their herding and trading lifestyle were more inclined to engage in trade and work relations with whites than the San hunter-gatherers, who could retreat to the Cape interior, and so the former were the first in this region to face the impact of white settlement.

THE FIRST FARMERS

The Bantu-speaking peoples who settled and developed complex chiefdoms across most of the rest of southern Africa comprised a large and diverse group of societies. We shall come to refer to them as the Tswana, Sotho, Pedi, Xhosa, Swazi, and others. These people had their origins elsewhere, and as they moved in slow, overlapping phases of interaction and expansion, their migration and settlement became known as the Bantu-speakers' migration. This migration was probably a series of overlapping streams of people who originated from a primary area in west-central Africa and flowed east and south from about 200 B.C.E. These movements were very slow processes which likely entailed much interaction and borrowing among groups as they settled the land over the next thousand years. Those who reached southern Africa by possibly as early as 500 C.E. brought with them the three hallmarks of their culture: cattle herding, farming, and iron technology. The ability to smelt iron was an incredibly important technology for these people. They associated it with wealth derived from farming with iron implements, and they thought they had the magical power to manipulate ores from the earth as well as to fashion weapons such as spears. Indeed, the founding rulers of many African kingdoms are associated with their ability to smelt iron or control blacksmiths. Yet, it was the diversity of their mixed farming and herding economy which gave these Nguni and Sotho-Speakers (as the variant families of southern African Bantu languages are termed) the ability to settle the land, farm intensively, and develop large chiefdoms and eventually larger political entities which we will refer to as states and kingdoms.

By about 1,000 C.E., the Bantu-speaking communities appear to have reached an economic threshold which enabled them to begin extensive trading, metalworking, and creating artistic pottery in what became continuous farming and herding settlements throughout South Africa, although they continued to accommodate more immigrants over time. They adapted to the local environments with a judicious balance of farming and herding. Along the coastal belt where the rains permitted, the Nguni-speakers such as the Xhosa undertook more farming than was possible inland on the highveld, where rainfall was less abundant. There the Sotho-Tswana-speakers relied primarily on cattle herding, with some limited farming. They introduced and adapted various indigenous crops such as millet and pumpkins, and they also readily accepted the later introduction of maize from the Portuguese to the northeast in modern-day Mozambique. Along the coastal belt from the Cape to modern Mozambique, mixed farming communities of Xhosa- and related Nguni-speakers took advantage of the well-watered lands and rivers and grew larger in size than other groups, eventually spreading out over the escarpment of the Drakensberg into the highveld.

The coastal Nguni developed small dispersed villages which allowed them to maximize their access to the land containing the finest soils and most abundant rainfall in the country. Their homes were built of strong laths stuck into the ground and bent over to form a domed support for a grass-thatched roof. While these were sound structures appropriate for an environment of heavy rainfall and heat, they were also easily removed and reconstructed whenever conditions or conflict dictated that a family move. On the central plateau of the highveld, the Sotho-Tswana speakers settled less well-watered lands closer to the desert region of the Kalahari. To cope with this environment, the Sotho-Tswana developed large towns situated near water sources such as streams or springs for their livestock and themselves. They built more permanent structures of stone and mud. Polished hard floors made from a mixture of mud and cow dung were common to both Nguni and Sotho-Tswana homes. The Sotho-Tswana did not grow or expand as quickly as the coastal Nguni and they were more isolated from each other. Nevertheless, there was a great deal of interaction and cultural synthesis among both the coastal and the highveld groups, and this increased over time. Trade, raiding, and political

amalgamation were all part of the fluid relations among these African communities. Mixed farming provided a stable surplus base upon which to build their
communities. In some early cases, major trading cities, led by a chiefly elite
and supported by extensive cattle-keeping, farming, and especially trade,
emerged in the central highveld of southern Africa. Beginning around 1,250
C.E., Phalaborwa and Mapungubwe, followed by Great Zimbabwe, were important centers for a lively trade in gold and copper to the Arabic-dominated
coast, but they declined from about 1,500 C.E. Thereafter, and prior to the
Bantu-speaking Africans' (hereafter, Africans) creation of larger, stable states
with a king as the established ruler, the herding and farming communities of
southern Africa organized themselves under the rule of chiefs.

FARMING SOCIETY

Although there were many local variations, mixed farming communities in
South Africa shared a number of common features. They were, on the whole,
more complex and stratified than the Khoesan hunter-gatherer and pastoral
societies. They had a clear social hierarchy which was based upon the dominance of senior patriarchs, especially married men who were the head of the
household or homestead, over subordinate women, youths, and children. Social relations were governed by elaborate and sophisticated rules, such as the
Zulu custom of *hlonipa,* which required subordinates to show deference to senior males, elder males, and ultimately the chief or king. **"Chiefdoms"** were
established by founding families or clans who could make a claim to some significant right to rule. In some cases, this claim was based on a founding myth
in which a family asserted to be the "first family" in the region or to have taken
the land first. In other cases, they claimed a particular power, such as the impressive and apparently magical ability to smelt iron, or the prowess of a successful warrior-conqueror. In any event, these claims enabled the ruling clan to
assert its authority and to differentiate itself from others. The leading family
took on a form of royal status and ruled other subordinate clans accordingly.
Thus, the senior male of a founding clan could establish himself as a chief and
thus could command the allegiance of the rest of the society, the commoners.
Yet chiefs worked through broad structures such as councils that included sub-
chiefs and through their *induna* or appointed deputies. The *induna* were se-
lected from loyal commoner families and represented the basic level of a
political office. They performed a range of important functions as military
leaders, official messengers, and collectors of tribute that was due from commoner families. Chiefs also held regular public meetings (*pitso* in Sotho,
indaba in Zulu) where the affairs of state were discussed and senior men
weighed in on decisions. Ultimately, the chiefs had the final say, and political
power rested with them.

Chiefs distanced themselves from commoners through the accumulation of greater herds of cattle, larger numbers of wives (as we shall see later, these were polygynous societies where a wealthy man could take more than one wife), and by customs that invested chiefs with an aura of power. For example, paramount chiefs and kings (those who led large states and ruled over many subordinate clan chiefs) had praise poets extol their virtues and prowess before assemblies of their followers, and they often refused to be seen eating in public. Chiefs, moreover, controlled key aspects of the religious beliefs and seasonal celebrations of their chiefdoms. There was a widespread belief in the importance of both ancestral spirits and nature and animal spirits or totems. These societies believed in an all-powerful creator spirit or god who was responsible for cosmological origins and in a broad range of nature and animal spirits which governed the balance of good and evil in the earthly world. This balance was essential to the well-being of the society and particularly its mixed farming activities. In consultation with their very powerful diviners, chiefs would decide upon key times for planting and harvesting and ritual sacrifices of cattle as well as keep an eye on the general balance between good and evil.

As far as the chiefs and diviners were concerned, evil could manifest itself in a number of ways, including as a challenge from a political competitor which might require the persons being "smelled out" as a witch and then banished or "eaten up," that is, having all their livestock taken and being broken economically. Ancestral spirits or "shades" included the spirits of all deceased family members. They were believed to inhabit both this world and the world beyond, and they too could strongly influence events through the manipulation of the balance between good and evil. Chiefs claimed special access to their royal shades who had more power and influence than commoner shades. These beliefs also related to the general state of health of the people and the community. Illness and calamity were understood in terms of the influence of evil spirits upon a person or community, and not just on the basis of a physical ailment. Chiefs, therefore, could work to restore health and well-being through their link to the shades and the nature spirits. Chiefs also governed commoner lives through the establishment of age-sets. These were cohorts for initiation and education purposes which only the chief could create. They were comprised of a group of similar-aged boys who had reached puberty and there were similar cohort sets for girls. Boys would go off into the bush under the supervision of an experienced elder who would teach them discipline and the traditions of the chiefdom. The elder would also perform the ceremonial circumcisions which would mark the boys' passage into manhood. The age-sets were an important tool for social organization, and they were later adapted to serve broader state needs such as military organization.

There were limits to the power of chiefs, and chiefdoms had to remain flexible. Chiefs extended their followings through their personal stature and, more significantly, their ability to provide cattle and grazing land. While a chief had considerable power to lead his people, he also had to maintain rule through a consensus, especially with the leading men of the community. Although a chief inherited his position, a chief was a chief by and for the people, according tradition. Chiefs did not command standing armies, but only called upon men to join forces for the purposes of raiding for cattle and land. Chiefs had no coercive means to control their followers and so men could refuse to join. The nature of the environment and the relatively low population density also allowed for an abundance of land. This meant that by tradition and custom, chiefs did not own the land, but rather held it in trust for the people, and each family was entitled to at least some land upon which to live and farm. The key to the success of a chiefdom was, therefore, the ability of chiefs to attract followers, since it was their labor which would till the soil, tend to the cattle, and provide tribute to the chief and his family. In order to allow for growth, chiefdoms accommodated extended kinship groups that combined real and fictive family relationships into a broader clan unit. In this way, African chiefdoms could over time incorporate a wide range of people, including newcomers and conquered people, as clients who could then be accepted into the group and take on its kinship identity. Indeed, the development of this identity was essential for helping to define chiefdoms and states, although these processes were subject to considerable change and manipulation over time. There were no crystalline "tribes" with unchanged essential features, but rather fluid and open extended clan-based chiefdoms that adapted to changing circumstances.

There were also fissiparous processes within chiefdoms that could lead to fragmentation and the creation of new chiefdoms. Clan members who aspired to chieftaincy but remained unfulfilled, generational tensions, and divisions between the wealthy and poor all led to the breaking away of groups and clans. There were also royal sibling rivalries over succession. Even though the rules of inheritance of power were clear, the nomination of heirs could change and lead to civil strife between aspirants for a chieftaincy. Moreover, since land was not owned outright and was comparatively abundant until some mixed farming communities started to form large states in the early nineteenth century, young men who were frustrated in their efforts to establish their own homestead independent of their father or unsuccessful claimants to chieftainships could relocate and establish their own family and clan groups. This was an important process for the expansion of African society, as was the case of the Xhosa paramountcy where two rival heirs to the founding Tshawe royal clan split off to establish their own chiefdoms. For young commoners, however, relocating inevitably meant having to come to terms with another chief who claimed rights to rule the new territory they had moved into. Nevertheless, chiefs relied wholly on the productive capacities and allegiance of their followers.

The basic unit of the mixed farming chiefdoms was the homestead, and the central pillars of the homestead economy were the productive and reproductive capacities of cattle and women. The homestead comprised the senior male as father and husband, his wife or wives, children, and often elderly dependents. These were polygynous societies in which men who had accumulated sufficient wealth in cattle could marry more than one wife and so extend the labor capacity of the homestead as their wives could do more work and provide more children, who also contributed to the labor-intensive household economy. There was a definite division of labor along gender lines within the homestead. Perhaps drawing upon practices from earlier societies based on male hunting and female gathering, men dominated cattle herding and women undertook the agricultural work in mixed farming communities. Women's cultivation of the garden was crucial to the homestead, for it provided basic food requirements such as sorghum, millet, pumpkin, melon, and maize. It also contributed extra items such as tobacco and *dagga* (cannabis or marijuana), as well as beer, which was important for social relations such as cooperative work groups and festivals.

Men subordinated women despite their importance for domestic work, agricultural production, and child rearing. Females had low status in this patriarchal hierarchy. Although they could own some limited amounts of property such as cattle and small stock like sheep and goats, women were effectively legal minors who came under the authority of their fathers and husbands. They did most of the heavy household work, including the arduous daily tasks of fetching water and firewood—often from a considerable distance—caring for the children, tending the crops, and preparing the food. Yet there was also a cooperative spirit where wives and daughters within and across homesteads would join together to do larger tasks such as harvesting. In contrast, men had greater power and status for they owned the bulk of the cattle and the agricultural produce. Although they shared in the heavier tasks of plowing and harvesting, much depended upon their status. A wealthier man would have a number of wives to cope with farming and their sons would tend the herds, leaving him free to attend to local politics and the acquisition of more cattle.

Cattle were central to the mixed farming societies. They had productive, reproductive, and significant symbolic social value. They supplied milk (which was intentionally soured), meat, hides, bones, and sinew, all of which were used to maximum effect for meals, clothing, tools, and weapons such as shields. Cattle also reproduced, and with twelve to fourteen or more cattle, a man could ensure a stable and potentially growing herd. Of course, not all families had this many cattle, and after the arrival of whites and the growing trade in cattle, increasing numbers of Africans owned no cattle. Such differentiation allowed wealthy men to rely upon his poor neighbors as clients to whom he could lend cattle. This relationship usually allowed the poor to use the milk (and meat and hides if a beast died) while they cared for the cattle, and to retain a calf or two from the natural increase of the herd. Because of the very real value of cattle, they were used in a wide range of social and economic relationships and so constituted a reproductive asset, or form of wealth, as well as a means of exchange or currency, although other items such as copper were used more appropriately for long-distance trade. Cattle were sacrificed to honor all major life events such as weddings and religious festivals, and they were the means of consolidating family relations.

Marriage was conditional upon the establishment and transfer of *lobola* (Zulu) or *bohali* (Sotho), known as bridewealth. Bridewealth was the pledge and payment over time of an agreed-upon number of cattle by a man to the father of his bride. This exchange was intended to compensate the father for the loss of his daughter's labor potential and to develop bonds between the husband's and bride's families since it was usually his family that came up with the cattle to be transferred over time. Yet *lobola* also served to concentrate cattle in the hands of the patriarchs, the fathers, as they were the ones who received and owned them. Chiefs especially profited from *lobola* because they could demand large numbers of cattle for their daughters on the basis of their elevated status. Similarly, wealthier men who had large herds of cattle could pledge more *lobola* to more fathers and thus marry more than one wife. Some powerful chiefs and kings married more than a hundred wives, and in some cases their betrothals later became annual events of state ceremony, such as the Zulu reed ceremony. Not surprisingly, young men were frustrated if their fathers withheld or delayed handing over the cattle they needed for *lobola* since it prevented them from marrying and establishing their own independent household. Over time, this would lead to increasing generational tension as fathers sought to keep their sons at home to help with the homestead while the young men resisted.

As we shall see, within the colonial context, young men took advantage of new opportunities to acquire money for cattle so they could come up with their own *lobola* payments. Yet, since there was no commercial market for cattle until the arrival of whites and their capitalist economy, African herders tended to try to accumulate as many cattle as they could. Effective herding strategies were, therefore, essential. Herding was undertaken primarily by young men and boys, and it required an intimate knowledge of the local environment in order to maximize the use of grazing areas on a seasonal basis and to avoid areas which might harbor disease. By maximizing cattle numbers rather than body size, they ensured that their herds could survive the rigors of drought and disease, even if they looked weak and emaciated during times of stress.

Overall, the mixed farming societies were strong and resilient, based as they were on the combination of chieftaincy, agro-pastoral production, and the foundation of women's domestic labor as well as men's hunting and defense of the community. The economy provided for an abundance of food and cattle in good years, and usually enough to see people through tough years. There were, of course, times of great stress when droughts and famine struck, although they rarely led to widespread deaths prior to the colonial period. Mixed farming societies sought ways to consolidate their holdings in order withstand these challenges. Nevertheless, through the seventeenth and eighteenth centuries, the mixed farmers expanded throughout South Africa to settle nearly all of the land that would support both farming and herding. They also started to specialize their crafts and manufactures. Basketry, pottery, and metal working—especially iron tools and copper ornaments—became more widespread, sophisticated, and decorative. Such specialized trade goods as well as other important trade items, such as salt, contributed to the development of trade networks. These networks traversed the entire southern African region and linked Bantu-speaking chiefdoms with Khoe and San groups as well as with the Portuguese, who arrived later on the coast to the north in modern-day Mozambique. Large states, such as the Mbo, probably began to form as they developed and controlled these long-distance trade routes. As we shall see, they declined and were replaced in the early 1800s as new, powerful African states rose.

As the mixed farming chiefdoms spread out, they developed new relationships with the Khoe and San. In some cases, the mixed farmers conflicted with these groups, especially the San, whose economy required them to have unfettered access to large areas that farmers wanted to settle, and who were inclined to raid pastoralists for their livestock. In such circumstances, the farmers would sometimes organize their forces and even join with Khoe bands to subdue the San and incorporate them as clients. In other cases, the Khoe and Nguni-speaking farmers shared common interests and a herding economy and so they intermingled more freely. This often led to either the farmers being incorporated into Khoe pastoral society, or the Khoe's adapting to farming society and joining an established group. Such relationships were often forged through marriage between leading Khoe or San and Nguni-speaking families, such as the case of the Xhosa chief, Sandile, who married a San wife. In general terms, mixed farming chiefdoms had the strength as well as sufficiently flexible political and social structures to accommodate and incorporate Khoe and San people into their communities as fellow members. The mixed farmers tended to dominate the well-watered coastal regions while the foragers and herders maintained their hold on the drier interior. Nevertheless, the overall pattern that emerged, until the arrival of the first permanent white settlers, was for the mixed farming societies to intermingle with the Khoe and San to such an extent that there was significant cultural and genetic transfer among these groups in a more or less peaceful process. As we shall see, this pattern was dramatically altered with the arrival of the Dutch in the mid-seventeenth century.

CONCLUSION

South Africa is a varied land, containing a range of geographic and climatic zones but with two major regions: the coastal belt and the highveld interior. These are separated geographically by the region's largest mountain range, the Drakensberg. At the southern tip of the African continent, the area of the Cape of Good Hope and the immediate interior is punctuated by high mountains and verdant valleys. It experiences a Mediterranean type of climate with cool, wet winters and hot, dry summers. These seasons in South Africa in the southern hemisphere occur during the opposite times of the northern seasons. As one moves first east and then north towards modern-day Mozambique along the Indian Ocean, the rest of the coastal belt gets gradually warmer as the climate shades from a Mediterranean-type to nearly subtropical in the northeast. Rainfall along the coast is relatively abundant and, despite the occurrence of severe droughts from time to time, the area provides ideal conditions for farming and herding of cattle and small livestock. The coastal belt is also cross-cut by numerous rivers. Although none of these allow for navigation or boat transport, they do provide useful regular supplies of water for livestock. Inland of the coastal belt, the average annual rainfall starts to decline as one moves toward the highveld, and this makes regular farming difficult. It requires that people and herders settle near regular water supplies. Overall, the land is rich in resources. There are vast mineral deposits of precious and useful metals as well as gems. The land supports a range of useful trees and grasses, from forested zones to savannahs. These zones play host to a broad range of flora and fauna, including large game animals which provide for food and tools for hunters, as well as small viruses and parasites such as malaria which could devastate human communities. Overall, however, the regions proved to be a suitable and productive place for human habitation.

South Africa has been continuously inhabited by indigenous people for a long time. Probably the earliest ancestors of modern humans emerged in South Africa over 200,000 years ago. Later, other people moved in to settle the region in overlapping phases of migration and settlement. These groups provided the foundation for the earliest communities of San and Khoe society. They were joined by later streams of people who were part of the Bantu-languages family which covers much of sub-Saharan Africa. The San and Khoe undertook foraging and herding, respectively, although there was much intermingling of communities and their economic strategies. They took advantage of the relatively abundant natural resources to provide for their daily needs; they also exploited valuable items such as metal ores and animal products which they traded with people in the interior. There were many conflicts as groups raided for livestock. In some cases, San people acquired cattle and sheep through trading and raiding and so they undertook herding. In other cases, Khoe herders lost livestock to drought or raids and they then relied upon foraging until they could re-acquire cattle. In all events, these societies remained fluid as the people interacted, formed, and reformed communities, and so they have been referred to as the Khoesan. On the whole, the resultant Khoesan herding communities tended to be larger and more organized than the small foraging-raiding bands of San. Both the San forager-raiders and the Khoesan herders struck new relations with the region's other inhabitants, the Bantu-speakers.

The Bantu-speaking peoples settled in southern Africa in slow, overlapping phases of movement which probably originated in west-central Africa. They later became known by the academic linguistic labels, the Sotho-Tswana group on the highveld and the Nguni group along the coast. There was, however, fluidity among these people and between them and the Khoesan, but they later became known for their specific languages such as the Sotho, Xhosa, and Zulu. They brought and developed cattle-herding, farming, and iron technology and adapted these to the South African region. These skills allowed them to make farming tools and to create a greater surplus which could support large, diverse communities. The mixed farming communities developed more complex and stratified societies than the Khoesan. There was a clear social hierarchy based upon the patriarchal authority of the chiefs and often a founding clan or kin-group. Chiefs ruled over the homesteads, allocating land and adjudicating law. They also accrued substantial wealth in cattle and through the multiple wives they could marry. They led the drive to acquire more cattle and grazing land through raids. Yet, chiefs' powers were also balanced and mediated by councils of leading men and public meetings where important affairs were considered. Chiefs who failed to provide for their followers, or who were too excessive in their demands for tribute, could find themselves losing followers to other chiefs, or to younger men who hived off to form their own chiefdoms.

Overall, these mixed farming communities were stable and very successful. The foundation of the chiefdoms was the homestead, which was the basic unit of production. New homesteads were formed through marriage, and even though women were subordinated to male authority, they were essential to the productivity and reproductivity of the homestead. This importance was signified by the exchange of bridewealth, usually cattle. The core of the economy was homestead production of farm crops and cattle which provided the staple food, milk, and also served as a form of wealth. The mixed farmers' herds were central to their economy and constituted the basic form of investment. Trade with other societies in southern Africa was also significant, and the exchange of ivory and iron aided in both the accumulation of wealth and the organization of larger polities. Individuals were integrated into the broader communities first through age-set groups or cohorts which were later incorporated into military organizations as regiments in larger states. These larger political economies expanded across the region, in some cases trading and intermingling peacefully with, and in others raiding and incorporating, Khoesan people. These processes continued to unfold as the first whites arrived and settled on the coast.

QUESTIONS TO CONSIDER

1. What are the most significant features of the South African environment, and how did these relate to human settlement?
2. Who were the earliest humans in the region, what strategies did they undertake, and why?
3. What were relations between the Khoe and San like?
4. Who were the Bantu-speakers, where did they settle, what strategies did they undertake, and how did these differ between the coast and the interior?
5. What were the major common features of the Bantu-speaking communities? How did they organize themselves socially and politically?

FURTHER READINGS

ACOCKS, J., *Veld Types of South Africa,* Second Edition (Cape Town, 1975). A very detailed account of the local environment, useful for its maps and for its clear sense of the different bio-climatic zones in the country.

BOONZAIER, E., MALHERBE, C., BERENS, P., and SMITH, A., *The Cape Herders* (Cape Town and Johannesburg, 1989). A simple but good overview of the Khoekhoe people with helpful illustrations and maps.

DEACON, J., *Human Beings in South Africa: The Secrets of the Stone Age* (Cape Town, 1999). A detailed analysis based on material evidence. This is perhaps too dense for the average reader.

GUY, J., "Gender Oppression in Southern Africa's Precapitalist Societies" in Walker, C., *Women and Gender in Southern Africa to 1945* (London, 1990), pp. 33–47. Sets out the basic patriarchal relationships within Bantu-speaking homestead economies.

HALL, M., *The Changing Past. Farmers, Kings, and Traders. The People of Southern Africa, 200–1860* (Chicago, 1990). An excellent illustrated guide to the earliest people based on meticulous archeological research.

HAMMOND-TOOKE, W., *The Bantu-Speaking Peoples of Southern Africa* (London, 1974). A still-useful anthropological overview of social relations and customs in the Bantu-speakers' communities.

INSKEEP, R., *The Peopling of Southern Africa* (London, 1978). A readable general work which still has value even though some aspects of the research have been revised by later scholars.

KLEIN, R. (editor), *Southern African Prehistory and Paleo-environments,* Balkema Press (Rotterdam, 1984). The most comprehensive collection of scholarly essays, particularly good for its information about the prehistorical environment.

MAYLAM, P. *A History of the African People of South Africa* (Johannesburg, 1986). An excellent general introduction to all the African societies in the country.

PEIRES, J., *The House of Phalo. A History of the Xhosa People in the Days of Their Independence* (Johannesburg, 1981). The definitive work on the early Xhosa chiefdoms and their founding. Also a good work for understanding relations within chiefdoms.

PEIRES, J., *Before and After Shaka. Papers in Nguni History* (Grahamstown, 1981). A good collection of scholarly essays which deal with important theories on prehistorical social, economic, and political relations in Bantu-speaking communities.

CHAPTER II

Early Conflict and Interdependence: The Khoesan, the Xhosa, and the Establishment and Expansion of the Cape Colony

A fter the turn of the seventeenth century, the societies of South Africa were linked to the wider world. Thereafter, European-dominated social, political, and economic forces would shape the country for the next 300 years. Engaged in a wider nexus of global merchant capitalism, the Europeans arrived at the Cape and transformed the development of indigenous African societies. Khoekhoe (or Khoe), San, and the Nguni-speaking Xhosa people who lived along the east coast now had to cope with powerful new forces that at once challenged, transformed, and ultimately destroyed their existing societies. Although early Portuguese maritime explorer-traders failed to secure a foothold at the Cape, Dutch commercial interests of the *Vereenigde Oostindische Compangnie* (Dutch East India Company or VOC) established an unintended long-term presence in Cape Town Fort at Table Bay in 1652. Initially, the Khoe and, to a lesser extent, the San communities, which were the first to confront white immigrants, took a cautious approach to the interdependent relationships that emerged with the fledgling European settlement. Indeed, early white settlers relied more on Khoesan knowledge of the local environment, and especially their pastoral economy, than the Khoesan needed the newly available European trade goods. It was, however, an ambiguous relationship that rapidly deteriorated as whites took over more control of the land

and the local political economy through the latter half of the 1600s and into the 1700s, leaving the Khoesan fragmented and subordinated to white society. There were, moreover, other problems in the emerging pluralistic society of the Cape colony. Cape society developed a new complex hierarchy, influenced by the advent of slavery and shifting European attitudes towards Africans. Although race, class, and gender were very much a part of this picture, the intersection of race and class, whereby social status was explicitly associated with one's perceived racial status, emerged slowly at the Cape. As European settlement by Dutch Boers (farmers) proceeded apace, and some whites moved beyond the confines of the colony as trekboers (trader-herders who moved beyond the settlement zone), the Xhosa and other African societies in the interior had to confront the challenges of adaptation and, later, conquest. Not surprisingly, a myriad of tensions, misunderstandings, and conflicts arose in this context. Although Africans employed creative strategies to cope with these challenges, the conflicts were eventually resolved by force of arms, and the indigenous societies ultimately lost their rights to the land and their political and economic independence.

The spatial, economic, and political transformation of the Cape region from the late fifteenth century until the beginning of the nineteenth century began with the establishment of an interdependent relationship between the Cape Khoesan peoples and newly arrived European merchants in the context of the emerging modern global trading economy. At the core of this relationship was the way in which indigenous people coped with the expansion of merchant activity under the VOC and how white settlement and expansion undermined Khoe society. Eventually, whites dominated the agrarian economy and this affected the social hierarchy at the Cape. An important feature of the new political economy was slavery and the implications it had for race, class, and gender relations in the country. Also fundamental were changes in the zones of interaction where white settlers developed interdependent relations with Africans as they sought to extend their claims to the Cape interior. The emergence of the mixed-descent Griqua communities was a product of this intermingling, as were the problems of the relations between Xhosa society and the trekboers beyond the settled zone of the Cape. The major themes of these developments are how control of land and spatial relations shaped the social and economic features of Cape society and how the interdependence between white and indigenous societies gave way to white racial and political domination.

EARLIEST CONTACT: PORTUGUESE FORAYS AND KHOE RESPONSES

As we have seen, the Khoe and the San communities had a flexible political economy, governed by kin relations and communal land use systems. They were in constant flux. Khoe and San people shifted patterns of land use for herding and foraging and formed or reformed clans and chiefdoms. These activities often mixed people from both societies, so while it is important to make a distinction between Khoe and San societies, there is evidence of combined Khoesan communities from the beginning of the colonial period. There was not, however, a single cohesive Khoe or Khoesan state. Khoesan people were opportunistic and employed multiple strategies to take best advantage of access to essential hunting and foraging grounds, water sources, and pastures in the arid interior of the Cape. Political relations reflected the ebb and flow of social and economic needs. The Khoe and San communities made alliances and shifted between cattle-herding and foraging, depending on the circumstances. These strategies had important implications for the ways in which indigenous people coped with the new European presence.

The Khoe and San communities were cohesive and strong enough to fend off the early Portuguese explorers and merchants who, from the later 1400s, made forays along the southern African coast in search of a productive foothold. In the age of sail, South Africa was a crucial replenishment point that linked European merchant centers with resource colonies in the Far East. The Portuguese maritime empire, however, was weak and poorly integrated compared to the later Dutch and British merchant and colonial empires. It was comprised principally of trading networks from the Indian Ocean basin to Asia and later, by the seventeenth century, of plantations in South America which were fueled by coastal trading for slaves and for gold in Africa. The Portuguese achieved no permanent establishment in South Africa, in part because they developed their interests elsewhere (farther to the north in Angola and Mozambique where they competed with and overcame Arabic Islamic and African merchants), and in part because of Khoesan resistance to their depredations. The Portuguese approach to the indigenous peoples in South Africa tended towards cultural chauvinism, arrogance, and aggression. Early contacts between the Khoesan and Portuguese explorers and merchants were characterized by suspicion, misunderstandings, and violence. Tensions mounted because of real and apparent threats to Khoe resources, especially water-holes, which were crucial for their cattle, on the one hand, and Khoe hostilities toward Portuguese incursions on the other. These tensions later developed into outright competition and conflict as whites sought to control land and pressed the Khoe to trade livestock.

The Portuguese were uninterested in establishing amicable relations with the Khoe because they considered them to be savages. Nevertheless, the Khoe were eager to trade for European goods, especially iron, which they fashioned into tools and spear heads, and copper, which was used for ornamentation and was traded extensively in the interior. It was probably these early Portuguese who first traded goods for cattle with the Khoe. Differing perspectives on trade relations inaugurated what became a long-term point of conflict between indigenous people and whites. The Portuguese tended to ignore Khoe customs and protocol while the Khoe resented Portuguese intrusions. For example, in 1487, the Khoe of Mossel Bay in the Cape repelled a ship's party from Bartolomeu Dias's expedition when the Portuguese crew took water from a Khoe well without following the local custom of first asking permission and offering a gift. Even when the Portuguese did offer trade items, they denigrated the Khoe and considered them unsophisticated traders who too easily parted with their valuable cattle in exchange for cheap European goods. The Khoe were unaware or unsure of Portuguese intentions, and probably often felt threatened by Portuguese advances towards their private domestic settlements. In some instances, the Portuguese responded to Khoe defensive acts by donning armor and firing crossbows. Such encounters demonstrated the extent of Khoe mistrust and apprehension of what they perceived to be Portuguese aggression.

As trade relations soured, shrewd Khoe traders began frustrating Europeans by refusing to part with too many animals, especially their best livestock. Relations deteriorated in 1510 when the Viceroy of Portuguese India, Francesco de Almeida, on a return voyage to Europe, stopped at the Cape to replenish supplies. After an initially friendly exchange of goods, Almeida's shore party seized a Khoe hostage in order to induce his people to bring more cattle for trade. The outraged Khoe attacked the shore party, which precipitated an aggressive Portuguese counterattack. The Khoe then drove the Portuguese back to their ship and in a skirmish killed a number of them, including the Viceroy. Thereafter, Portuguese and other merchant expeditions, fearing the Khoe, avoided the Cape until the 1650s, when the Dutch established a trading fort at Table Bay. The prejudicial tone of fear, mistrust, and loathing set between whites and indigenous people, however, had ominous implications for future relations.

THE DUTCH EAST INDIA COMPANY (VOC) AND COMPANY RULE

The Khoe and San communities faced even greater challenges and opportunities when, in 1652, the VOC, a Dutch merchant firm with extensive interests in Indonesia, Java, and the Malay peninsula, established a replenishment station and fort in Table Bay at the Cape. This ushered in a new trade economy which inextricably linked South Africa and its people to the wider world and the vagaries of developing commercial relations. The VOC initially had no intention of penetrating into the interior and settling the Cape. It was merely a convenient stopping point on the long voyages between Europe and the Far East where passing ships stocked water and left mail to be forwarded home. However, the company's rising demands for meat to supply its merchant fleet led to increasing entanglements with the Khoesan.

The VOC foothold soon became a permanent facility that developed into Cape Town and the foundation of the Cape colony. A significant feature of this settlement was the fort which served to protect Company employees and servants, some of whom were Khoe, from possible Khoesan raids. The VOC was more successful than the Portuguese at developing its foothold in South Africa, in part because of the fort, and in part because of its approach to trade. The Company initially fostered an interdependent relationship with the Khoe, who increasingly sought goods of European manufacture in exchange for live-stock. While some historians have suggested that the fort tended to segregate whites from indigenous society, there was significant interaction between the two cultures. A number of Khoe worked and traded at the fort and thus con-tributed to the expansion of Cape Town. Despite official company policies de-signed to protect trade relations with the Khoe, the burgeoning economy put enormous pressures on indigenous societies and their economy. VOC traders disregarded Khoe etiquette and practices designed to safeguard their herds and continually pressed them for more and better cattle. Although some Khoe em-braced the new opportunities to engage in trade and European material cul-ture, relations deteriorated as Khoe society resisted white intrusions and the increasingly imbalanced terms of trade. In keeping with established practice among their own clans, some Khoe and San raiding parties menaced the settle-ment and stole back the cattle. This reinforced the white society's perceptions of a growing cultural difference between Cape Town society—which included some Khoe who had embraced acculturation and accepted European ways—and the indigenous people of the Cape interior (see Map 2–1).

As VOC shipping needs rose, the fort settlement expanded. Khoe commu-nities, however, were unwilling and unprepared to cater to the escalating de-mands for livestock from the VOC. Cattle provided dairy foods and meat when needed, and they reproduced to increase Khoe wealth in herds. Parting with too many animals would have undermined their entire economy. In order to compensate for insufficient supplies from the Khoe, the Company sent em-ployees out beyond the confines of the town, where they invaded Khoe grazing lands and established agricultural farms. Overall, this period was characterized by a clash of cultures and the competing economic systems of intensive Euro-pean mercantilism and agriculture and less intensive Khoe pastoralism, both of which required control of the land. This clash led to violence between the two societies, although the lines of conflict were not clearly drawn between whites and indigenous people. Ultimately, the combined forces of the new economy and conquest fragmented and destroyed Khoe communities and subordinated these people to a white-dominated society. Nevertheless, the Khoesan were in-dispensable for the foundations of the Cape colony because of their knowledge of the local environment and their herding expertise.

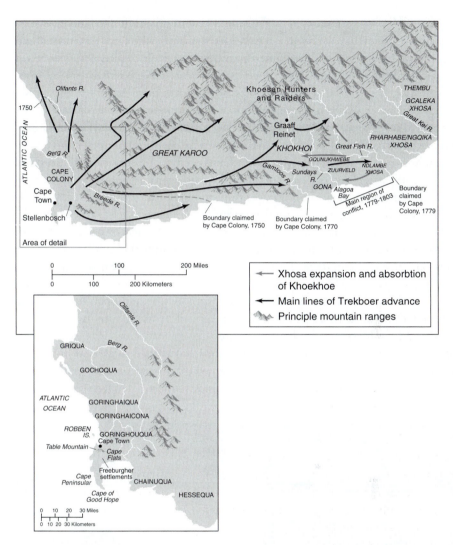

Map 2–1   The Early Cape Colony Showing African and Boer Settlements. *Adapted from K. Shillington, History of Southern Africa. Addison-Wesley. Edinburgh. 1997.*

    While the Khoe were the majority population in the interior of the Cape, by the 1650s the VOC and European culture began to dominate early Cape Town society. This was an uneven process, conditioned by the erratic effects of the new economy, the modest resilience and resistance of Khoe society, and ambiguous VOC policies. While white society was comprised of various Europeans, the Dutch language and especially the power of the Calvinist Dutch Reformed Church (a conservative Old Testament-based form of Christianity), increasingly predominated in the Cape. The church and the language supported a sense of European group exclusiveness along the lines of cultural and theological chauvinism. Christianity became one possible cultural determinant of social status that tended to separate European colonists from indigenous people, that is, the Christian from the so-called heathen. Although the VOC, which was governed by a board of directors in Amsterdam, was subject to the economic imperatives of the profit motive, it still had to contend with its relatively weak position in South Africa. It depended upon Khoe society and so to a certain extent it adapted to the local context. Khoe herders initially provided the bulk of cattle needed for meat. They also had an intimate knowledge of the local environment, including the location of water sources and grazing lands. Moreover, they were central to the trading economy. Indeed, the Company relied on the ability of some important Khoe to learn Dutch and English in order to facilitate trade. Almost no whites learned the challenging Khoe click-sound-based language. This was another indication of European cultural chauvinism.

Early Cape Town society was more accommodating and open for the Khoe than it later became. Khoe people were regular visitors to the fort and a few even embraced Dutch culture and became part of Company society. From the earliest days of VOC trading, a number of these Khoe individuals played an important role as "compradores" (indigenous people who cooperated and collaborated with colonizers) who facilitated trade and understanding between the two cul-

THE FORT AT CAPE TOWN   Built to defend VOC interests in the region, the fort was the center of both trade and tension in Cape society. *Source: National Archives of South Africa.*

tures by interpreting and communicating information about Khoe and Dutch ways to both societies. In some cases, they helped establish political and trade alliances with the Dutch in order to get firearms and gain an advantage over other Khoe clans, although the Dutch mistrusted them. Moreover, they hastened the expansion of the limited local market economy, which increased the range of European goods available to the Khoe.

The compradores were neither outright traitors to the Khoe, nor fully adapted to or accepted by the VOC society; they were sophisticated and complex individuals who sought to take advantage of new opportunities. Dorha (called "Klass") of the Chainouqua, for example, gained official status as a "captain" of the VOC by helping the Company establish a lucrative cattle trade with other friendly clans. Dorha and 250 followers then allied with the Dutch in a war against a rival Khoe group, the Cochoqua, and he was duly rewarded with looted cattle and sheep. As with many of his counterparts, however, the alliance turned sour. He was attacked and arrested by VOC Governor Van der Stel in 1693, in part because of Dutch concerns about his rising influence and wealth and in part because of the jealous accusations of other Khoe trading clans. Although he was later released on Company orders, the effect of his arrest was the loss of his wife, his status, and his livestock. In 1701, he was killed by a rival Khoe chief. Clearly, the alliance had not served him well. Other Khoe such as Doman and Krotoa of the *Strandlopers* (Khoe "beach rangers" of the Cape) not only learned to speak Dutch and English (in some cases by living briefly overseas in European society or on merchant ships), but later developed a keen understanding of whites and their motives. This knowledge allowed them to capitalize on trade and enhanced their ability to lead resistance when the tide of cooperation turned to conflict.

Krotoa had important connections to various Khoe herding groups and was about ten years old when she was placed with Jan van Riebeeck's family as a domestic servant and protégé. Moreover, her sister was the wife of Oedasoa, the chief of the important Cochoqua band. This royal connection enhanced her prestige and usefulness to the Dutch because it afforded her special access to the Khoe leaders. While with the van Riebeecks, she was formally educated and quickly learned to speak both Dutch and Portuguese; she also acquired a taste for European clothing and Dutch cuisine. Unlike most Khoe girls in her position, Krotoa was encouraged in the Christian religion and was eventually baptized. As Krotoa grew older, however, she was torn between her life within VOC society and her links with Khoe society to which she frequently returned, re-adopting their dress and customs. She did try to get some of her poorer relatives involved with the lucrative livestock trade, but with little success. Moreover, she was not fully trusted by the Dutch, nor was she completely accepted by the Khoe who remained suspicious of white motives. After van Riebeeck left the Cape, Krotoa's fortunes improved for a time when she married the Danish soldier and physician Pieter van Meerhoff in 1664. The stresses in her dual life, however, provoked her to abuse liquor which was then widely available, and she was often reported to be publically drunk. The prejudices of Dutch society provided her little comfort and yet she was rejected by the Khoe. In her final years, she was described as an adulterer, a prostitute, and an alcoholic. At various times, she was arrested and imprisoned, ironically on Robben Island where she had once been the superintendent's (van Meerhoff) wife. She died there in July 1674, and despite her public ignominy, was given a Christian burial within the castle which replaced the old fort in Cape Town (see Map 2–1 on page 30).

White Settlement and Khoe Resistance

Beginning in the late 1650s, two new Dutch initiatives—increased white settlement and the use of slaves—set in motion the destruction of Khoe society and the more general subordination of "black" peoples at the Cape. Since the Khoe would not part with cattle essential to the survival of their herds to meet VOC demands, the Company, contrary to its policy in the Far East, decided to allow some employees to move onto and farm Khoe lands. In 1657, the first twelve "free burghers" (farmers released from company duties) settled beyond Table Mountain in the Liesbeck Valley on land granted to them by the VOC under a loan-farm system. More settler farmers followed, and they gradually transformed the political and economic geography of the region. They staked out vast farms in the fertile valleys of the Cape and instituted a European-style system of land leases and ownership which was alien to indigenous society in which land was held in trust for communal use. Moreover, settlers worked the land intensively and developed regular, market-oriented production of livestock commodities (wool, meat, and hides) in addition to grapes for wine and substantial amounts of grain, principally wheat. The Cape was thus transformed into a more intensive and commercializing farming settlement colony.

A significant feature of increased white settlement was a decided gender imbalance because the overwhelming majority of newcomers were men. In the absence of European women, the men established liaisons with Khoe women. Some of these were official marriages, as with Krotoa, which gave some Khoe women social status within colonial society, but most were informal relationships bordering on exploitive concubinage. In any event, the offspring of such relationships inherited their mother's social status, and this was significant for the emergence of the "bastaard" (later Griqua) communities of mixed-race descent. As Khoe society deteriorated, it was Khoe women who were the first absorbed as domestic servants in white households. Thus white male Company officials and employees dominated the patriarchal Cape Town society. These men, nominally controlled by the VOC, proceeded to press increasingly unfavorable terms of trade on the Khoe and, more significantly, to dispossess them of their land. When pressure on the Khoe to trade failed, some burghers resorted to raiding Khoe communities. Thus, burghers established **"commandos"** (unorganized militias which often included acculturated Khoe servants) and attacked the Khoe along the emerging zone of interaction. In retaliation for Khoe cattle, raids, the commandos terrorized Khoe communities, looted for cattle, and abducted women and children to be used as bonded labor under informal contracts on white farms.

Since the Khoe could still muster potentially powerful resistance, the VOC sought to avoid costly military conflicts which would undermine profits and draw critical attention from the Company shareholders and directors. Indeed, this consideration and the fact that some Khoe communities were still important trading allies (as long as they continued to meet VOC demands) led the Company to enact laws protecting the Khoe from settler predations. Under official orders, Company governors, beginning with van Riebeeck, tried to prohibit independent trade between the free burghers and the Khoe since it threatened the VOC monopoly. The ban on cattle trading, for example, was lifted and reimposed five times over the next fifty years with the effect that standard trading practice between whites and Khoe was sometimes illegal and sometimes legal. Not surprisingly, both Khoe and settler traders resented this government interference. Moreover, the Khoe were protected against enslavement by whites, although this did not prevent their being exploited as laborers, auxiliary soldiers, and servants. The fact that these laws were inconsistently applied had ominous implications for the Khoe.

Over the next hundred years, Khoe society was consistently eroded and destroyed as more whites invaded their territories and settled the land. Khoe grazing lands, water sources, and trade routes were brought under settler control and Company authority with the establishment of European-style political districts in Stellenbosch (1685), Swellendam (1745), and Graaf-Reinet (1785). Moreover, the imposition of these European names added a cultural and temporal dimension to Dutch control of the landscape. In 1688, the VOC settled some two hundred French Huguenots, refugees from religious persecution in Europe, who brought their expert knowledge of viticulture and established South Africa's wine industry on former Khoe lands. Moreover, the combined effects of drought and a series of devastating smallpox epidemics, beginning in 1713, further weakened Khoe society and their ability to resist. As white settlers pressed along the well-watered arable lands of the eastern Cape coast, they intensified their commando raids, hunting Khoesan people as sport which approached the level of genocide, fragmenting their communities, and either absorbing individuals as subordinate laborers or driving them onto land held by powerful Xhosa and Tswana chiefdoms. Although the settlers had now established their command over the Khoe and their lands, there remained the critical problem of securing sufficient labor to meet the demands of the expanding economy. By law the Khoe could not be enslaved, but they could be bound in servitude under informal contracts. Despite the collapse of Khoe society and the concomitant increase in the number of them potentially available to work for white settlers, too few of the reluctant Khoe offered themselves for service to satisfy white demands. A labor shortage became a significant and persistent feature of the South African economy as indigenous peoples resisted and then sought to control the terms on which they engaged in the labor market. Whites, therefore, had to find other sources of cheap labor.

SLAVERY AT THE CAPE

Almost from the inception of the VOC colony, whites turned to the use of slaves to meet their labor demands. As with other slave-based societies, notably in the Americas, this had significant and ominous implications for Cape and later South African society. Perceived physical or racial characteristics were not the determining feature of social status at the Cape, for some Khoe women did marry white men and were accepted into VOC society. The use of slaves, however, critically influenced the intersection of race and class even though it was still illegal to enslave the local Khoe. Although early VOC officials had debated the possibility of creating a white labor force, the plan never materialized because they believed imported white workers would be too expensive. Whites, moreover, tended to avoid manual farm labor in the employ of others. Moreover, established white settlers sought a cheap and malleable work force for profitability.

Consistent with a global trend in European-dominated colonies, servile labor in South Africa was increasingly associated with people of color and their enslavement. In 1658, the VOC imported its first shipment of slaves from Angola and west Africa. For the next 150 years, more slaves were brought in from Madagascar, Mozambique, and VOC holdings in the Far East. They included a multi-racial blend of mostly African, Indonesian, Malay, and some Indian and Chinese people who contributed to the vibrant religious and ethnic diversity of the Cape. Slaves with different African beliefs co-existed alongside those very few who were converted to Christianity and the substantial number of Muslim slaves who established wider social and religious networks through Islam. They influenced everything from local cuisine and language to architecture and agricultural techniques. While the majority of slaves were kept by burghers in the farming region, most of the slaves within Cape Town were held by the VOC and maintained in the Company's slave lodge.

Although slave labor in South Africa never approached the numbers exploited in the Americas (there were under 20,000 slaves by the 1770s and only about 40,000 near the end of the slave period in the 1810s), it was nevertheless a pernicious system. The absence of wide-scale plantations, as in Brazil and the American south, meant that fewer slaves were needed. They were more evenly distributed among whites, and there was perhaps less systematic control of them. Nevertheless, the lives of slaves in South Africa were miserable. They were often torn from their families, held in bondage, and were used predominantly for arduous physical work. Through an established code of paternalism and the law, masters could beat and punish their slaves. Slaves' transgressions of a master's orders or their attempted escape, which was a real threat to the order of slave society, led to branding or the brutal amputation of a leg, ear, or nose.

Previously, historians perceived slave society in South Africa to be more flexible and benign than other slave-owning societies. This was in part because the early Cape was characterized as open and tolerant and in part because of a policy of manumission and the existence of a "free black" community which included Malay and Chinese people but not Khoe people. Some slaves did become skilled artisans and craftspeople who could gain modest wealth from their own wages. In a few cases, they bought their freedom and held slaves themselves. But this was rare outside the colony, where whites demanded much in the way of hard labor. In these interpretations, much emphasis is given to the ambiguous Dutch Reformed Church doctrine, which stated that Christianity and slavery were incompatible and that the baptism of slaves led to their emancipation. Scholars now recognize that there was never any official policy that all baptized slaves be freed and, overall, rates of manumission remained much lower than in other slave-owning societies in the Americas. For the significant number of Muslim slaves, moreover, emancipation by baptism was not a possibility. The few manumitted slaves were those owned and converted by the VOC because Company officials encouraged this policy in the vain hope of developing a free, stable, and productive workforce. Free blacks remained a small and politically powerless segment of society. Private slave-owners, however, were not very interested in baptizing their slaves, as there was little missionary spirit in the burgher community and they feared losing the ability to control and sell Christian slaves. Farmers, most of whom were separated by long distances, generally held small numbers of slaves on their farms. This prevented slaves from mounting any major, organized rebellions, such as the ones in the late eighteenth- and early nineteenth-century Caribbean. Until the arrival of the British raised hopes for abolition, slaves were limited to minor forms of resistance on a day-to-day basis and a few minor mutinies on remote farms.

Although slavery in South Africa was a minor affair when compared with the vast plantation systems of the Americas, it was a rigidly closed and controlled slave society. This had an enormous impact on South African society. In addition to the inhumanities of slavery, the company-sponsored immigration of significant numbers of European women in the late eighteenth century further contributed to the cultural chauvinism and the hardening of racial attitudes in Cape Town. The newly arrived white women sought to establish their elite status against the local population of African and mixed-race women. The VOC then officially excluded children of mixed marriages from full legal rights and, by 1765, social and cultural distinctions were added to the classification of race and class groups. Similar to European sumptuary laws for maintaining class difference according to the cost and types of dress people wore, the VOC prohibited even free black women from wearing lace and hoopskirts, which were the privileged domain of white women. Coloured domestic servants were further denigrated and openly referred to as *skepsels,* or "living tools." Moreover, the patterns of labor coercion and control established by whites over black people through slavery and informal contracts with the Khoe in the early Cape persisted.

RELATIONS IN THE ZONES OF INTERACTION

As white settlement expanded, trade and political relations between Khoe and whites and among indigenous societies shifted. Whites developed very negative views of the Khoe in part because of Khoe resistance, and in part because of European cultural values. Reminiscent of the culture contact and relations in the Americas between white settlers and Indian societies, the burghers considered that indigenous people were savage and stood in the way of commercial progress. Moreover, because of the understandable Khoe reluctance to abandon their way of life to work for often exploitive whites, they were perceived to be unfit laborers. These attitudes were reinforced by the institution of slavery at the Cape which associated servile status with people of color, by the relative weakness and eventual collapse of Khoe society, and by the Khoe being absorbed into colonial society as subordinates. In some cases, Khoe communities sought or were forced by circumstances to make alliances with the Dutch until their wealth in cattle was eroded and they were replaced by other Khoe groups. Other Khoe clans attacked competing Khoe and San communities in order to gain pasture land or to control trade with the Dutch and the interior Nguni peoples. In the long term, however, the Khoe were forced to either stand and resist white encroachment, or retreat to the interior where they often reformed with San communities and undertook foraging and raiding strategies.

Organized Khoe military resistence demonstrated the extent to which the Khoe had struggled to adapt to the rapidly changing political economy. It was limited, however, and largely ineffective against determined white assaults.

Nevertheless, because of Khoe raids and a widespread (although largely un-founded) belief that they harbored fugitive slaves, whites escalated the scale of conflict with the Khoe through settler expansion, domination of trade, and, more significantly, a series of wars. In 1659, most of the Cape Khoe groups in-tensified their raiding activities with stealthy guerrilla tactics. Not surprisingly, some of the most successful resistance leaders were former compradores who had gained valuable knowledge about Dutch military capabilities. Doman of the Goringhaiqua, for example, led raids in rainy weather when, he knew, Dutch match-lock powder-muskets would not fire. Indeed, the combined ef-forts of the Goringhaiqua, the Gorachoqua, and the Cochoqua nearly suc-ceeded in driving the Dutch out. However, it was too difficult for the Cape coastal Khoe to sustain the war and, by the end of a second war in 1677 they were subdued and absorbed into the Company's expanding colony, as were a succession of Khoe groups over the next century.

The driving force behind this expansion was a new type, the trekboer. These herders moved into the interior in search of trading opportunities and land for stock herding. By about 1700, the combination of intensive settle-ment of fertile lands close to Cape Town and unusually large settler families forced the poor or adventurous young men of the colony to search for new op-portunities. Many set out eastward as would-be stock farmers with a meager inheritance of a wagon, some oxen, a few slaves, and Khoe servants. The trek-boers developed a unique lifestyle and consciousness in the interior. They had a fiercely independent attitude and began referring to themselves as **"Afri-kaners,"** ostensibly indigenous white people of Dutch-European descent who had made the continent their home. While they embraced the tenets of Dutch Calvinism and its attendant attitude of Christian superiority over indigenous heathens, even if they were not studied in it, they rejected VOC interference. They remained only partially tied to trade with Cape Town for a few essentials such as weapons and gunpowder.

In the interior, the trekboers adopted indigenous strategies of survival, and they relied upon Khoe society for servants, wives, knowledge of the environ-ment, and livestock trade for cattle and sheep. As with the Khoe in the more arid interior, they tended to engage in hunting, raiding, and long-distance herding rather than intensive farming. Until whites conquered and completely subjugated the Africans and then established a colonial government in the dis-tant regions of settlement, the VOC had only nominal control of the trek-boers. They were rugged, land-hungry men who often ignored the Company policy stipulating payment of an annual fee for the vast areas of land (up to 6,000 acres) which they claimed under the VOC loan-farm system. In a region with few roads or towns, the trekboers could not effect total political control the way the VOC did later. Even so, they expanded their claims and settlement rapidly. With large, organized commando raids, they easily displaced or pressed into service the remaining Khoe communities of the near Cape interior. Settlers, however, met more concerted resistance from Khoe and San people entrenched in the Great Karoo Mountains, and from the more powerful Xhosa kingdom to the east of the colony.

For much of the later 1700s, African society had a strong influence on the trekboers to the north and east of Cape Town, as indigenous people stalled white expansion and developed their own forms of interdependence. Despite trekboer expansion, from about 1770 until after the turn of the century, the area beyond the colony was an open, fluid zone where neither whites nor Africans commanded sufficient power to assert total economic or political control. It was, instead, a region of contrasts. Trade and violent conflict, shifting alliances and reconfigured communities, Boer commandos, and Xhosa cattle raids all were a part of life in the zones of interaction. While the VOC sought to regulate the area beyond the colony, the interior region and the settlers were beyond their practical control. Relations between settlers and indigenous farmers shifted from remarkable interdependence and profitable trade to outright violence and aggression as whites struggled to control the land and resources of the interior. These relations contributed to the whites' notions of cultural difference and their belief in their superiority, and yet there was no evidence of explicit racism based on biological difference. Both African and white remained open to interaction and the possibilities of profits to be had, but they also sought to assert or defend their own interests.

North of the colony, determined Khoesan groups who had retreated from the settled region of the Cape forced many white farmers to abandon their land altogether. Here, with the aid of a VOC deserter, Jan Bloem, the Khoesan acquired guns and also displaced the Rolong, a Sotho-Tswana chiefdom. By 1778, they emerged as the powerful Kora chiefdom. (A chiefdom is a political unit in many African societies. It consists of a number of clans which are subordinate to an established dominant chiefly clan and the leader or chief. Chiefdoms claim control over defined territories which can be expanded by settlement or conquest. Clan members are related through kinship, real or fictive, and their basic social organization is based on family relations within homesteads. This contrasts with the chief, who controlled the political relations for all the clans.) In the east, however, the Khoe who had acted as middlemen in a growing trade between settlers and the expanding Xhosa were pushed back. A number of stable Khoe chiefdoms settled for a time in the region between the Gamtoos and Sundays rivers. The Gonaqua, a significant fragment of displaced Khoe, withdrew to the area between the Fish and Keiskamma rivers where they were absorbed by the dominant Xhosa and reemerged as the part-Khoe, part-Xhosa Gqunukwebe chiefdom. As these Khoe struggled to settle, they were caught between the expanding white settlers from the Cape and the expanding Xhosa chiefdoms to the northeast.

A XHOSA HUNTING PARTY   The Xhosa chiefdoms were confronted by White settler expansion on the eastern Cape region. *Source: National Archives of South Africa.*

WHITES AND THE GRIQUA IN THE INTERIOR

Another significant, though unintended, development of relations beyond the colony was the emergence of the Griqua communities. The Griqua were a cultural and biological blend of white settlers, Khoesan, Africans, and free blacks who, along with others of mixed descent, were later referred to as the "Coloured" (or Cape Coloured) people. Within the settled parts of the colony, intensified competition for land and resources contributed to a growing white prejudice against people with a darker complexion. Competition also tended to reinforce the low economic standing of people of color and left only servitude as the way of life for most indigenous people, thus encouraging them to seek an independent footing in the interior. The Griqua had their origins in the crucible of the zone of interaction where economic and social features were more important determinants of status than race. There, the fluidity of social relations often allowed people of mixed-race descent to be incorporated into white society just as some whites were accepted into Khoe society. No firm racial classifications yet existed, which suggests that, whatever the perceptions of physical type, concepts of race were socially constructed. Unlike the custom in parts of the Americas, heterogeneous origins, did not necessarily dictate a person's social status. Nevertheless, there were social categories for groups with defined legal and ethnic characteristics. The Bastaards (or Basters) were a product of marriages between settlers and indigenous people who aspired to citizenship and property rights through their association with Christianity and

European culture and language. A subsidiary category of Khoe and Khoe-white people who had lost their economic independence and become dependents of settler farmers were known as *Oorlams,* and they too were a part of the cultural blend beyond the colony. Along with an assortment of white adventurers—some of dubious character—free blacks, and escaped slaves, they formed the distinct Griqua communities.

The Griqua were an integral part of the gun-toting commando culture of the lawless area north of the Cape in the later 1700s. Some sought to create stable herding and ivory trading communities while others concentrated on the illicit gun trade, hunting and, where feasible, raiding. In some cases, capable Griqua leaders who managed to circumvent colonial laws limiting their access to firearms, aimed particularly at potentially hostile indigenous people, gathered substantial followings of Oorlams and San, and established powerful family clans. The Koks, under Adam, a manumitted slave, and his sons Cornelius and Solomon, and the Barends, led by brothers Klaas and Piet, for example, acquired extensive farms along the Orange River and developed a lucrative trade in ivory and cattle with Sotho-Tswana people, particularly the Thlaping, who controlled routes to the elephant-rich interior. Thereafter, the Koks and the Barends developed good relations with the colonial government and were among the pre-eminent Griqua families.

Other maverick Griqua clans emerged under the patronage of well-capitalized white settlers. Petrus Pienaar, a minor white official who owned several farms along the Orange, provided Jan Bloem the support which enabled him to help establish a Griqua commando and lead the powerful Khoe chiefdom of the Kora mentioned earlier. His alliances eventually fell apart and he later died of poisoning. Pienaar also acquired the services of another important Griqua leader, Klaas Afrikaner and his son Jager, with ill-fated results. While Klass was on a raiding expedition, Pienaar is said to have assaulted his wives and children who remained on the farm. On his return, Klass and his men killed Pienaar, then, fearing a colonial reprisal, fled with his clan to an island refuge further up the Orange River. From this stronghold, the Afrikaner clan fended off the Barends, who had been sent in pursuit to punish Klaas, and gathered a large following of Khoe and some displaced Xhosa. Klaas's clan then established their hegemony as raiders in the northern reaches of the Orange River Valley and successfully defended their territory against colonial forces and combined Griqua-settler commandos in a minor war.

The Griqua inhabited a violent region where raiding by commandos from various communities and illegal gun trading were common occurrences. The entire region north of the Cape was in upheaval through the turn of the nineteenth century despite the efforts of colonial officials and some Griqua clans to stabilize it. Some well-placed Griqua families, such as the Koks and the Barends, sought to formalize their position in colonial society by adopting aspects of the language and culture of the white settlers, by registering their land titles (which was still legal for people of mixed parentage), and by cultivating alliances with those settlers. Others maintained a more independent stance and considered raiding and trading possibilities in the interior rather than attempting to create settled society. They were encouraged, no doubt, in these endeavors by the increasing hostility of whites to their enterprises as well as the settlers' demands that the Griqua carry identification passes as well as subject their children to labor apprenticeships for whites. Nevertheless, the Griqua played a leading role in the expansion of the northern zone of settlement and, as we shall see later, they were also involved in the turmoil of labor raiding in the interior during the *difaqane*. With the advent of British rule and the arrival of missionaries, however, the Griqua became embroiled in the machinations of colonial politics.

The Xhosa and the White Settlers

The area to the east of the Cape was initially a porous zone where expanding Xhosa chiefdoms interacted and competed with advancing white settlers. Xhosa society, however, was still undergoing political re-alignment in the mid-eighteenth century and did not constitute a single cohesive polity. The original Xhosa chiefdom of the Tshawe royal lineage, under pressure from drought and a rapidly increasing population, was forced to extend its settlement over larger grazing areas. During this period, the Xhosa chiefdoms split and fragmented into new segments as younger brothers sought to usurp legitimate heirs and minor chiefs split off to establish their own chiefdoms. A major schism between two royal brothers, Gcaleka and Rharhabe, led to the establishment of two major chiefdoms named for the founders. The Gcaleka chiefdom dominated the area east of the Great Kei River, and the Rharhabe chiefdom settled the land between the Kei and Fish rivers. In the next generation, a regent, Ndlambe, governed the Rharhabe while his nephew, the heir Ngqika, was still a child. When Ngqika came of age in 1800, Ndlambe wanted to retain power and broke away to establish a rival chiefdom. By the time the Trekboers had arrived in the 1760s, six other minor independent Xhosa chiefdoms, dispersed from the internal conflicts, had settled permanently between the Fish and Sundays rivers. Here they absorbed the fragmented Khoe chiefdoms and controlled the important *zuurveld* (literally "sour grazing land"; grasses essential for seasonal patterns of grazing) zone. A relatively small number of white settlers then disbursed along the still sparsely populated *zuurveld* and traded with the Xhosa until competition over grazing land led to conflict.

As with the Khoe and the expansion of the Cape, mutually beneficial trade relations between whites and Xhosa were often characterized by suspicion and misunderstanding, but for a time, neither group upset the balance of power. On the one hand, some undisciplined and aggressive settlers pressed exploitive terms of trade and, more significantly, raided for cattle as they sought to gain access to *zuurveld* grazing. On the other hand, Xhosa groups raided unprotected white farms to retrieve their stolen cattle and to assert their rights to the land. The tension between the groups was a product of competition between similar economic communities, not overt racism. Indeed, most of the Boers developed a lifestyle which closely approximated that of the local Xhosa, including herding, hunting, and trading for metals and stock. A few Boers adapted to the local culture to such an extent that they were completely immersed in the Xhosa political economy. For example, the rough and ready frontiersman, Coenraad de Buys, married Ngqika's mother and several other Xhosa women and later played a significant role in shifting alliances. For the majority of the white settlers, however, major cultural and political differences changed competition into open conflict. Most settlers believed it was their right to take outright the land they had claimed. This was a concept as alien to the Xhosa as it had been to the Khoe. Moreover, despite their aversion to Company authority, settlers eventually demanded and received VOC support. Officials were concerned that settler belligerence would provoke organized Xhosa retaliation and lead the VOC into a costly war against a much more powerful African society than they had faced previously. The Company, therefore, developed a policy to restrain the settlers, establish a firm border, and to reduce white entanglements with the Xhosa, but it was ultimately ineffective.

The relative strength of the Xhosa chiefdoms, the aggression of the independent-minded settlers, and a complicated series of shifting alliances all conspired to prevent the VOC from settling the area. In 1778, Governor van Plettenburg attempted to extend the Cape colony border to bring the settlers and their lands under Company control. After discussions with some minor Xhosa chiefs, he claimed that he had secured rights to the *zuurveld* and he proceeded to extend the official boundary of the colony to the Fish River. However, the Xhosa, including the Gqunukwebe who settled the area, did not recognize the claim since the chiefs whom van Plettenburg consulted had no authority over the region. In any event, under Xhosa law there was no precedent for anyone to cede land since it was held in communal trust and could not be alienated or owned. Thus the proclamation had little immediate effect on the Xhosa, who continued to inhabit the land and to trade with willing settlers. Nevertheless, the VOC established its jurisdiction by appointing local military commandants to settle the area. This had dire consequences for the Xhosa. In 1780, there was a series of unauthorized commando raids against the Xhosa, including a particularly vicious one led by Petrus Ferreira. The whites killed many Africans and looted hundreds of their cattle. This provoked a massive Xhosa retaliation which threatened to overwhelm white settlements in the area.

In an effort to restore order, the VOC dispatched its local commandant, Adriaan van Jaarsveld, to negotiate peace and persuade the Xhosa to retreat beyond the Fish River. This was significant because it established a policy of territorial segregation between whites and Africans which reflected the general European belief that the two cultures could not co-exist. Van Jaarsveld was far from an ideal choice, for he was notorious among indigenous people for earlier brutal expeditions against the San. Contrary to orders, he ambushed a Xhosa group who had been induced into the open by an offering of tobacco laid on the ground, and he later attacked Xhosa settlements and seized hundreds of cattle. This incident sparked the first of nine wars between the Xhosa and the colonists. In this first campaign, settler forces were unable to dislodge the Xhosa. The region was later the scene of more complex conflicts as the Rharhabe Xhosa made an alliance with some Boers in an effort to drive their mutal rivals, the Gqunukwebe, from the *zuurveld*. While the Boers shared in the spoils from the successful military thrust of the alliance, they coincidently further destabilized the region as the Gqunukwebe fled into the colony where they started to raid isolated white farms.

The Xhosa kept the upper hand until the next war in 1793, despite a renewed effort by the VOC to settle the area. Indeed, white settlers who made repeated requests for official intervention were even more frustrated with the newly appointed magistrate, H.C.D Maynier. Maynier was an able but paternalistic administrator. He sought to uphold the rule of Company law by prohibiting unauthorized commandos against or alliances with any section of the Xhosa. Moreover, he hoped to stabilize labor relations within the colony to discourage disgruntled Khoe from deserting their contracts. He allowed Khoe servants recourse to his court for their complaints of mistreatment by their white employers. The settlers resented both initiatives because this limited their ability to loot cattle, to claim more land, and to control their workers as they saw fit. In response, the settlers continued their raids against the *zuurveld* Xhosa, which provoked a wide-scale retaliation. The magistrate resorted to organizing a pacifying commando which forced the Xhosa to sue for peace. The magistrate realized, however, that he could not muster sufficient forces to pressure the Xhosa to quit the contested area. In the peace negotiations, he accepted that the Xhosa would retain the *zuurveld,* but he warned that they could only remain subject to peaceful behavior. This agreement further embittered the settlers who demanded the right to settle on Xhosa lands. In 1795, inspired by radical republican ideals loosely derived from the philosophy of the French and American revolutions, two settler communities rebelled, drove out Maynier, and proclaimed the independent republics of Swellendam and Graaff-Reinet. This was an important indicator of the extent of settler agitation and the lengths to which they would go in asserting their independence from official authority. These problems remained unresolved by the VOC, for the Cape was taken over by the British (see Chapter 3, "The British and the Expanding Cape: Continuities and Contrasts") in the same year; and they too joined the protracted struggle to settle relations with the Xhosa and other African societies as they tried to rein in the settlers.

Conclusion

The early foundations of Cape society rested on an interdependence between the African peoples and the newly arrived European merchant interests. Interdependence gave way to mistrust, tension, and eventual conflict because of contending social and economic interests. The aggressive and unsuccessful bid of the Portuguese to gain a foothold in South Africa set the tone for later relations between whites and the indigenous Khoe and San. Thereafter, the VOC's (Dutch East India Company) establishment of a permanent trading fort at the Cape dramatically changed the lives of the Khoesan peoples of the region. Company rule relied upon compliant Khoe compradores as interpreters and trading agents in order to secure livestock and water from Khoe communities to supply the VOC shipping fleet. This mutually beneficial trade relationship, however, deteriorated when the Dutch began escalating their demands beyond what Khoe society could accommodate. Dutch efforts to get cattle, either through coercive terms of trade or outright force, led the Khoe to resist. Faced with decreasing supplies from the Khoe and the potential for the still-powerful Khoe to defend their interests and lands, the VOC sought to improve its position with the importation of white settlers.

Increased white settlement had several significant implications for the escalation of conflict with the Khoe and changing white attitudes about indigenous people. First, more white settlers meant that they could press their interests against the Khoe with force. Second, an increase in the number of white men meant an expansion of the colony and new relations with Khoe women. The result was an ambiguous combination of intensified white hostilities against Khoe resistors on the one hand, and increasing trade contacts and interrelations between white male settlers and Khoe women on the other hand. Ultimately, Khoe society could not withstand the impact of white expansion. Coupled with devastating smallpox epidemics, the white settler commando raids drove Khoe communities into collapse or withdrawal from the Cape. Almost from its inception, the Cape colony relied upon slave labor. The VOC experienced a significant labor shortage in part because of increasing demands for agricultural and livestock products, and in part because the Khoe resisted employment by whites, preferring to retain their economic independence. As a result, the Company turned to the use of imported slaves. Brought into bondage from other parts of Africa and Asia, these people provided a significant source of malleable labor and contributed to the Cape's ethnic diversity. The expansion of settler farming under the VOC's free burgher loan-farm system only served to increase the demand for slaves, and the Cape took its ignominious place in history as one of the world's most ruthless slave-owning societies. These developments had important implications for later race relations in South Africa, since they meant that whites began to associate people of color with servile work and slavery.

Meanwhile, the eastern Cape emerged as an open, fluid zone where white Trekboers and Africans intermingled through trade and conflict. One by-product of these relations was the establishment of the mixed-descent Griqua peoples. The Griqua played an integral role in expanding trade and social relations into the interior through raiding and trading. A broader front of interdependence and conflict emerged in the eastern zone of the Cape when Trekboer farmers encountered the expanding Xhosa chiefdoms. The Xhosa were a more powerful and politically organized polity than the Dutch had yet confronted. Although trade relations between Xhosa and white Trekboers were an important aspect of economic activity in the eastern Cape, the deciding feature was competition over the valuable *zuurveld* grazing lands. While the VOC vacillated between a policy of neutrality and pacification, settler aggression forced the Company to attack and attempt to subdue the Xhosa in an attempt to gain control of Xhosa lands. As we shall see in Chapter 3, until the nineteenth century and the arrival of the British, the Xhosa held firm and the eastern Cape area remained a contested region where republican-minded settlers vied with the Xhosa for economic and political control.

QUESTIONS TO CONSIDER

1. What were the VOC's initial interests in South Africa, and how did these change as company employees interacted with the Khoe? Compare this with the relations between the Portuguese and the Khoe.
2. How was the VOC interdependent with the Khoe, how did the Khoe respond to and shape this interdependence, and how did this relationship change to one of resistance and conflict?
3. Discuss the nature of slavery at the Cape and what implications it had for South African society.
4. What impact did white settlement have on the interior? Who were the Griqua, and what role did they play in changing the social, economic, and political relations beyond the Cape colony?
5. How did the Xhosa shape and resist the expansion of white settlers into their territory?

FURTHER READINGS

ELPHICK, R., *KhoiKhoi and the Founding of White South Africa* (Johannesburg, 1985). A recently revised work which is the best comprehensive analysis of Khoe societies and their economic, political, and social relations with whites.

ELPHICK, R., and GILIOMEE, H. (editors), *The Shaping of South African Society, 1652-1840* (Cape Town, 1989). A collection of essays covering the period from the establishment of VOC rule through the period of the British takeover and slave emancipation. It has excellent pieces on the frontier relations among Khoe, Griqua, whites, and Xhosa by the leading scholars in the field.

ELDRIDGE, E., and MORTON, F. (editors), *Slavery in South Africa: Captive Labor on the Dutch Frontier* (Pietermaritzburg, 1994). A good recent collection of essays which re-invigorates debates about the nature of slavery in early colonial South Africa.

LAMAR, H., and THOMPSON, L., *The Frontier in History: North America and Southern Africa Compared* (New Haven, 1981). A still-useful collection of essays which applies a re-interpretation of the frontier thesis to both countries in comparative perspective. It would especially be of interest to American students.

KEEGAN, T., *Colonial South Africa and the Origins of the Racial Order* (Charlottesville, 1996). A well-researched and detailed analysis of the emergence of racial attitudes and societal constraints in early colonial South Africa. This is a challenging work with a strong structure and argument.

MARKS, S., "Khoesan Resistance to the Dutch in the Seventeenth and Eighteenth Centuries," *Journal of African History,* Vol. 13 (1972). The best early work on resistance studies in South Africa by the leading figure in this field.

NEWTON-KING, S., *Masters and Servants on the Cape Eastern Frontier, 1760-1803* (Cambridge, 1999). An important re-evaluation of relations between white settlers and black on the frontier and in the colony. It has set a new tone and put forth a very convincing new argument about social and economic relations between whites and their bonded workers.

PEIRES, J., *The House of Phalo. A history of the Xhosa People in the Days of Their Independence* (Johannesburg, 1981). The definitive work on the early Xhosa chiefdoms and their founding. Also a good work for understanding relations within chiefdoms.

ROSS, R., *Cape of Torments: Slavery and Resistance in South Africa* (London, 1983). A still very insightful analysis of slave resistance in the Cape. Well written and very readable.

Ross, R., *Adam Kok's Griqua: A Study in the Development of Stratification in South Africa* (Cambridge, 1976). An important analysis of the fluidity of relations in the interior and the emergence of new communities which complicated notions of race, class, and culture in early South Africa.

Switzer, L., *Power and Resistance in an African Society. The Ciskei Xhosa and the Making of South Africa* (London, 1993). A fine application of the frontier thesis to developments along the eastern frontier. It has very good coverage of the role of missionaries and western education on African society.

Worden, N., *Slavery in Dutch South Africa* (Cambridge, 1985). A powerful assessment of the making of a race-based slave society. It examines the foundations and causes of slavery in South Africa as well as the nature of the dominant white society.

CHAPTER III

The British and the Expanding Cape: Continuities and Contrasts

Towards the end of the eighteenth century, the revolutionary forces of the European Enlightenment and, more importantly, industrialization, transformed Britain into a powerful modernizing force in the world. Intensified British imperial activity soon brought South Africa to the center of these tumultuous changes after Britain acquired the Cape and introduced new settlers and a colonial government. British policies for South Africa were conditioned by two new political philosophies: liberalism and humanitarianism. Liberalism emphasized equality and individual rights based on merit rather than birth, but these values were not extended to the indigenous peoples of the empire. British liberals sought to champion the middle class, their rights to private property, and to free speech. They also believed in representative democracy and in restraining government from interfering in the lives of individuals. In addition, they sought to advance free market relations and open competition within a capitalist economy. Humanitarianism was a symbolic system associated with liberalism which provided the British with an ideological purpose for their new political and economic order.

Humanitarianism conjoined the values of the new Christian evangelical revival, which was spawned on both sides of the Atlantic in Europe and New England, with the values of commerce and personal accumulation based on hard work. Humanitarians were also concerned with the social and political ills of bondage and privation. They endeavored to "uplift the heathen savages of Africa" through spiritual and economic "improvement," although this also legitimized paternalism and the hierarchy of class rule. Significantly, the humanitarian movement converged with the ideology of free trade and fair competition, especially as it sought to extend human rights and freedom to people subjected to coerced labor. Contained within the ideology of humanitarianism, however, was the rising strand of "utilitarian liberalism" which emphasized efficiency, production, and profit and which eventually outweighed more philanthropic concerns. The imperatives of a free market system, however, also meant that many people in Britain questioned whether it was appropriate to maintain colonies such as South Africa at all, especially if they were a drain on the treasury.

While British rule appeared to differ from the stringent commercial imperatives of the VOC, for Africans there were more continuities than contrasts under British rule when it came to the effects of white domination at the Cape. This was particularly true of British abolition of the Atlantic slave trade in 1807, and of the use of slaves within the British colonies in 1834. Abolition freed the Africans who were held in bondage; first, it freed them from the wretchedness of slavery and secondly, British liberalism and humanitarianism appeared to provide some protection and opportunities for the "upliftment" of African workers who were prepared to embrace "Christian Civilization." African workers, however, were to experience more open and rigorous forms of control under expanding British capitalism than they had previously experienced with the Dutch. Moreover, because of strategic concerns, the British were determined to create a permanent, peaceful, and ordered colony in South Africa. This entailed both the introduction of a significantly increased number of settlers and the forcible resolution of troubled relations with African societies such as the Xhosa.

British rule and the attendant settler and merchant forces both impinged upon and created new opportunities for indigenous people. In addition, the new Christian evangelical movement created a great wave of missionary activity which flowed across South Africa and the continent. African communities and individuals at various times resisted, adapted to, or retreated from missionary activity and the burgeoning white capitalist-dominated society as they sought the best advantage in trying times. For some indigenous peoples, these new forces provided markedly improved access to European material culture; for others, they were the harbingers of dispossession and economic dislocation. British colonial rule also challenged the established Dutch-speaking Afrikaner-Boer settlers of the VOC period. Although the Afrikaner elite managed to establish a working relationship with the British, most Boers, and especially the trekboers, resented British policies and political ideals. Many trekboers perceived British rule as a threat to their rugged independence and subversive to the racially ordered hierarchy they sought to entrench. This was especially true of the new laws designed to safeguard indigenous people and stabilize the black labor force. While these policies were aimed at settling the country and,

more significantly, calming the relations between Africans and whites, they
were often inconsistently applied and instead served to create unintended tensions beyond the colony. African people had to confront a confusing array of
often contending influences, policies, and powers. These ranged from an imperial metropolitan government in London to local colonial officials, from
merchants, settlers, and missionaries on the ground to newly emerging and
transforming indigenous communities. Each of these groups had its own stake
in the land and in the control of the country. Not surprisingly, there was a
myriad of tensions, misunderstandings, and conflicts in this context. Despite
the attempts of Africans to employ creative strategies to cope with these challenges, the conflicts were ultimately resolved by force of arms. In the end, indigenous societies near to the Cape lost their rights to the land and their
political and economic independence.

THE ARRIVAL OF THE BRITISH

In 1795, Britain first acquired the Cape as a function of European conflict.
Then, after it reverted to the Dutch Batavian Republic (as the United Netherlands was then known) for a brief time from 1803–1806, the British reacquired
the colony permanently in 1806. Earlier, in 1792, a longstanding rivalry between France, which was still under revolutionary leadership, and Britain boiled
over into a war involving several European nations, including the Netherlands.
After France occupied the Netherlands in 1794, the exiled Dutch leadership invited Britain to invade the Cape for strategic reasons, and British troops quickly
secured the colony in order to safeguard its trade route to India. During the
first British occupation, although the new administration retained many features and personnel from the VOC period, it also sought to reform the corruption and nepotism which characterized much of the earlier company rule. Yet
the first British governors, many of whom were military men, enjoyed wide-
ranging powers and ruled in an autocratic fashion. This had significant implications for the colonial government's relations with the established Boers.
Established white settlers had resented the previous VOC government's attempts to restrain their drive to expand into African lands. They turned this
same rejection of government interference in their affairs against the British.

British imperial rule helped set in motion the development of the South
African economy. As Britain's maritime empire rapidly expanded in the eighteenth century, its mercantile system fueled its industrial revolution. This economic power drove new markets, the demand for resources, and new labor
relations. However, until the discovery of mineral resources—specifically diamonds and gold—after the 1850s, South Africa contributed little to the British
economy, and it did not attract significant investment compared with other
parts of the empire. Nevertheless, the British administration implemented a

new land tenure system in the country. This provided for the private ownership of farms in place of the old VOC loan-farm system which had hampered entrepreneurial agriculture. British merchants also promoted the rapid development of the Cape wine industry. Wine production rose over eighty percent in the first twenty years of British rule. By the 1820s, imported merino sheep contributed to the gradual increase in wool exports, which dominated the Cape export market by 1870. Although wheat remained an important crop, harvests were unreliable and insufficient for the development of significant exports.

In order to develop the Cape economy and to bring it in line with imperial and humanitarian policies, the British made significant changes which had an enormous impact on South Africa. The first was the attempt to reform labor relations; they abolished the slave trade after 1807, and by 1834, slaves were no longer used in British colonies. The second was to significantly increase the number of white British settlers through a series of immigration schemes. The abolition of slavery exacerbated the problems that whites already faced in securing workers and, as white settlers increased, made acute the labor shortage. Influenced by the humanitarian movement, British officials felt that further entanglements with Africans would lead to complications and conflict. They therefore sought to keep the majority of Africans out of the colony by developing a policy of non-interaction or segregation between whites and Africans. In addition, African societies in the interior had yet to be broken up through conquest and so their labor was unavailable to the colonial economy. Consequently, whites began to more thoroughly exploit their slave and contracted Khoe workers. In response, British reformers sought to improve conditions for slaves (until their full emancipation) and workers within the colony.

ABOLITION

In 1808, Britain ended its involvement in the capture and transportation of bonded humans as part of the humanitarian reform movement, but the use of slaves in South Africa continued. The institution of slavery, however, was beyond reform; humanitarian pressures, the changing economy, and increasing tensions between owners and slaves all contributed to the ending of open slavery in South Africa. British officials compromised their reforms, which were intended to improve working conditions and thereby stabilize the labor force. Although ex-slaves and Khoe workers did experience some improvements, overall the transition to emancipation would lead to equally restrictive labor relations for the colony's working classes.

Between 1816 and 1830, the Cape government introduced a series of measures intended to reform slavery in South Africa. First, owners had to register their slaves. Then, an 1823 proclamation set standards for food, clothing, hours of work, and prohibited the breakup of slave families. The proclamation also limited slaves' physical punishment and allowed them access to Christian rites such as baptism and marriage. They were afforded certain legal protection and could now own property and testify in court. After 1826, slaves could purchase their freedom at a fair price. They also had an official protector who monitored conditions, and, by 1830, checked the record book of punishments compulsory for every slave-owner. Increasingly, during the process of abolition, slaves more openly resisted their owners. They made recourse to the courts and new laws which could afford them some protection. They sought to keep their families together and to resist the worst excesses of their owners' abuse. In these ways, British humanitarianism opened the door for slaves to challenge the dominant world view of their owners. Abolitionists hoped that reforms would lead to the eventual end of slavery, while slave-owners hoped they would sustain the institution in the face of humanitarian opposition. There remained, however, abuses because many slave-owners were able to ignore the regulations.

Although the abolition of slavery under the British Emancipation Act of 1833 was primarily focussed on plantations in the West Indies, it nevertheless had a significant impact on South Africa. Abolition represented a convergence of interests. It was inspired by the humanitarians desire to extend liberty and equality to all peoples and it freed the slaves from the wretchedness of human bondage. It also served the new industrialists' demands for a "free labor" market where workers could move to the jobs of their choosing. In theory, workers would be happier, work harder, spend their cash wages on manufactured goods, and contribute to an efficient economy. The economic motivation to free slaves from bondage was perhaps less important than the ideological imperative for the British to create a new moral order for the colony. For slave-owners, however, emancipation meant the loss of valuable property and an ensuing struggle to attract free labor. The British sought to lessen the impact of abolition by providing for a four-year apprenticeship of slaves to their owners. Nevertheless, slave-owners were frustrated by the stipulation that monetary compensation for freed slaves was payable only in London and most could not afford the voyage. Many received only a fraction of their slaves' value from unscrupulous agents.

As talk of reforming slavery circulated through the colony, slaves and contracted Khoe workers became increasingly agitated about their social condition. Concern among slave-owners that their supplies of labor would vanish led them to exact an even greater toll from their workers. Slaves also resented the proposed apprenticeship period which would perpetuate their owner's claims to their labor even after emancipation. In response, slaves took advantage of the legislation to defend their legal rights in court; they resisted their owners' demands or ran away. In 1808, just after the ending of the British sea-trade in slaves, over three hundred slaves and Khoe workers left their masters' rural farms and marched on Cape Town. Although they were dispersed by the colonial militia, their attempted assault sent a disturbing message to the colonizers. Increasingly, the reforms both undermined slave-owners' control of their slaves and apparently encouraged slave defiance. By the 1820s, resistance soared and culminated in the Bokkeveld Revolt in 1825. This insurrection was led by the slave Galant, who had complained in vain to the local authorities of ill treatment and floggings by his owner, Willem van der Merwe. Galant and a number of fellow slaves and Khoe servants seized some guns, killed van der Merwe and his wife and then attacked some neighbouring farms. The rebellion was quickly put down by a commando. At his trial, Galant claimed he had been inspired by the rumours about abolition, and a fear of his master, who, he claimed, had vowed to kill his slaves rather than let them go free. The British sought to suppress both slave insurrection and the excesses of masters. Indeed, in 1822, Willem Gebhard was sentenced to death for killing his father's slave, although his execution was also intended to appease the humanitarians. By the 1820s, however, the colony's transition to the use of free, contracted labor was underway.

REFORM AND LABOR

The corollary to British abolition was a reform of labor relations and employment practices. The new "free market" capitalist system of labor exploitation bound African people to white employers under stringent and pernicious contracts. There were numerous ambiguities and contradictions within this system. On the one hand, British liberalism and humanitarianism appeared to provide some protection and opportunities for the "upliftment" of African workers who were prepared to embrace "Christian civilization." On the other hand, increasing numbers of African workers experienced more open and rigorous forms of control under the British than they had previously. Despite these changes, the colony still experienced an overall labor shortage. By the time of the British arrival, the appalling relations between whites and the Khoe, especially in the interior, had deteriorated into anarchy and threatened to undermine the peace and prosperity of the colony. The settlers blamed the missionaries (see "The Missionary Enterprise" later in this chapter) for disruptions to their labor supplies because these humanitarians had petitioned for abolition and reform. Yet the missionaries and their allies back in London continued to press for reform.

In response to the missionaries and in the wake of a major Khoe rebellion and upheaval on the frontier in 1799, the Earl of Caledon, British governor of the Cape (1807–1811), issued a new code to govern employers (masters) and

Khoe workers (servants). This "Hottentot Proclamation" provided for the registration of all Khoe workers within the colony, and required that they carry identification passes which stated their "fixed abode" and their place of work. Caledon's code was also intended to protect Khoe workers and to make employment in the colony more attractive to them. It enforced the timely payment of wages by employers, outlawed debt slavery, and allowed for the prosecution of masters who abused their servants. Following Caledon's tenure, missionaries succeeded in getting the new governor, Sir John Cradock (1811–1813), to institute an improved court system to enforce the new laws. Although this innovative circuit court allowed for Khoe testimony, it did not render many judgments in favor of Khoe plaintiffs, nor did it appreciably change the prevailing settler view that the Khoe were inherently inferior. In fact, many Afrikaners bitterly resented the court's intervention and the consequent rise in Khoe accusations against their masters, some of which were without foundation. Many whites felt that such government meddling undermined the class and cultural hierarchy of the colony. They referred to the court as the "black circuit." It was these sorts of settler resentments that eventually led to rebellions and ultimately, culminated in the exodus of many Afrikaners from the colony.

Despite humanitarian pressures, British reforms were not intended to fundamentally alter the social and racial order of the Cape. They were aimed, instead, at settling the rather chaotic labor relations between whites and blacks and thus ensuring a stable supply of labor. In many ways, the new laws were very restrictive, and they reinforced employers' control over their African workers. In 1812, governor Cradock instituted a series of "apprenticeship" laws which allowed local officials to bind over, as workers, Khoe children between 8 and 18 years of age to any farmer who had maintained them. This was, in effect, a legally disguised form of forced labor. "Apprenticeships" would come to have ominous implications for Africans in South Africa as they did elsewhere in colonial Africa. Similarly, during the abolition of the slave trade, colonial labor shortages were alleviated by the introduction of "Prize Negroes." These people were former slaves who had been "liberated" by the British from slave ships and then forcibly indentured to settler farmers for a fixed period. Overall, the new "free market" for labor was far from free, and was accompanied by an intensifying exploitation of the workers who were available to colonists.

Through the 1820s, the British worked to reconcile the colonists' increasing demands for labor and labor control with the missionary movement's pressure for reform. At the forefront of the reform movement in South Africa was John Philip, a director of the powerful London Missionary Society (see "The Missionary Enterprise" for more information). After his arrival in 1819, Philip quickly realized that the plight of Khoe workers was inextricably bound up with the question of abolition and slavery. He sought to improve their powerless and menial status through his tireless lobbying in the British parliament and the publication in 1828 of his influential book, *Researches in South Africa*. Philip, in conjunction with Andries Stockenstrom, the commissioner-general of the Eastern Cape, was successful in convincing a receptive acting governor, Richard Bourke (1826–1828), and the British government to implement safeguards for the Khoe in 1828. The result was the Cape Governor-in-Council Ordinances 49 and 50. Ordiance 49 protected Khoe contract workers. Ordinance 50 removed all pass and vagrancy laws which had been established under Caledon's code. It also abolished summary punishments without trial and any compulsory work demanded by local officials.

Perhaps more significantly for the Cape's social hierarchy, Ordinance 50 placed the Khoe, and eventually ex-slaves as they gained their freedom after 1834, on the same legal footing as whites. They could now buy and own land, their employment was governed by legal contracts (the vast majority of which were monthly verbal agreements) and their children could no longer be indentured without parental consent. Ordinance 49 sought to address the acute labor shortage. It provided for the entry of Africans from beyond the colony, especially Xhosa from the east, as long as they took out an official pass to seek work. This was a decided departure from the earlier British policy of non-interaction between settlers and Africans from outside. It did, however, confirm the existing state of affairs in the 1820s when many Africans sought refuge in the colony from conflicts in the interior.

The theory behind Ordinance 50 was not as benevolent as it seemed. The humanitarians' intention for this reform was to raise what they claimed were the "indolent and barbaric" Khoe to a "productive and civilized" level. In the eyes of missionaries and their merchant allies, Ordinance 50 would attract Khoe workers and allow them to contribute to a profitable free market economy without relying on inefficient coercion. Not surprisingly, settler farmers were deeply shocked by the legal revolution. The government's elevation and protection of Khoe status fundamentally challenged the social hierarchy which settlers had established. Many Afrikaners complained bitterly that they could no longer afford to hire workers, and that they and their families now had to work like "slaves." Despite the provisions of both ordinances, settlers also claimed that "vagrancy," insubordination, and theft were rampant. They demanded a new vagrancy law, but were rebuffed. Their complaints were not entirely supported by the facts.

Ordinance 50 was very difficult for the authorities to enforce, and many farmers continued the exploitation of their workers as before. Some Khoe, however, took advantage of the new law to leave those farms where the conditions were poor. They either moved to other farms where they could secure more favorable terms of employment or onto mission stations where they could get access to land. In any event, few Khoe found any improvements in their economic status outside of the mission stations. By 1835, settler demands for improved labor controls led to a new apprenticeship ordinance which enhanced the power of employers to control their Khoe workers with the lash if deemed necessary. In 1841, the Masters and Servants ordinance further buttressed white employers' powers to control contracted workers. This effectively nullified Ordinance 50 which had safeguarded Khoe rights, and reinforced the racial hierarchy, although the new legislation did not refer to racial categories. Overall, Ordinances 49 and 50 did not significantly improve labor relations in the colony. They certainly did fuel the intensifying feelings of resentment and alienation which Afrikaner farmers felt, and these feelings were compounded by the arrival of large numbers of British settlers (see Map 3–1 on page 55).

BRITISH SETTLERS

The arrival of more than 4,000 British settlers in 1820 significantly changed the social and economic relations in the Cape and along its frontier. This 1820 settlement scheme was born of a British imperial desire to populate the colonies with productive white settlers and a Cape colonial desire to settle the interior. As a sop to the humanitarians, the imperial government had considered emigration schemes for industrial Britain's growing number of poor and unemployed. Earlier emigration schemes mounted by private concerns or self-funded individuals had added only small numbers of primarily British males to South Africa, compared with the more than one million people who left Britain for other colonies such as Canada and Australia between 1814 and 1840. The cost of sending out these earlier British settlers was offset by selling their indenture to local employers. They were quickly absorbed into the colony, but a number broke their indenture and absconded from their employers in order to set up working on their own. An unexpected vote of £50,000 from the normally parsimonious British parliament set the much larger 1820 scheme in motion. Close to 90,000 people applied to settle in South Africa, which propagandists had portrayed in glowing terms as an ideal destination. The government accepted about 4,000 emigrants, and roughly another 1,000 self-funded settlers joined the group. Each successful applicant was granted a 100-acre farm with the understanding that he must settle the land and undertake farming. The scheme, however, did not work out as intended.

The imperial and Cape colonial governments had intended for the 1820 settlers to establish a form of English rural society, by creating a landed gentry as a bulwark against African expansion along the eastern frontier. This unrealistic plan was never to materialize. The majority of the settlers were artisans, tradespeople, and merchants who came from the ranks of Britain's lower and middle working classes. They had no real knowledge of farming, especially in

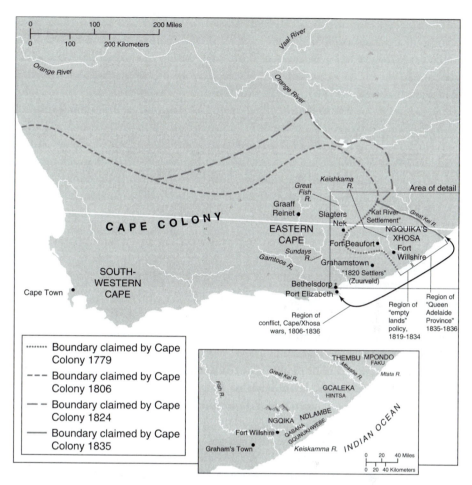

Map 3–1   The Cape Colony under British Rule. *Adapted from Shillington, History of Southern Africa. 1997; and C. Hamilton, The Mfecane Aftermath. London. 1995.*

the difficult soils and climate of South Africa. Most did not have the financial resources to hire workers in an increasingly competitive Cape labor market, and many of the workers indentured to them absconded. Moreover, the government did not inform them that they were sent to settle the *zuurveld* area in the eastern zone of interaction, which was still contested by Xhosa and Khoe-Xhosa communities. As they struggled to establish viable farms in this recently named Albany district, they had to perform extra duties as part-time soldiers to defend their claims to the land. Not surprisingly, the combined effects of drought, crop disease, and floods, on top of the stresses of living in a hostile region, led to the failure of their agricultural endeavours. Frustrated in their aspirations to become a landed gentry, some of the settlers agitated against the colonial government for more support and controls over labor. However, these "Albany Radicals" were quickly suppressed by Governor Somerset, who would not cater to their demands. Instead, the colonial government intervened to subdue the region by military force (see "Xhosa Crises: Interaction with the Settlers and Civil War" for more information).

Despite the failure of their attempts at farming, the 1820 Albany settlers were a significant force in expanding British culture, which would add further complexity to an already complicated multicultural society. As their farms failed, many would-be settlers moved off into the burgeoning frontier towns of Port Elizabeth and Grahamstown. There they turned to crafts and trades of various types, but most engaged in merchant trade, especially with Africans who had previously been on the periphery of the Cape economy. Supported by the new reformist Methodist brand of Protestantism established by John Wesley, which spoke to aspirant middle-class values, many settlers saw their future financial success in commercial profit and accumulation, not agriculture. For others, accumulation of wealth would be achieved through a return to pastoral activities which were more appropriate for the region. They introduced and rapidly developed merino sheep herds that provided valuable wool which came to dominate the Cape export economy. The mainstay of the economy for settlers in the interior was mercantile activity and trade with the Xhosa. Such activities, however, soon led to further entanglements between whites and Africans, and there were increasing demands by the settlers to push Africans farther into the interior and to extend British control. Although the British settlers sought the same things as their Dutch-Afrikaner predecessors, namely, land and labor—they were, of course, forbidden by law to own slaves—they were a culturally distinct group. Successive colonial administrations supported the extension of English as an official language, a point which greatly irritated the Afrikaners and gave an advantage to the British immigrants over those who spoke other European or African languages. The settlers also believed in the superiority of their evangelical Protestantism and had great faith in the power of merchant capitalism to transform South Africa. The new settlers did not mix or intermarry with the established settlers, referring to them as "Boers," which came to have a derogatory meaning, compared with the term "Afrikaner" preferred by the Dutch-descended immigrants. The protestants were also less inclined to adapt to indigenous culture as they sought to imprint their ways on the African landscape.

THE MISSIONARY ENTERPRISE

Christian missionaries were a major force in the transformation of South African society. They had a significant influence on white politics and laws, labor relations, and social relations within African societies. They arrived in

South Africa during the first decades of British rule, infused with newly emerging humanitarian ideals derived from the European Enlightenment and with philanthropic notions about how to uplift the "African heathen" through "Christian Civilization." Their efforts were as practical as they were spiritual. Indeed, for many members of the early missionary societies such as the Scots Presbyterians, the Wesleyan Methodists, the Anglican Church Missionary Society, and the influential London Missionary Society Congregationalists, spiritual awakening went hand in hand with individual rights, equality, and freedom.

Missionary activity, however, produced ambiguous results. On the one hand, many African people benefited from the material and social advantages of life on protected mission stations. Some Africans were able to enhance their own learning and experiences with Western education, which enabled them to better adapt to the colonial context and the new capitalist economy. Other Africans, however, especially those men such as the chiefs who had a large stake in the established indigenous forms of spirituality and patriarchy, were less embracing of the mission enterprise. On the other hand, some missionaries challenged and undermined the emerging racial social order in South Africa, thus threatening to undermine the social status and identity of white

AFRICANS BEING BAPTIZED Many Africans, especially women, embraced the spiritual and material culture associated with the missionary enterprise. *Source: National Archives of South Africa.*

settler society. Over time, African society began to affect and influence missionary activity as much as Christian "civilization" influenced it.

By the 1790s, mission societies had established a number of mission stations for Africans on two fronts. The first was among the Khoe near Cape Town and the Griqua people to the north. The second major missionary initiative was along the eastern zone of interaction with the Xhosa. Early efforts by George Schmidt of the German Moravian mission to establish stations among the Khoe within the colony faltered. Settler hostility forced the Moravians to abandon the station until 1792, when it was revived and achieved some limited long-term success under the name Genadendal. As British influence at the Cape increased, missionaries were able to expand their activities with the protection and support of metropolitan imperial interests.

The most influential of the new societies which rode in on the wave of British humanitarianism was the London Missionary Society (LMS) under the leadership of T. J. van der Kemp. Van der Kemp sought to establish mission links with the Xhosa as a stepping-stone to other African societies in the interior. His initial attempt at mission work with people living under Ngqika, the nominated heir to the **Ciskei** (the Xhosa region of the Cape side of the Kei river, hence, cis -near, side- kei) Xhosa, failed. This was due, in part, to the machinations of Ngqika's ally, the white frontiersman Coenraad de Buys, who did not want to compete with missionaries for the chief's favor. It was also a function of the relatively well-integrated nature of Xhosa society and spirituality. By comparison, rates of conversion among the scattered Khoe were higher than for the cohesive Xhosa. The local colonial government was also wary of any further entanglements with the Xhosa and instead encouraged the LMS to work among the eastern Khoe. Officials felt that missionary influences would help the Khoe adjust to colonial rule following the crushing of their rebellion in 1799. It was not until well into the 1820s and later, after renewed wars which atomized the Xhosa communities, that Europeans established the highest concentration of missions in the Ciskei and beyond. By the 1830s, other Western-nation missions would join the scramble to convert and transform African societies in the interior, including the American Board Mission, the Paris Evangelical Missionary Society, and the Berlin Mission Society.

Missionaries could also be deeply subversive of the colonial order. Colonial officials were concerned that missionary activities would upset the balance of white domination. Indeed, as we have seen, Dr. Philip was instrumental in pushing through the abolition of slavery, which greatly upset settlers. Although British commercial interests welcomed and supported missionaries who aided in the expansion of their markets among Africans, many colonists did not care for the creation of potentially financially independent African competitors. It was the missionaries' encouragement of African farming on the stations, and the sale of the produce to the colonial market, which white farmers later came to resent. For example, with great zeal, van der Kemp established Bethelsdorp as a model Christian society for the destitute and destabilized Khoe. He believed, as other early missionaries did, that their efforts would be successful only if they separated their stations from the corrupting influence of European civilization. The experiment at Bethelsdorp, however, was a radical challenge for colonial society. The mission station was a place where the Khoe were baptized, learned to read and write, and became familiar with the egalitarian principles of the gospel and the civilizing mission, all of which threatened many Boer ideals for a white-dominated social order. For them, Christianity was the privileged domain of the "civilized." Van der Kemp's marriage to a 14-year-old slave girl whose freedom he had purchased was one indication of the extent to which he had been influenced by the local context and how his practices reinforced ideas of equality with African people. Moreover, the separatist station was a haven from settler demands for Khoe workers. While missionaries sought to protect indigenous people, settlers criticized the stations for bottling up labor. Despite Khoe converts and LMS efforts, however, Bethelsdorp did not have sufficient arable land to support the community. The station would remain poverty-stricken and ridden with alcoholism. Colonial critics referred to it as "beggars town."

Missionaries of the LMS then turned their attentions to the fledgling Griqua communities in the north and the Nguni-speaking communities of the interior. Their mission work among the Khoe fueled the expansion of evangelical work by Khoe and Griqua agents. As we have seen, the mixed-descent Griqua, who left behind the limitations of white-dominated society at the Cape and settled across the Orange River, already had some of the trappings of European culture. The Griqua (the term was the LMS missionary John Campbell's corruption of the name of a Khoe band) seemed an ideal community for conversion and "upliftment through Christian civilization." Political tensions among the leading Griqua families, the Bergenaars, the Koks, the Waterboers, and the Barends, and their involvement in trading disposed them to take advantage of missionary protection and connections to the colony. What emerged were three main independent Griqua communities sponsored by the LMS. Cornelius Kok led the Campbell community, Adam Kok II and the Bergenaars settled at the mission station of Philippolis, and the Waterboers developed the new settlement at Griquatown. Dr. Philip helped transform these communities with various improvements in housing and agriculture, but he then turned his attentions to the larger issue of abolition.

Settlers and colonial officials alike condemned these stations for harboring runaway slaves, indentured workers who had deserted their employers, and criminals. Both Governors Cradock and Somerset sought to bring these mission stations under colonial control and demanded that they turn over deserting workers. The local missionary, William Anderson, refused to comply; in any event, he lacked the manpower or resources needed to enforce authority so far beyond the colony's border. Thereafter and until after 1820, officials refused to give permission for LMS missionaries to work beyond the colony and instead supported missionaries who would act as compliant colonial representatives to indigenous people. By the later 1830s, many humanitarians capitulated to the merchant and "liberal" settler philosophy that Africans were an irredeemable underclass who required coercion to integrate them into the colonial economy so they could benefit from Christian civilization and the capitalist work ethic. Thus the purely utilitarian aspect of liberalism took over as the whites, buoyed by their successes in controlling Africans, grew increasingly pessimistic about the short-term upliftment of African people.

While Philip remained in the colony and worked through conventional channels to uplift the Khoe and push for emancipation, others sought to develop self-reliant missions beyond the colony. Robert Moffat, who was often at odds with Philip, took over the LMS station at Kuruman across the Orange River, well outside the confines of the colony. Here, he and the far more celebrated missionary-cum-explorer, David Livingstone (who married Moffat's daughter), embarked on an ambitious program of immersion into the Sotho- and Tswana-speaking communities of the region. They believed that for Christianity to take root in these African societies, it had to do so independently of colonial influences and coercion. Livingstone especially felt that for Christianity to flourish, Africans had to embrace it on their own terms, lest they develop a false consciousness driven by constant colonial supervision. While these unconventional, adventurous men were committed to spreading Christian spirituality, they nevertheless remained firmly convinced that the extension of "British civilization" to Africans through trade and commerce went hand in hand with their mission. Yet they remained largely frustrated (as Livingstone attested in his *Travels and Researches in Southern Africa*) in their early efforts to transform the Tswana from a predominantly pastoral society into a settled agricultural society along British lines. The trade items which missionaries could provide proved far more attractive to Tswana chiefs. The chiefs readily accepted gifts and goods, but steadfastly refused to allow the missionaries access to their people for conversion. Yet, it was in this way that the LMS stations of Philipolis and Kuruman became the jumping-off points for the expansion of trade to the interior. Driven by Griqua and "Coloured" converts who became transport riders and merchants who had access to colonial goods through their missionary allies, British commerce rapidly expanded across the northern and eastern boundaries of the colony.

Although not all Africans embraced Christianity—some preferred their own faith or viewed this new religion as threatening—many of those on the margins of African society did seek asylum within the world of the missions. Many women in particular had reason to want to escape the African patriarchal system. Young women who refused to accept arranged marriages and widows who faced the levirate—the custom of marrying their deceased husband's brother—were probably among the largest number of those seeking refuge with the missionaries. Other Africans who were somehow stigmatized—whether physically disfigured, handicapped, or accused of witchcraft or having a spiritual abnormality—also joined in significant numbers. Periodically, wars generated large numbers of refugees who could not sustain themselves within African society. Thus, the wounded and sick, orphans, the elderly, and the homeless also flocked to missions. Others, such as the Griqua and some shrewd African chiefs, sought out relations with missionaries in order to gain access to trade goods, particularly guns, and to enhance their understanding of colonial politics. They knew well that one of the main aims of the humanitarians was to protect Africans from the excesses of colonial subordination. By at least professing some interest in missionary activities if not a wholesale acceptance of Christian civilization, African leaders could hope to gain some safeguards against settler demands. They could use the missionaries, who had an intimate knowledge of the machinations of colonial politics, as negotiators as well as advisors on matters ranging from land policy to the use of modern weapons. These features of missionary activity had great importance in the various abilities of African societies to come to terms with the colonial world.

For many Africans, missionary Christianity was often at odds with the most fundamental features of their social and cultural practices. Christianity sought to supplant African beliefs, which, in many cases, emphasized the importance of the "Shades," that is, the ancestral spirits who influenced people's lives rather than the Christians' creator god. African divining and healing practices were condemned as witchcraft, as were rainmaking and spiritual efforts to manipulate the environment. The missionaries also stressed the importance of the individual over the communal African ideal. This tended to threaten especially the chiefs who maintained traditions and were believed to embody the spiritual center of the community. Thus, the chiefs of well-integrated African communities who commanded strong leadership powers sought to limit the extent of the missionary influence. Missionaries also worked to transform African lives in other ways. They prioritized agriculture, customarily done by African women, for men over their usual domain of cattle herding and encouraged people to accept Western practices of commerce, medicine, "civilized" square houses, and European forms of dress and behavior. Where Africans lived according to patterns of seasonal time, engaged in dancing, communal beer drinks, polygamy, and sexual behavior which appeared to differ from European norms, the missionaries sought to implant industrial time and encourage temperance and sexual inhibition, as well as monogamy and the nuclear family. The stations were intended to be places of refuge from both what missionaries perceived as the excessive demands of the settlers and the "primitive" patriarchy of African chiefs. On the mission stations, proselytizing was combined with the practical transformation of Africans' daily lives and activities.

The two features of mission life which had perhaps the greatest impact on Africans were agriculture and Western education. Mission stations provided Africans with more secure land tenure as individuals than they could find under a chief, who held the land for communal use. As noted earlier, African men, rather than women, were encouraged to undertake "progressive" agriculture as part of their commitment to a "civilized" work ethic and a commercial culture. Over time, many Africans embraced this avenue of accumulation and eventually developed into a vibrant **peasantry** that produced an agricultural abundance for colonial markets. Missionaries also used Western and Christian education as a vehicle to transform African lifestyles. Literacy and English were essential for Africans who sought to embrace "Christian civilization." The primary focus of early mission schools was religious and bible studies. They began training African men as lay ministers and ordained preachers, and later extended education to include the majority of women and children members of the stations. The focus of mission education, however, remained the training manual laborers under the guise of "industrial training." Nevertheless, some Africans were able to make much of the opportunities which mission education afforded. Over time, mission schools expanded their curriculum to include more traditional forms of academic training, which included the preparation of African teachers. Some mission stations offered both English and African language newspapers. Some of these then developed into vibrant African newspapers, run by African editors trained on mission stations. For example, Tiyo Soga, a mission-trained Xhosa minister, later became the leading figure in early African literature for his work in revising a Xhosa-language bible and translating British writer John Bunyon's classic, *Pilgrim's Progress*. Eventually, African ordained ministers and other African Christians took the seeds of missionary activity to sow the growth of their own independent African Christian and Zionist churches.

Xhosa Crises: Interaction with the Settlers and Civil War

British colonial officials had to contend with the major challenge of rising tensions between white settlers and the Xhosa along the Cape's eastern frontier. Although the British vacillated between a humanitarian-influenced policy of protection for the Africans and their potentially costly subjugation, the Xhosa would ultimately be conquered and incorporated into the colonial economy. Meanwhile, the republican-minded Afrikaners continued to agitate to subdue the Xhosa and take their lands as they had done during the VOC administration. The result was that for the next thirty years, the Xhosa steadily lost their struggle to hold their own against the forces of settler capitalism and colonial conquest. The establishment of British rule and, more importantly, the arrival in South Africa of imperial troops, tipped the balance of power to the east of the colony decidedly in favor of the white settlers. Although the British authorities and especially the British parliament were not necessarily disposed to attacking African communities beyond the colonial boundary, the rising tide of white settler activity provoked official intervention. The Afrikaners pressured colonial authorities to allow them to gain the upper hand against the Xhosa and to press beyond the colony into fertile Xhosa grazing lands beyond the Fish River. The Afrikaners called for official support, yet they bitterly resented the way the British handled the situation.

It was Afrikaner rebelliousness which provoked British reprisals and led to another war. As the British instituted reforms (noted above), Afrikaner settlers became increasingly concerned with their access to land, their social status, and their control of African workers. Although these settlers acceded to British rule, they agitated for more independent political authority and for official support in their efforts to press beyond the border into the African lands. For example, Adriaan van Jaarsveld, infamous for his earlier brutal attacks against the Xhosa, challenged British authority and was arrested for forgery. After a group of fellow Afrikaner dissidents freed van Jaarsveld and rose up in rebellion, the British responded with force. Early in 1799, they sent a combined group of Khoe and British imperial troops which quickly suppressed the rebellion. The appearance of a large, armed force of Khoe troops along the frontier, however, led to further upheaval. Many Khoe servants, emboldened by the arrival of Khoe troops sent to punish the white rebels, attacked their employers and fled to the protection of the British forces. Then, in response to British efforts to drive them from the *zuurveld,* the Gqunukwebe teamed with fleeing Khoe servants and Xhosa to raid many white farms. When the British troops returned to Cape Town, they abandoned their Khoe contingent who in turn joined the attacks on the settler farms. Widespread raiding ensued along the entire frontier, and many whites were forced to retreat. British reinforcements under General Dundas were able to bring about peace in this "third frontier war" only with the assistance of H. Maynier, magistrate and trusted confidante of the Khoe. Maynier convinced the Khoe to abandon their alliance with the Xhosa and to quit raiding, with the promise of protection from abusive employers and unfair contracts. Maynier's reforms, however, raised the ire of Afrikaners who resented safeguards for the Khoe, especially his decision to allow the Khoe to worship in church. By 1801, agitated Afrikaners again rose up in rebellion in the town of Bruintjies Hoogte and demanded the removal of Maynier as well as to be allowed to raid into Xhosa lands. Although the British put down the short-lived rebellion after they replaced Maynier, in the eyes of some Afrikaners the incident was yet another example of British interference in their lives.

Prior to the arrival of the Albany settlers in 1820, the eastern region of the Cape remained an unsettled zone as hostilities between the Xhosa and the settlers escalated. Although white settlement steadily increased along the frontier between the Sundays and Fish Rivers, settler numbers ebbed and flowed as they faced problems of drought and pressure from the Xhosa. Following the third frontier war, the Xhosa chiefs sought to recoup their losses. They stepped up raiding parties into the settled areas and they steadfastly refused to quit the *zuurveld* which provided their followers, who were also increasing in number and in need of land, with crucial seasonal grazing. By 1809, British colonial officials were concerned that continued tensions along the frontier would prove costly, so they sought a solution. After a tour of enquiry in the eastern zone, Colonel Collins recommended to Governor Caledon that a firm policy of non-interaction and segregation be applied to the region. He called for the *zuurveld* to be cleared of the Xhosa and asked that they be pushed behind a firm boundary along the Fish River. He also advised that the region be occupied by British settlers who would bring peace and economic stability to the area.

Within Xhosa society, political tensions rose among the three main power brokers: Ngqika, the heir to the Rharhabe chiefdom, Ndlambe, his uncle and former regent, and Hintsa, chief of the Gcaleka Xhosa, who lived east of the Kei River (the Transkei.). Ngqika, who had pretensions to become the paramount Xhosa chief west of the Kei River, first faced off against Hintsa and then forced Ndlambe west across the Fish River. As Ndlambe fled, he drove the Gqunukwebe deeper into the farming area of the colony. The upheaval caused by these maneuvers provoked some Khoe and Xhosa to form raiding parties which attacked isolated white farms. Ngqika then further inflamed the unsettled state of affairs by abducting one of Ndlambe's wives, a serious crime in Xhosa society. Many Xhosa lent Ndlambe support as he waged a retributive battle against Ngqika. Over time, Ngqika steadily lost popular support, but there remained for a time a balance of power between these two contending chiefs. Ngqika then devised another ill-fated strategy. He cast his lot with the British in a dubious alliance and announced he would accept the Fish River as the westernmost boundary of Xhosa lands, thereby leaving Ndlambe and his people within colonial territory.

In 1811, Colonel John Graham executed the Governor's order to clear the *zuurveld*. With great brutality, Graham led some 1300 well-armed British troops, settlers, and Khoe recruits as they drove over 20,000 of Ndlambe's followers from their homes and fields. Most Xhosa families lost their cattle and were unable to reap their crops, and so suffered the loss of their food sources in the upheaval of their retreat. The British then imposed severe demands on the Xhosa and their supposed ally, Ngqika. They established a series of forts and military outposts along the Fish River frontier from the town of Cradock in the north to the main trade town of Grahamstown in the south. Governor

Somerset crudely misread Ngqika's authority within Xhosa society. He fixed the responsibility for all Xhosa border violations on Ngqika as the paramount chief, whereas in reality it was the Gcaleka chief Hintsa who had the authority. Not only was Ngqika unlikely to be able to restrain all Xhosa transgressions, but also the other chiefs did not accept Ngqika's authority, and they resented his pretensions to power as well as his alliance with the British. The tide began to turn against Ngqika. In 1818, the Xhosa prophet Nxele ("the left handed," also known as Makana) joined Ndlambe and roused his people to unity in the struggle against white expansion. Nxele, who had been influenced by Christian missionaries, preached a message of restoration, saying that if people returned to traditional moral values, their heroic ancestors would return to aid them in driving whites from their land. Nxele also directed his message against Ngqika for his dalliances with the British, and he drew deserters from Ngqika as his popularity grew. Under Nxele's leadership, the aging Ndlambe and the Gcaleka combined forces and defeated Ngqika, who escaped and fled into hiding. Ngqika then appealed to the colonial authorities for support.

British involvement in African politics and determination to control the interior region to the east ultimately caused the demise of the independent Xhosa chiefdoms. Their downfall was also due to the combined effects of a rapidly expanding colonial economy, white settlement, and mission Christianity which eroded and transformed Xhosa society. In 1818, British troops came to Ngqika's aid against Ndlambe, Nxele, and Hintsa, but the Xhosa chiefs did not engage in battle. Ngqika, however, took advantage of British cover to raid his adversaries and loot over 20,000 cattle. His attack was so vicious that the British commander had to confiscate arms from their former ally, Ngqika and his forces, lest they do even greater damage. Devastated and impoverished by the assault and a drought as well, Ndlambe and Nxele rallied their people to mount a counterattack against their foe. After driving Ngqika from the lands he had re-occupied, Ndlambe's forces pushed into the colony and began raiding for cattle. Before the British could muster their defense, Ndlambe mounted an attack against the main colonial stronghold of Grahamstown in this war of 1818–1819. With nearly 6,000 men (plus women and children aiding with supplies), the largest African force yet assembled against colonial invaders, Ndlambe was nearly successful at taking the town, but his strategy of attacking en masse proved to be folly against the heavily fortified British position. Having secured the town, British forces then swept the *zuurveld,* burning homes and looting cattle along the way as they methodically drove the Xhosa back in fragmented groups. Nxele gave himself up and later drowned while trying to escape from Robben Island (which would later house many African resistors as prisoners). For the demoralized Xhosa, his name became synonymous with unfulfilled expectations.

As the victors, the British dictated a harsh peace which set the stage for the fuller expansion of colonialism in Xhosa territory. First, the colonial government turned against Ngqika and established a neutral belt on his lands—including his birthplace—to act a buffer between the white farms and the Xhosa. The British intention all along, however, had been to consider this strip of land as ceded to them, rather than as a vacant area where Xhosa and colonists could meet and exchange trade goods. This treachery was compounded by the arrival of Afrikaners and over 5,000 British settlers from 1820. The colonial government allowed Ngqika's son and heir, Maqoma (1798–1873), to occupy ancestral lands along the Kat River in the northern part of the ceded territory for a time, but, in 1829, they forced him to abandon them to make room for the settlement of the destitute Khoe and Coloured settlers. This Kat River Settlement was to be a model Christian mission community of loyal converts who could act as a buffer against Xhosa efforts to regain their land.

Xhosa society was further eroded and diluted as Christian missionaries and British settlers dug into the region. Settler demands, moreover, prompted the formalization of trade relations between whites and Africans. Within the ceded territory, the British established weekly trade fairs at Fort Wiltshire. These controlled fairs were a vain attempt on the part of the government to contain illegal trading relations between the settlers and the Xhosa which rapidly expanded along the entire frontier. From the major centers such as Grahamstown and Port Elizabeth to the bourgeoning mission stations, trade in cattle and ivory virtually exploded in the 1820s and 1830s. The Xhosa, despite their defeats, took advantage of their strategic location between the colony and the trade routes to the riches of the interior. The British policy for the expulsion and segregation of the Xhosa from the colony clearly could not prevent the realities of settler participation in the lucrative African trade. Spurred on by missionary agents, settler-African trade became the main focus of the new colonial economy until white-dominated mining and commercial agriculture took over in the latter half of the nineteenth century. Ultimately, however, British expansion and settler demands for African land and labor were aimed more at the dispossession and subordination of the Xhosa than the development of commercial interaction. The situation along the eastern and northern borders of the colony and in the interior was further complicated by the upheavals due to African state building and settler expansion. By the middle of the 1800s, the Xhosa would be overwhelmed by new arrivals and British conquest.

CONCLUSION

The arrival of the British, including colonial rulers and the attendant missionaries and settlers, transformed South Africa and enhanced its links to the wider world. The British introduced new ideas about the nature of the economy and society based on features of the European Enlightenment. They sought to rationalize South Africa and to order its society in keeping with the demands of industrialization and a capitalist economy. They put in motion a number of new forces and plans which started to change the economy from one based on trade and herding to one based on commercializing agriculture. They also shaped the social composition and outlook of the colony by introducing large numbers of white settlers and by abolishing slavery. These projects were bound up in the overarching idea of "British Civilization" which brought together notions of political liberalism, humanitarianism, and utilitarianism. This entailed the restructuring of economic and labor relations with an emphasis on free-market capitalism, free labor, and greater efficiency.

In keeping with its broader policies for the Atlantic world, the first major British initiative in South Africa was the abolition of slavery. First, Britain abolished its involvement in the slave trade in 1807 and then, in 1834, it ended the owning and use of slaves in all its colonies, including South Africa. Abolition resulted from the convergence of pressures and interests both in South Africa and in Britain. First, humanitarian groups, especially missionaries, argued that slavery was immoral and abhorrent and that blacks must be freed first if they were to be uplifted by the British "civilizing mission." Second, new economic relations born of the industrial revolution and the rise of merchant capitalism demanded both expanding markets and free labor which could be allocated by employers as needed. This suggested that free blacks would work more efficiently for wages and would also make good consumers. In this way, there was a convergence of interests between merchants and missionaries for the "upliftment" of the blacks. There was, moreover, the rising force of black resistance to slavery both within South Africa and in other British colonies. As blacks rose to challenge their masters over the way they were treated and over their bonded servitude, British officials saw the need for change and reform. The British intended to reform labor relations for the sake of improving the efficiency of the economy rather than for purely philanthropic reasons. They did not fundamentally alter the emergent racial order or the hierarchy of masters and servants. Instead, they provided for some protection of servants' rights in order to pre-empt further agitation and to ensure that labor was forthcoming. In many respects, the subordination and exploitation of black workers continued and was made more efficient under the new British system of free labor.

British rule also brought the new social forces of English-speaking settlers and missionaries to the country. Part of the British colonial agenda was to make South Africa more settled and civilized along British lines. This entailed the immigration of significant numbers of white settlers, both male and female. These settlers altered the balance of white settlement in favor of British culture and away from the emerging Afrikaner culture. The new European missionaries were also an important and influential force. They sought to "uplift" the blacks to Christianity in a particular fashion. They emphasized industry and "civilized" culture as the best ways to modify African lifestyles. This enterprise included introducing Western Christian education and literacy to black people. Missionaries also sought to safeguard blacks from the vagaries of colonial rule, and especially the impact of white settlement. The missionaries' paternalistic efforts to "protect" blacks often led them afoul of both black leaders and colonial officials. On the one hand, British officials sought to counteract what they perceived as missionary efforts to undermine the colonial racial order. On the other hand, many chiefs resented and resisted missionary efforts to convert their followers and entice them away from their rule. For many Africans, Christianity was at odds with both their established faith and their way of life. It sought to change patterns of marriage, agriculture, and patriarchy, and often male household heads were deeply suspicious of the new faith. Although not all Africans embraced Christianity, many—especially from the margins of society—embraced the new faith. Women and the infirm were particularly interested in Christianity and the new opportunities it provided. Although the British sought to rationalize the colonial order and to lessen the tensions between blacks and white, which were costly in terms of labor relations and the suppression of conflicts, they became increasingly drawn into settling affairs in the interior. This was particularly true of relations between the white settlers and the Xhosa. Along the eastern frontier of the colony, independent-minded Afrikaners sought to press into Xhosa lands and this often led to conflicts. British attempts to restrain the settlers' expansive and aggressive tendencies only served to provoke the Afrikaners. There remained, moreover, the problem of rising tensions with the Xhosa. The British policy of non-interaction between whites and Africans failed. Trade and raiding between whites and blacks continued, and in many cases led to further wars. As the Xhosa sought to assert their authority in the zone of interaction, they came into conflict with both the settlers and the British troops. The British relied on political alliances with some Xhosa under Ngqika in their attempt to control the zone of interaction. In response to the increasing pressures of colonialism, other Xhosa under Ngqika's adversary, Ndlambe, mounted a major offensive. British officials on the ground in South Africa later altered the imperial policy in an effort to settle the frontier once and for all as they undertook the conquest and subordination of the Xhosa chiefdoms adjacent to the colony.

Questions to Consider

1. What new ideas and initiatives did the British bring with them to South Africa?
2. What were the economic, political, and social reasons for abolition and what impact did abolition have on South Africa?

3. How did the British seek to reform labor relations and how different were conditions of employment for blacks after abolition?
4. How did the arrival of large numbers of British settlers change the social and economic make-up of the colony?
5. Who were the missionaries and how did they convert blacks to Christianity?
6. Why did the British change their policy for the zone of interaction between whites and blacks on the eastern frontier of the colony?

FURTHER READINGS

BEINART, W., *Settlers, Livestock, and the Cape Environment, c. 1770–1950* (forthcoming). An insightful analysis of the interrelationships between the white settlers, the new herding economy, and the South African environment by the leading social and environmental historian of South Africa.

CRAIS, C., *White Supremacy and Black Resistance in Pre-Industrial South Africa: The Making of the Colonial Order in the Eastern Cape, 1770–1865* (Cambridge, 1992). An excellent localized study of the interaction of whites and blacks in the process of the subordination of blacks to a new racial hierarchy. It highlights the intellectual dimensions of British policy initiatives and how they came to be seen through their application to the eastern Cape region.

ELPHICK, R., and DAVENPORT, T. (editors), *Christianity in South Africa: a Political, Social, and Cultural History* (Berkeley, 1997). A comprehensive, well-edited collection of essays which thoroughly covers the introduction and development of Christianity in South Africa and how it shaped the country's history.

ELPHICK, R., and GILIOMEE, H. (editors), *The Shaping of South African Society, 1652–1840* (Cape Town, 1989). A collection of essays covering the period from the establishment of VOC rule through the period of the British takeover and slave emancipation. It has excellent pieces on the frontier relations among Khoe, Griqua, whites, and Xhosa by the leading scholars in the field.

KEEGAN, T., *Colonial South Africa and the Origins of the Racial Order* (Charlottesville, 1996). A well-researched and detailed analysis of the emergence of racial attitudes and societal constraints in early colonial South Africa. This is a challenging work with a strong structure and argument.

MARKS, S., and ATMORE, A. (editors), *Economy and Society in Pre-Industrial South Africa* (London, 1980). This excellent collection of essays ranges from topics from the nature of African societies and their economies to issues of culture contact and frontier relations. It is a very useful teaching tool.

MOSTERT, N., *Frontiers, the Epic of South Africa's Creation and the Tragedy of the Xhosa People* (London, 1992). A moving account of the plight of black communities struggling with the impact of white settlement and the integra-tion of the interior of South Africa with the wider capitalist economy.

Ross, R., *Beyond the Pale: Essays on the History of Colonial South Africa* (Johan-nesburg, 1994). A good general collection of essays which covers most aspects of recent scholarship on the early colonial period.

Shell, R., *Children of Bondage: a Social History of the Slave Society at the Cape of Good Hope, 1652–1838* (Hanover, 1994). An insightful analysis of the inter-nal social dynamics of slave society in transition to the point of emancipation.

Switzer, L., *Power and Resistance in an African Society. The Ciskei Xhosa and the Making of South Africa* (London, 1993). A fine application of the frontier thesis to developments along the eastern frontier. It has very good coverage of the role of missionaries and Western education on African society.

Worden, N., and Crais, C. (editors), *Breaking the Chains: Slavery and Its Legacy in the Nineteenth-Century Cape Colony* (Johannesburg, 1994). A finely edited collection of essays dealing with issues of bondage and emancipation from leading scholars.

CHAPTER IV

The Making of New States

The first half of the 1800s witnessed a series of interrelated dramatic developments in the interior of South Africa. First, before the turn of the nineteenth-century, the Sotho-Tswana-speaking people in the central interior and the Bantu-speakers in the northeast had begun transforming their communities. With the expansion of settler forces engaged in trade and raiding, there came an ensuing upheaval of wars and mass movements of people. This period and process have been referred to by some historians as the **Mfecane**—pronounced mmm-fah-kan—along the coast and the *Difaqane*—pronounced *Dee-fah-kan*—in the interior region of the Orange and Caledon River Valleys. (*Mfecane* is a term with no definite origins which has been interpreted to mean variously the time of troubles, the crushing, those who crush others, wandering hordes, wars, the weak and famished. *Lifiqane* has been said to mean "wandering horde"; it has been used to refer to movements and conflicts in the interior highveld region.) It comprised two broad developments. First, the African chiefs started to forge their communities into a series of major African states and polities. Second, waves of people of mixed descent from the Cape expanded into the interior with the aid of the powerful combination of horses and guns. They sought their fortune through trading and raiding, largely for cattle and labor, as they confronted those people seeking to settle in safe havens. The white settlers who had invaded the Cape and spread out to the eastern frontier faced economic difficulties, drought, and an overbearing British colonial government. Their frustrations reached a peak by the mid-1830s, leading to a major exodus of many Afrikaners, known as the Great Trek. They sought to establish independent states of their own in the interior, far from British interference. The new Afrikaner trekker states, however, closely resembled the established states of their African neighbors, and the two clashed over land and resources. These developments, some of which were part of long-established processes of African state-building, had profound implications for the social, political, and economic structures which would emerge in the nineteenth century.

These were times of courageous peoples and their great, creative leaders; times of drought and famine; raiding and refugees; battles, victories, and defeats; submission and state-building. From the northern Cape throughout the southern interior of the continent, new political and social organizations emerged and rose to power. For this brief period of the first half of the nineteenth century, upheavals and mass movements reconfigured the entire way of life for South Africans. These were processes that had been in motion since the middle of the eighteenth century, as whites and Africans intermingled along the uneven frontiers. Trade, raiding, and social interaction had long been central to the communities of the interior. Although this period had previously been characterized as one of unprecedented violence, driven either by bloodthirsty Africans or predacious whites, more recent analyses have emphasized the creative efforts of many great chiefs to sustain or build enduring states and their efforts to take advantage of contacts with settlers and colonial forces. Major African states established their new political identities and their rights to the land. Afrikaner settlers would then arrive and collide with them as they sought to do the same. In both cases, these state-building processes came to play significant roles in shaping the mythology and ideology of later white and African nationalist identities. Clearly, there were continuities with previous efforts at state-building in the interior, and yet these new states created a significant and lasting legacy throughout southern Africa.

As we have seen in Chapter 1, "The Setting: Climate, Geography, and People in South Africa," by the later 1700s, the African farmers, who established the Nguni-speaking communities in what became the Natal-Zululand region, had started to forge powerful chiefdoms. During this period, African homesteads considerably expanded their production of both cattle and grain agriculture. While cattle-keeping may have suffered as the population of the region increased, the pressure to find grazing land for cattle alone did not provoke any major re-organization of society. Although there were intermittent periods of severe drought, more intense use of the land for cultivation rather than for grazing appears to have satisfied the overall needs of these communities. In addition, the process of smaller chiefdoms amalgamating for unity and strength helped communities sustain themselves during periods of stress. In the area north of the Thukela River, major chiefdoms such as the Methethwa and Ndwandwe began to expand in size and dominance as they sought greater control over the land, resources, and labor of the region.

These processes had ambiguous results. They brought both conflict and the creation of new states. While some historians have argued that this process of African state formation was a product of internal developments within African societies, others point to external factors. Those who emphasize external factors claim that the European trade for ivory—and especially for slaves—was violent and provoked the African communities to respond defensively or with a military re-organization of their society. Although it appears that the Europeans facilitated a trade in slaves from Delagoa Bay, just north of the region where the Zulu state emerged, the slave-trading remained insignificant prior to the period when the Nguni-speakers began to re-organize their communities into major states. Nevertheless, European slave-trading along the southeastern coast of Africa was later responsible for untold violence, and it may have prompted African communities to develop extreme defensive measures, although these did not contribute to the formation of the Zulu and other kingdoms in the region.

The contending view insists that the process was driven by Africans from within their own communities or by internal climatic and environmental factors. Why are these contending views important for South African history? They are at the heart of a still-simmering debate about the implications of the concept of the *Mfecane*. There are those who feel that it celebrates the great achievements of African leaders in constructing their own states, whereas others feel that it was a myth created by European colonizers and their white descendants to cover up the violence perpetrated by white slave raiders. This latter view, it is argued, reveals the truth about white attempts to justify racism and segregation. One way at looking at the controversy is to consider that, on the one hand, those who support external factors desire that we not perceive Africans as inherently violent people who instigated the entire upheaval of this period. They argue that the interpretations of Africans as violent led white South Africans to fear them, and later encouraged the government to implement the racist policies of apartheid in order to keep "dangerous" and "primitive" Africans separate from a white-dominated society. They prefer that we accept the view that the Europeans had a significant role in instigating both the violence which provoked African communities to develop militarized states and in creating myths in which Africans are seen as violent and savage. On the other hand, those who argue for an African initiative feel that it is important to credit great African leaders with significant achievements such as forging major kingdoms. Most recently, however, historians have presented alternative theories which synthesize a wide range of factors and emphases. These include consideration of environmental factors such as drought, economic factors such as access to crucial grazing lands and control of trade routes, and social issues such as increasing social stratification, all of which could have provoked intense competition and conflict.

NGUNI-SPEAKING CHIEFDOMS

Increasing tensions among African communities over resources during times of drought and environmental stress appear to have been the central features of the development of new polities and states. In a process which became acute during severe droughts in the periods 1800–1803, 1812, and again from 1816–1818, many African chiefs sought greater control over land and cattle. Normally, the land in northeastern South Africa could probably have accommodated its increasing population, but when drought struck, the parched land could not sustain all the people and their cattle. During these periods, more powerful chiefs took advantage of their access to land and cattle. They and their followers thrived while others did not. This produced a cycle of increased socio-economic stratification because of inequities in the accessibility of resources by different peoples. Many successful chiefs asserted their power to extend their control over more good grazing and farming lands. As a result, weaker groups were forced to submit to their more powerful neighbors, flee, or fight. It was definitely to the advantage of the chiefs to increase the number of their adherents since this enabled them to either defend their lands or attack their neighbors in order to gain more land. In addition, more adherents meant more people to cultivate the land, which was especially important when agriculture became more intensive on the available land. Increasingly, the poor and the weak had to submit to powerful leaders under an organized political authority if they were to avoid starvation, even if it meant living under an oppressive ruler.

The development of a lucrative regional trade in ivory was another important factor in the emergence of more centrally organized African states. Ivory had long been sought in Africa. It was in high demand by Asian artisans in the Far East, and increasingly by the more affluent classes of Europe. Just to the north of what became the center of the Zulu kingdom, first English and then Portuguese traders began taking out substantial quantities of elephant tusks, surpassing 100,000 pounds a year by the 1770s. As this trade unfolded, the Africans sought to re-organize their societies into hunting and trading parties which could track and kill elephants for their valuable tusks, and efforts were made to control the routes along which the ivory was sent to coastal towns. As with land and cattle, the more successful chiefs gained control of this valuable resource and the people needed to facilitate its trade.

The rising ivory trade coincided with an increasing militarization of the chiefdoms as they competed against each other for control of the lucrative trade routes, cattle grazing, and agricultural lands. Although a number of larger southern African societies such as the Pedi re-organized their social institutions in order enhance their political power and stability, it was among the Coastal Nguni that these changes had the greatest effect. In established practice, the Nguni-speaking chiefs created cohorts for circumcision initiation rituals, known as *butho* (pl. *amabutho*), by banding together young men of roughly the same age for the rites of passage between youth and adulthood. With increasing pressure to amalgamate smaller communities into chiefdoms for the purpose of competing effectively for resources such as ivory, the *amabutho* were transformed into military units called together to serve a chief. Chiefs who commanded more ivory could convert it into other forms of traded wealth such as iron tools and beads. With these items they could attract increasing numbers of followers and thus enhance their prestige and power. As the chiefs enhanced their command over the *amabutho*, they also increased their ability to turn these groups against their neighbors in the struggle for land and cattle.

By the end of the eighteenth century, rivalries between chiefdoms over attracting followers and controlling the ivory trade had escalated into full-blown competition and violent conflict. In, the northeastern part of southern Africa, four chiefdoms emerged as the main contenders for its domination. In what is now southern Mozambique, the Mabhudu broke from the Thembe paramountcy and asserted its power over the Delagoa Bay region. The Dlamini began establishing its presence in what became southern Swaziland. And farther south, in what became the heart of the Zulu kingdom, the Ndwandwe and Mthethwa rose to prominence. The rivalries among the trading chiefdoms intensified as droughts exacerbated their need to control the grazing and agricultural lands. The ensuing conflicts provoked two major changes for African society in the region. First, there was increasing social stratification as chiefdoms attacked rivals and then incorporated the vanquished as subordinates within their social ranks. Second, in order to survive in these trying times, chiefdoms had to amalgamate and organize themselves into larger, more militarily powerful units. As we shall see, those that were unprepared to defend their interests were forced to flee the region or submit. What eventually emerged were fewer, more powerful, and more stratified states.

THE RISE OF THE ZULU KINGDOM

As the processes of competition, conflict, and political amalgamation unfolded, a handful of powerful states and kingdoms emerged. First, in the region roughly bounded by the Phongola River to the north and the Thukela River in the south, two powerful chiefdoms—the Ndwandwe under Chief Zwide kaLanga and the Mthethwa under Chief Dingiswayo kaJobe—vied for control over essential grazing lands and ivory trade routes. Two significant developments occurred in the wake of the Ndwandwe-Methethwa conflict. First, Shaka kaSenzangakhona led his relatively minor Zulu chiefdom to power and prominence. Shaka was probably born in 1787, the illegitimate son of the minor chief Senzangakhona. After his father cast him out to be raised by his very independent mother, Nandi, in other chiefdoms Shaka quickly distinguished himself as a skilled soldier. Dingiswayo made Shaka chief and encouraged him to extend his chiefdom as a tributary client of the Methethwa against the Ndwandwe. Upon Dingiswayo's death, Shaka killed the legitimate heir to the Methethwa chiefdom, took power, and then set about extending his rule. Over time, Shaka would become perhaps the most celebrated and mythologized African king in South African history, based on the numerous images and perceptions of him. Second, Zwide and other chiefs failed to resolve their conflicts through the established practice of diplomacy and marriage. Instead, violent conflict arose among the Ndwandwe and the neighboring chiefdoms of the Ngwane under Chief Matiwane, and the Dlamini under Chief Sobhuza. Rather than face ongoing violence, these chiefs left the area and led their followers in search of good grazing lands. Sobhuza struck off to the north into the region in which he established the Swazi kingdom. Matiwane re-established his chiefdom in the upper Thukela valley before he embarked on a trying odyssey to re-establish it in the interior of South Africa. The movements of these people became part of a much wider upheaval of mass movements and parallel state-building in the interior and throughout southern Africa.

As conflicts escalated around the turn of the century, the chiefs in this region employed long-established fighting techniques and introduced some

SHAKA ZULU   The mythologized first King of the Zulu is seen as both a hero and a tyrant. *Source: South Arfican Library, Cape Town.*

modifications to the ways in which battles were conducted. First, the *amabutho* regiment system, which had already been in wide use for some time, became the standard way that chiefs transformed basic cohorts into fighting units. Throughout many chiefdoms, military training became more rigorous and the consequences of conflict more telling. Battles which previously had produced small numbers of wounded now accounted for a significant number of deaths. As we shall see, the ambitious Shaka managed to make the most of these tactics as he raised fighting to new levels of intensity and ruthlessness. Instead of employing the usual arsenal of throwing and stabbing spears, he required his soldiers to utilize a short stabbing spear exclusively. Along with the effective use of the common body-length cowhide shields, his regiments were well-organized and trained to engage in battles at close quarters.

Shaka emphasized stealth and surprise in his attacks. His Zulu regiments became renowned for descending at night upon the enemy, torching their villages and killing the dazed and confused occupants. He also developed an extremely effective battlefield strategy referred to as "the horn of the bull." This formation comprised several *butho* forming a central block of troops called the "chest," with seasoned veterans termed the "loins" following in reserve. Other regiments known as "the horns" flanked this central formation and moved ahead of the main body, endeavoring to encircle and pin the enemy as the "chest" advanced to slay them. And yet, as with all the other chiefs who vied for control of the cattle, the grazing lands, and the human labor power needed to sustain them, Shaka sought not to destroy all his opponents, but rather to undermine the competing chiefs while trying to attract and accumulate more followers from them. It did not profit a chief to eliminate all of the potential followers in battle when in fact his power rested on the number of young men and women whose labor he could command.

In early 1819, Shaka's forces retreated from Zwide's Ndwandwe in a feint and then maneuvered into a counterattack to overcome them. Shaka then set about consolidating his position by raiding southwards. He drove out some opponents while subordinating others to his rule and enlisting their support in his opposition to the Ndwandwe. In both cases, he enriched the Zulu with cattle taken as booty. The Ndwandwe became fragmented, probably as much for internal reasons as for the rise of the Zulu. Along with the other chiefs, Zwide left the territory between the Thukela and the Phongola, leaving it to the Zulu, yet, both Zwide's people and King Sobhuza's Dlamini lineage remained on the fringes of the Zulu kingdom. Over the next few years, while Ndwandwe opposition to the Zulu melted away, Sobhuza's descendant, Mswati, established the Swazi Kingdom to the north. Nevertheless, by this time, Shaka's Zulu were the predominant power in the region and his impressive kingdom remains the best-known example of the sort of state-building that Africans throughout southern Africa achieved during the early 1800s.

As with other major African polities at the time, the Zulu kingdom relied on the king's and a chief's command of the cattle and the allegiance of the labor force which these valuable animals attracted. Cattle became even more central to social, economic, and political relationships than they were previously. As we have seen, cattle were a form of productive and reproductive wealth, for they provided milk, meat hides, and calves. They were extremely important for household survival; they consolidated marital and political relations, and they were central to the overall economy. Kings and chiefs used them to support their expanding *amabutho* systems. These military regiments could then be turned against neighboring communities in order to capture even more cattle and thus expand the power and influence of their state. Kingdoms grew larger, more complex, and more powerful. They also became increasingly stratified both within and between the more and the less powerful chiefdoms.

In the Zulu kingdom, Shaka pressed these tactics to the highest degree. He sent his soldiers out against neighboring chiefdoms in order to raid for cattle and to win or force their allegiance as clients and buffers against potential enemies beyond. Within the kingdom, the Zulu became differentiated by discrete social and economic categories. At the center were the king's family, his extended royal kin group, and the associated aristocratic chiefdoms. The bulk of Zulu society comprised the *amantungwa*. These were people with status as full subjects who originated from the chiefdom that had allied with them or had been incorporated into the kingdom in its earliest days. As the Zulu developed their sense of identity, they considered the most recently conquered chiefdoms and those who lay on the fringes of the kingdom as the *amalala*, or subordinated menials. The *amantungwa* and the *amalala* developed their own separate identities based on different dialects, customs, and social status. As we shall see, these different identities contributed to increasing tensions within the kingdom and to the friction among the factions within the ruling elite. At this time in history, one of the chiefs' greatest achievements lay in their ability to attract and control followers. Shaka achieved this by inculcating in his followers a profound sense of national identity through his sophisticated political and spiritual leadership. He cultivated a Zulu identity through the military system through the use of the term *Zulu*. The name, meaning "the heavens," conveyed an association of the Zulu people with the literal meaning of the word. Shaka also claimed command of supernatural forces and of the diviners, who could communicate with the ancestors, could summon the rains, and could "smell out" (i.e., identify) a political opponent such as a witch. He organized and managed a very effective centralized kingdom. The chiefs served at the pleasure of the king, yet many were prominent leaders of clans such as the Qwabe, which had been incorporated into the kingdom as an important ally and who retained authority over its followers. Each person in each homestead within the kingdom knew that he or she had to pay deference to his or her chief, and ultimately to the king, and to render labor—instead of simple taxes or tribute—to support the ruling elite. In return, people expected their chiefs to defend their interests, loan cattle or give out food in times of need, and to provide opportunities to raid for cattle and booty. Although reciprocal relations between king or chiefs and their subjects were supposed to exist, in reality, the ruling elite gained wealth from their followers through the extraction of tribute.

The key to the relatively smooth operation of Shaka's increasingly militarized kingdom was the institution of the regimental system. This system comprised both male and female units, housed separately in barracks, or *amakhanda*. The *amabutho* did away with, and thus transcended, the earlier social and regional differentiation of local chiefdoms, although these local allegiances remained strong for some of the more powerful chiefdoms when they were incorporated into the Zulu kingdom. Now, however, all the young brought into the kingdom by conquest or incorporation were expected to focus on the king and their Zulu identity. The *amabutho* regiments were stationed at strategic locations around the country, with many concentrated around Shaka's great capital, Bulawayo. Each regiment was overseen by a trusted *induna*, or military official. The men served as a sort of standing police force, and they enjoyed access to the large herds of royal cattle, from which they sustained themselves.

The king rewarded successful *induna* by giving them cattle and allowing them to build up a personal following. More importantly, at short notice, the king could call upon the *amabutho* as a well-disciplined fighting force to raid for cattle. Their female counterparts tended to crops and maintained the *amakhanda*. Both groups were subject to strict royal oversight, and the king retained control over when they could marry and establish their own independent households. For young men, the incentive to serve was that when the king retired an active regiment, he rewarded the men with sufficient cattle and access to land to establish their own independent households. In addition to the *amabutho*, the king maintained the *izigodlo*, which housed his extended entourage of women. More than just a stable of concubines, the *izigodlo* consisted of young women presented to the king as tribute or for political reasons. These women, who performed important domestic and agricultural functions, also represented the king's other "daughters" or dependents. As such, he arranged marriages for them to important men, and thereby both consolidated political relations and received cattle in bridewealth. Thus, these women were an important political and economic resource for the king. In these ways, the Zulu king integrated all his subjects into a military system which combined a common identity with a way of controlling their life activities and the means to provide for their material needs in land and cattle.

As with other African states such as the Swazi and the Sotho, there were limits to the extent that the Zulu kingdom could exercise or project its power. First, there were practical geographic limits on the distances which the Zulu army could travel and still sustain a military campaign. Troops could be expected to travel fifty or sixty miles and still do battle, but beyond that limit, the men would require costly provisioning with herds of cattle. Moreover, shrewd African statesmen sought not to kill but rather to capture cattle and a labor force. It profited rulers little if they annihilated opponents when their kingdoms needed more people, land, and cattle. Many leaders, therefore, sought to keep their distance and stay just beyond the reach of other powerful states' raiding capacities. This made it extremely unlikely that a settled state such as Shaka's would set off on expeditions of pure conquest instead of more profitable, calculated raids for cattle. In any event, the Zulu kings could not extend their reach of governance too far. While Shaka mounted cattle-raiding campaigns against the chiefdoms adjacent to his kingdom to sustain his regimental system, he could not command allegiance nor control the internal politics of other powerful states.

The remaining years of Shaka's short-lived reign were fraught with tensions and conflict. His centralized rule, especially the highly regulated army, created more rigid lines of difference in the regional hierarchy between chiefs and commoners, as well as between the Zulu and client chiefdoms. In 1827, following the death of his much beloved mother, Nandi, Shaka called upon the kingdom to observe a customary period of mourning. He then embarked upon what colonial sources described as a notorious killing spree designed to rid the kingdom of his political opponents. Perhaps he was angry about his army's failure to successfully raid an old adversary, Shoshangane, for cattle. This created new fault lines, and he sought to purge the kingdom of his opponents. Moreover, Shaka became increasingly consumed by the drive for war, in part because of the competitive nature of statecraft at this time, and in part because of the pressing need to provide more cattle-raiding opportunities for his troops. He raided far and wide and encouraged his men to take large numbers of cattle from the Pondo in 1824. By this time, however, Shaka had made new allies among the fledgling British trading community at Thekweni or Port Natal (so named by the early Portuguese explorer, Vasco da Gama, for his sighting of the region on Christmas Day, the *Natal*, and later named Durban after the Cape Governor and military commander, Major General Sir Benjamin D'urban). This relationship established a growing British interest to intervene in the Zulu Kingdom that would persist through the colonial period.

Shaka had accommodated the British Cape traders, Henry Francis Fynn, Francis Farewell, and others for many of the same reasons that other chiefs sought out white merchants: to get guns and information. Fynn, Farewell, and their hapless competitor-associate, James King (who had been stranded on the northeast coast after his ship foundered during an earlier reconnaissance mission), established the trade settlement of Port Natal in 1824 in order to gain access to the lucrative ivory and hides trade through Delagoa Bay. Beyond direct British support and authority and unable to fend for themselves entirely, the traders came to rely on Shaka's benevolent support. The Zulu king granted them permission to occupy the area around Port Natal and to trade, as well as provided them with cattle to sustain their party. Farewell and King would later parlay this permission into claims for an outright grant of land from Shaka, and this eventually laid the foundation for formal British intervention in the area. Reliant as they were on Shaka, these men assumed the guise of client chiefs, married Zulu wives, and embraced the local customs. As for furthering Zulu interests, the traders did prove extremely useful as well-trained, gun-wielding raiders. Shaka first induced the Port Natal traders into making a raid with their rifles against his Khumalo rivals as a condition of a pardon he had granted to them after two of them raped a chief's wife. Thereafter, Shaka recognized the phenomenal power of firearms. He called upon the traders to provide the decided advantage of their guns when the remnants of the Ndwandwe attacked but were defeated in 1826. Fynn and his compatriots also proved extremely effective allies when Shaka made a major raid to the south against Chief Faku's cattle-rich Pondo.

By 1828, Shaka had gained an ambiguous reputation which would persist and grow to mythological proportions. Thanks in part to the power of the white traders' guns, and in part to their (and later, white settlers' and missionaries') propagandizing Shaka as a mighty and terrible ruler, the Zulu king was thereafter known as both tyrant and statesman. In both cases, he has been given an undue share of both credit and responsibility for the emergence of new states and the violence associated with it in a "Zulucentric" perspective on this period. Nevertheless, his seemingly relentless prosecution of raids also created rifts within the kingdom. In September 1828, as most of Shaka's soldiers were far away in the north in a vain attack against Shoshangane (the former ally of the Ndwandwe who established the Gaza state to the north), others plotted against the king. It was Shaka's half-brothers, Dingane and Mhlangana, along with Mbopha, the king's personal assistant, who assassinated him. Beyond their greed for power, their apparent motive was to end the seemingly ceaseless raids that left countless men dead on the field and mourning wives and children back in the homesteads. After more calculated killing which left only one brother, Mpande, as a possible heir to the throne, Dingane emerged as the paramount chief of the Zulu. It would be for him to contend with the powerful array of new forces, the Boers, or Afrikaners, and the British who invaded his lands in the 1830s and there after (see Map 4-1).

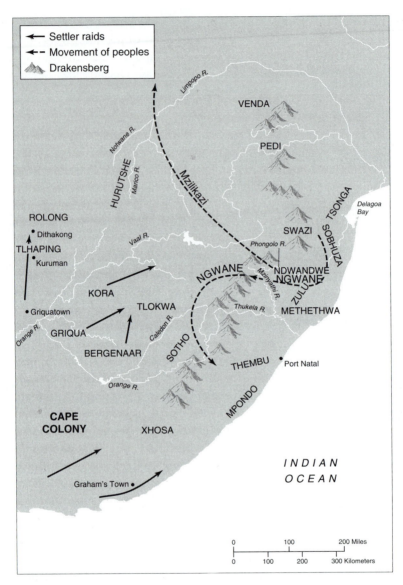

Map 4–1   The Making of New States: African States. *Adapted from Hamilton, History of Southern Africa. 1995.*

Developments in the Interior

There were other powerful forces at play in the interior. By the early 1800s, a diverse group of whites, Africans, and people of mixed descent transformed the economic and political relations in the interior. In so doing, they contributed to the forces which shaped the building of new states. European merchants, adventurers, and colonial officials had developed a growing interest in the resources of the region beyond the confines of the Cape colony. Moreover, British officials were increasingly wary of the potential for cross-border raiding, provoked by settlers in the north, to spill over into the Cape colony, as it had done along the eastern frontier with the Xhosa. They expected the Griqua and the Kora to act as a "semi-civilized" (employing their usual deprecating colonial parlance) buffer against African incursions. Such policies of separation, as we shall see, inevitably did not work.

As the British phased out slavery, the more highly capitalized European farmers and merchants pressed not only for new avenues of trade with the powerful African kingdoms of the interior, but also, more ominously, for new sources of malleable labor. Moreover, even poorer Boer farmers started to "trek" (literally the command to pull a wagon with oxen) or move beyond the confines of the colony in search of grazing land and possibly cheap labor. These *trekboers* took with them their flocks of sheep, some cattle, perhaps a few servants, and their guns. More affluent Afrikaners sought to establish larger farms. Together, they were a formidable force when organized into a commando. As they had done previously against the San and the Xhosa, the northern commandos sought to assert Boer claims to the land and the labor of the area. The overall effect was to intensify the competition for grazing resources in the more arid interior. In turn, the Europeans involved Khoe and the descendants of their marriages with Boer frontiersmen in their bid to secure workers—coercively, if necessary. They began to intensify their trading and raiding beyond the Orange River and deep into the Caledon River Valley. Along with increasing numbers of Afrikaner adventurers, these men were part of a broader vanguard of gun-wielding raiders and traders who altered the balance of power in the interior. It was, however, the increased use of guns, introduced by the whites and so sought after by the Africans, the trekboers, and the Griqua and the Kora alike, that contributed most to the intensification of violence as well as to the defensive political responses to it.

It was a diverse assemblage of people of mixed descent and cultural inheritance that helped drive the upheavals along the Orange and Caledon Valleys and on the highveld. Some of the major Griqua and Kora family dynasties, such as the Koks, the Barends, the Waterboers and Jan Bloem's Springbok Kora, originated from the freed slaves or employees of Cape farmers. In their own view, they were outcastes from colonial society seeking to escape persecution for their mixed heritage by moving ahead of the expanding Afrikaners. Their understanding of colonial society and language, plus their command of firearms and knowledge of the trade routes through which they circulated, made these men popular and successful leaders. Men such as Jan Bloem and Adam Kok II were particularly effective at developing raiding techniques, as were their Afrikaner counterparts, such as Coenraad de Buys. They took advantage of their horses and guns, which were expensive commodities on the frontier, to prosecute ruthless raids for cattle and people as slaves, either the young as bonded workers or the women as "wives." They struck terror into the minds of the African chiefs upon whom they descended. In this way, Griqua, Kora, and Boer raiders alike stabbed into the heart of the interior and forced the established Sotho-Tswana-speaking African communities to either adapt, retreat, or be torn asunder.

The ebb and flow of relations in the interior provided for more than just the explosive force of Griqua, Kora, and Boer raids. The chiefdoms of the interior took advantage of the new opportunities and challenges to re-organize their polities and engage with the new forces. The main stimulus to this re-organization was the opening of new trade opportunities in ivory and hides along routes to the coast in the northeast, and back in Cape Town. Some chiefs created alliances with Griqua and Kora forces through political marriages. Others thought it more prudent to retreat and avoid direct conflict. In so doing, however, they risked the fragmentation of their societies. The Rolong chief, Tau, for example, saw his followers split into five separate groups in the wake of attacks from a combined Kora and Thlaping (competitors of the Rolong) force.

In many cases, raids for cattle and women preceded or followed the lines of trade. Trade flourished between the various Sotho-Tswana-speaking chiefdoms and the Griqua and the Kora. For the Griqua, manufactured goods, tobacco, and livestock from the Cape brought highly prized ivory, animal hides, and iron goods from the major Tswana chiefdoms upcountry. Increasingly, however, Tswana chiefs sought the guns and horses that could empower them over other groups. Those who secured guns could then set off on raids against neighboring competitors. In turn, successful raiders accumulated more cattle and were thus more attractive to new followers. In this way, the initial thrust of Griqua, Kora and Boer frontier raiding and trading set in motion successive raids and counter-raids as the Sotho-Tswana chiefdoms sought to recoup their losses. By the early 1820s, these raids reverberated across the interior beyond the Orange River. Moreover, the widespread use of guns contributed to an arms race as chiefs from the interior sought more powerful weapons to counter Griqua and Kora raiders and to assert their control over territory. British Government prohibitions against trading arms to Africans forced the chiefs to turn to Griqua traders. Ultimately, however, the chiefs were too poorly armed and prepared to turn this firepower against the more organized militia of the Afrikaner trekkers.

Missionaries played an ambiguous role in this projection of power into the interior. On the one hand, they sought to wrest indigenous peoples from their established spiritual practices by substituting the Christian gospel and tools of the "civilizing mission"—the Bible, the plow, and western material goods. On the other hand, they asserted themselves as guardians of African people, and sought to safeguard them from the depredations of colonial forces and settlers. In the face of increased settler and official pressure to trade and supply labor, some Griqua resisted and broke away farther, beyond the Orange River to the Hart's River, where they established a new and more independent community known as the Hartenaars. By the 1790s, the Griqua and the Kora, however, had presented themselves first as ideal collaborators in the expansion of trade and religion. Just as some chiefs of the major African states would later seek to make alliances with missionaries, so too did the Griqua and the Kora. As inheritors of many features of Afrikaner culture, including the language of Afrikaans and Christianity, they made entreaties to the men of the London Missionary Society to recognize their "civilized" status.

By 1802, influential missionary men of the LMS such as John Campbell, John Philip, the society's general superintendent, and Robert Moffat of the northern Kuruman mission embraced this opportunity to gain a stake in the interior with a view to reaching the large number of potential converts among the Bantu-speaking communities there. They set about developing alliances with the more powerful Griqua leaders and also with some of the smaller splinter groups such as the Hartenaars and Bergenaars. As we have seen, they established some major mission stations such as Cornelius Kok's Campbell community, the Bergenaars' mission station of Philippolis, and the Waterboers' settlement at Griquatown. These missions also became important sites for the dissemination of missionary ideals and for trade. Settler farmers, however, viewed the stations as refuges for what they claimed were indolent Griqua and Khoe. They railed against missionary efforts to make these communities self-sustaining and at the refusal of those who lived on the stations to work for them. Their complaints became even more vociferous as slavery was phased out after 1807 (in part because of the missionary and humanitarian lobbies) and the labor shortage became more acute.

Despite settler farmer hostility, the Griqua were able to take advantage of the links which British missionaries had to the Cape markets and especially to the illegal arms traders. This allowed the Griqua to circumvent official, but largely unenforceable, prohibitions against the trading of guns to Africans and people of mixed descent. Similarly, LMS missionaries largely turned a blind eye to the escalation of the Griqua's brutal commando raids into the Caledon Valley and beyond. By 1820, the mission stations served as the major staging points for Griqua and Kora raiding against a range of Sotho and Tswana chiefdoms. The raiding for cattle and labor had important implications for the escalation of violence which ultimately led to the formation of new states in the interiors. First, the Griqua represented a significant outside influence in the processes referred to as the *Difaqane*. The Griqua linked the interior to the external agents of trade and missionary activity. As the missionary at Kuruman,

Robert Moffat surmised, however, LMS support of the Griqua raiders also undermined their efforts to win over many Sotho and Tswana converts. Moreover, although not officially sanctioned, these alliances and other British missionary activities eventually laid the foundation for British imperial intervention north of the Orange River, based on their interest in protecting the rights of these frontier groups.

The effect of Griqua cavalry and firepower in association with missionary activity proved a powerful combination against the less well-organized refugees of battles on the highveld. For example, Griqua raiding abilities and missionary efforts to safeguard peoples in the interior for potential evangelical activity converged at the Thlaping town of Dithakong in 1823. At that time, a substantial mass of destitute and wretched folk were approaching the Thlaping town after having scoured the Vaal River Valley to the north for food and cattle. This was a unique force which had coalesced from the effects of the severe drought and raiders to the north and east (probably including MaNthatisi's Tlokwa and Matiwane's Ngwane) and had started to flow down the valley. Although not well-armed or organized, this band of possibly tens of thousands presented a formidable force. As news of their approach reached Robert Moffat at Kuruman, he immediately called upon notable Griqua leaders to provide men for the defense of the town which was within Moffat's zone of missionary activity.

In short order, the Koks, Waterboers, and Barends mustered about eighty men in the hopes of grabbing some booty from the marauders. Although eyewitness accounts are not clear, it appears that both the Griqua and Moffat achieved their aims. The combined Griqua-Thlaping defenders killed more than 500 of the invaders without sustaining any losses. Moreover, they captured and kept more than one thousand head of cattle for their efforts. There is no convincing evidence to support the notion that Moffat and the Griqua had actually instigated the battle as a raid to take captive labor. The inevitable by-product of the conflict was, however, destitute and famished prisoners, only some of whom were transported back to the Cape and ended up in the hands of frontier farmers as contracted workers. Most of the invaders either fled the scene, or were attacked by vengeful Tswana. The remaining "horde" appears to have then melted away, and the people were absorbed by the more stable new and rising states of the interior. Still, the impact of Griqua raiders and white traders who could provide guns for highveld conflicts was significant for the ways in which the new states emerged.

Mass Movements and New States

It would seem that the emergence of major new states in southern Africa was a product both of external forces and local agencies. Trading, raiding for slave labor, and guns were the thrusting external hand of colonial commerce and expansion which contributed to increasing violence in the interior and which forced communities to adapt or fragment. How local communities coped with these external forces was a matter of internal initiative. The rise of charismatic African statesmen and the movement of their followers in search of a secure place with sufficient good agricultural and grazing land to sustain their mixed farming and cattle economies were the key features of the local factor. These were, of course, part of a long-standing process of the formation and reformation of states in the region that can be traced back to the twelfth century and the emergence of the Mapungubwe and Zimbabwe kingdoms. From the later 1810s, however, there was a significant range of new communities on the move in search of a place to settle and call home. From the east across the Drakensburg came the Nguni-speakers who mixed and blended with Sotho and Tswana speakers into the interior. Various communities were on the move on the highveld. Some of them were torn asunder by the ruthless raiding of colonial forces and their allies; others were intact or enlarging as successful chiefs captured more cattle and garnered more followers. Similarly, Afrikaners, particularly the more impoverished frontier settlers of the Eastern Cape, attracted by reports of empty lands, set off in large numbers to lay claim to the grazing resources of the highveld. Although the number of Afrikaners who invaded the interior was not as great as the number of Africans there, they nonetheless proved to be a formidable force. There then emerged a major confluence of people and their livestock in the central region along the Caledon River Valley, bounded by the Orange and Vaal Rivers.

MOSHOESHOE AND THE SOTHO

The Sotho statesman Moshoeshoe was among the most successful chiefs to weather the challenges of the early 1800s and to create a flourishing state in the Caldeon River Valley. Born of the comparatively minor Mokoteli chiefdom, Moshoeshoe took advantage of the impressive natural resources of his region, won over followers, and bested his competitors. The Caledon provided good sources of water, fine grazing, and most importantly, excellent defensible positions in the surrounding mountains; Moshoeshoe made the most of all three. He exhibited considerable mental toughness and remarkable military and political skills. Aware of the centrality of cattle for the local economy, and the need to be prepared to take and defend herds, he honed his skills as cattle-raider to the extent he became known as Moshoeshoe, "the cattle razor," who cut away opponents' herds as neatly as a shave. He made successful raids from the highveld against the Thembu, who held large herds along the other side of the Drakensburg, and thereby established his reputation. He did not, however, simply hoard his raided cattle. Instead, he applied them to the complex fabric of cattle exchanges by using the established practices of *mafisa* and *lobola* (i.e., the loaning of cattle and the provision of bridewealth by a would-be husband to his prospective bride's family). These practices were based on the productive and reproductive capacities of cattle which signaled their status as accumulated wealth. In this way, Moshoeshoe enhanced his economic and political standing among an increasing number of followers.

Those who joined Moshoeshoe's ranks came from the fragments of the various Sotho chiefdoms which had been assaulted first by the Hlubi and then by Mshoeshoe's main competitor, the Queen-regent of the Tlokwa, Ma-Nthatisi. She, along with her son and heir to the chieftaincy, Sekonyela, continued to attack Moshoeshoe's people in their stronghold of Butha-Buthe. Moshoeshoe then shrewdly chose to lead his followers to Thaba-Bosiu, an impregnable natural fortress on a flat-topped mountain. From there, he developed his kingdom around both cattle-clientage and an inclusive administration. Most of the fragmented chiefdoms were allowed to retain some

MOSHOESHOE   The gifted diplomat and statesman who founded the Sotho state. *Source: National Archives of South Africa.*

autonomy, and he bound them to his rule through political marriages and the *Pitso*, a form of national council which operated at the village level and at the capital, Thaba-Bosiu. Moshoeshoe was also a pragmatic statesman. He initially paid tribute to his powerful neighbor, Matiwane and his Ngwane, but gradually shifted his allegiance to the Zulu when the Ngwane became too demanding. Moshoeshoe conspired with the Zulu to attack Matiwane in 1827, and this enabled him finally to push the Ngwane from his region.

Moshoeshoe also developed tactics and policies that enabled the Sotho state to survive while others were conquered and collapsed. First, he adopted one of the tactics of the competing white and Griqua raiders: He acquired a horse from a successful raid on a Boer farm and soon encouraged his people to breed ponies. The Sotho then developed an impressive mounted force which easily navigated their local mountain terrain. Perhaps his most astute move was to enlist the aid of French missionaries. In 1833, after Moshoeshoe played the different factions off against each other, he welcomed members of the Paris Evangelical Missionary Society at Thaba-Bosiu in the Sotho kingdom. They were suitably impressed by his detailed understanding of regional and international politics, by his guns, European clothes, and manufactured goods. They remained hopeful that they could create a complete Christian state out of Moshoeshoe's kingdom but they were ultimately frustrated.

Moshoeshoe continued to take full advantage of the French missionaries. He persuaded them to appeal to the Griqua and Kora raiders as self-proclaimed fellow Christians in a bid to keep them in check. Moreover, he used them as vital intermediaries with the British at Cape Town where he sought political influence and access to guns. He also allowed them to build a string of mission stations. These helped link his kingdom together and were sites for European Christian schools, which were attended by many Sotho, including his own sons. The French missionaries, therefore, became important allies for Moshoeshoe and they wrote their own glowing history of his accomplishments. Although their efforts did not prevent British Wesleyans from gaining a foothold in his territory, they did help considerably with the Sotho's successful effort to prevent the wholesale annexation of their mountain kingdom by settler forces.

MZILIKAZI AND THE NDEBELE

One of the most harrowing journeys which led to the development of a major African state was that of chief Mzilikazi and his Ndebele state. Mzilikazi's story exemplifies the important processes of state building which unfolded in the interior during the first half of the nineteenth century. Mzilikazi emerged from a rather unpromising situation as chief of a minor group, the Khumalo, sandwiched between Shaka's Zulu and their competitors, the Ndwandwe. Originally, the Khumalo paid deference to the Ndwandwe, but Mzilikazi, perhaps predicting events to come, switched his allegiance to Shaka during the early wars between the Zulu and the Ndwandwe. Mzilikazi then thought himself on sounder footing and asserted his independence by retaining raided cattle and grazing land which Shaka wanted. Shaka responded with two successive attacks, and sometime after 1822, Mzilikazi prudently distanced himself from the Zulu state. Although it is not clear when he quit the coastal belt, Mzilikazi and about three hundred followers did set off across the Drakensburg in search of sufficient pasture to sustain their cattle and attract more followers. They arrived on the highveld by 1825 and tried to establish a stable community. Once on the highveld, the Sotho-speaking inhabitants labeled Mzilikazi and his Khumalo followers the *Matabele* or "Ndebele", which was their generic term for alien invaders, and so the Ndebele became confused with a range of refugees who were on the move.

Over the next decade, with remarkable statesmanship, Mzilikazi set about trying to consolidate his kingdom despite being buffeted by raiders and competitors. First, he enforced his strong centralized rule over regimental towns based on the Ndwandwe model. He then sent out his *amabutho* to raid for cattle and to demand tribute from subordinated chiefdoms while he absorbed local Sotho-Tswana people into his rapidly swelling kingdom. His rule was marked by a balance of sophisticated political indoctrination and terror. Public executions of enemies and criminals were tempered by the development of a corporate spirit in which all Ndebele learned to speak Zulu and to embrace the coastal culture which Mzilikazi brought with him from the region of the Ndwandwe-Zulu chiefdoms. What sustained the Ndebele, however, were lightning-fast cattle raiding and Mzilikazi's remarkable ability to keep pace with the rapidly changing and violent politics of the highveld. Through the later 1820s, the Ndebele raided over a vast area. They forced the Hurutshe chiefdom to submit and pay tribute, and then successfully defeated and took massive numbers of cattle from the substantial Pedi chiefdom to the north.

Mzilikazi also soundly routed the Taung forces of Moletsane which had repeatedly raided the Ndebele and eventually forced them from the region. He was sorely tested, though, when Griqua and Kora raiders with their horses and guns descended upon Ndebele cattle settlements. In 1828, Jan Bloem's Kora allied with the Taung and forced Mzilikazi to retreat into the central reaches of the Vaal River. In order to survive, the Ndebele sustained their cattle raiding against northern Tswana and Rolong chiefdoms The Ndebele were, however, driven back by a well-prepared force under Moshoeshoe when they attempted to strike at the Sotho stronghold of Thaba-Bosiu in 1831. Mzilikazi did manage to recoup most of the cattle that Barend-Barends Griqua commando took in a massive raid later in 1831.Yet the threat of Griqua and Kora raiding persisted. Before the Ndebele could deal with the Griqua harassment, a large Zulu army attacked. The Zulu raided across a broad swath and looted numerous Ndebele settlements, perhaps in a vendetta for old transgressions, but more probably to keep the now powerful Mzilikazi in check. After an indecisive battle, the Zulu withdrew. In response, Mzilikazi immediately sent out more raiding parties to restore lost cattle, and then he relocated the Ndebele to the Marico Valley, farther from the reach of Zulu and Griqua raiders.

In order to contend with the challenge of the well-armed Griqua horsemen, Mzilikazi sought the aid of missionaries just as the Griqua and the Kora had done. It was not just access to the Cape gun market which Mzilikazi sought from the Wesleyan Missionary Society and Robert Moffat of the LMS. He hoped that by striking up a friendship with Moffat, he could gain his assistance, and that of the influential LMS, in controlling the actions of Griqua raiders and greedy white frontiersmen. He also accommodated members of the Paris Evangelical Society, whose abject failure to make any converts frustrated them to the point where they abandoned their efforts among the Ndebele. Unfortunately, for him, Mzilikazi, did not reckon on the missionaries' inability to provide guns, nor on their vilifying the king and portraying him as a bloodthirsty tyrant, in the same fashion that some missionaries portrayed Shaka. Nevertheless, in 1835, after yet another damaging raid by the Griqua, Mzilikazi relied on missionary guidance in working out a treaty of friendship with the Cape colony in the vain hope of securing its protection. By 1835, as we shall see, the Ndebele were again forced to move—this time beyond the highveld entirely—but not by the usual host of local raiders. By then the configuration of power on the highveld was altered by the arrival of large numbers of white settlers, the Afrikaners. Nevertheless, Mzilikazi is rightly credited as being a brilliant statesman and military leader, the equal of any other leaders in the region at this time.

MATIWANE'S NGWANE AND THE BRITISH

Matiwane, the chief of the Ngwane, did not fare nearly so well. On his arduous trek, he and his followers were caught in the web of conflict that pitted colonial forces against the African states, the Zulu and the Xhosa, which threatened settler interests along the eastern frontier zone. In the early 1820s, Matiwane led his followers away from the orbit of Zulu power across the mountains in order to establish his own independent rule. En route to the highveld, Matiwane overwhelmed the Hlubi (who had moved to the foothills of the Drakensburg in the wake of Shaka's rise to power) and killed their chief Mpangazitha. Once on the highveld, Matiwane was remarkably successful at asserting his power and equally remarkable for losing it. At first, following a routing of the Tlokwa, he made an alliance with Moshoeshoe, who paid him tribute. As Ngwane demands became excessive, however, Moshoeshoe called upon the Zulu to keep Matiwane in check and Shaka complied, probably for his own interests in gaining cattle. In order to recover from the losses sustained from the Zulu attack, the Ngwane imprudently tried to repair their losses with an attack on Thaba-Bosiu, Moshoeshoe's mountain fortress. Matiwane himself did not wish to attempt such an attack, but a rebellious group of his followers distrusted the Sotho and coveted their cattle. Facing the potential of increased internal dissent, Matiwane then chose to leave the area and to take his loyal followers in search of a fresh start.

It was at this point that the Ngwane became embroiled in a confused state of affairs involving British colonial forces, the coastal chiefdoms of the Thembu, Pondo, and Xhosa, and the raiding Zulu. As Matiwane sought a new place to settle, he led his followers south and east in order to avoid direct conflict with the predacious Griqua raiders of the interior. His people then undertook the same tactics of the highveld which had sustained the Sotho and Ndebele—cattle-raiding—and they descended upon the coastal chiefdoms of the Thembu, Faku's Pondo, and their subordinate clients, the refugee *Mfengu*. As the Ngwane successfully raided the coast, they joined groups such as the Sotho, who attacked across the mountains and were referred to as *Fetcani*, a catch-all term for such raiders. Matiwane could not have known the extent to which these raids contributed to an unsettled state of affairs along the frontier between the Cape and the Xhosa, Thembu, and Pondo chiefdoms.

British officials, with their rather paranoid colonial imagination, were concerned that such raids would further destabilize the border Xhosa chiefdoms. They worried that this would precipitate a widespread movement of Xhosa into the colony and force their intervention to safeguard white farms. But it was the Zulu that the British were directly concerned with, not Matiwane. As we have seen, in July 1828, Shaka had sent a massive raiding party not against the Xhosa next to the colony, but against the Pondo, farther north. British military men went in search of the Zulu forces, whom they feared were on their way to attack the Xhosa. Shaka had, however, sent an embassy to the British informing them of this action and that his intentions were otherwise peaceful as far as the Xhosa and the British were concerned, just as he had shown with the Port Natal settlers. In a sudden move, Colonel Somerset's forces, which included British regulars as well as Xhosa and Thembu troops, swooped on the Nganwe encampment at Mbholompo, assuming them to be Zulu. Once the smoke had settled and many of the Ngwane lay dead, the Xhosa took their pick of Ngwane cattle as booty, and Somerset escorted the Ngwane survivors back to the Cape to work on settler farms. Although the British action was not a planned labor raid, Somerset's professed offer to accommodate the Ngwane refugees belied his motive to take them back as captive workers for the labor-hungry settlers of the Cape.

Clearly, settler demands for labor in light of the anticipated abolition of slavery far exceeded the small number of Africans who offered themselves for work. This was true even after the promulgation of Ordinances 49 and 50, which, as we saw Chapter 3, "The British and the Expanding Cape: Continuities and Contrasts," were designed in part to encourage an increase in the availability of free contracted workers (Ordinance 50) while also seeking to protect the status of Khoe workers (Ordinance 49). Following the brutal attack, a broken and dispirited Matiwane fled with the remnants of his followers to Zululand. Once there, Dingane, the Zulu king, had Matiwane executed as a potential competitor for power; his son was later allowed to establish a modest chiefdom in the region.

BRITISH POLICY AND THE XHOSA

By the early 1830s, the colonial and settler pressure on the Xhosa had risen to intolerable levels. Prior alliances and treaties between the Cape government and Xhosa chiefs such as Ngqika could not withstand the combination of settler demands and the determined machinations of British military commanders to control the region through might. Moreover, a long string of Methodist missionary stations now stretched deep into the Transkei region. The missionaries were daily petitioning the chiefs for permission to preach while also simultaneously demanding more support from British officials to safeguard their interests against "hostile native chiefs." Increasing numbers of British and Boer settlers raided for cattle and, more menacingly, asserted claims to permanent rights on Xhosa lands. Moreover, as we have seen with the fate of Matiwane's people, white settlers expected the colonial government to aid in their acquisition and control of contracted labor. These pressures were compounded by a severe drought in 1834, and tensions rose to the point where the Xhosa made a series of widespread incursions into the colony before British troops could reinforce the frontier.

In response, under the new governorship of the military-minded Sir Benjamin D'urban, the British made a retaliatory strike which led to the Sixth Xhosa War of Resistance. This was more than just an effort to resettle the frontier. British forces struck deeply into Xhosa territory in a punitive campaign which devastated the people. In a move that shocked and dismayed missionaries and the humanitarian lobby, colonial forces seized the Gcaleka chief, Hintsa, as a hostage. When the British caught him trying to escape, they decapitated Hintsa and brandished his head as a trophy. Determined to settle the land, D'urban then placed *Mfengu* refugee chiefdoms on Xhosa land between the Keiskamma and Kei Rivers. He claimed this land as a prize of the war and termed it the Ceded Territory.

D'urban's intention was for the Ceded Territory to act as a buffer between the now severely weakened and demoralized Xhosa and the settlers. D'urban added insult to injury when he annexed this territory to the colony as Queen Adelaide Province (named in honor of the British King, William IV's wife). His purpose was to move from a policy based on the peaceful segregation of white settlers and the Xhosa according to earlier treaties to one in which he had complete authority to settle whites on their lands and force the remaining Xhosa into submission. Once the liberal administration in London got wind of D'urban's actions from the humanitarian lobby, the Imperial government forced him to abandon Queen Adelaide Province. This signaled a significant shift in British policy. Previously, officials could take action beyond the confines of the frontier to aid settler and colonial interests and even to extend the colony. By 1835, the British Parliament wanted no more embarrassing and costly entanglements with African states in the interior. Although missionaries then clamored for greater intervention and protection for African interests, the best they could get was the Cape of Good Hope Punishment Act of 1836. The Act stipulated that British subjects could be tried for illegal acts, even if committed beyond the Cape up to 25 degrees South, approximately the line of the southern border of modern-day Botswana. This shift was symptomatic of long-term vacillations in British policy between a reluctance to intervene beyond their colonial possessions and their desire for a immediate response to demands from settlers and missionaries to extend British power and authority. Overall, it was apparent that, by the 1830s, the British were determined to assert their authority in the colony, whether over Africans or Afrikaners, and their heavy-handedness was a contributing factor in the movement of many of the Afrikaners.

THE BOER/AFRIKANER GREAT TREK

From 1836 to 1838, by the time many African leaders had already established or reconfigured their states in the interior, a new massive wave of Boer or Afrikaner families from the eastern frontier embarked on another trek. The eight to ten thousand people, including some Khoe servants and slaves (the 1834 Act of Abolition was not enforced until 1838) of the families, who set off on this Great Trek (as it was later called) were of mostly modest means. In some respects, their exodus was an acceleration of the processes of frontier expansion that had been going on for some time. They left the confines of the colony for many of the same reasons that earlier Boer *voortrekkers* had wandered into the interior: to find land and economic opportunity away from the controlling hand of the Cape government, be it Dutch or British. They differed from earlier trekkers in that they left with a view to establishing permanent homes in the interior, and they developed a decidedly idealistic vision of their mission. By the mid-1830s, however, there were new challenges and opportunities for these settler invaders of the highveld. These included a more interventionist British colonial government that had greater ability to shape the political economy than the VOC, and a powerful humanitarian-missionary lobby which appeared determined to interfere with settler society. There were also, as far as the Boers could see, new possibilities for trade and settlement in the interior. On the basis of various reports, they conjured up images of vast tracts of fertile grazing land (which did exist), devoid of any African settlements or political authority (which was not the case), ripe for their taking.

The Afrikaner families who left the Cape in these tumultuous years were motivated by a need for land and were spurred on by a severe drought in 1836. As we have seen, the processes of segmentation, whereby each Afrikaner's son believed it was his birthright to stake out a vast farm along the frontier, had contributed to overcrowding, raiding, and a series of brutal frontier wars with the Xhosa. The reports of fertile open land filtered that back to the Cape from hunting parties, and particularly from Dr. Andrew Smith—the British secret agent who toured the interior in 1832—and Piet Uys—an advance trekker—stimulated great interest among frontier families in the pastoral potential of the lands across the Orange River. The families hoped to claim farms and establish lucrative trade relations with the wealthy African kingdoms in the interior. Other economic reasons for the trek included the Afrikaners' concerns about cattle lost in Xhosa raids and the insecurity of their land tenure in the frontier zone. In the early phases of the Great Trek, there was no clear sense of group identity or Afrikaner nationalism, nor any set of guiding principles derived exclusively from their Calvinist faith, although leaders and historians would later attribute both of these to the movement. There was, however, a broad sense of grievance against the British for their handling of the frontier.

The Afrikaner trek movement was also fueled by a growing sense among less well-to-do farmers that the British colonial government would not necessarily support the type of white-dominated settler society they wanted. Frontier Afrikaners were concerned about the apparent indifference of the colonial government to their economic plight, about British policy changes, and the increasing influence of missionaries. Of great concern to the Boers was the reversal of D'urban's annexation of Xhosa land as Queen Adelaide Province at the behest of the humanitarian lobby. The settlers had hoped the annexed territory would provide new lands for white settlement, and the return of the land signaled for them that the British were abandoning their interests. Earlier policies for the protection of Khoe and Africans in the colony (Ordinance 50 and the Black Circuit Court) had rankled Afrikaners who sought to keep the upper hand with their employees, as had the heavy-handed British suppression of Boer republican rebellions such as Slachter's Nek.

The impending abolition of slavery, or at least the talk surrounding it, may also have been a factor that influenced slave-holding Afrikaners. Nevertheless, most of the wealthy slave-holding Afrikaners, who had settled on large farms near Cape Town, did not leave on the trek. The trekkers themselves claimed that they were compelled to leave because their lives had become intolerable under the British. A later trek leader, Piet Retief, published a manifesto aimed at justifying rather than instigating the movement; he claimed that the colonial government had abandoned the Afrikaners. He argued that the British did not support their livelihood or the "proper" handling of master-servant relations, in which white settlers were expected to have unquestioned authority. He further claimed that they had offended God for allowing the missionaries to interfere in these "proper" relations. He did, however, profess the loyalty of the trekkers to the British government in the hope that it would eventually come to their aid in support of the white settlers claims to the land in the interior.

The trekking parties, which set off as independent groups under the leadership of a single patriarch, had an impact disproportionate to their numbers. This was in part because they came to the interior with a new set of ideas about the outright ownership of the land, and in part because they brought the terrifying means to achieve their goals: guns, cannons, and horses. They also prided themselves on their self-sufficiency and their fiercely independent spirit. As they entered the interior, they did adapt increasingly to the local African context, "learning the lay of the land," so to speak; yet they still retained their religion, their technology, and the military strategies which would set them apart from African societies. The lands of the interior appeared uninhabited to their settlers' eyes, and they did not take notice of the sometimes subtle African systems of land use in which seasonal grazing patterns and hunting strategies left large tracts undisturbed for certain times of the year. Moreover, they did not figure on African political authority which may have projected power into areas far beyond the immediate range of settlement. Once they arrived on the highveld and along the Natal coast, their interests and activities placed them immediately in potential competition with the African states.

Among the early trekking groups were some folks who were completely unaware of the hazards of the interior of South Africa. Louis Trichardt and Johannes van Rensburg, for example, led two ill-fated parties. Trichardt was wanted by colonial authorities for slaving and illegal gun-running. When the British offered a substantial reward for his capture, he fled from the Cape colony with about fifty people. After meeting up with van Rensburg's party, the entire group traveled across the Orange River in search of a route to the trading port at Delagoa Bay in Portuguese territory. Following a quarrel over leadership, van Rensburg split from Trichardt, and subsequently led his party toward the coast, where they reportedly were wiped out by one of Shoshangane's Gaza regiments. Trichardt fared no better. Unaccustomed as he and the Afrikaners were to the terrain of the region, Trichardt retained a Sotho-speaking guide and yet still ran afoul of the local disease ecology. He report-edly lost a whole team of oxen to sleeping sickness after he went in search of salt in a tse tse fly- (the carrier of sleeping sickness) infested marsh. After con-siderable effort, his party crossed the Drakensburg and descended to the coast, where he and most his party succumbed to malaria and eventually died.

The first major trekking party of 1836, led by Hendrick Potgieter and joined by Sarel Cillier's group, laid the foundation for permanent Afrikaner settlement across the Orange River through political organization and military tactics. They divided up their authority, as other trekking groups would do, placing military power in Potgieter's hands as commander of the *krygsraad*, or war council, and then establishing a civil authority, the *volksraad*, under Gerit Maritz. Their combined group was welcomed by the missionary, James Arch-bell, and the Rolong chief, Moroka, at Thaba Nchu near the western Lesotho mountains. As to some other Sotho and Tswana chiefs, the Afrikaners ap-peared to Moroka as potential allies whose guns and horses could prove deci-sive in future raids against powerful kingdoms such as Moshoeshoe's or Mzilikazi's. However, Moroka and the other African chiefs were unaware that these white settlers' profession of friendship belied their real motive to take the land and get labor for their farms.

Mzilikazi, whose Ndebele still commanded much of the highveld, was more wary. His spies informed him that Potgieter's group was no raiding party. They had arrived with all the trappings for establishing a settlement—wagons, families, servants, and personal effects—much the way he had done a decade earlier, and so constituted a far greater threat than the Griqua. Mzilikazi made a pre-emptive strike against the Afrikaners' encampment to prevent their set-tling in. Potgieter's forces then split, with one group returning south and the other moving on to a place called Vegkop. It was here in October 1836 that the Afrikaners showed the devastating potential of what would become the hallmark of their military tactics: the *laager*. Before Mzilikazi's troops arrived, the trekkers draped heavy animal hides over their wagons, placed them into a tight square formation, and filled the gaps in with thorn bushes. In the center of the formation, they made a final redoubt for the women and children, even though they would be kept busy reloading muskets and reinforcing breaches as the attack progressed.

When Mzilikazi's force of some 5,000 men attacked, they were repulsed by the awesome firepower of only forty Afrikaner defenders secure behind the wag-ons. Hundreds of Ndebele lay dead within a few hundred yards of the *laager*, while only two defenders were killed and fourteen wounded. The retreating Ndebele did manage to steal as many as 6,000 cattle and tens of thousands of sheep and goats, but at too great a cost to human life. Realizing their phenomenal advantage, Potgieter then regrouped his forces and, with Rolong and Griqua as allies, made a major assault on Mzilikazi's settlement in the Mosega Valley. The alliance was very successful, and they made off with more than 7,000 cattle. Potgieter then made grandiose claims to vast stretches of the highveld, far beyond what his followers could hope to occupy. Mzilikazi was severely compromised and forced to retreat. He was then harried from the highveld by the Zulu king, Dingane, who, in 1837, launched an audacious long-distance raid to capture cattle from the weakened Ndebele. Potgieter then mounted another commando with the help of cavalry from the newly arrived Piet Uys. They finally drove Mzilikazi far to the north where he established his permanent capital for the Ndebele Kingdom at Bulawayo in modern-day Zimbabwe (see Map 4–2 on page 99).

PIET RETIEF AND THE ZULU KINGDOM

Following the news of Potgieter's great victory at Vegkop, other trekkers set off to find their fortunes beyond the colony. Chief among them was Piet Retief, who had already established himself as one of the most respected leaders of the trekker movement in the Cape, with his earlier manifesto, his considerable wealth, and his political savvy. Upon his arrival across the Orange River, over a thousand Afrikaner families atop their wagons met Retief and proclaimed him governor and military commander of their forces, while Gerit Maritz retained civil authority as president of the *volksraad*. Potgieter was left out of the new dispensation. Retief then pledged himself to lead the Afrikaners to Natal, where he claimed there were excellent grazing lands and great opportunities for trade. Potgieter, however, warned that the British had designs on Natal, and so he decided to remain in the Transvaal—the highveld region beyond the Vaal River—where, as we have seen, he had successfully pursued Mzilikazi. By this time, Retief was in communication with the British Port Natal traders who were trading ivory, running guns, and even making raids on behalf of Dingane's Zulu Kingdom. They encouraged Retief to join them and thus presented possibly lucrative commercial opportunities for the Afrikaners. The Port Natal men were ostensibly under the watchful eye of Captain Allen Gardiner, a self-styled missionary-cum-adventurer. (He had permission from the British to oversee their subjects in the area under the provisions of the Cape of Good Hope Punishment Act.) Retief lost no time in leading the majority of the trekkers across the Drakensburg and down to Natal.

Retief realized that the real center of power in the region lay with the Zulu king, Dingane, to the north across the Thukela River. He sent emissaries to Dingane to arrange a discussion of a land grant. Dingane was all too aware of the potential threat posed by Retief's party, especially after the news of the Xhosa war, and the news of Potgieter's victory had also reached him. Dingane stalled for time by stating he could not meet with Retief until the matter of some cattle, allegedly stolen by Afrikaners, had been settled. When Retief arrived at Mgungundhlovu, Dingane's capital, to discuss the matter of the

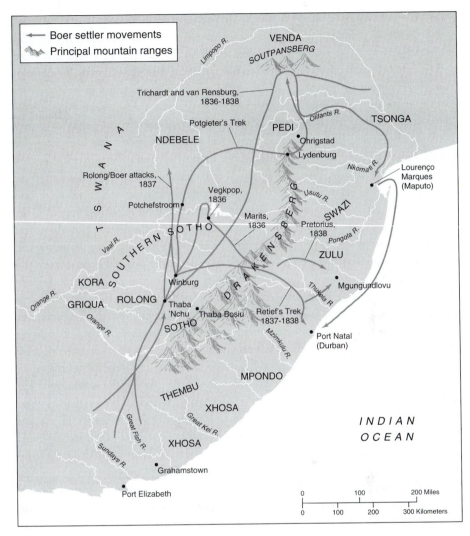

Map 4–2   The Making of New States: Boer Movements. *Adapted from Shillington, History of Southern Africa. 1997.*

stolen cattle, he was received with a great fanfare intended to both intimidate and impress. Dingane put on a great display of Zulu power, parading 6,000 men in front of his "guests." Retief pledged to resolve the matter, and claimed that it was in fact an old Zulu rival, the Tlokwa chief Sekonyela, who had stolen the cattle. Retief and his men then set upon the unsuspecting Sekonyela, with whom he had earlier made a treaty of friendship, and tricked him into putting on some handcuffs. Once the Tlokwa chief was in captivity, Retief demanded a ransom of 700 cattle and some guns, far in excess of the number stolen. By the time Retief was set to deliver the cattle to Dingane, the

Zulu king had become alarmed by the increasing number of Afrikaner families who had invaded his lands; it was a mass movement reminiscent of the settlers who had provoked war with the Xhosa. He also feared that he could not trust Retief, who so easily had thrown off his treaty of friendship with Sekonyela. Dingane planned to do away with the threat before it was too late.

Dingane invited Retief and his men to return the cattle in February 1838. Upon their arrival, the Afrikaners sought to demonstrate their prowess with a display of horsemanship and firing guns of guns as they drove the cattle into the capital. They were, however, forbidden to bring their weapons into the King's enclosure. Once inside, Dingane struck. He called out for the "criminals" to be killed as his men set upon Retief's party. With a flash of spears, seventy-one trekkers were killed in an instant. What was remembered by Afrikaners as Dingane's treachery was, in fact, a measured response to the threat posed by the combined force of the settlers' guns and their determination to dig in and settle the land. As Retief and his men fell dead, Dingane sent out his regiments to attack the Afrikaner camps back across the Thukela river. The Zulu struck quickly and efficiently, killing more than 500 men and capturing 25,000 cattle. In response, the terrified Port Natal settlers teamed up with the remaining Afrikaner families and a number of Natal chiefs who had grudges against Dingane in order to recoup their losses and defend their settlements. They were joined by Piet Uys and Hendrick Potgieter, who heard the news of Retief's murder and the attack on their fellow settlers. Dingane was prepared for the retaliation. He laid an ambush for the combined settler forces and managed to kill Uys. Potgieter shortly decided to leave the coast and he returned to the Transvaal, regretting the whole affair. Dingane then turned to punish the Port Natal settlers who had abrogated their treaty of friendship by attacking with the Afrikaners; he took tens of thousands of their cattle after burning their homes.

Despite their losses to the Zulu, and the recent reversal of policy which meant that the British wished to prevent entanglements between the settlers and the Africans, the Afrikaners were determined to remain in Natal. They boldly declared the annexation of Port Natal to their authority, the United Laagers. The Afrikaners were in a precarious position, facing the might of the Zulu in renewed raids and contending with serious disease among their cattle. Nevertheless, they went on the offensive to strike at the Zulu and drive them back once and for all. In November 1838, a new leader, Andries Pretorius, arrived with reinforcements from the Cape. They assembled their forces in December and reportedly gathered to make a vow to God that if they were victorious against the Zulu, they would observe that day in honor of their faith as the Day of the Covenant (or Vow). Dingane sent out a strong force to meet and attack their forces in a *laager* on the Ncome River. Dingane's men were, however, no match for the Afrikaners' guns, secure within the *laager*. By the end of the battle, more than 3,000 Zulu lay dead.

What transpired became enshrined in later Afrikaner mythology as the "Battle of Blood River," so named for the water which ran red with the blood of so many fallen Zulu. The Afrikaners then set off in hot pursuit of the remaining Zulu, massacring even more of the retreating force. The commando pressed on, routing Zulu at their capital and forcing Dingane to capitulate. They also claimed to have conveniently found a document purported to be the Zulu king's official cession of vast tracts of Natal and Zululand to Retief's party. Just after the battle, a small British force arrived under orders to keep the peace between the settlers and the Zulu. By that time, all they could do was preside over the peace negotiations. Dingane was forced to make massive reparations in cattle and to give over a further large cession of land to the trekkers.

In the aftermath of the battle on the Ncome River, there was a new spatial deployment of power in Natal. The Afrikaners spread out across the lush valleys of the Natal interior and built their capital at Pietermaritzburg (named for the trekker leaders, Piet Retief and Maritz). They remained in an uncertain state, however, for they did not have the means to fully settle the land which they had claimed, and also because the Zulu kingdom remained intact to the north. The British too started to take a more active interest in the region, in part because of policy imperatives for keeping the peace in the interior, and in part because of the economic possibilities for trade and farming. They maintained a continued presence in Natal.

The Zulu kingdom was in an uneasy state. Dingane was in desperate straits, facing not only having to recover from the devastating losses against the Afrikaners, but also growing disgruntlement from his followers. He called for a series of attacks on the emergent Swazi kingdom to the north. This was done to raid for cattle and to push the Swazi back to make room for Zulu families who were forced to leave their land in the southern parts of the kingdom that had been ceded to the Afrikaners. Dingane's plans put too great a strain on the already compromised kingdom and it fractured into civil war. Dingane's surviving brother, Mpande, rebelled rather than accepted Dingane's order to move his people from their ancestral lands along the Umfolozi River, the new border with the land ceded to the Afrikaners. Mpande, who had gained great popularity and a substantial following as his brother struggled to rule, then made an ill-fated alliance. He set off for Port Natal where he struck a deal with the former enemies of the kingdom to aid him in his claim to the throne in return for booty and yet more land. These proposed cessions of land were not, strictly-speaking, allowed under Zulu law. By custom, the king was supposed to hold the land in trust for his people and he could not alienate it in any way. Nevertheless, agreeing to the deal, the Afrikaner leader Pretorius assembled a commando of some 400 mounted men. In January 1840, they set off on a course parallel to Mpande's invading column. In the ensuing battle there was no need for the commando.

Mpande's forces won an easy victory as many of Dingane's men deserted to his brother's cause. Dingane, anticipating a rout, had already fled to Swaziland where, it was claimed, he was killed in retaliation for his earlier raids. The commando still exacted its price, and made off with more than 40,000 cattle. In a practical compromise, Mpande allowed the Afrikaners to proclaim him king, thus conceding their authority. He pledged never to attack the trekkers in Natal but managed to secure the Thukela River, to the south of the previous line, as the border of his kingdom.

CONCLUSION

The period from 1800–1840 witnessed the emergence of major new states and a reconfiguration of power in the interior. These processes were the culmination of long-standing processes of amalgamation which originated in the mid-eighteenth century. Great African statesmen such as Shaka, Moshoeshoe, and Mzilikazi took advantage of the many new opportunities and challenges presented by settler forces such as the traders and the missionaries, just as they worked to cope with the problems of climate and the environment. The critical feature of state-building was the ability of the chiefs to contend with the needs of their followers for cattle and grazing land. There were, however, new forces in the interior. The armed commando raiders of Griqua, Kora, and Afrikaners had a significant impact on power relations. They undermined some chiefdoms while provoking others into more defensive—and ultimately secure—positions. British colonial forces also played a part in state-building through policy initiatives which created new demands for bonded labor, and through increasing intervention beyond the Cape colony. Their actions also contributed to the emergence of a new settler vanguard, the trekkers.

Frustrated in their efforts to gain a secure economic footing along and across the eastern frontier, the Afrikaner trekkers set off in search of new lands to settle. Despite the considerable odds against them, the trekkers had managed to gain a foothold in the interior, and they were determined not to relinquish it. These Afrikaners had proven the phenomenal success of the *laager* and they would rely upon it again in the future. Their ability to withstand attacks from major African armies fundamentally altered the balance of power on the highveld in their favor. No longer would the African states be able to recover from the basic cattle raid or remain settled on the land. The *laager* would moreover serve as a sort of ideological metaphor for future Afrikaners who claimed that they were besieged by the majority African population. This *laager* mentality suggested to some Afrikaners that they should withdraw to an inward-looking defensive position and their views of their exploits were later enshrined in the Voortrekker Monument see photo in Chapter 9, "Apartheid and South African Society." By the 1840s, the interior had been reconfigured by local African agencies and external forces alike. Now the Sotho, Zulu, Griqua, and Afrikaners would all vie for control of the land, and the British would feel compelled to intervene.

QUESTIONS TO CONSIDER

1. What are the different ways that scholars have viewed the emergence of new African states and what are the implications of these views for South African history?
2. After considering the example of the Zulu kingdom, discuss how African states developed and were organized.
3. How and why was Shaka mythologized?
4. What role did the Griqua and the Kora communities play in the developments in the interior?
5. Compare and contrast how African leaders such as Moshoesho, Matiwane, and Mzilikazi fared in the making of their states.
6. What were the reasons for and conditions behind the Afrikaner trek, and what relations did the trekkers develop in the interior?

FURTHER READINGS

COBBING, J., "The *Mfecane* as Alibi: Thoughts on Dithakong and Mbolompo," *Journal of African History*, 29, 1988. The controversial article which is credited with fomenting the debate about the *Mfecane*. Cobbing rejects the entire concept of the so-called *Mfecane*, and instead argues that it was whites who instigated violence in the region.

DELIUS, P., *The Land Belongs to Us. The Pedi Polity, the Boers, and the British in the Nineteenth-Century Transvaal* (London, 1984). An excellent, comprehensive micro-study of the Pedi and the their relations with encroaching white settlers during the period in question.

DUMINY, A., and GUEST, B. (editors.), *Natal and Zululand from Earliest Times to 1910: A New History* (Pietermaritzburg, 1989). A very useful general textbook for the region. It contains some important essays about the early period of Zulu history, including a chapter by C. Hamilton and J. Wright, two of the leading scholars on the so-called Mfecane.

ELDREDGE, E., *A South African Kingdom. The Pursuit of Security in 19th-Century Lesotho* (Cambridge, 1993). Another excellent micro-study which sets out the African perspective on relations with the forces of imperialism and colonialism. This work emphasizes the African initiative, but also takes into account the powerful forces arrayed against Africans in enclave states.

ETHERINGTON, N., *The Great Treks: The Transformation of Southern Africa, 1815–1854* (London, 2001). A new revisionist interpretation of most of the mass movements of the period. Etherington has taken a fresh new approach which de-centers the debate and emphasizes African initiatives and the local context.

ETHERINGTON, N., *Preachers, Peasants, and Politics in Southeast Africa* (London, 1978). A sound, well-researched, and well-written analysis of the forces shaping the region in question. It is one of the finest regional studies in South African history.

GILIOMEE, H., *Afrikaner Political Thought* (Cape Town, 1983). A good overview of issues surrounding Afrikaner interpretations of the Great Trek and its causes. It emphasizes the political ideology which was imposed on the events of the trek and so is important for understanding the mythology of the event and how it articulated with the mythology of Shaka.

HAMILTON, C., *The Mfecane Aftermath. Reconstructive Debates in Southern African History* (London, 1995). The most comprehensive collection of schol-arly essays surrounding debates over both the *Mfecane* and the so-called *Difaqane*. It contains essays on the broadest range of aspects of the issue, but Cobbing declined to contribute a piece. It is essential reading.

HAMILTON, C., *Terrific Majesty: The Powers of Shaka Zulu and the Limits of Historical Invention.* (Cape Town, 1998). This is an excellent deconstruction of the myths surrounding Shaka and the Zulu kingdom. It considers a range of interpretations of the myths and shows how they have been constructed by various groups to serve changing needs over time.

MARKS, S., and ATMORE, A. (editors), *Economy and Society in Pre-Industrial South Africa* (London, 1980). This excellent collection of essays ranges on top-ics from the nature of African societies and their economies to issues of culture contact and frontier relations. It is still a very useful teaching tool.

OMER-COOPER, J., *The Zulu Aftermath: A Nineteenth-Century Revolution in Bantu Africa* (London, 1966). This book sets out the argument for the African initiative and the "Zulucentric" approach to the issue and emphasizes Shaka's role in the *Mfecane*. It is the key book against which Cobbing and others argue.

WEBB, C. DE B., and WRIGHT, J. (editors), *The James Stuart Archive of Recorded Oral Evidence Relating to the History of the Zulu and Neighbouring Peoples*, Five Volumes (Pietermaritzburg, 1976–2001). A wonderful primary resource. This richly textured and insightfully edited series provides a range of views on Zulu history as recorded from the oral evidence of the Zulu people.

CHAPTER V

Africans, Afrikaners, and the British in the Interior, 1830–1870

F ollowing the emergence of the new African states, the trickle of raiding and trade which had brought white invaders to the interior became a stream and eventually an overflowing river. Everywhere, settlers spilled over into the interior to make claims to the land, implant their economy, and inscribe their political states onto the region. Although they were far fewer in number than the established African inhabitants, they brought with them the same white-dominated racial social structure and commercial imperatives which had developed in the Cape. They also brought with them the means and the will, in the form of guns and horses, to extend their control over African societies and their land. The processes of "pacification"—the forcible subordination of Africans—and white settlement, were, however, just beginning; they would remain uneven for decades to come. The African states shaped these processes through outright resistance and creative politics and diplomacy. In some ways, they collaborated or co-operated to gain advantages in resisting in other ways. Despite their brave efforts, African societies faced an overwhelming and relentless force with the rising tide of white settlers. Yet, by the mid-nineteenth century, the outcomes of the white invasion were not yet clear. A number of powerful African states, the Sotho and Zulu included, managed to remain largely intact. Moreover, humanitarian pressures and British policy changes also tempered the effects of rapacious settler expansion.

As with the zone of interaction between the whites and the Xhosa a generation earlier, no one group was yet able to assert complete authority over the interior, but the British, with their powerful imperial government, were gaining over the Afrikaners and the Africans. The initial reluctance of the British to intervene and become embroiled in costly entanglements beyond the Cape slowly gave way to local exigencies. Not only did the British colonial government claim responsibility for its subjects' actions, Afrikaners included, across the Orange River, but also increasing numbers of British settlers started to infiltrate the region. The colonial government was caught between acquiescing to settler demands and imposing imperial-humanitarian imperatives to keep the peace and safeguard African interests. Missionaries sought to co-opt African converts, most of whom were women, and bring them under the "protection" of the British crown, which would ultimately lead to their loss of sovereignty. Similarly, as the imperial government conceded the need to stake official claims to the land, it annexed new territories in the eastern Cape and Natal.

British colonial officials introduced a new bureaucracy and grafted new legal and commercial systems onto existing African societies. Thus, the British "civilizing mission" was ambiguous. On the one hand, it afforded Africans some protection from settlers bent on wresting the land away from Africans and forcing them into servile labor. On the other hand, the British brought a more systematized way of imposing a "civilized" state on the region. It would take some time, however, before the British could effectively occupy the lands they governed. The paper claims to African lands did not necessarily lead directly to the intensive use of it by the white settlers. For a period, white land claims fell to the hands of well-capitalized speculators, some of whom were financed by joint stock companies (at the time, this was a new investment strategy which pooled monies from various smaller investors). These absentee landlords actually stood in the way of the white settler farmers. They bought up vast tracts of land, They then kept their vast land holdings tied up in anticipation of higher prices in the future. In the interim, they allowed the original African inhabitants to remain on their land. The Africans were, however, not fully aware of the changed status of their rights to the land. When the new landlords demanded rents, in labor, kind, and cash from their African tenants, many resisted, while others accommodated them.

AFRICAN STATES AND THE TREKKER REPUBLICS

In the wake of the first Zulu civil war, in which Mpande drove his brother Dingane from the throne in 1840, the Afrikaners struggled to consolidate their state in Natal. Under Andries Pretorius' leadership, they established the Republic of Natalia. It was governed from the capital, Pietermaritzburg, by a *volksraad* (or *Raad*) of 24 elected men and a council of war. Local officials and magistrates (the *landdrosts* and *veldkornets*) carried out district administration in the same manner as it had been done along the eastern frontier. The democratic *Raad,* did not, however, extend the voting franchise to any African or outsider, and the restriction of this vote to white, Afrikaner men became a defining feature of the trekker republics. The Natal trekkers also claimed a substantial land grant from the Zulu. Mpande, the Zulu king, had struck a costly alliance with the trekkers for their support in overthrowing Dingane. Although he retained authority over the Zulu land north of the Thukela River, he had ceded vast stretches to the Afrikaners in the south. More significantly, he had permitted them to weigh in on Zulu political affairs when they proclaimed him king—a precedent that would influence Zulu politics thereafter. Pretorius also managed to negotiate a pact to create a form of joint government with the leader of the highveld trekkers, Hendrick Potgieter. This was a short-lived effort. Tensions over questions of leadership, the great distance between the highveld and Pietermaritzburg, and the Afrikaners' limited political and economic resources undermined both a broader political framework and the survival of Natalia.

By 1840, tensions within the Republic started to fray the Afrikaner state. First, the Afrikaners were unable to manage their government or the land they claimed. Initially, there was a scramble for land. A small number of wealthy and influential Afrikaners managed to acquire title to most of the land ceded by Mpande while most of the settlers could not make good their claims. A large number of these families remained bitter about the Republic's inability to manage land allocation as the speculators held onto their vast tracts. Similarly, the wealthy managed to gain a disproportionate number of the vast herd of cattle raided from the Zulu during the civil war, leaving the other whites poor and dissatisfied. More significantly, as the Afrikaners settled in, tens of thousands of African families who had been in hiding or had retreated from the area during the upheavals of state formation returned to their homes. They resettled the land that the Afrikaners now claimed but could not occupy for lack of numbers and resources. The few Afrikaner families who had taken up residence complained to the *Raad* of Africans squatting on their farms and of repeated cattle raids. These problems threatened to escalate and destabilize the region just as they had affected the relations between the Boers and the Xhosa in the eastern Cape. In an effort to address these grievances, the *Raad* made two plans. First, they organized a large cattle raid against the small Bhaca chiefdom of Ncapayi which they accused of having raided Afrikaners for cattle. Second, they developed a scheme, though far beyond their capacity to ever execute, for the removal and resettlement of the returned Africans, which they deemed "surplus," onto land held by the Pondo chief, Faku, to the south of Natal. Both of these plans aroused strong responses from the British.

The Afrikaner policies prompted direct British intervention in Natal. The humanitarian lobby roundly condemned the commando attack against the Bhaca. They characterized it as yet another example of Afrikaner settler hostility to Africans coming on the heels of the massive herd taken from the Zulu just a year before. British officials and military strategists evinced even greater concern over the contemplated relocation of thousands of Africans to Faku's territory. They were convinced that such a plan would set off tension and conflict among the Pondo and the Xhosa. They argued that this would, in turn, spill over into the Cape colony and force a costly British intervention. Both British traders and missionaries had long made a case for intervention in order to open up the region to their activities. In response, in May 1842, the British Cape governor, Napier, ordered a small force of some 200 troops to occupy Port Natal and prevent further Afrikaner raids on African chiefdoms to the south. The British force was besieged by the Afrikaners. If it had not been for the English trader, Dick King, the soldiers might have been overwhelmed. He managed to evade the Afrikaners and made a legendary ride of 600 miles from the port to the British garrison at Grahamstown to get relief.

British reinforcements arrived by ship in June and quickly forced the Afrikaners into submission. Local British officials then convinced a reluctant imperial government that Natal should be annexed to the Cape. They argued that, without British involvement, the Afrikaners would continue to provoke the Africans, leading to instability which would threaten British strategic interests. The Afrikaner settlers were divided over the annexation of Natal to the Cape in May 1844. Some felt that they needed the British in order to gain security and a stable government. They recognized their inability to administer the territory or to deal with the large African population. In the peace negotiations leading to the annexation, they struck a deal where they retained some degree of local authority while accepting British rule. This local Afrikaner administration, however, rapidly deteriorated because of internal arguments and their inability to contend with Africans returning to the land. As conditions worsened, most of the Afrikaners left Natal in disgust. They felt they could not tolerate the imposition of the same government which they had sought to escape when they left the eastern Cape a few years before. They trekked back over the Drakensburg mountains to join their fellow Afrikaners in the highveld, a territory now surrounded by African states and British colonies.

The trekkers had some measured degree of greater success establishing republics on the highveld, yet these states remained internally divided and weak. Their primary concerns were undertaking effective occupation of the land they claimed, establishing trade links with coastal ports, attracting African labor, and contending with their powerful African neighbors. In the region north of the Orange River, Afrikaner trekkers had been settling on rented or purchased Griqua lands since the 1820s. By the 1850s, there had been an influx of large numbers of Afrikaners. Their challenges to the main Griqua chief, Adam Kok, III's authority in the region, and their demands for land forced Kok to sell all their remaining lands and relocate across the Drakensburg mountains. There, under British protection, he established Kokstad, the capital of what became the new state, East Griqualand, adjacent to the Pondo. Meanwhile, the Afrikaners in the region between the Orange and Vaal Rivers, Trans-Orangia, were still subject to British authority. As we shall see, it was not until the British relinquished their claims to administer this region (see the Bloemfontein Convention, mentioned later in this chapter) that the Afrikaners were able to assert their own state authority.

THE AFRIKANER REPUBLICS

The Afrikaners declared the independent Orange Free State Republic in 1854 and drafted their constitution based on their past experiences as trekkers, with ideals cobbled together from the American republican constitution. Although many in the Free State maintained close connections with the British Cape, many more developed a fiercely independent spirit, fueled by repeated British interference in their affairs. Indeed, many in the Republic longed for unification with the even more independently-minded Afrikaner groups to their north across the Vaal River in the Transvaal.

The Transvaal was beset with leadership squabbles and fragmentation. Initially, the scattered Afrikaner trekkers who left Natalia established a center at Potchefstroom just north of the Vaal. Hendrick Potgieter, who had bested Mzilikazi and claimed much of the Transvaal, was not content to remain tied to the interior. He led a group of followers far to the northwest in the vain hope of finding a short, safe route to the Portuguese trade port of Delagoa Bay (a strategic goal which the British suspected to be an Afrikaner motive to break free of imperial commercial and political power). They failed to establish a permanent settlement at the town of Andries-Ohrigstad. This was partly because of malaria, and partly because paramount chief Sekwati of the local Pedi people resisted their demands for labor, even though he had allowed them the right to use land, though not to own it as the Afrikaners assumed. The Transvaal Afrikaners and the Pedi were on a collision course as settlers claimed more of their land, and the Pedi acquired guns through migrant work in the Cape. Potgieter then faced political challenges to his authority and he moved his followers once again, this time north to Soutpansberg, where they enjoyed a lucrative ivory and gun trade for a time. The remnants of the Ohrigstad party relocated to nearby Lydenburg, where they set up another republic. Meanwhile, Andries Pretorius returned to the Transvaal from Natal to champion the original trekker goals: independence from the British and political unification.

Following Pretorius' death in 1853, it was his son, Martinus Pretorius, who persuaded the *volksraad* leaders in the Transvaal republics (Lydenburg, Potchefstroom, and Soutpansberg) to create a unified stable republic under one constitution. The new state was known as the South African Republic (SAR). They agreed to have their capital at Pretoria, and they agreed upon a single constitution with suffrage limited to white adult males who elected a republican president, M. Pretorius being the first. Pretorius then pressed ahead with his ill-conceived plans to unify the Orange Free State and the SAR. There was still significant interest in a union of the two republics among people in the Free State. In a feat of political daring, he managed to get elected president of both the Free State and the SAR, but was forced by the *volksraad* leadership to chose one. Relying on his reputation, he had retained the Free State presidency (leaving it to W. Van Rensburg) in the vain hope of maintaining his influence in the SAR. Divided loyalties in both republics, and especially the problems of relations with the Sotho, conspired against Pretorius' plan. Unity was not achieved. As Pretorius resigned from the Free State presidency to resume his post in the SAR, the Free Staters, under President J. Brand, again looked to the Cape for financial and political support, while the SAR remained aloof. In contrast to the Free State where trade and wool production for the Cape market led to a boom, economic conditions declined in the SAR. The SAR suffered even greater problems with land speculation than had Natal, and increasing numbers of farmers lost their land. These landless *bywoners* were forced into harsh tenancy arrangements and they became a grave embarrassment to the Republic. For most of the next few decades, the government remained in debt, unable to administer the vast stretches it claimed. Its greatest challenges, however, were its relations with the British and its African neighbors, as we shall see.

The Africans viewed the arrival of the the Afrikaner trekkers and their states with concern. Although some local Tswana and Sotho chiefdoms initially welcomed the trekkers for their ability to drive off the overbearing Ndebele, and for the willingness of some Afrikaners to trade guns (in defiance of colonial and republican law), their view soon changed. The Afrikaners sought to recreate the sort of racially-based master-and-servant relationship between white employers and African workers which had prevailed at the Cape. As with Natal (see the discussion in the next section), however, white settler farming did not satisfy the needs of the burgeoning white population, and the trekkers relied upon African producers for much of their food requirements.

In order to bolster their livestock holdings, and especially to get African labor, the trekkers resorted to further commando raids of the surrounding chiefdoms. The results were mixed. On the one hand, the Afrikaners did capture some cattle, and they took many youths and children as "apprentices" or *inboekselings* (a thinly veiled cover term for a slave-like labor contract which bound an African youth to a white employer for many years). On the other hand, the Africans acquired more guns, albeit old and unreliable ones, from illicit traders who began circulating through the region. These guns considerably enhanced their ability to withstand further settler depredations. Most Africans, however, did not have sufficient resources or knowledge to use and repair these weapons in order to block the later invasions of settler and imperial armies. Nevertheless, in one form or another, the highveld chiefdoms and kingdoms of the Venda, the Tswana, the Pedi, and the Sotho all managed to survive the arrival of the trekkers. Many remained relatively intact and fended off the raiding Afrikaners into the 1870s. They did so with creative combinations of the use of guns, the aid of missionary advocates, and their own skills at surviving in a region and climate where drought and disease often overwhelmed the whites (see Map 5–1 on page 112).

AFRICANS AND BRITISH POLICY INITIATIVES:
SEGREGATION AND INDIRECT RULE

The British annexation of Natal was part of a broader pattern of intervention beyond the confines of the Cape, although there would be future vacillations and reversals of British policy. Within Britain there were powerful advocates of a non-interventionist, free-market approach to the empire. They called for the British to cast aside the costly encumbrances of colonies in general and to avoid any further involvement in the interior of South Africa in particular. They held sway for a time during the 1850s and into the 1860s. Nevertheless, the overall trend was for settlers and missionaries, as well as developments in the interior, to force an otherwise reluctant imperial government to increase its role in the region. As more British settlers arrived in South Africa, they voiced increasing demands to be granted authority over their own affairs, including relations with African societies, just as many trekboer Afrikaners had done previously. It was still imperative, however, for colonial officials to develop policies which aimed to keep administrative costs down and to reduce the number of entanglements between settlers and Africans which could lead to friction. British officials started to experiment with various methods of reducing tensions, protecting Africans, and keeping the peace. The practice of keeping black and white people separate from each other—segregation—would prove to be more difficult than it first seemed, not least because of the decidedly unfair ways it was applied. Nowhere was this more true than in the new British colony of Natal.

British officials faced considerable challenges from an uncertain economy and an overwhelming African majority in the fledgling colony of Natal. First, the problems of land speculation which had emerged during the creation of the South African Republic intensified. Investment companies such as the Natal Land and Colonization Company took over many of the land claims left by the emigré trekkers while the colonial government parceled out vast stretches of "crown land." The companies were bound by agreement to encourage white settlement, and with a severe depression gripping Britain during the early 1850s, they succeeded in bringing nearly 6,000 immigrants to Natal by 1852. These new settlers brought with them a significant baggage of British culture, including sports, gardening clubs, private educational facilities, and

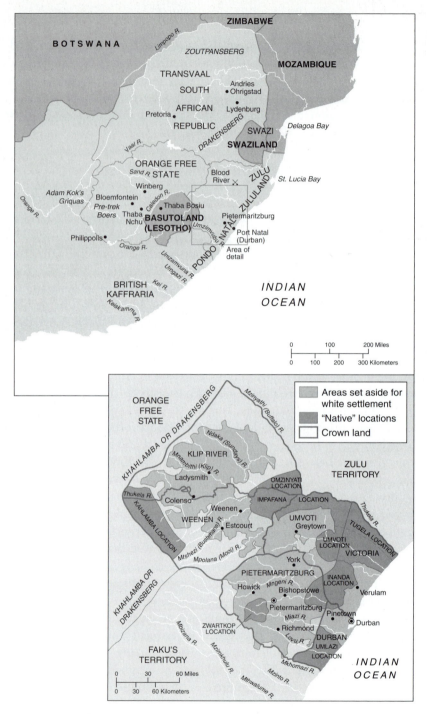

Map 5–1   Afrikaner Trekker Republics and Segregation in Natal. *Adapted from Omer-Cooper, History of Southern Africa, 2/e. 1994; and A. Duminy and B. Guest, Natal and Zululand From Earliest Times to 1910. University of Natal Press. Pietermaritzburg, 1989.*

the religious traditions of Methodism and Anglicanism, which later contributed to a unique British colonial Natal mentality. They did not, however, have the wherewithal to undertake their intended work: agriculture. Indeed, many of the early Natal colonists abandoned farming for more lucrative work such as merchant trading. From the 1850s, more capital-intensive farming developed along the lines of plantation agriculture for sugar cane, but this required large amounts of land and labor. As in the Cape, sheep farming for wool later became a mainstay of the settler economy.

The driving force of the agricultural economy in Natal during this period, as it would be in other parts of South Africa, was the emergence of a vibrant African peasantry (a peasant is a producer of an agricultural commodity or food who has one foot in the capitalist market economy, and one foot in a customary, African, or traditional economy). Conditions in Natal were just right for the rise of an African peasantry. Most of the land was held by absentee speculators, and most of the settlers did not engage in food production. Since the speculators acted as landlords, they demanded a rent from their African tenants, who once again found themselves liable to some form of payment simply to remain on their land. It is not surprising that accomplished African farmers, who knew the land and climate of the region, were best able to respond to an increasing demand for food products from the settlers.

There were many industrious African farmers who could easily meet the initial demands for rent and colonial taxes by producing maize (corn) sorghum and cattle for sale in the growing colonial markets. Christian missionaries, who emphasized the "civilizing" influence of farming and agricultural education, also helped foster thriving communities of *kholwa* (Christian Africans), who invested their meager peasant earnings in land and plows. In both communities, women played a vital role in homestead farming and in producing commodities such as beer and tobacco for the market. While these endeavors afforded some women a measured degree of economic independence, most women were still subordinated to their fathers and husbands within family homestead farming. Thus, despite increasingly vociferous cries for an increase in taxes to drive Africans out to work for wages, most African families jealously defended their independent economic status. They eschewed poorly paid work on white farms, preferring instead to grow produce for the market.

The resistance of Africans in Natal to employment within the colonial sphere was so strong that Natal officials were driven to recruit labor from abroad. The colonial government organized the importation of Indian indentured workers, or *grimitiyas* (a Hindi adaptation of the word "agreement") to Natal beginning in the 1860s as part of a wider Indian-British imperial plan. These mostly poor, lower-caste people arrived, bound to work under a government contract of indenture, more commonly to a settler employer, for ten years. After this period, they could either claim free passage back to India or remain to make a new life. (In some cases, they could claim land in lieu of the passage back to India.) In all, over 75 percent chose to remain. Despite suffering harsh conditions and harassment from a hostile settler community, they made a significant contribution to the building of the colony, especially in the sugar industry and government railways. They also made for a diverse and cosmopolitan society in Natal, especially as the earlier Hindu (who made up about 86 percent) immigrants were joined by Muslims (about 12 percent). The later immigrants were predominantly Muslim Gujerati merchants. Referred to as "passenger" Indians because they paid their own way over, they were free from contracts and so could set up their own thriving businesses. After their periods of indenture, most of the workers settled into market gardening in the Durban (Port Natal) area while others, primarily Muslims, undertook commercial and professional work. In both cases, they had to compete against Africans and whites and this eventually led to tensions and conflict. The system of indenture persisted until 1911, when the Indian government intervened to stop it on behalf of immigrants who complained of abuse, including floggings and unfair wage payments by employers in Natal. Throughout the period, white shopkeepers agitated against the vibrant Indian community in Natal (and later in the Transvaal). They resented the success of many Indians and sought to force them to return to India on the completion of their indentures. Having failed in this, the white Natalians worked to curtail Indian political rights. Once Natal achieved responsible government in 1893, they succeeded in effectively excluding Indians from the franchise. Natal also encouraged them to return to India with the institution of an excessive £3 poll tax on those who did not renew their indenture contracts. These abuses set the scene for later widespread Indian agitation against the increasingly racist colonial governments.

The question of how to manage the majority African population remained a problem for the new colonial administration. In 1846, colonial sources estimated that nearly half of the original ninety-four tribes or chiefdoms that had existed in Natal prior to the rise of the Zulu kingdom had survived and taken up their lands around the area. Their numbers would swell from 100,000 to more than 250,000 by 1870. Notwithstanding the problems of land speculation in Natal, the British were still required to administer the colony and its African inhabitants with a view to encouraging white settlement and in keeping with "civilized" standards for peace and security. More importantly, Natal was expected to pay its own way. To deal with these daunting tasks, the British appointed Theophilus Shepstone as Diplomatic Agent to the Native Tribes of Natal in 1846. Shepstone was the son of a Wesleyan missionary and had some experience on the eastern Cape frontier. He brought with him to Natal a decidedly paternalist approach to dealing with African affairs, and his hubris grew as he made claim to knowing the "native mind."

Shepstone developed a remarkably effective administration based on one of the earliest variants of indirect rule. The driving force behind the Shepstone system, as with other forms of colonial indirect rule, was to control Africans with as little cost and as little disruption as possible. His system relied heavily upon African society to conform to the new colonial demands. It also rested on an unquestioned colonial assumption that African and settler societies were so different that they required separation, or segregation. Although some of the roots of segregation in South Africa could be found in the early Cape, the Natal system of indirect rule undoubtedly played a major part in the unfolding separation of whites and Africans. Shepstone was faced with the problems of very limited resources and a parsimonious imperial government. Thus, the Colonial Office rejected his early schemes to bring "Christian civilization" and law to the Natal Nguni-speakers through a series of industrial schools as too costly.

Shepstone's eventual plan was simply to provide Africans with enough land to satisfy their needs so that white settlement would not provoke the same sorts of violent convulsions that had plagued the eastern Cape. An 1846 commission laid out a series of "locations" in areas where Africans lived but

THEOPHILUS SHEPSTONE   The architecture of segregation in colonial Natal, he acted as "supreme chief" over Africans. *Source: National Archives of South Africa.*

whites had not yet claimed the land. In this way, Shepstone inscribed a new colonial patchwork of various forms of land ownership onto Natal. All the land which Africans had previously understood to be theirs was now under one form or other of colonial control. In addition to the locations, there were white farms, land owned by absentee white speculators, and government-owned crown land. With considerable diplomacy and some pressure, Shepstone managed to encourage many Africans to abandon their homes on white farms and retreat to the locations. These areas, which were in some cases so fragmented that parts of some chiefdoms were separated from each other, were not sufficient for the whole African population. Many thousands of Africans remained on government crown land or on farms which would not yet taken up by settlers for many years.

Whether in the locations, or on white-owned land, Africans would be subject to "Native Law" as understood and ultimately enforced by colonial officials through their new agents, the appointed African chiefs. This was Shepstone's paternalist system of indirect rule. He created a political and legal hierarchy in which African commoners remained subject to their chiefs' patriarchal authority, but only insofar as it conformed to colonial demands for the rule of law and the payment of taxes to support the colony. The system also set up a potential convergence of interests whereby white male officials worked with African patriarchs in order to control the youth, and especially the women. Shepstone thus referred to himself as in terms of a grand patriarch, the "Father of the Zulu." Shepstone allowed chiefs to rule on the basis of traditional African law. He did so, however, only as he and other colonial officials interpreted it, and only when it did not contravene "civilized" standards. In the cases where a legitimate chief refused to work with the system, he was removed promptly and replaced by a compliant government-appointee. In other cases, only fragments of tribes remained and so Shepstone, the expert in "native affairs" took it upon himself to amalgamate the fragments and invent new tribes where none had existed.

There was clearly a paradox inherent in this Shepstonian system of African law which was taken over by white officials and was enforced ultimately for colonial ends. There was also the provision—which ran against the tide of emerging segregation—for Christianized, "civilized" Africans to be exempted from "Native Law," based on their culture and means. A substantial minority of over 5,000 Africans, most of whom had escaped chiefly authority on mission stations, were exempted by the end of the century, but the vast majority, Christian converts included, remained under the chiefs' jurisdiction. Moreover, for the convenience of the administration, Shepstone enforced "tribal (collective) responsibility" as another tool of domination. This meant that if one or a few members of a tribe, whether a longstanding one or recently created by the colonial government, broke the law, the whole tribe and the chief would be held responsible and punished together. These contradictions and the lack of uniformity in the application of these laws served to promote abuses which ended up driving people away from the chiefs' courts. Moreover, all the chiefs and their officials were subject to oversight by white officials, with Shepstone himself as the Secretary for Native Affairs having the power to rule by decree (which he justified as being the way the Zulu kings ruled) and the colonial Lieutenant-Governor taking on the thinly veiled guise of "African authority" as "Supreme Chief." These titles and rules were applied in order for colonial officials to appear to Africans as if they had some legitimacy. Their manipulation of the system, however, had a more ambiguous effect. While some chiefs accommodated the new system, for it enhanced their power and wealth when they imposed fines for infractions of "Native Law," others rejected it outright and were removed. In most cases, however, people resented a chief who too openly embraced the colonial regime and they often defied him or sought to leave his jurisdiction. In the long term, Natal officials would continue to seek legitimacy in the eyes of their subjects by invoking claims to "traditional" African authority. As we shall see, the more they did so, the less effective they became.

Finance was the master-stroke of Shepstone's administration. In order for the colony pay its own way, Shepstone tapped into the expanding African-driven economy through taxation. This was possible only because Natal Africans had quickly came to terms with the colonial world, including the new capitalist economy, demands for wage labor, and a new work regime patterned on industrial time. In addition, as we have already seen, they responded with alacrity to new opportunities for marketing their produce. Although they managed to resist and shape some labor relations on white farms and in towns, and many remained independent peasant producers, they could not escape colonial taxes, tariffs, duties, and fines. It seemed that everywhere there was another chief or official demanding some form of payment. Moreover, the government imposed a wide and increasing range of import duties, primarily on goods used exclusively by Africans, such as wool blankets, hand-held hoes, and trade beads. Africans bitterly resented the increasing imposition of these payments, and they were often the spark of broad protests. They nevertheless managed to finance the entire colony and provide a phenomenal surplus for Shepstone's administration.

It was here that the inequities of Shepstone's system become most glaring. By the end of Shepstone's tenure in Natal, in 1872, the balance sheet showed that Africans had contributed about 75 percent of the total revenue to colonial coffers. Expenditure on whites compared with Africans was, however, grotesquely disproportionate. Of the approximately £150,000 expended, less than £6,000 was spent on Africans and their locations. The other sum of over £144,000 paid for the colonial government, white officials' salaries, white schools and education, hospitals for whites, colonial defense, and infrastructure in white towns.

It was African workers who not only drove the economy with peasant produce and wage labor, but also supported almost the entire colonial state with their taxes and duties. Not surprisingly, white settlers resented African productivity and competition. Despite conditions which favored white farmers (including access to land and government loans as well as the use of the colonial infrastructure of roads and towns) and which worked decidedly against Africans in the locations, whites started to mount a growing protest against the location system. They argued that the locations allowed Africans to escape having to work for whites, and they demanded that the locations be broken up. As we have seen, the government turned to outside sources of labor, including Indians and migrants from beyond the colony, rather than dismantle the location system and risk an African reaction. However, white farmers continued to demand that Africans be forced off the land they coveted and into working for them. They were later able to enforce these demands as the imperial government granted them increasing responsibility over the colony. As was the case in the Cape, the minority white settler population demanded and was given representative political institutions with an executive and legislative council advising the governor from 1856, although the British did not relinquish control to a "responsible" elected local government until 1893.

AFRICAN STATES, WHITE SETTLERS, IMPERIAL AUTHORITIES, AND THE XHOSA CRISIS

By the end of the 1830s, state authorities, both black and white, had to address the impact of increased numbers of white settlers in the interior and their demands for cattle, land, and labor. African statesmen grew very concerned about how white activities threatened to fundamentally alter their societies through both the loss of land and the assimilation of the people which placed them in a subordinate status in the colonial world. The underlying question for British officials was whether the two societies could be separated or whether white society would continue to penetrate into African society and change it. In the wake of the Sixth Frontier War between the British and the Xhosa, and the return of Queen Adelaide Province, the British experimented with a new treaty system for the separation of the Xhosa chiefdoms from the colony. It was the relatively liberal and enlightened Andries Stockenstrom— who had just given damning testimony about settler predations against the Xhosa to the Aborigines [protection] Committee of 1836—who administered the treaties. Under the treaty system, Stockenstrom oversaw the creation of boundaries between the colony and Xhosa territory and the settlement of complaints of cattle theft and encroachment between whites and Africans. The treaty system, however, was doomed to failure.

In yet another reversal of policy, D'urban and two succeeding governors, Napier and Maitland, chose not to honor the spirit of the treaties, and they continued to provoke the Xhosa by siding with the settlers in matters of dispute. The Xhosa chiefs then stepped up their raiding into the colony. When a young Xhosa accused of stealing an ax from his white employer was arrested, they struck. A small band of Xhosa attacked the police to free their compatriot and then their chiefs refused to turn him in upon the demand of colonial officials. In 1846, in a pre-empting maneuver, the Xhosa invaded the colony along a broad front precipitating the War of the Axe.

The British struck back swiftly and decisively and forced a beleaguered Xhosa leadership to accept terms. Sir Harry Smith, a disciple of D'Urban's, stepped in to administer the conquered territory—comprised of the old Ceded Territory and all the rest of the land between the Keiskamma and Kei Rivers— and it was annexed as the Crown Colony of British Kaffraria. Smith applied a more ruthless direct approach to the settlement of the new colony. A good portion of the new territory was given out as farms to whites and, under the auspices of extending British "protection," he settled refugee *Mfengu* chiefdoms to act as a buffer between the Xhosa and the settlers. Moreover, he circumvented chiefly authority and disregarded Xhosa customs of law and inheritance as he rigorously applied colonial laws. The Xhosa were then inspired by the prophet, Mlanjeni, who invoked aspects of Christianity in his message of resistance against the settlers. Mlanjeni claimed that God had told him he was angry with the whites for having killed his son, Jesus, and that he would therefore aid the Xhosa against them. Mlanjeni's war, 1850–1852, ended badly for the Xhosa and the British settled more whites and "loyal" Africans in their midst. But Smith was eventually recalled by the British for having pressed the Xhosa too far and a new tack was taken by Governor Sir George Grey.

Beginning in 1854, Grey developed a policy of "civilizing" which pushed the Xhosa over the edge. His "mingling" policy, which he adapted from the advice of missionaries, sought to maximize the integration of whites and Africans in the frontier zones of interaction, primarily through the assimilation of the Xhosa. He believed that the Xhosa would become more useful servants and consumers of British goods if large numbers of whites, who could teach them about Christian civilization and European habits of farming and industry, settled among them. Although some aspects of Grey's policy may have seemed somewhat benevolent, for they sought to "uplift" the Africans, it ultimately undermined Xhosa society. Grey's approach ran rough-shod over established Xhosa values and traditions, and, more significantly, put too great pressure on the already overcrowded land. By this time, Xhosa society was in crisis. They

had withstood the relentless encroachment of white settlers, a colonial administration which was at best indifferent, and at worst hostile, and repeated wars
which had exhausted their resources as well as prevented them from recovering
from their losses. Perhaps more importantly, the entire fabric of their society
and beliefs was under attack. The chiefs, who had been the central figures of
both the belief system which venerated ancestors and natural spirits and of the
military resistance against colonists, appeared to some as if they had lost their
initiative. Colonial officials had usurped their authority, and missionaries had
provided alternative views of religion. The Xhosas' growing resentment of settler predation and Grey's policy erupted in a crisis of tragic proportions.

In 1857, in a desperate response to mounting pressures, the Xhosa heeded
the prophecy of a young woman, Nongqawuse, and engaged in the mass
slaughter of their cattle to cleanse their land of evil. Their hope was that this
act of sacrifice would resurrect their ancestors, especially the heroic chiefs of
the past. They believed that only the ancestors could provide them with food
and restore their nation to a "happy state," the way it was before the coming of
colonialism. This was a fascinating episode of a genuine millenarian movement
in which aspects of Christian cosmology blended with Xhosa beliefs in a desperate attempt to cope with the crisis. Nongqawuse and her uncle, the prophet
Mhlakaza, who had spent some time with missionaries, clearly drew upon
Christian ideas when they referred to a resurrection and when they depicted
Governer Grey as "Satan."

The form of the movement, the cattle-killing itself, was also shaped by a
virulent epidemic of cattle lung-sickness which had arrived from Europe in
1855. The epidemic swept like wildfire through the region and predisposed
many to consider ridding themselves of infected cattle to contain the spread of
the disease. There emerged, nevertheless, a genuine and passionate belief in the
prophecy which split the Xhosa and led to catastrophic results. Many prominent chiefs, including Sarhili of the Gcaleka and Sandile of the Ngqika, embraced the prophecy and slaughtered their stock, even if some were uninfected.
Others, the hard unbelievers, refused, hoping to retain as many cattle as they
could in the wake of the epidemic; the believers condemned them as selfish.
By early 1857, the movement had reached a fever pitch. Thousands of believers slaughtered their cattle, destroyed their grain stores, and purged their
homes of colonial goods.

Xhosa society collapsed in the wake of the cattle-killing. By the end of the
movement in early 1858, the Xhosa had destroyed over 40,000 head of cattle.
Tragically, perhaps as many 45,000 Xhosa died of starvation, although this was
in part because of the collapse of agriculture from drought and in part because
of a broader economic downturn. As overwhelming grief and despair gripped
the land, a further 35,000 people sought to escape the shattered economy
by moving into the colony, where they took jobs under white employers.

Although there is no evidence to support Grey's allegation that the Xhosa chiefs or even Moshoeshoe had masterminded the cattle-killing (nor indeed, as the Xhosa supporters claimed, that Grey had plotted it), Grey did take full advantage of the ensuing chaos. He forced masses of the destitute Xhosa onto white farms as cheap labor when he blocked relief to them, and he grabbed yet more land for a new group of white settlers. Moreover, he further undermined the chiefs by working through his own officials and their appointed African assistants instead of the chiefs. By 1866, the Ciskei (the Cape side of the Kei River) Xhosa lost all hope of retaining an independent authority or economy when the whole territory of British Kaffraria was given over to the settler-dominated Cape colony, while the Transkei (across the Kei river) retained some autonomy and avoided widespread white settlement. Even before the cattle-killing, the British feared that upheavals similar to those with the Xhosa would erupt in the interior, so they tried to find some way of consolidating white authority there.

The Sotho, the Afrikaners, and British Intervention on the Highveld

It was across the Orange River and in the environs of the Caledon River, where the Afrikaners were encroaching on Moshoeshoe's Sotho kingdom, that the British were drawn, sometimes reluctantly, into ever greater intervention between whites and Africans. As we have already seen, Moshoeshoe was successful in carving out for his people a strong, defensible kingdom along the western side of the Drakensburg mountains. By the later 1830s, large numbers of *voortrekkers* had encroached upon his territory, as they had on the lands of a number of other chiefs (including Adam Kok II who left the region, as we have seen in Chapter 4, "The Making of New States"). Under the Cape of Good Hope Punishment Act, the British claimed authority over their former Afrikaner subjects across the Orange River, and they also concluded a series of treaties recognizing the local Griqua and Sotho chiefs' authority over and against the Afrikaners. Both these provisions failed to prevent conflict. For example, when Adam Kok II sought to enforce colonial law by arresting a *voortekker,* the Afrikaners responded with force. After quelling the ensuing skirmish between the Griqua and the Afrikaners, the British felt compelled to try to prevent future fights with a territorial separation.

At a meeting of all concerned chiefs in 1845, the British persuaded the chiefs to concede the practical reality of white settlement. Following the trend for the segregation of people, the British officials proposed that each chief set aside "alienable" land which whites could acquire, and "inalienable" land which no white could gain access to. The British provided Major Warden as the resident in charge of whites on the "alienable" lands, while the chiefs retained their power over the "inalienable" lands. The situation proved unworkable because Warden did not have the resources to keep the peace, and many Afrikaners bitterly resented having a British official in control. Moreover, Moshoeshoe, a key signatory of the treaty, did not have absolute power over some of his allied and subordinate chiefs. Although he did agree to open some "alienable" lands to white settlers, he dared not risk an internal rebellion or the fragmentation of his rule by forcing any of his followers to give up any more land. It was then that the cavalier new governor, Harry Smith, stepped in to precipitate even greater confusion and tension. Convinced of his own power to settle the matter, Smith surmised from a hasty assessment of Sotho and Afrikaner opinion that it was direct British administration which was lacking.

In 1848, Governor Smith summarily declared Britain the paramount authority in the region now referred to as the Orange River Sovereignty. Major Warden was retained as administrator of this territory, which had an ill-defined status within the British empire. He set about defining segregated territories for whites and Africans with the "Warden line." Warden knew he had to maintain good relations with the white settlers because they were his chief means of support, and so he sought to contain the powerful Sotho. His "line," however, set up tension by significantly reducing Moshoeshoe's territory and giving much of it to the settlers and to other Sotho adversaries, the Kora and the Rolong.

Moshoeshoe, ever the shrewd statesman, initially welcomed the implementation of British authority, although it placed him in an invidious position. On the one hand, he knew he could not contain the various chiefdoms in the region and also contend with Afrikaner encroachments on his lands. He also knew from his missionary advisors that the humanitarian lobby was strong in Britain and that they would provide his best chance of some form of imperial protection from white settlers. On the other hand, Moshoeshoe feared that the concessions of land which Warden demanded for the establishment of the Sovereignty would lead the various chiefdoms of his kingdom to abandon their loyalty to him. There were no precedents for the outright alienation of African lands by a chief or king, and, according to custom, all rights conferred on newcomers were for use, not ownership. This had certainly been Moshoeshoe's intention in the case of the rights to his lands he had initially conferred on the first transitory Afrikaners. Consequently, Moshoeshoe had to turn a blind eye to continued raiding of white farms by his subordinate chiefs. Major Warden could not countenance the flagrant disruptions to the peace in which both white settlers and the Sotho were engaged. He decided to support the settler cause, and so he marshaled an inadequate force of combined British and African troops to bring the Sotho into line. Moshoeshoe's men overwhelmed Warden's troops and forced them to retreat, yet the Sotho statesman did not press his advantage and raid too widely; thus he avoided provoking further British reprisals. The Orange River Afrikaners, however, remained vexed with the Sotho.

British Policy Reversals and the Sotho-Orange Free State War

By the early 1850s, leaders in Britain began questioning the policy of humanitarian support for Africans, and the concomitant imperial intervention to enforce this policy. They grew tired of the seemingly endless conflict between the whites and the Africans and the apparently insoluble boundary disputes in regions which showed no immediate profits or potential for investment. At the same time, local developments in the Cape colony disposed the imperial authorities to consider reducing their involvements in South Africa, and to retreat from their interventions across the Orange River. By this time, the *voortrekkers'* failure to find an independent route to the sea via Portuguese territory in Mozambique to avoid trade and customs duties at the Cape eased British imperial strategic concerns about a competing white state in southern Africa. Also, in the period of relative prosperity during Governor Grey's tenure, especially from a booming wool industry, the local whites grew increasingly interested in gaining more control over their own political affairs. From the 1820s, there was increasing agitation among the settlers for some form of representative political institution. By the 1850s, many felt that the humanitarian lobby had already achieved its goals through abolition and other measures safeguarding the indigenous people in the empire, and so, they argued, imperial oversight was no longer necessary. Although the imperial government made some concessions to the settlers by forming local town councils and a legislative council to advise the governor, there was still no elected representative legislature.

The British government eventually recognized that it could reduce its responsibilities and costs by devolving power to the colonists themselves. It finally allowed for the creation of the Cape Parliament in 1853. A critical question for the humanitarian lobby, however, was whether a settler-dominated Cape would still provide for African upliftment. The Cape politicians argued that they had a long established liberal tradition, although it would dissipate later. This liberal tradition, they claimed, was based upon interactions with Khoe and Africans and the policies of Governor Grey, who followed missionary ideals and sought to assimilate Africans into British "civilization" through a policy of "mingling." Moreover, in order to assuage imperial concerns, Cape leaders agreed to the British demand for a color-blind voters franchise. Wealthy English-speaking settlers, however, argued for very high property or income qualifications for the vote.

In an unusual alliance, less well-off Dutch (Afrikaans) speakers joined with missionaries and the Cape Coloured people to protest the high qualifications.

In the end, the liberals prevailed, and a relatively low rate of £50 annual income or a home worth of £25 was established, allowing a substantial number of Coloured men and later African men to join the voters' roll in the Cape for a time. This foundation of the Cape liberal political tradition did not accommodate poor Africans or women, who together formed the majority of the population. This property qualification was, however, much the same as those in many other democracies at that time in history.

As a result of these policy changes, the British abandoned the extension of their authority and power to the interior. First, under the Sand River Convention of January 1852, Britain renounced all claims to authority across the Vaal River and recognized the Afrikaners' efforts toward establishing their own republic. This was done, in part, because the Transvaal Afrikaners threatened to side with the Sotho against the British in the Orange River area. The Afrikaner trekkers were now finally free to create their own government and to deal with the African people as they saw fit. Later that same year, the new British governor, George Cathcart, surmised that Warden's line and British attempts to keep the peace in Moshoeshoe's lands along the Orange-Caledon River area were futile. He did, however, want to give the Sotho a last chance to humble themselves to British and settler power.

Cathcart issued an ultimatum for Moshoeshoe to hand over 10,000 head of cattle as reparations for his resistance to Major Warden. Although Moshoeshoe made a good faith effort to send some cattle, he failed to meet Cathcart's deadline, and British forces once again moved in. Following an indecisive battle in which the Sotho lost cattle but held their ground, the Sotho king made a conciliatory gesture by conceding "defeat" and calling on Cathcart to accept his friendship in order to ensure continued British sympathy. Cathcart, who wanted to avoid the potentially costly embarrassment of having to stage a prolonged campaign against Moshoeshoe's mountain fortress of Thaba-Bosiu, accepted the Sotho gesture. Not that it really mattered. By this time, the British had determined to leave the highveld altogether, at least for a time. In 1854, they ratified the Bloemfontein Convention, rescinding all previous treaties with African rulers north of the Orange River and recognizing the independence of the Transvaal republics and the Orange River Afrikaner government. This ignored some settlers' desires to retain the British presence in the region, as well as Sotho hopes for British protection. The British did guarantee the Afrikaners' access to the Cape markets for ammunition—which was a crucial bargaining chip for the British—in return for a pledge that the Afrikaners would respect the remaining Griqua land claims. Now the Sotho were left to face the Afrikaners on their own, or so it seemed.

Within just a few years, continued boundary disputes and raiding drove the new Orange Free State (OFS) Afrikaners and the Sotho back to the brink of war. The new OFS president, J. Hoffman, took a conciliatory tone with

Moshoeshoe. His gift of gunpowder to the Sotho king, however, seemed too much like giving aid and comfort to the enemy for most Afrikaners, and he was forced out of office. The Afrikaners then called upon the British (with whom they wished to maintain good relations for trade and military support purposes) to resolve the boundary disputes. The still-interventionist British governor, George Grey, was happy to oblige. Grey added a nominal amount of land to the Sotho side of the already agreed-upon boundary of the Warden line in the 1858 Treaty of Aliwal North. Despite his best efforts, Moshoeshoe could not restrain his people behind the line. Population increases in the areas of white settlement, but especially among the Sotho, led to greater competition for grazing land and rising tensions.

Moshoeshoe embarked on a calculated but still risky strategy to save his kingdom in the territory of Lesotho (called Basutoland—"place of the Sotho people"—at the time). He mounted a propaganda campaign as his people's raids led them and the Afrikaners to war. With the help of the French missionaries, Moshoeshoe produced a well-publicized manifesto. In it he argued that the Afrikaners were the aggressors, that he sought only to safeguard his land for his people, and he implored the British to come to his rescue. There was no immediate aid and the Afrikaners overwhelmed the Sotho, burning crops and leaving the people destitute and on the verge of starvation. Moshoeshoe then took another gamble. He agreed to yet another treaty which gave the Afrikaners almost all of the Sotho agricultural lands. Satisfied, the Free State troops withdrew to plan the settlement of their new farms. In the interim, the Sotho returned to these lands and resumed farming. As the Afrikaners mounted another offensive to enforce the treaty, Moshoeshoe applied his fail-safe strategy of retreating to defend the mountain fortress of Thaba-Bosiu, leaving the Afrikaners in a stalemate.

Moshoeshoe then resumed his strategy of trying to gain British support, and he eventually convinced them to reverse its policy again. This time, however, he sought to play one group off against another. Moshoeshoe was a consummate statesman, and he knew that the local Natal settlers also had an interest in his land, principally as an outlet for its "surplus" African population. He made overtures to the Natal government to annex his kingdom, and the British imperial government actually agreed to this as it did not entail any direct action or cost on its part. The governor, Philip Wodehouse, stepped in at the last minute to amend the deal, principally to address the Sotho concerns about being handed over to the settler-dominated colony. Instead of Natal annexing Lesotho, Wodehouse arranged for Britain to take over the kingdom directly as a High Commission territory in 1868, and so protect it, in theory, from settler incursions. The Free State Afrikaners, under their new president J. H. Brand, were outraged, and Wodehouse managed to keep them in check only by first threatening to cut off their access to the Cape ammunition market and then agreeing to define a new boundary for the High Commission Territory of Basutoland. Although the Sotho lost slightly more land to the Free State, their great king, Moshoeshoe, "the razor," had bequeathed to them an integrated kingdom after his death in 1870. The territory was administered by the Cape from 1871–1884, but Basutoland (Lesotho) would, despite further settler incursions and wars of pacification, eventually gain its independence from Britain in 1966.

Conclusion

The British had come full circle with the annexation of Basutoland. Developments on the ground, such as the increase in white settler activity and trade in the interior, had prompted the British to get involved beyond the confines of the Cape. Initially, imperial authorities had reluctantly bowed to humanitarian pressure to safeguard the Africans from the vagaries of white settlement. There had also been a strategic interest as well. Imperial military men were concerned that the Afrikaners would become too independent and escape the draw of the Cape market. Moreover, the Afrikaners' conflicts with powerful African states threatened to spill back over into the Cape. The Afrikaners seemed to have enough firepower to establish their footholds in the interior, but not sufficient resources to create stable states. As a result, the British developed grand schemes to draw lines on maps and then convince the parties concerned to accept wholly impractical settlements of the land. These were manifest especially in the case of the Orange Free State and Basutoland boundary.

There were also some British interests already established in the interior. Some in the Free State remained loyal to the Cape despite a growing movement for the independence of the trekker republics. There were British merchant interests, also in Natal, and they managed to convince the British government to support their cause. In all of these cases, the British intervened to settle disputes. The most significant features of these developments were the ways in which the British implanted their colonial structures on the land and over the people. The imposition of British colonial rule, including the Shepstone system in Natal and the annexations of British Kaffraria and Basutoland, as well as the emerging designs on the federation of the whole region, had a profound impact on the people and the political geography of South Africa. Ultimately, expediency won out, and the imperial government was increasingly willing to accede to settler demands for land, labor, and responsible government. These developments had important implications for how gold and diamonds would be managed and how African society would be forced into the colonial world which claimed these new resources.

QUESTIONS TO CONSIDER

1. What were relations like between the various African polities such as the Pedi and the Zulu and the Afrikaner trekkers?
2. How did British policy develop in Natal and how did Shepstone develop his system?
3. Why were African productivity and society so important for the development of segregation, and how did segregation alter aspects of African society?
4. What pressures led to the Xhosa cattle-killing and why did this crisis take the form that it did?
5. How did Moshoeshoe seek to take advantage of British policy changes and intervention?

FURTHER READINGS

BEINART, W., *The Political Economy of Pondoland* (Cambridge, 1982). A landmark study of an African polity in the region between the Cape and Natal. Beinart's work is important for its analysis of rural political economies in South Africa and for understanding South African social history.

DELIUS, P., *The Land Belongs to Us: The Pedi Polity, the Boers and the British in the Nineteenth-Century Transvaal* (London, 1984). An excellent, comprehensive micro-study of the Pedi and their relations with encroaching white settlers during the period in question.

DUMINY, A., and GUEST, B. (editors), *Natal and Zululand from Earliest Times to 1910:* (Pietermaritzburg, 1989). A very useful general textbook for the region, it contains some important essays about the early period of Zulu history, including a chapter by C. Hamilton and J. Wright, two of the leading scholars on the so-called *Mfecane*.

ELDREDGE, E. *A South African Kingdom: The Pursuit of Security in Nineteenth-Century Lesotho* (Cambridge, 1993). Another excellent micro-study which sets out the African perspective on its relations with the forces of imperialism and colonialism. This work emphasizes the African initiative but also takes into account the powerful forces arrayed against the Africans in enclave states.

MARKS, S., *Reluctant Rebellion* (London, 1970). This groundbreaking work by a leading scholar on Natal-Zululand and South African history is an analysis of the patterns of pressure and resistance which led to the 1906 African uprising known as the Bambatha rebellion in Natal. Marks has provided an insightful explanation of the events and an excellent analysis of black-white relations in the region.

MARKS, S., and ATMORE, A. (editors), *Economy and Society in Pre-Industrial South Africa* (London, 1980) This excellent collection of essays ranges on topics from the nature of African societies and their economies to issues of culture contact and frontier relations. It is still a very useful teaching tool.

PACHAI, B. *A Documentary History of Indian South Africans* (Johannesburg, 1985). A comprehensive collection of early documents dealing with Indian immigration and indenture in South Africa. It does not have as much editorial analysis as one might like and so is not a good introductory work, but it is a useful work.

PEIRES, J., *The Dead Will Arise: Nongqawuse and the Great Xhosa Cattle-killing Movement of 1856–1857* (Johannesburg, 1989). A masterful account of the cattle-killing. Peires, who has written extensively on the Xhosa, has gone to the heart of the issue with extensive research, and he has clearly shown the importance of the historical context for understanding Xhosa motives and actions as well as colonial motives and actions.

SHILLINGTON, K., *The Colonization of the Southern Tswana* (Johannesburg, 1985). This is an eloquently written account of imperial and settler actions and the impact they had on African communities. While it does not emphasize African initiative as much as some other studies, it does capture the complexities of interactions on the settler frontier.

WEBB, C. DE B., and WRIGHT, J. (editors), *The James Stuart Archive of Recorded Oral Evidence Relating to the History of the Zulu and Neighboring Peoples,* Five Volumes (Pietermaritzburg, 1976–2001). A wonderful primary resource. This richly textured and insightfully edited series provides a range of views on Zulu history as recorded from the oral evidence of the Zulu people.

WELSH, D., *The Roots of Segregation: Native Policy in Natal, 1845–1910* (London, 1971). A sound early work dealing with the politics of Shepstone's system and the implications it had for segregation policy in South Africa. It does not consider all of the economic implications as later works did.

CHAPTER VI

The First Phase of South African Industrialization

Diamonds are primarily a luxury good used in jewelry. They had few uses until the industrial-era application of smaller stones and dust for industrial purposes. In the 1870s, they were nevertheless in high demand and their discovery near the confluence of the Vaal and Orange Rivers in the interior had a profound impact on the South African political economy. Their high value drove an intensification of British involvement in the interior and the rapid, exponential growth of industrial capitalism. Just as settler farming and especially sheep-herding transformed the patterns of land use and the relations between whites and Africans in the rural areas of the Cape and Natal, so too would diamond mining change the patterns of living and the spatial relations of Africans and white society. Initially, the discovery of diamonds set in motion a scramble for digging claims among whites and Africans alike in the area along the lower Vaal. Since there was no dominant political authority in the area, the British felt obliged to step in to settle disputes and ensure the maximization of profit from the new commercial enterprise. The diamond fields had to be directly connected to the wider capitalist world. This was to ensure not only that labor, machines, and the diamonds themselves could be moved about, but also to make certain that the fields were tethered, via the Cape and Natal, to the British imperial world.

Imperial strategists believed that these valuable resources had to be managed by the expert bureaucrats of their colonial administration, not the poorly organized and undercapitalized Afrikaner republics. So, rather suddenly, imperial strategists started to plan for the political incorporation of the interior into a wider British-dominated confederation. Their plans unfolded as the London- and Cape-based industrial capitalists—Cecil Rhodes chief among them— started to connect the fields politically and physically to the British-dominated port cities of Durban and Cape Town and to mobilize a highly controlled African industrial workforce.

Although agriculture remained an important part of the South African economy, it was soon outpaced by the mining of diamonds and later gold (see Chapter 7, "The Second Phase of South African Industrialization: Gold Mining and the Creation of a Unified White State"). The mines inaugurated the implantation of industrial capitalism. They also stimulated new economic developments in the interior. In addition to agricultural and herding production, new markets for trade goods and services emerged. More significantly, the mines started to intensify the exploitive nature of labor relations throughout southern Africa. Later, gold mining changed this exponentially. Although the population remained primarily rural and based on farming, mining began to draw large numbers of people into the rapidly expanding port towns, and especially into the mining centers. The urban centers created a huge demand for produce and other commercial endeavors. As in Natal, Africans responded by increasing their agricultural output. Also during this period, the rise of white settler farmers changed the farming economy from one which was dominated by African peasant production to one in which Africans were displaced in favor of white commercial farmers.

Africans had been mining rich mineral deposits in the region long before the arrival of Europeans. Iron mining and smelting had ancient roots throughout the continent and were factors in the establishment of early states. Similarly, copper and gold mining were carried on at various sites and also contributed to the wealth of important prehistoric African civilizations. The discovery of diamonds, and later of gold by the white settlers however, transformed the African role in mining in South Africa. Increasingly, Africans would be subordinated to the demands of the white state, the white farmers, and especially the white mining industrialists. First, however, imperial designs, driven largely by British officials and settlers in South Africa, demanded the conquest and dismantling of the powerful African states.

Various groups had an interest in the conquest of the numerous African kingdoms which they thought stood in the way of "progress." Some humanitarians, for example, argued that the kings and chiefs continued to prevent them from getting access to the African people, and that those in control were pagan tyrants who resisted the evangelical message. Settler farmers wanted to wrest the land from the Africans and then force them to return as tenants and workers under new white landlords. Mining industrialists wanted to induce the Africans to work for them under harsh and highly controlled conditions. Finally, in order to try to reconcile these sometimes contending interests, the imperial strategists, both in London and in South Africa, wanted to create a uniform British bureaucratic policy for the entire region. They envisaged the expansion of British civilization through industrialization, but they felt that this would require making Africans compliant by extending the empire. Some imperialists were also concerned about the potential enormous cost of administration. They reasoned, however (and thereby abandoned most imperial-humanitarian safeguards for Africans) that the responsibility of managing the new areas could be passed on to the local colonies where the settlers were fast gaining political power. Now the whites would have two trajectories open to them. One was grounded in the rural areas where an improving but still tense relationship had emerged between the whites and the Africans competing to farm the land. The other was wrought from a massive undertaking: the capital-intensive transformation of the very bedrock of the country through mining. In both cases, the white-dominated structures of capitalism and the state shaped the ways in which the Africans were forcibly incorporated into the colonial world

Diamond mining took off in 1867 with the discovery of alluvial diamonds near the confluence of the Orange and Vaal Rivers. Then in 1869, a Griqua man found what would become the Star of Africa, a fist-sized uncut diamond which he traded to a local white farmer for some oxen and a flock of sheep. The news of these discoveries raised great interest among whites and Africans who knew that the commercial value of such gem stones was great. Near the initial sources along the Vaal River, others discovered that there were more than just dry diggings or alluvial surface deposits in the region. In 1870, they found the exposed ends of massive "pipes" of diamond-bearing ore which ran deep beneath the surface. Within a few short months, thousands of people flocked to the area and with a few tools and their brawn, they started to un-earth what would become one of the world's largest man-made surface mines, the "Hole" at Kimberley. Prospectors' or diggers' claims to the land prolifer-ated at an exponential rate as men from all over the region scrambled to ac-quire title to the diamond-rich land at Kimberley. This flurry of activity, and especially the potential value of the diggings drew the attention of the sur-rounding states.

Control of the diamond fields, which were located in the southwestern corner of the Orange Free State, had been contested by various groups. The in-digenous Tswana chiefdoms as well as the Griqua under chief Waterboer, Jan Bloem's Kora, and the Afrikaners of the newly established Orange Free State, as well as those in the trans-Vaal South African Republic, all made claim to the area. As we have seen, the British had recently pledged to quit the area as part of their imperial retreat from the interior of South Africa. When chief Water-boer employed a cunning Cape lawyer to assert his claims to the land, a com-plex dispute arose and the British used this as a justification to intervene once again. In a bold ruse, the British governor, Henry Barkley, used Waterboer's claims against the Republicans. When they called for an objective arbitration of the disputes, Barkley appointed the British Natal Lieutenant Governor, Robert Keate, to hear the evidence. Not surprisingly, Keate sided with British-Cape interests to keep control of the lucrative trade and labor recruiting routes

DIAMOND MINING AT KIMBERLY African labor was essential to the development of mining but Africans were excluded from ownership of the diamond claims. *Source: National Archives of South Africa.*

to the interior known as the "road to the north" out of Afrikaner hands. Keate upheld Waterboer's claims to the diamond fields as well as Tswana claims to the land that the Transvaalers wanted. Barkley conveniently persuaded Waterboer to call for British protection against the angry Afrikaners. To ensure imperial interests, the Cape governor declared the diamond fields British territory in the 1871 annexation of the colony of Griqualand West. This act was clearly a reversal of the policy of retreat. It was conditioned, however, by a new imperial strategy for the federation of the white states. British politicians believed they could reduce their responsibilities in South Africa by uniting the territories and relying on the local British settler colonies of the Cape and Natal to undertake the costly and burdensome administration of newly acquired colonies. Initially, however, the Cape legislature refused to take over control of Griqualand West, and so it remained under imperial control.

THE DEVELOPMENT OF DIAMOND MINING

The demand for diamonds was so great that initially thousands of men worked claim properties, but the economics of the industry were such that they were forced to give way to the organization and control of mining by big capital.

Almost all the early diggers were white, though they relied on African employees to do the actual work of digging the diamonds out. Some Africans did own or rent claims but primarily in the less productive areas. Most diggers came as poorly-funded entrepreneur-adventurers, and most ended up destitute or deeply in debt when they could not find enough diamonds in time to pay their costs. As competition and cost led to the redivision of mining claims, many were barely large enough for a man to stand upon and dig without falling into a neighboring hole. Many claim-holders were soon squeezed out, and the number of owners dropped sharply from nearly 2,000 in 1872 to only 130 by 1879, although the number of men working the claims continued to increase.

There was little organization at the four main mine areas, and local committees struggled to coordinate mining activities among all the diggers. Although they did manage to agree to leave some land untouched between the claims to act as rough roadways, their greed drove them to ignore safety and good planning. As a result, many claims collapsed or flooded, and roadways were either eaten up by claims, or they too collapsed. As the claims got deeper, each digger erected his own wire pulley system to haul buckets of earth up to the surface, creating a vast web of lines (see cover photo). Later, some miners cooperated in order to erect larger hoists and to purchase horses to haul larger buckets up from the deepening hole. Soon, some wealthier claim-holders introduced steam engines to power the hoists, but even this large improvement could not satisfy the growing needs of the industry. By the mid-1870s, the whole affair was becoming increasingly unorganized, dangerous, and costly.

Within a few years, the white diggers who sought to install the white-dominated racial hierarchy of the Cape agreed that Africans must be excluded from claim ownership and reduced to unskilled workers. The whites feared competition from the larger number of African workers, and they claimed that the Africans stole diamonds to sell illegally. As a result, the white diggers managed to get British officials to enforce the otherwise color-blind law (stated so as to appease the humanitarians) in such a way that all Africans were excluded from ownership. The white diggers formed the Defense Association to safeguard their interests against African workers, and in 1875, they rose in armed insurrection against the imperial administrator, Lieutenant Governor Robert Southey. After the British troops restored order, the government allowed the color bar against Africans to stand. Moreover, to prevent theft, only Africans were subject to summary inspection of their whole body. White employers and magistrates also had the power to control the African workers' movements with passes (official written permission to be in the area for work purposes only). In these ways, the mining industry started out as a major force in the increasing differentiation of whites and Africans in terms of both work and social relations. Now that there was so much more wealth at stake and more whites in the country, with more pouring in every day who wanted to control it, there was a great incentive to cut out the Africans altogether. Moreover, since Africans comprised the majority of the workforce and whites had come to rely upon them, the whites had a definite interest in finding ways to control them.

As the small individual claims became more dangerous and harder to work, a few well-placed individuals took advantage of the highly speculative nature of the industry. They realized that with steam-driven hoists and deeper diggings, the diamond mines were becoming increasingly industrial in nature and that this required a larger economic scale of organization and a huge investment. In the unregulated claims market, men such as the London investor, Barney Barnato, and the German diamond merchant, Alfred Beit, engaged in rapacious tactics to acquire claims. They bought up and amalgamated most of the properties so that by 1880, there was only a handful of companies controlling all of the claims. Chief among these was the De Beers Mine owned by Cecil Rhodes. Rhodes had come to South Africa in 1869 for his health. His entrepreneurial spirit led him to the diamond fields where he quickly parlayed a small amount of capital into control of De Beers. He then formed an alliance with his competitor, Beit, and they gained substantial financial backing from the Rothschilds in London.

Rhodes and Beit soon realized, though, that the fledgling South African diamond mining industry was on precarious footing. World diamond prices fluctuated dramatically, and the discovery of massive numbers of diamonds in Kimberley—where soon more than 90 percent of the world's gem-quality diamonds would come from—forced prices to tumble. Rhodes and Beit reasoned that what was needed was monopoly control in order to stabilize the market and keep prices up. Rhodes squeezed out Barnato and then set about buying up all the companies in Kimberley. By 1889, his De Beers Consolidated Mining Company controlled all of the South African diamond production. By the mid-1890s, De Beers had established monopoly control of diamond marketing through London as well as production in South Africa. The company eventually tried to buy up nearly all the diamond mines ever found, and it strictly limited the number of diamonds sold in order to keep prices high. This strategy of controlling the bulk of the world's diamond supply, and thus controlling the market by limiting the number of stones sold, has been De Beers policy ever since.

Once Rhodes and his associated mine owners took control of the mines, they transformed the industry through heavy investment and the intensification of labor control in order to realize even greater profits. Rhodes brought in heavy machinery to aid with deep-level mining so the workers could reach the entire pipe of diamonds. The large hoists and machines, however, required huge amounts of fuel. Initially, the local whites and Africans produced most of the high-quality charcoal which the mining industry needed, but as supplies dwindled, prices rose too high for the mine owners. They pressured the Cape government to invest in the extension of the railroad from Cape Town to Kimberley—which was completed by 1885—and this enabled them to purchase cheap coal from overseas. Over time, the mining industry's demand for fuel and supplies drove the rapid expansion of the South African railways from other coastal cities such as Port Elizabeth and East London, as well as to new coal fields in Natal. In this way, mining and industrialization linked the interior to the coast, and cheap goods as well as cheap labor flowed into the region at a much faster rate than was previously possible.

AFRICAN MEN AND WOMEN AND THE IMPACT OF DIAMOND MINING

Diamond mining stimulated a range of new economic and related political changes. The mines at Kimberley became the center of a web with strands stretching back to the white-dominated port cities and out across the entire southern and central parts of the continent. They attracted three things: people, investment, and imperial intervention. As the population and commercial needs of the digging fields grew (Kimberley had more than 30,000 people by 1880 and was second in size only to Cape Town at the time), they stimulated unprecedented growth in the import trade from Cape Town. The trade routes to Kimberley then swelled with mining equipment, stores and provisions, alcohol, and guns. Moreover, the city provided a voracious market for agricultural food products. As in Natal, most of the farmers in the region were still African, primarily Sotho and Tswana.

MEN SORTING DIAMONDS AT KIMBERLY   Whites monopolized the well-paid skilled jobs and the profits in mining. *Source: National Archives of South Africa.*

These peasants, many of whom were the wives and daughters of those who had access to land, responded to the growing demand by increasing their production of grains, fodder for livestock, milk, hides, and meat. Women were especially significant for producing beer and growing tobacco. They then shrewdly invested their profits in transport wagons for goods or charcoal and in plows. They also bought a range of new imported manufactured goods such as blankets, clothing, liquor, and especially guns. The Afrikaner settlers in the region also sought a stake in the agricultural market on the backs of African workers. They started to enforce their ownership of the land, which had often been won at gunpoint, by demanding that African tenants work their farms for them instead of paying a rent. As the market demands and profits grew, the Afrikaner farmers demanded more of their African "labor tenants." Alternatively, the white farmers allowed their tenants to farm freely, but then they took up to half the crop for themselves as a sharecropping rent. Over time, the city of Kimberley also provided a broad range of other support services. Hotels, eating houses, the building trades, transportation, prostitution, and entertainment all employed thousands of people outside of the mines.

It was the implementation of segregated migrant wage labor in the mines which had the most profound effect on southern African society. For the mine owners to extract the kinds of profits they demanded out of Kimberley, they had to find cheap labor that was easily controlled because the machinery and production costs were so high. Initially, both African and white workers were used, but as we have seen, the whites sought to assert a racial labor hierarchy in the country. With the advent of mechanization in drilling and digging there came new skilled white workers from Britain and Europe. They arrived with the expectation of high wages and a good living, and they did not seek to extend their privileges to African workers. The white workers fought for and won an extension of the color bar which forced virtually all Africans into the ranks of unskilled manual laborers. This racial hierarchy was reinforced by the fact that most African mine workers were male migrants. They came from outside the colony and so had no political power there. White workers took advantage of their political influence to ensure that they remained a privileged labor elite. With this policy in force, the consolidated mining companies sent labor recruiting agents out all over southern Africa into the distant lands of African kingdoms to attract workers down to the mines. The allure of substantial cash wages, from £2–£4 per month (this amount was far below that paid to fellow white workers and inadequate to support a family), and the possibility of adventure drew many thousands of Africans into the mines. Some men journeyed for weeks from as far as 600 miles away to take a contract and earn wages. Paradoxically, while Africans provided the vast majority of the labor power for the mines, it was the whites who profited disproportionately.

Once at the mines, African workers were subjected to rigorous controls and appalling living and working conditions. Each miner was required to sign a contract, either in his home area, where the recruiters worked through the local chiefs who helped to find able workers, or in Kimberley. The contracts, which were often misrepresented to African workers, stipulated from three to six months of work at a set wage per month. Initially, in many cases there was tension over the length of time of the contract since African workers measured time according to their own agricultural lunar cycles, not the industrial time of the Christian seven-day week (although Africans showed less resistance to these new measures of time in the mines than when working on white-owned farms). Africans complained of being cheated when they had to work what they believed was extra time to fulfill their contract in order to get paid. African workers were also subjected to humiliating and dangerous living and working conditions. There were virtually no safety precautions for miners in the ground, and there were often mine tunnel collapses and flooding, or accidents with heavy machines.

Workers were also not allowed to bring their families to the mine areas, and this was particularly hard on them because it severely disrupted normal family life (as we shall see in Chapter 7) and prompted the growth of both female prostitution and homosexual relationships in the compounds. The mines provided very crude accommodation for men in cheap single-sex barracks which were eventually contained in compounds adjacent to the mines. The mine owners prevented Africans from leaving the compounds for the duration of their contracts. Although they claimed that this was necessary to reduce theft, it was actually enforced to ensure that the workers remained near their place of work and could be easily monitored. All African workers were subjected to the ignominy of strip-searches for stolen diamonds. African workers also endured the most deplorable conditions. The mine compounds were notoriously overcrowded and poorly maintained by the owners. They became terrible places of filth and disease. In 1883, for example, more than 500 African miners died of smallpox. These appalling conditions also contributed to high death rates from pneumonia; widespread venereal diseases also plagued the miners and circulated back to their rural homes at the end of their contracts. These circumstances persisted and extended later to gold mining where even more African migrant workers faced these and worse problems. The return journey home from Kimberley also proved to be a hazardous gauntlet. The Afrikaners sought to exact their toll, and they subjected African migrant workers to the theft of their goods and wages earned at the mines, the confiscation of purchased guns, and the payment of return pass fees as they made their way through the republics.

Despite their long journeys to Kimberley, the rigorous demands of mine work, and the wretched living conditions there, increasing numbers of

Africans continued to make their way to the diamond mines. They sought cash for purchasing power because there were new market opportunities and cash demands in South Africa. In the colonial areas such as Natal, and the Cape and Ciskei, African men were subjected to various taxes and rents. Moreover, there were expanding colonial commercial towns and a burgeoning livestock market, which allowed Africans to purchase a whole host of goods as well as to acquire cattle and sheep, which were necessary to marry and establish their own homesteads. These were part of broader strategies for coming to terms with the new world of colonial industrial capitalism. Yet the system of migrant labor also required Africans to maintain a stake in the rural areas, where family life was principally held together by women. Although the wages paid in Kimberley were better than on white farms, they were still not sufficient to support a whole family. Most men still relied upon their chiefs to provide their families access to land in the rural areas so that their wives, mothers, and daughters could farm there. In some cases, the chiefs took advantage of this system and called upon young men to take jobs in Kimberley in exchange for payments from mining company labor recruiters.

Those Africans who engaged in migrant labor did not necessarily want to abandon their rural links. They simply wanted take advantage of the new economy to enhance their status. Moreover, workers' links to the rural chiefdoms also operated at a collective level. Migrant workers maintained relationships with their wives and children, their extended kin (real and fictive), and their linguistic and chiefly networks. This helped them keep a stake in the rural areas so they could easily return when they finished in the mines, and it also helped them form support groups in the mines. Young men from the same rural areas often traveled and worked together. This was in part because this gave them group support from familiar people, and in part because the mine owners learned to view these identities as another means of controlling the men. The mine owners tried to play one ethnic group off against another in order to prevent widespread worker organization. This became even more important in the gold mining industry.

Many shrewd chiefs, especially the Pedi and Sotho, sent their young men down to Kimberley to get sufficient money to buy a gun, which cost about £4, or about one or two months' wages. By the early 1870s, white traders were selling more than 100,000 guns pen year to Africans, and probably more were sold at various towns throughout the region. These guns constituted considerable firepower, and they were far more effective in battle than spears and clubs alone. Migrant labor, therefore, was an important part of initial African strategies of resistance since, as we shall see, the guns they acquired were used to fight off colonial forces later on. The chiefs saw wage labor as a crucial means of defending their chiefdoms from settler incursions through the purchase of guns. In this way, mining initially helped create the conditions for Africans to

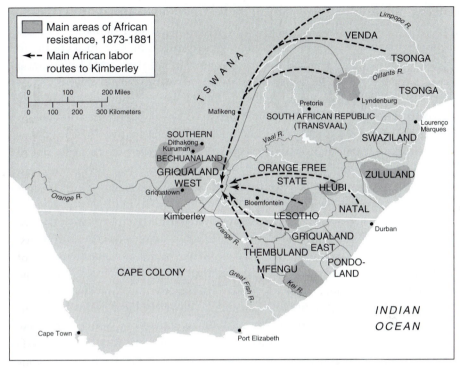

Map 6–1   Mineral Discoveries and African Labor. *Adapted from Shillington, History of Southern Africa. 1997.*

resist the impact of white invasion. Ultimately, however, it was the ability of the independent African states to arm and protect themselves which finally brought the full might of imperial Britain down upon them (see Map 6–1).

IMPERIAL DESIGNS, LOCAL POLITICS, AND CONFEDERATION SCHEMES

As mining in South Africa expanded, imperial strategists came to believe that they had to formulate a comprehensive political policy for the full exploitation of the labor and resources of the region. This thinking was driven by a growing belief, evinced especially by Cecil Rhodes, in the power and importance of "British civilization" for the transformation of the entire African continent. There was also an undercurrent of a crude settler mentality that Africans could not be left to their own devices or be trusted, and that only the British "race" could save the country from African "savagery." Yet, now that there was real wealth to be made in the country, there were different interests and problems to be reconciled. Powerful local politicans, principally Rhodes, wanted to ensure that they controlled development in the region. Local settlers, both British and Afrikaner, wanted to safeguard their farming and commercial interests. Missionaries were still largely frustrated with African leaders in the interior who were reluctant to promote missions in their domains. Imperial authorities wanted to prevent foreign powers from getting a foothold in the region. Of course, Africans and the Afrikaners still had their vested interests in the interior. As far as the imperial strategists were concerned, however, it appeared as if the African states and even the Afrikaner republics stood in the way of their genuine progress. Lord Carnarvon, newly appointed in 1874 as British Secretary of State for the Colonies by a conservative British government, and other colonial officials reasoned that the best way to make the region safe for mining, and for the British, was to federate the colonies and Afrikaner republics under one white government.

The schemes for the confederation of white rule in South Africa reflected both the demand for a cheap, easily controlled African labor force and an affirmation of a racial hierarchy. There were also the problems of cost and African resistance. The British conservative government would not countenance the expenditure of vast sums to bring under control and administer the various independent African states. This accounted for the continued vacillation on the part of the imperial government. Ultimately, however, local events conspired to bring the British fully into a commitment to controlling South Africa. For Carnarvon (who had been instrumental in the recent confederation of Britain's Canadian colonies), confederation meant less imperial involvement and more local responsibility. He hoped to get the Cape and Natal to bear the cost by taking a greater role in local administration. In 1872, the British managed to get the Cape to accept local government and all the costs for defense and administration which this entailed by giving it more power under its own "responsible government" assembly. The imperial government also started to turn over to the Cape certain African territories such as Basutoland in 1871. These developments were significant because they represented a marked increase in the power and influence of the local settler minority over the Africans.

Local Cape interests became even more influential in British strategies when Rhodes entered Cape politics and was elected to the Assembly in 1880. Rhodes become increasingly influential in asserting his own brand of Cape "sub-imperialism." He created a grandiose vision of extending his version of British "civilization" under the "Teutonic races" (both British and Afrikaner) from "Cape to Cairo," fueled by the profits from mining. He was instrumental in expediting the construction of rail and telegraph lines to link the mining areas to the coasts and the rapid expansion of capital-intensive development. In this way, he left his monumental mark on the southern part of the continent. He also precipitated greater imperial involvement in South Africa through his cavalier adventurism and the provocation of Afrikaner resistance. Despite these local developments, confederation was far from a foregone conclusion. There remained three major issues. First, there was the extreme volatility of the Kimberley diamond fields and the problems of ensuring that African labor would continue to flow to the region. Second, there was the related issue of powerful African states which could and did resist increasing settler demands for land and labor. The fact that the Africans had guns of course fueled colonial paranoia about being overrun, although ironically, it was the whites who continued to invade African land and make demands. Finally, the Afrikaner republicans wanted to remain independent of British rule. They wanted to use their wealth derived from mining toward this end, and the British feared they would succeed in breaking free of British markets and authority and forge an alliance with another European power.

BRITISH IMPERIALISM, AFRIKANER REPUBLICAN RESISTANCE, AND THE PEDI KINGDOM

As part of their belief in the superiority of a racial solidarity of whites over Africans within a confederated South Africa, the British felt they must bring the Afrikaner republics in line with imperial policy. Lord Carnarvon made overtures to both the Transvaal (South African Republic) and the Orange Free State to join in a British-led federation. Again, the chief concern was the creation of a single policy to control the Africans and ensure that they provided the labor needed for mining. A number of British industrialists, particularly Rhodes, believed that the Afrikaners were incapable of creating conditions favorable to their needs. They complained that the Afrikaners always mismanaged their relations with the Africans, and that their harassment of migrant workers with taxes and the confiscation of guns as they passed through the republics served to discourage them from going to the mines. They wanted to see British rule extended over the interior, not just confined to the mines, to ensure that their economic interests were served. Carnarvon was convinced that both states had a real interest in federation since it would link them with the power and wealth of the British empire, and thus enable everyone white to consolidate their control over the Africans and build a "white civilization" in the interior. While the Free State appeared to be amenable to economic cooperation, it and the Transvaal both balked at surrendering their political independence. At a meeting in London to discuss these issues, the Free State agreed to a substantial cash settlement for the loss of its claims to the diamond fields, but showed no interest in political union. Despite facing considerable political and economic problems, the Transvaal also rejected the scheme. Indeed, by the mid-1870s, the Transvaal was struggling and in its compromised state, it presented a threat to British interests.

The Pedi kingdom was the greatest challenge to the Transvaal. In the 1860s, the Pedi had successfully fended off an attack by the Afrikaners and their Swazi allies from a mountain stronghold. By this time, the Swazi had consolidated their kingdom under Mswati, Sobhuza's heir, north of the Zulu and to the east of the Transvaal. Mswati had deftly navigated complex diplomatic terrain by making an alliance with the Afrikaners of Lydenburg in the Transvaal against the Zulu, but at the cost of substantial land on the Transvaal side of his kingdom. Under the alliance, the Swazi and Afrikaners planned to take the Pedi and divide their land and cattle. Once they foiled the plan, the Pedi started to re-occupy the land sought by the Afrikaners. At the same time, a small deposit of gold was found in the Lydenburg area and, until the vast deposits of the **Witwatersrand** were discovered, this sparked great hopes in the economic future of the area. Both Afrikaner farmers and miners, who feared that the Pedi would ally with Zulu against them (although there was no firm evidence of this) now had a great interest in conquering the Pedi. The Pedi, under chief Sekhukhune, however, had acquired a large number of guns with money earned in the diamond mines and so were able to withstand the next assault. In 1876, the Transvaal assembled a massive force of nearly five thousand troops, half of which were Swazi. The Pedi won with shrewd tactics. They managed to prolong the campaign with a series of feints and retreats. The Afrikaners, many of whom were pressed to return to tend their farms, could not afford to remain at war. They quit after agreeing to a vague peace treaty which left no one in power. While the Pedi remained independent and rebuffed the Afrikaner demands for labor and taxes (as we shall see, it would take the British imperial army to conquer them), the Afrikaners' economy languished.

The war with the Pedi was costly for the Transvaal because it contributed to their mounting debts and precipitated British intervention. The republican president, T. F. Burgers, had sought to counter their losses and realize Transvaal economic independence from the Cape by building a rail line to Delagoa Bay, in Portuguese territory to the east. His plan caused great concern for the British because in 1875, an international tribunal had confirmed Portuguese claims to Delagoa Bay. This meant that the Afrikaners could potentially get access to a port independent of the British and thereby avoid Cape tariffs as well as open the door to the region to a competing European power (which was a continuing British concern). Following the defeat by the Pedi, the funding for the rail line collapsed and left the Afrikaner government financially embarrassed. Although the Transvaal was known for its opposition to the confederation scheme because it threatened its independence and its fierce spirit of emergent Afrikaner nationalism, the British felt they could overcome this.

Seeking to take advantage of Transvaal weakness, in 1877 Lord Carnarvon devised to send Natal's Theophilus Shepstone to quietly convince the republic's leaders to accept British rule. Failing that, he was to annex the territory even without popular consent. Shepstone had his own and Natal's interests at stake. Unlike the Cape, Natal favored confederation because it provided the means for a possible outlet for their "surplus" African population. If they could join with the other white states, Natal officials believed, they could push their way north through Zululand and the Transvaal to get access to more African land and labor. As we shall see, for Shepstone and his political ally, the lieutenant governor of Natal, Garnet Wolseley, the annexation was part of a larger strategy to deal with the powerful African states, specifically the Zulu. Shepstone nevertheless failed to gain any support from the Transvaal *volksraad* despite their difficult circumstances and the clear offer of British aid. Not surprisingly, the English-speaking community, which had grown to significant numbers by this time, responded enthusiastically.

Shepstone summarily declared the Transvaal to be British territory in a precipitous move. Although the Afrikaners in both republics had no means to openly oppose the annexation, and they did benefit from the British settling their debts, they bitterly resented the intervention. While the British merchants and miners applauded the move, Afrikaners all over the country condemned the annexation, mainly because the British had made no provision for a local representative elected assembly, and their anger began to fester. In the Cape, Afrikaner protests against the annexation laid the foundation for a new political movement, the Afrikaner Bond. The Bond, led by S. du Toit (and later taken over by the influential leader of wealthy Afrikaner wine farmers, Jan Hofmeyr), was inspired by past experiences and new resentment of British meddling, which was articulated in a decidedly anti-British Afrikaner nationalism. These Afrikaner sentiments fueled open resistance to the British annexation and confederation scheme and would eventually lead to war.

In 1880, just as the British were overcoming African resistance to conquest in a series of defensive wars, they faced an open rebellion from the Afrikaner republicans in the Transvaal. The Afrikaners were angry at the British refusal to allow them a greater measure of political power. Indeed, British officials packed the local appointed legislature with men favorable to imperial interests with no consideration for the Afrikaners. In response to British intransigence, Paul Kruger, a new, charismatic, and strong-willed military leader, emerged to take up the Afrikaner cause. Kruger and his supporters were inspired by a growing ethnic nationalist consciousness which was articulated by Afrikaner intellectuals such as Dr. S. J. Du Toit. They based their nationalism on highly selective interpretations of history, on their language, and on a fervent belief in a mythology of the Afrikaners as God's chosen people who were destined to carve out and rule their own white state in Africa.

The British rebuffed Kruger's diplomatic efforts, including a widely-supported petition which he took to London. Afrikaner resentment boiled over when, in a move reminiscent of other imperial follies in the Americas, British officials seized a wagon and oxen belonging to a modest farmer for his refusal to pay taxes. The Afrikaners, returning to the tried methods of the commando, swept in on horseback to retrieve the confiscated goods and rode off to rise in armed rebellion. In this First Anglo-Boer War (as the Afrikaners renamed it), the Afrikaners won stunning victories against surprised imperial forces at Laing's Nek and Majuba Hill. A new liberal administration in Britain sought to compromise and negotiate peace even before it sent in reinforcements to contain the rebels. Despite objections from humanitarians, who feared that the Afrikaners would gain license to ill-treat the Africans, and even from the British sovereign, Queen Victoria, who lamented the loss of imperial prestige, the British officials agreed to leave the Afrikaners to themselves within the republic. In the settlement of the Pretoria Convention of 1881, the British conceded independence to a republican government under newly elected President Kruger and sought only to retain some vague authority over the Transvaal's external relations with European powers. This retreat from a forward imperial policy for confederation was also conditioned by even more embarrassing military defeats for the British against some African states.

THE FINAL PHASES OF CONQUEST

It was guns and the (short-lived, as it turned out) independence that they afforded Africans which presented the first challenge to a settler-colonial controlled confederation in South Africa. As noted earlier, Africans had managed to earn sufficient wages to purchase a considerable number of guns by the early 1870s. Indeed, it was a policy of the Pedi, for example, to send out their young men with the express purpose of buying guns in order to fend off Afrikaner encroachments on their land. Others, such as the Tswana, Sotho, and Natal Nguni and even the distant Ndebele chiefdoms, also bought guns with migrant earnings in order to raid or defend their lands from African neighbors. As we have seen, the Afrikaners objected to the Africans having guns, especially as they traversed the Republics, and their efforts to take away the guns was part of a broader pattern of harassment which served as a disincentive for workers to go to the mines. Still, enough Africans managed to keep their guns to pose a challenge to both settlers and imperial strategists. Most African workers acquired these weapons as members of independent organized African states and chiefdoms, while some lived under chiefs within colonial Natal and the Cape. For African men, guns became a symbol of status and independence which put them on a par with whites. Indeed, as they lost their guns, they also lost political power within the colonial arena.

Already by the early 1870s, as the Hlubi chiefdom of Natal discovered, armed Africans posed too great a threat to settler society. As far as whites were concerned, just as independent armed kingdoms would pose an obstacle to confederation and would require removal, so too did armed Africans within the colonies require a remedy. In 1873, chief Langalibalele of the Hlubi was caught in the coming storm of heavy-handed settler politics and the gun issue. Theophilus Shepstone, secretary for native affairs in Natal and the high-minded pragmatist who had implemented indirect rule, summoned Langalibalele to Pietermaritzburg. The chief was ordered to explain himself for having refused to heed the orders of the local magistrate to have his followers turn in all unregistered firearms, as required by Natal Native Law. Langalibalele, who was a respected hereditary chief and powerful rainmaker, chose not to comply with either demand. He knew that he could lose his authority and prestige if he demanded that the young men of the chiefdom comply with a colonial law which ran counter to their interests. Moreover, the chief feared a trap if he presented himself. He remembered an incident years earlier in which Shepstone's brother had tried to trick a neighboring chief into an easy arrest. The chief evaded the trap, but colonial police killed more than thirty of his followers.

By the time Langalibalele had ignored his third summons, Natal settler society was in a nervous mood. There was already near hysteria over rumors of African men raping white women (though there were very few actual cases of this), and the idea of armed Africans refusing to comply with the demands of the colonial minority set off a panicked response. Rather than face hostile Natal officials, the chief decided to flee. He gathered some followers and cattle, perhaps with a view to establishing a new chiefdom, and took refuge with the Sotho chief Molapo. He was pursued by a colonial force aided by African auxiliaries. Molapo, fearing colonial reprisals, turned in his guest to the Natal authorities, but not before they were cornered and faced off in a skirmish in which the Hlubi men shot and killed five of the colonial troops, including the son of a prominent official.

Natal officials, influenced by settler fears, overreacted in an extremely heavy-handed fashion and drew imperial censure. Following Lanaglibalele's capture, Natal troops quickly moved into the Hlubi location and commenced attacking the remaining elderly, women, and children, killing over 150 people in the maneuver. They then applied excessive measures of punishment by enforcing a strange variant of tribal "collective responsibility." Chief Langalibalele was banished from Natal and handed over to the Cape for imprisonment on Robben Island, his chiefdom was broken up, the land was sold to whites, and his people's cattle were distributed among the "loyal" Africans who had aided the colonialists. The chief's sons and over 200 hundred of his followers were also incarcerated for varying periods. Not surprisingly, these harsh measures drew immediate criticism from humanitarians. Moreover, as far as British imperial authorities were concerned, Natal officials had overstepped their authority in dealing so harshly with the Africans, and they had clearly shown that settler society was ill-prepared to cope with its African neighbors without provoking a major crisis. In the end, the effect of the Langalibalele affair was to raise white settlers' fears of African rebellion. It also disposed the settler society in Natal and the Cape to consider the need for a uniform policy, backed by imperial authority, for dealing with Africans across the region. Finally, it confirmed imperial views that the best solution to local problems in the region was to empower a federation of white states with a single "Native Policy."

It was, however, the economic and political independence of the African states that most concerned the imperialists. They realized that, in the long term, integrated African kingdoms such as the Zulu and the Sotho not only posed a potential military threat, they also could resist the extension of the white-dominated capitalist economy. As the African states sought favorable terms for their participation in the new economy, they retained control of the land and labor which the white farmers and the industrialists continued to need. Imperialists felt that such an array of contending political economies was not conducive to the creation of a uniform policy to control the Africans and recast them as workers in a white colonial state. As a means to an end, the imperial authorities on the ground in South Africa and local settler interests precipitated local developments into a series of major wars against the African states. They saw these campaigns as prerequisites for the creation of a broader "Native Policy" under a federated white British imperial state, and, more significantly, as a way to free up African land and labor for use by the whites.

Although the conquest of the powerful African states transpired quickly, it was not a foregone conclusion. As we shall see, the Africans put up a spirited and strategically sound resistance. Perhaps their most important achievement was that they did not lose all of their traditional institutions despite the ultimate outcome of their military conquest. In each case, although they had been rendered compliant and were brought under the overarching control of the British—particularly the demands of industrial and settler capitalism—the resilient African states had retained at least some features of their pre-conquest societies by the end of the period of conquest in the 1880s. Indeed, the Africans kept their unique forms of African chieftaincy and many aspects of their cultures, languages and religions, and even access to some of their land. Ultimately, however, even these features of African society would be eroded, corrupted, reconfigured, and made compliant with the demands of the white state and capitalism. All that would remain for the Africans after conquest was some meager means of contesting and negotiating their subordination. The military campaigns were of necessity conducted in a piecemeal approach because the Xhosa, Sotho, Pedi, and Zulu remained separate and entrenched on their lands, which ranged from the eastern Cape region to the interior to the far north of the settler colonies. Moreover, each war was brought about by local factors as much as by imperial design, though both were required to override the ever-present humanitarian objections as well as the British government's continuing concerns over cost.

By the 1870s, in the eastern Cape, the policy of an earlier governor, Sir George Grey, to "civilize and subordinate" the Xhosa started to unravel under the pressures of the Cape settlers' demands. As we have seen, Grey took advantage of the devastation of the Xhosa in the aftermath of the cattle-killing to settle the region with *Mfengu* people. The *Mfengu*, who had been "loyal" to their British protectors, enjoyed the provision of even more land among the Xhosa in the territory of Fingoland. So did loyal Thembu in Thembuland and emigrant Griqua whom the British encouraged to leave the Orange Free State and settle in Griqualand East adjacent to the Pondo and Xhosa lands. Such large numbers of new African and Coloured settlers in the area naturally led to increased competition for land and subsequently friction. As the African peasants in all these communities increased agricultural production and vied for the burgeoning Cape and Kimberley markets, tensions flared into open conflict.

In 1877, fighting broke out between Xhosa and Mfengu at a beer-drinking party. These were common social gatherings where Africans met friends and family and engaged in contests of strength and prowess through stick-fighting. These contests were normally full of harmless bravado, but in the colonial context, economic pressures sometimes pushed people over the brink into more violent fighting over land and resources, as was the case here. As the fighting escalated, the new high commissioner for South Africa, Bartle Frere, who was committed to confederation and to bringing Africans under imperial control, intervened. Frere believed that only after all Africans had been disarmed, wrested from their own leaders and states, forced to pay taxes, and work for whites would South Africa become a valuable civilized place. Frere took the opportunity of the unsettled state of affairs to press his plans for the reorganization of the region. He summoned the Xhosa Gcaleka chief, Kreli, and when the chief refused, Frere sent in the troops.

Just as the combined force of imperial soldiers and *Mfengu* and Thembu auxiliaries "pacified" the Gcaleka Xhosa in the Transkei, and the Ngqika Xhosa in the Cape colony, other rebellions broke out. Within a year, the Cape government, which had resisted confederation schemes for political reasons, began to look favorably upon imperial intervention and unity in order to deal with the problem of resistance. In 1878, the Griqua and the Pondo in the Transkei area rose in protest against white colonial storekeepers and the Griqua in Griqualand West engaged in a futile rebellion over the loss of their land to settlers. In both cases, the Africans and the Griqua were resisting the expansion of settler capitalism whereby whites were given unfair advantages in getting land and licenses to trade. As the frontier economy expanded, the colonial government issued licenses for trade in the Cape to whites only. These granted the settlers a virtual monopoly on business in African areas of the colony and beyond, and would-be African competitors rose in rebellion. As the rebellions flared, Frere stepped in to select a new prime minister for the Cape government, Gordon Sprigg, who was more amenable to imperial desires for confederation. Now Frere was able to press ahead with his plans, even though they contravened many imperial policies for non-intervention and the protection of Africans. With his support, the new Cape government crushed the Xhosa and forced them to submit to colonial officials as it annexed more parts of the Transkei. By 1885, the Cape had annexed and governed almost all of the Xhosa, Mfengu, Thembu, and Pondo lands. More ominously, the Cape passed the Peace Preservation Act in 1878 which aimed to disarm all Africans who were under Cape authority. Just as the Afrikaner republicans were trying to keep guns out of the hands of the Africans, so too did the British embark on a concerted campaign to wrest firearms away from all Africans.

THE SOTHO AND ZULU RESISTANCE

By the late 1870s, leading African statesmen such as the new Sotho paramount, Letsie (who succeeded Moshoeshoe in 1870), could clearly see the emerging patterns of British expansion and conquest. Yet, despite their best efforts, there was little they could do to avoid a collision course when local imperialists were so determined to ignore humanitarian concerns and to break African independence in order to serve the confederation strategy. As we have seen, the British annexed Basutoland and handed it over to the Cape, which had recently passed the Peace Preservation Act with the aim of disarming Africans and extending its control over the interior. However, Cape rule of the Sotho, as with other colonial forms of indirect rule, was incompatible with the authority of the independent chiefs. One such chief, Moorosi of the Phuti (a quasi-independent chiefdom within the region), was consistently frustrated by the local Cape magistrate who had repeatedly been at odds with the chief and always undermined his rule. Moorosi responded to the colonial demands to amend traditional law along lines acceptable to the Cape with increasing defiance. Cape authorities then called upon Letsie to bring Moorosi under control. Letsie thus faced a new but increasingly common problem of African paramounts: internal dissent which put the kingdom at odds with the colonizers.

The two choices for Letsie were to comply and face possible resistance from his people, or to support his subordinate chiefs and face certain reprisals from the colonial state. In 1878, Letsie, who feared the loss of even more land from the severely curtailed kingdom, forced Moorosi to submit and accept a hefty fine for his defiance of colonial authority, although the magistrate in question was removed. Cape colonial officials were determined to show who was in charge. They placed a new magistrate over Moorosi who was even more bent on humbling the chief. The official arrested the chief's son, Lehana, on a trumped-up charge of horse theft. Lehana was found guilty and sentenced to four years of hard labor. Moorosi freed Lehana before he was taken away and then, defying a colonial order to surrender his son, the prisoner, the chief, and his followers retreated to a mountain stronghold. Chief Letsie felt he had no choice but to fall in line and support the colonial forces sent to capture Moorosi. He was particularly concerned that his failure to aid the Cape forces would be seen as a form of resistance. Colonial officials had given the Sotho the impression that as long as they remained loyal, they would remain independent, and, more importantly, would be allowed to retain their guns upon which they depended to defend themselves against the Afrikaners. Letsie's hopes were in vain.

The Cape imperialists forced the Sotho into an open war of resistance. During a protracted campaign, Letsie's Sotho soldiers helped in the taking of Moorosi. The colonial forces made macabre sport of the victory and capture, killing many of Moorosi's followers, and mutilating the chief's decapitated body in front of the Sotho. The British high commissioner, Frere, then pushed the Cape to extend and enforce the Peace Preservation Act on the Sotho. In the spring of 1880, the Cape called upon all Sotho, even those who had actively participated in the campaign against Moorosi, to surrender their guns. This threat to their sense of having an independent life as armed individuals who could protect their lands, combined with their misgivings about the fate of Moorosi and their wider fears of the motives of Cape imperialists, proved too great for the otherwise loyal Sotho. It also created a broad sense of unity among a range of chiefs who previously had pursued their own individual interests.

Nearly every Sotho chief protested against the extension of the act. With the exception of Chief Jonathan, who hoped to gain colonial support in his bid to win a succession dispute, they rose in a defensive rebellion known as the Gun War. Much to the embarrassment of the Cape colonial forces, the Sotho conducted a masterful war strategy. Rather than directly confront the colonial troops who had superior firepower, the Sotho took advantage of the mountainous terrain of their country. They used their sure-footed ponies to move from mountaintop to mountaintop, always one step ahead of the invaders. When faced with the certain loss of a fortress, they quickly abandoned it until colonial troops had moved on, then re-occupied it. With stealth and guerilla tactics, the Sotho eventually exhausted the colonial forces, who were also forced to contend with parallel rebellions in Griqualand East and the Transkei. By 1881, the Cape agreed to a British imperial government-sponsored peace treaty, which allowed the Sotho to retain their guns as long as they were registered in exchange for the Sotho's payment of war damages. The Cape's embarrassing loss had the effect of significantly reducing the colony's willingness to take on imperial objectives for confederation for a time. Basutoland was handed back to the British government in 1884 and it remained a British protectorate until independence in 1966, although it would have to submit to the demands of the broader South African economy.

Perhaps the most famous African war of resistance was that of the Zulu kingdom against British imperial conquest. The Anglo-Zulu war of 1879 was largely the product of a concerted local propaganda campaign designed to portray the Zulu kingdom as a savage state led by a villainous ruler. It was the bellicose machinations of the overly ambitious high commissioner, Bartle Frere, and his Natal collaborator, the "Father of the Zulu," Theophilus Shepstone, who pressed the reluctant Zulu into a defensive war. They managed to concoct a false presentation of the Zulu as a warlike kingdom which was in alliance with the Pedi and the Sotho in a region-wide conspiracy to rid the land of whites. They further argued that the Zulu were driven to violence by their martial past and that this would be soon directed against Natal, despite clear evidence to the contrary. Moreover, they whipped up sufficient settler paranoia to generate vociferous demands from white farmers and missionaries for the conquest of the Zulu kingdom, although the ulterior motives were to open the territory to evangelical activity and commercial sugar cane agriculture, which was already developing in coastal Natal. These demands fed into the wider imperial discourse about the need for confederation. For Frere, Shepstone, and—ultimately—the British, the prestige and power of the independent Zulu state threatened Natal security interests, provided a potential outlet to the sea for the Afrikaners, and stood in the way of the advance of industrial capitalism. Once the kingdom was conquered, the British could contain the Afrikaners and open Zululand to missionaries, settler farmers, labor recruiters, and taxation.

On the eve of the war, the Zulu kingdom was uneasy. A new Zulu king, Cetshwayo, took the throne in 1872. He had replaced his father, Mpande, following a bitter succession dispute which had erupted in civil war in 1856. Cetshwayo's supporters, the uSuthu, beat out the other pretender to the throne, his brother Prince Mbuyazi. Cetshwayo became the effective ruler although Mpande remained as a figurehead. Yet Cetshwayo's position remained precarious. First, he strengthened the kingdom through his enhanced control over Zulu homesteads, marriage, and the transfer of cattle for bridewealth so that he could maintain a powerful army of up to 35,000 men. Before becoming king, he had worked to get support in fending off contending factions, in part through dealings with the Transvaal Afrikaners and in part through overtures to the British in Natal. He sought to keep good diplomatic relations and a non-aggression policy with Natal through Shepstone just as his father had done. Cetshwayo had even made an agreement with Natal in 1873 to facilitate the passage of migrant workers from southern Mozambique into the colony.

In order to strengthen his hand in the earlier succession dispute, Cetshwayo also accepted Shepstone's offer to affirm him as the heir apparent. As we shall see, this was a dangerous precedent for the Zulu, for it convinced Shepstone and later Natal officials that it was they who conferred legitimacy on the

Zulu paramount. Indeed, following Mpande's death in 1873, it was Shepstone who proclaimed Cetshwayo king at an installation ceremony full of the pomp and circumstance which were the hallmarks of British imperial rule. Although the king had actually been proclaimed before his people at a Zulu ceremony some days before Shepstone arrived in Zululand, Cetshwayo deferred to Shepstone in order to keep friendly relations and to satisfy Natal interests. Cetshwayo had also sought to learn more about colonial Natal by allowing a friend and advisor, the trader John Dunn, to set himself up in southern Zululand. Dunn was a self-styled adventurer who, with Cetshwayo's permission, remade himself as a white Zulu chief and attracted a considerable Zulu following, including numerous wives.

It was a dispute with the Transvaal over land which the Afrikaners claimed that Mpande had ceded to them which opened the door to Natal intervention and led to the undoing of the Zulu. In 1878, Frere, Shepstone, and the British suddenly reversed their previous support of the Zulu and prepared for war. Following his annexation of the Transvaal, Shepstone told the Zulu that the Afrikaners' claim to their land was legitimate, even though he had previously supported the Zulu protests against Afrikaner expansion in the area. Then, contrary to imperial desires for the land dispute to justify suppressing the Zulu, a Natal government commission investigating the boundary found in favor of the Zulu. Despite the commission's findings and Cetshwayo's obvious desire for peaceful relations, Frere suppressed the commission's report. He then began rattling sabers in support of Natal missionaries and sugar cane planters who wanted the Zulu king to be removed and the kingdom dismantled. Frere found the pretext for war when the Zulu chief Sihayo had two women put to death for infidelity after his men captured and returned with them from Natal where they had fled with their lovers. Despite the fact that colonial forces had often entered Zululand to retrieve criminals, the British treated the Sihayo case as a major offense, first, as a border violation and second, as a contravention of civilized law.

The British rebuffed Cetshwayo when he tried to explain the harsh treatment of the women in terms of Zulu law and offered some cattle in compensation for the perceived offense. In December 1878, at Frere's behest, Shepstone presented a Zulu delegation which had gathered to hear the good news of the boundary commission's findings with an egregious set of demands in an ultimatum calculated to provoke war. The British ordered that, in addition to turning over Sihayo's men who had violated the border within twenty days, the Zulu king must provide 600 cattle in compensation, admit missionaries and a British official to oversee the kingdom, and conform to the "coronation laws" for civilized behavior that Shepstone had proclaimed at Cetshwayo's coronation. The most excessive demand—for Cetshwayo to disband the Zulu army—was tantamount to calling for the complete dissolution of the kingdom. Cetshwayo of course had to reject these most unreasonable terms and the British got their war, though it was not the one they had hoped for.

The war itself was far from the easy victory of an industrialized nation over a traditional African military system which the British had hoped for. Under the command of Lieutenant General Sir Frederick Thesiger, 2nd Baron of Chelmsford, more than 17,000 troops invaded Zululand. Of these, less than half were white, including some 5,700 British regulars and the rest were assorted colonials. Over 9,000 of the force were also Zulu-speaking Africans of the Natal Native Contingent, which gives some indication that a united black race conspiracy against whites was truly a product of a terrified colonial imagination. The Zulu forces, which significantly outnumbered the invaders and had the home-ground advantage, nevertheless could not sustain the fighting. They did not take full advantage of their outmoded firearms procured through trade, and they were constrained by Cetshwayo's defensive strategy. The Zulu king, baffled by British aggression, still hoped to negotiate an end to the hostilities. This may account for reports that the Zulu *impi* (army) simply melted away after heavy engagements rather than take the offensive, although heavy casualties and the need to tend to cattle and crops were more probable factors. It is also significant, however, that the Zulu army was substantially smaller than previously. The forces of change wrought by a new colonial economy had atomized Zulu society, altering the focus for young men away from the traditional *amabutho* (a military regiment) system and toward individual interests. The king could no longer command the entirety of Zulu men in battle. Nevertheless, the Zulu had put up a formidable resistance which tempered the peace in their favor.

Chelmsford's advance was hampered by poor organization, logistical problems of supply over difficult terrain and, more importantly, shrewd Zulu tactics. Overly sanguine about their chances for a short and successful war, myopic British officers discounted reports of Zulu forces where they were not expected. Chelmsford then broke a cardinal rule of engagement by splitting his forces. He took half of his own column in pursuit of a small Zulu reconnaissance party, leaving the rest encamped at Isandlwana. It was here, on 22 January 1879, that a force of some 20,000 Zulu struck their most telling blow of the war, annihilating over one-third of Chelmsford's force. Following this massacre, a Zulu reserve force under Cetshwayo's brother, Prince Dabulamanzi, abandoned the defensive strategy to besiege the fortified depot at Rorke's Drift just inside Natal. A Welsh regiment of 150 men, demonstrating the deadly effect of modern weapons, put up a heroic defense, inflicting 500 casualties out of an estimated two or three thousand Zulu attackers. The British garrison lost only 17, but won 11 Victoria crosses for heroism, the most ever awarded for a single engagement. Clearly, the war was far more difficult than the imperial strategists had bargained for. The Zulu managed one more major victory, overwhelming a cavalry force at Hlobane. Thereafter, the Zulu defenses fell away. The British forces pressed on to Cetshwayo's capitol, oNdini, in July and their mopping-up operations lasted until September.

The war ended in British victory with the burning of Cetshwayo's royal homestead in July and his capture in August 1879. Thereafter, the British established their authority over the Zulu through the suppression of the Zulu monarchy, the political division of the territory, and the stationing of a British Resident there. It culminated in the annexation of the former kingdom in 1887. The postwar colonial settlement, however, was an expedient marked by an equally remarkable Machiavellian quality. It divided the vestiges of the kingdom against itself and served British interests for the political subordination and fragmentation of Zululand. At the end of the war, the Zulu retained their land and formal independence, but at the cost of their monarchy, their military system, and their political cohesion. Cetshwayo was exiled, and the ensuing British settlement of Zululand ultimately caused the destruction of the kingdom. Sir Garnet Wolseley, the new High Commissioner for South Eastern Africa, influenced by practices elsewhere in the empire and by the decidedly anti-Zulu monarchist, Shepstone, devised the notorious division of the kingdom into thirteen chiefdoms. By re-creating and exploiting long-standing divisions within Zulu society, the local Natal officials supported compliant and self-aggrandizing appointed chiefs such as Zibhebhu kaMaphitha and the white chief John Dunn against the remaining Zulu royalists.

The British settlement failed and the result was a protracted and bloody civil war. In the interim, Cetshwayo and his missionary allies, Bishop Colenso of Natal and his daughters, Frances and Harriette, successfully petitioned the British government—which now had flagging confidence in the settlement— for the restoration of the exiled king, albeit with drastically curtailed powers and territory. This and the imposition of British administrators and a Reserve Territory as a buffer between the Zulu and Natal only served to exacerbate the violence. Both Cetshwayo and his rival Zibhebhu enlisted the aid of white mercenaries in continued fighting. After Cetshwayo's sudden death in February 1884, it was his son and successor, Dinuzulu, who turned the tide of the civil war. He engaged a formidable force of Boers, who had been encroaching on Zululand for decades, to support the royal cause. The exorbitant price for their success was the unprecedented cession of vast Zulu lands to the Boers to the northwest as the New Republic and along the coast. Faced with the rapidly deteriorating conditions and coupled with imperial anxieties over a Boer-German alliance which could provide these colonial adversaries with access to the sea, the British intervened. After recognizing limited Boer claims in the interior of Zululand, imperial authorities formally annexed the remaining territory in 1887. Thereafter, colonial officials intensified the integration of a devastated Zulu society into the wider colonial political economy. Thus, the

British finally crushed Zulu independence with an administration which retained only certain features of the pre-conquest kingdom and by the imposition of taxes paid for by migrant wage labor, which redirected the productive
forces away from the monarchy system to the service of the colonial state.

The Pedi suffered a similar fate. In late 1878, following his annexation of
the Transvaal, Shepstone referenced unfounded rumors of a Pedi alliance with
the powerful Zulu kingdom and provoked yet another war when he demanded
the payment of a fine in cattle, which had accrued from the previous war between the Pedi and the Afrikaners. This was coupled with the imposition of a
burdensome "hut tax" levied against every adult male. As with the ultimatum
presented to the Zulu a year later, Shepstone's demand was impossible for the
Pedi paramount, Sekhukhune, to fulfill and was thus calculated to precipitate
conflict. British imperial forces under Sir Garnet Wolseley's command invaded
in October 1878 and finally conquered the kingdom by September 1879. The
British then broke up the Pedi and relocated them to two distant reserves, thus
ending their independent kingdom.

Conclusion

The advent of diamond mining in the interior of South Africa ushered in two
powerful new forces: industrial capitalism and British and colonial imperialism
under the guise of confederation. These were the twin powers which started
the forcible integration of African and Afrikaner people into the wider world
economy. Diamond mining began the most profound reconfiguration of the
social and political geography of the region. It directly linked, through road
and rail, the emerging urban centers in the interior, specifically Kimberley, to
the coast and the outside world. Moreover, many African people, increasingly
from distant lands, began to move into the area. They transformed the social
geography of the land, bringing in new labor power and skills to mining, as
well as contributing to the development of a thriving peasant agricultural
economy. Yet these processes also unfolded in a unique way in South Africa.
Mining, industrial development, and profits had to work in a context shaped
increasingly by race and ethnicity. Diamond mining was but one, albeit central, pillar of the new imperial superstructure of confederation. Confederation
was a policy designed to bring the region under the overarching power and influence of British civilization. Its proponents sought to create a uniform policy
of treatment and control of the Africans in order to avoid conflict, bring about
a compliant and cheap labor force, and to make the region safe for investment.

To this end, there was a belief that whites—English and Afrikaner together—must control the country. There remained a definite difference of

opinion between the Afrikaners and the British about how this was to be achieved. Afrikaner republican interests did not necessarily converge with imperial designs, and their resistance provoked a strong British reaction in the First Anglo-Boer War. These tensions grew as the economic stakes got higher. The independent African states, moreover, were seen not just as obstacles to confederation, but as dangerous, violent entities which threatened white interests. The destruction of these states—the Xhosa and the eastern Cape peoples, the Sotho, the Pedi, and the Zulu—was part and parcel of the imperial imperative: The Africans would have to be subordinated to white interests in order for the country to progress. Yet conquest was not so easy as was hoped. The Africans stung the Afrikaner, British, and allied forces in many battles. Moreover, while the African kingdoms ultimately lost the wars, they did give the British, and their alter-ego missionary consciences, reason for pause. Not only did the Africans show their military prowess (which of course only provoked the British), but they also managed to retain certain features of their states and cultures which could be used defensively again in the future.

QUESTIONS TO CONSIDER

1. How did diamond mining and industrial capitalism develop in South Africa? What impact did this have on African communities and workers?
2. How did the new economic relations of industrial capitalism influence imperial policy? What was the meaning of confederation in South Africa?
3. How did the Afrikaner republicans respond to imperial initiatives?
4. Why did Chief Langalibalele run away, and what effect did his resistance have?
5. Compare and contrast the conflicts between the British and the Xhosa, Sotho and Zulu. Why did the British seek to conquer these African states?

FURTHER READINGS

BEINART, W., DELIUS, P., and TRAPIDO, S. (editors), *Putting a Plough to the Ground: Accumulation and Dispossession in Rural South Africa* (Johannesburg, 1986). A fine collection of revisionist chapters dealing with the struggle of African producers to live off the land. It also deals with the nature of the Afrikaner agro-pastoral economy in the interior.

BUNDY, C., *The Rise and Fall of the South African Peasantry* (London, 1979, 1988). A classic materialist account of the black peasantry. Bundy's landmark work is excellent for its detailed analysis of African producers, their contribution to the South African economy, and their struggle to remain economically independent.

COPE, R., *The Ploughshare of War: The Origins of the Anglo-Zulu War of 1879* (Scottsville, 1999). An excellent and very well-researched analysis of the politics and events leading to the precipitation of the Anglo-Zulu war and the imperial factor in general. Cope has provided compelling arguments and evidence for the theory that the British clearly precipitated the war, and he has deftly shown how the Zulu and Pedi sought to deal with the challenges before them. The African initiative is well-covered here.

GUY, J., *The Destruction of the Zulu Kingdom: The Civil War in Zululand, 1879–84* (London, 1983). A groundbreaking study of the impact of colonial policy and the manipulations of Zulu politics which led to the undermining of the Zulu kingdom after the conquest. Guy's work puts the Zulu at center stage and explains how it was the wider patterns of change in the political economy of imperial industrial and settler capitalism which led to their fragmentation and subordination.

DELIUS, P., *The Land Belongs to Us: The Pedi Polity, the Boers, and the British in the Nineteenth-Century Transvaal* (London, 1984). An excellent, comprehensive micro-study of the Pedi and their relations with encroaching white settlers during the period in question.

LABAND, J., *Rope of Sand: The Rise and Fall of the Zulu Kingdom in the 19th Century* (Pietermaritzburg, 1996). A very thorough and balanced account of the history of the kingdom from its early days to its collapse under the weight of colonial rule. Ladand is a leading historian of the Zulu and their wars.

MARKS, S., and RATHBONE, R., *Industrialization and Social Change in South Africa, 1870–1930* (London, 1982). This is an excellent collection of essays covering everything from the nature of mining to African society and culture to gender issues. It is still essential reading for the period in question.

MAYLAM, P., *Rhodes, the Tswana, and the British* (London 1980). A well-crafted analysis of Rhodes' policies and the impact on the Tswana. Maylam writes clearly and concisely and his work brings out the importance of the African initiative in the story of unfolding imperialism.

ROTBERG, R., *The Founder: Cecil Rhodes and the Pursuit of Power* (New York, 1988). A comprehensive and well-researched biography. Rotberg not only encapsulates and builds upon other biographies of Rhodes, he also provides a clear sense of the context in which he emerged.

SCHREUDER, D., *The Scramble for Southern Africa, 1877–95* (London, 1980). A classic account of the imperial factor in the region. This book is more concerned with grander political designs than the local factors or African actions, but it is still a useful guide to imperial motives during the period.

WORGER, W., *South Africa's City of Diamonds: Mine Workers and Monopoly Capitalism in Kimberley, 1867–1895* (Johannesburg, 1987). A balanced account of the early mines with a keen insight into the mechanics of mining and the challenges for African workers. It has a series of excellent photographs.

CHAPTER VII

The Second Phase of South African Industrialization: Gold Mining and the Creation of a Unified White State

In 1886, gold was discovered in what turned out to be vast, deep deposits of gold-bearing ore in a seam or "reef" on the Witwatersrand (white water's ridge) or *Rand* in the central Transvaal. This discovery accelerated the transformation of the South African economy and led to the domination of African people within a unified white state. Although small surface deposits of gold had been found at Lydenurg and other places on the highveld, nothing compared with the potential of the "reef." It provided one of the world's richest sources of gold during a time when gold was extremely valuable not only for jewelry, but also as the world's standard currency of finance. Gold's rarity and high value made it an ideal commodity for many governments to use to back up the value of the paper currency they issued. This created significant demand for this precious metal and made the *Rand* gold deposits very important to the world economy as more countries went onto the gold standard. It also led to a shift in the focus of the South African economy.

Although diamonds remained important, gold mining now commanded the attention of the industrialists and financiers as well as the politicians. As the emergent giant of South African industry, gold mining also reshaped the entire region spatially. The mines became the geographic center for a wider nexus of labor recruitment and for transportation routes which brought people and infrastructure to the highveld in unprecedented volumes. Indeed, the movement of African workers to and from the mines and other industries would take on nearly continent-wide proportions. The mines were also the launching pad for Rhodes' schemes for the spatial extension of his own brand of British imperial civilization. Thus mining led South Africa to play an ambiguous role in Africa. It fostered the country's ability to attract large numbers of workers to its urban centers and to repel people from the increasingly racist and pernicious political economy that supported mining.

The location of the *Rand* in the Afrikaner-controlled Transvaal (South African Republic) and the nature of the deep deposits of ore required the industrial capitalists who owned the mines to develop new economic and political associations. Deep-level mining required massive infusions of capital to buy the heavy machinery needed to crush and process the ore. Similarly, increasing numbers of white farmers sought to capitalize upon the burgeoning market for produce. They clamored for land and political support in order to gain a greater stake in the economy just as their African counterparts, the peasants, struggled to retain their niche in the face of expanding white commercial agriculture. Above all else, the industrialists' demands for great profits from the gold mines required the exploitation of massive amounts of cheap African labor, and this became an obsession of both the South African state and the mine owners. These demands, however, were made within the context of a region dominated by the British imperial government. As we have seen, the British were convinced that the region, and especially its economy, required a uniform policy for dealing with the African states and their peoples and that this could best be achieved through white unity in a confederated state. At the same time, there was still a sense that the imperial government should continue to safeguard African interests along humanitarian lines.

Some of the British political and humanitarian philosophies, however, were quickly subordinated to the demands of industrial capital. Thus gold and diamond mining shaped the forging of a unified white state. Paradoxically, there were definite limits to this racial solidarity. British imperial strategists, spurred on by metropolitan investors and nationalists as well as by local Cape and Natal interests, especially those of Cecil Rhodes, demanded the British conquest and control of the region. This included the subordination of white Afrikaners to the exigencies of mining. Yet the Afrikaners would eventually be accommodated in ways that were never extended to Africans. Not surprisingly, this led to rising tensions between Africans and whites.

THE NATURE OF GOLD MINING AND AFRICAN MIGRANT LABOR

The *Rand* gold mines provided great long-term potential for mining, but the profitable realization of this mineral resource required a revolution in mining techniques as well as the transformation of political, social, and

AFRICAN MINERS DRILL INTO THE ROCK AT THE SUB NIGEL EAST GOLD MINE   African gold miners experienced harsh conditions in the highly controlled migrant labor environment. *Source: Getty Images, Inc./Hulton Archive Photos.*

economic relationships needed to support the industry. The gold ore in the *Rand* reef deposits contained small amounts of pure gold compared with other deposits around the world. Only some of these deposits were near the surface. Most were found later, deep in the earth, and miners had to sink long shafts down to the ore-bearing seams. In order to rend the gold from the ore, it first had to be dug up, hauled to the surface, crushed into manageable chunks, and then treated with expensive chemicals. These were costly processes. Moreover, gold was sold at a fixed price in order to ensure the stability of the gold standard. Even if mining costs such as for machinery and labor went up, the profits from the sale of gold stayed the same. This meant that in order for the South African mines to show a profit, the owners had to find a way to process huge amounts of ore and yet keep their production costs down. This entailed the development of mining companies which could strike a complex balance between the use of expensive heavy machines and the employment of very large numbers of cheap African migrant workers.

In order to achieve this balance, prospective mine owners needed to raise vast amounts of investment capital, and they needed the cooperation and support of a strong central government. These companies benefited from the earlier developments of migrant labor and diamond mining at Kimberley which generated some of the profits used to finance mining on the *Rand*. In 1887, the mine companies also helped create a stock exchange in Johannesburg, or *Egoli* (*Egoli* is the African name for the place or city of gold), the city which started to grow up around the mines. The stock exchange helped raise considerable sums of money, both locally and from abroad. Early on, speculation ran rampant and many companies went bankrupt when they could not produce sufficient gold to pay off their huge investments in the mining operations. What remained were a few large, powerful companies, led by the Wernher-Beit company and Cecil Rhode's own Consolidated Goldfields of South Africa, Ltd. Within a short time, they consolidated their hold on the industry and colluded to form the Chamber of Mines in 1887. The Chamber later acted as a powerful lobby group and cooperative regulatory body for common aspects of mining such as wages and labor recruitment. All the Chamber members then benefited from these common policies for ensuring a steady supply of workers and for keeping wage costs down.

Labor was the crucial factor for the South African mining industry. So many questions turned upon how it was to be managed, but there was little doubt in the mine owners' minds that Africans should and would be used as the main source of the cheap unskilled labor force they demanded. The mines and the machinery used in them required only a small, specially skilled—and therefore highly paid—work force. Most of the men initially brought in for these jobs were experienced whites who came from mining areas in Europe. Although they shared many concerns regarding the deplorable work conditions with their fellow African workers, they increasingly came to see themselves as a special labor caste, distinct from Africans. What ultimately separated African and white workers was the fact that the whites had political power and the Africans did not. The mine owners therefore found it far easier to exploit the African workers than the whites, who could vote for change. As with diamond mining, the gold mines came to rely upon African men as migrant workers although they did not originate this form of labor. Africans had engaged in patterns of labor migration for some time prior to the advent of mining. Since early in the nineteenth century, they had made their way onto white farms and into the towns of the Cape to engage in seasonal or short-term labor before returning home to their families. They did so in order to purchase the newly available range of goods, including guns, which arrived in large quantities with the settler merchants.

African Society and Migrant Labor

Although over time the colonial government did much to force Africans to participate in migrant labor because of its conquest of the African states and the dispossession of African lands, as well as its imposition of various taxes and regulatory laws, many Africans had their own incentives for engaging in migrant work. In some cases, they sought to earn wages which gave them some degree of economic independence from the confines of the rural African communal economy which was dominated by the chiefs. For most, however, migrant labor did not mean a breaking away from their rural ties. Migrant earnings could be plowed—literally—back into the land with the purchase of farming implements. The chiefs still held sway over the release of people into migrant wage labor from the rural areas since they controlled the allocation of land to the families.

African migrant labor was predicated upon the division of labor in the foundation of the family homestead economy (see Chapter 1, "The Setting: Climate, Geography, and People in South Africa"). For this reason, it was predominantly young men who went off to the mines. Although women had participated in various forms of migrant labor in the towns of the colonial world and would do so increasingly, on the whole, they supported the homestead economy with their agricultural work. As senior men sought to maintain their authority over the homesteads, they sent out their sons to work for wages because this was the least disruptive to the rural society and economy. Their wages could be used for the acquisition of bridewealth cattle, thereby reducing the burden on the fathers to provide it from his herds, or it could be applied to the bridewealth for daughters and therefore, also end up in the fathers' hands. Moreover, migrant labor allowed African men to stay in touch with the culture and traditions of their communities when they regularly return to their rural homes. Over time, it became increasingly important, even necessary, for African migrants to maintain their links to the rural area, and so they oscillated between the towns, where they were prevented from gaining a permanent foothold, and their rural homes. Overall, following the conquest of the African states, most African workers resented and resisted the ways and terms by which they were incorporated into the white-dominated capitalist mining economy more so than the mere fact of their participation in it.

The Chamber set about developing a system of uniform labor recruitment and wages. Yet the mine owners struggled to find sufficient regular supplies of labor at the wage rates they wanted to satisfy their demands. The Chamber first tried to reduce costs by controlling wages at a low level. It bound its members to a maximum wage agreement in 1890 to ensure that no single mine could attract more or better workers than others with higher wages and thus force up wage rates. In this area, they were effective, driving average real wages for Africans down by nearly 50 percent by the turn of the century. This was made possible by finding new sources of labor, intensifying recruitment, and by a sudden downturn in the rural economy. In 1896, the devastating stock disease, rinderpest, hit South Africa. This cattle disease was particularly hard on African herders who did not have access to veterinary help, and for whom the costs of restocking were high. Indeed, the impact of rinderpest lingered for many years; Africans struggled to recoup their losses, they turned up to work in the mines in increasing numbers despite the downward spiral of wages. The Chamber also enlisted the direct support of President Kruger's Transvaal government in labor recruitment and for a pass law which allowed for the apprehension of workers who broke their contracts. When this proved insufficient, the mine owners approached the Portuguese government and won the right to create a single recruitment agency for their Mozambican territory. Mozambique then became the single most important source of African migrant workers for the mines for the next twenty years, supplying over half of the total labor force. There remained, however, for the mining industry the problem of politics in the Transvaal (see Map 7–1 on page 164).

THE POLITICS OF MINING: THE AFRIKANERS, THE BRITISH, AND RHODES

The discovery of gold in the Transvaal threatened Britished interests in the region and would once again draw the imperial factor into the interior. Tensions between the Afrikaners and the British had remained high following the first Anglo-Boer war, and both were deeply suspicious of the other's motives. Many Afrikaners, throughout the country, resented the British for their high-handed imperial policies which ran counter to republican interests. Such sentiments had earlier (see Chapter 6, "The First Phase of South African Industrialization") culminated in the emergence in the Cape of the nascent Afrikaner nationalist political association, the *Bond*. Now the mines suddenly provided Transvaal president Paul Kruger with the means to realize the Afrikaners' aspirations for independence and expansion. Yet, Afrikaner aspirations for expansion challenged imperial and especially Cape interests. First, the Germans, a rival European power which appeared sympathetic to Afrikaner aspirations, gained a foothold on the South West African (now Namibia) coast in 1883. Kruger then approved the annexation from Tswana and Korana chiefs of two minor independent settler states, Stellaland and Goshen. Immediately, British missionaries, traders, and investors claimed that this move threatened their interests along the "road to the north" (i.e., the route into the interior of Africa).

Britain responded by resuming its forward policy of intervention to hem in the Afrikaners. In order to safeguard potential future interests in the region, and to keep a British-controlled route to the interior open, they sent in the troops and annexed British Bechuanaland from some Tswana chiefs. The

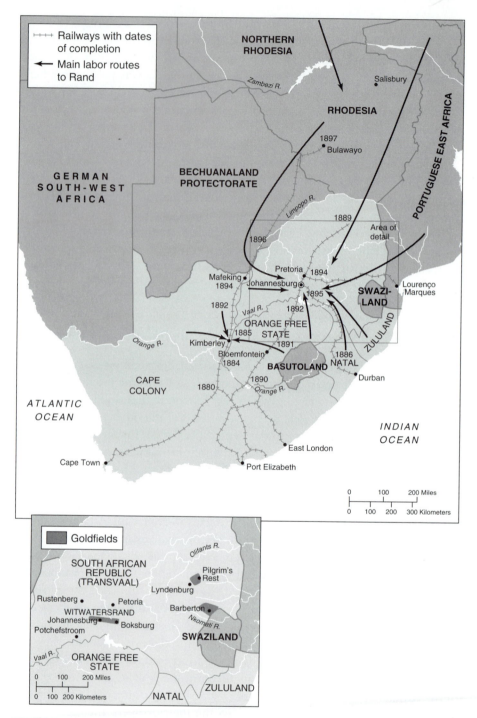

Map 7–1 Transportation and Labor Routes to the Rand Goldfields. *Adapted from Shillington, History of Southern Africa. 1997.*

imperial government made a settlement with the Afrikaners in the London Convention of 1884 which prevented further expansion of the Republic. Six years later, other Tswana chiefs—Sechele, Kgama, and Gaseitswe—were encouraged to apply for British protection from Transvaal expansion. The imperial government was happy to oblige the contrivance and so annexed the territory as the Bechuanaland Protectorate (now Botswana). Later, Kruger made inroads into the Swazi kingdom with the connivance of the British. It was Theophilus Shepstone's son, Offy, who as the supposed advisor to the Swazi king, Mbandine, facilitated the almost wholesale giving away of his country through concessions granted to the Transvaal Afrikaners. The British conceded Transvaal authority over the kingdom which it practically controlled in 1899, but only after they ensured that the Afrikaners had no independent access to the coast.

Kruger worked to enhance Afrikaner power in an independent Transvaal. Although most of the rural settler farmers in the Transvaal were Afrikaners who controlled local politics, Johannesburg and the mines were increasingly overtaken by vast numbers of Africans and whites from other European countries, primarily Britain. While there was no question in the Afrikaners' minds that African workers would be denied political rights, the white outsiders, or *uitlanders* in Afrikaans, posed a threat as a majority block which could vote in the interests of mining rather than for Afrikaner farmers. In order to prevent these fellow whites from gaining political power, Kruger's government quickly passed legislation which increased the residency requirements for whites to vote from five to 14 years with a stiff £25 fee for new citizens. Moreover, Kruger sought to sideline *uitlander* politics by creating a largely powerless local municipal government for the white outsiders only in Johannesburg. Nevertheless, the majority of Afrikaners wanted to ensure mining, and the huge tax revenue which it generated remained productive, and so they passed laws which safeguarded mining interests. At the same time, they wanted to benefit from the profits, even if most Afrikaners remained outside the ranks of the mostly British "Randlords" who owned the mines; nor were the Afrikaners part of the group of well-paid, skilled white miners and managers. Kruger provided for the establishment of monopoly concessions for key sectors of the economy. Soon, Afrikaner investors came to control water delivery, the sale of alcohol, and especially the very lucrative production of dynamite, which was essential for blasting mine shafts. With monopoly control, the Afrikaners were able to drive up their prices to phenomenal levels. At the same time, Kruger's government started to raise customs tariffs and duties on all goods entering the Transvaal, including the already very expensive mining machinery.

Perhaps the greatest threat to British mining interests was the planned railway monopoly. Although British-financed rail lines from the Cape and Natal had progressed into the interior, the Orange Free State and the Transvaal prevented them from penetrating their territory. Kruger felt that if he was to realize Transvaal independence, he would have to find his own route to the sea, free from British control. He granted a monopoly concession to the Netherlands South African Railway Company to link up with a line which originated in Delagoa Bay on the coast of Portuguese Mozambique. When the construction of this line faltered in 1890, however, the Randlords demanded that Kruger allow the British Cape line into the Transvaal in order to keep rising transport costs in check or their industry would collapse. He relented, allowing the Cape line to reach Johannesburg by 1892, but not before ensuring that the independent Mozambique line would be completed as it was in 1894.

Kruger further frustrated British merchants by closing river crossings into the Transvaal to them as they sought to avoid costly rail tariffs by transporting their goods by wagon. Such brinksmanship inflamed the British and threatened to provoke war until Kruger reduced the duties. These policies were intended to favor the rural Afrikaner farmer by raising prices on imported goods and keeping Afrikaner produce competitive. Similarly, another major threat to the mining industry was the Transvaal government's refusal or inability to provide and manage a steady supply of African labor. Indeed, its priority was to ensure that as much African labor as possible was available to the Afrikaners' farms. The Transvaal passed restrictive pass and tenancy laws similar to those in the British colonies which sought to force at least some Africans to remain on white farms while most African workers sought the better and higher-paying jobs in the mines, on the rail lines, and in the city. These policies and the increasingly independent status of the Transvaal provoked a severe British reaction.

The British responses to the mining problems in the Transvaal were driven by two related forces, one based in the Cape politics of Cecil Rhodes, the other in imperial strategies. Rhodes, who left a monumental imprint on southern Africa—from his domination of Cape politics to the establishment of colonies which bore his name (southern and northern Rhodesia, now Zimbabwe and Zambia)—rose quickly from the ranks of diamond mining magnate to Cape prime minister. The sharp-witted, heavy-drinking Rhodes, who played politics hard and fast, had grandiose ambitions and the means to try to realize them. When the Transvaal mines appeared inhospitable to Rhodes and his plans to link the Cape to Cairo faltered, he sought alternative ways of pushing north through the interior. First, he set about cultivating a curious political relationship with the now powerful Afrikaner Bond in the Cape. Hofmeyr, the Bond leader, realized that his supporters could benefit from an alliance with Rhodes, who supported their interests in gaining farm land and in a reduction in Transvaal tariffs which impeded the sale of their goods on the Rand, while Rhodes needed the broader political base which the Bond could provide. Rhodes also appealed to Bond members' desire to unify white interests and to further limit

CECIL RHODES   The archtype of unrestrained imperialism, Rhodes sought to further the British Empire through the engine of mining capitalism. *Source: National Archives of South Africa.*

African political power in the Cape. As he cemented this political alliance, Rhodes sought to further his industrial capitalist base by laying claim to African lands beyond the Transvaal.

Lobengula, who succeeded Mzilikazi as independent king of the Khumalo Ndebele (who were of Zulu origins, as discussed in Chapter 4, "The Making of New States") north of the Limpopo River, was drawn into the ambit of the southern African mining industry by Rhodes. Rhodes and others in the Transvaal believed that the land of the Shona, adjacent to the Ndebele, which had provided the foundation of the ancient gold trade at Great Zimbabwe (see Chapter 1), still contained enough gold to support a second gold reef like the Rand. In order to forestall Transvaal interests in the kingdom, Rhodes first got John Moffat, son of the missionary Robert Moffat who had advised Mzilikazi, to persuade Lobengula not to deal with the Afrikaners. Rhodes then sent two agents, C. Rudd and R. Maguire, to the king. They convinced a nervous Lobengula that his best chance of avoiding an Afrikaner invasion was to accept British "protection." Through deceit and calculated pressure, Rhodes' agents persuaded Lobengula to sign the "Rudd concession." This document gave Rhodes ostensibly only the mineral rights—although he would far exceed the authority conferred in these dubious rights—to the land in the neighboring Shona territory, over which even Lobengula did not have sovereign power.

Rhodes ultimately managed to convert the spurious document into the creation of what amounted to his own private colony. On the basis of the concession, he convinced the imperial government to grant him a royal charter for the British South Africa Company (BSA). The BSA satisfied the British government's desire to see imperial interests furthered without bearing the financial burden. Yet this empire-building by chartered company came at the cost of the loss of all control over the profit-driven cavalier adventurism of Rhodes and his financial backers. In 1890, without any imperial oversight, Rhodes sent a "pioneer column" marching north to establish the BSA capital at Fort Salisbury. By 1893, the BSA realized there was no gold and there would be no second Rand. The company then turned its attentions to the herds and grazing lands of the Ndebele as compensation for its considerable expenditures. The BSA handily won the war it provoked with the Ndebele with the assistance of the deadly Maxim gun. Thereafter, a flood of white settlers swooped in to wrest the land away from both the Ndebele and the Shona people. By 1897, the settlers had brutally suppressed widespread uprisings and established the new colony of Rhodesia, which persisted as a white minority-dominated state until it became the independent Zimbabwe in 1980.

Rhodes was frustrated in the failure of his schemes to the north, but bolstered by his successes in the Cape. He consolidated his political base in the Cape where, with the backing of the Bond, he was elected prime minister in 1890. He set about furthering his alliance with the land-hungry Bondsmen by first supporting Dutch-Afrikaans language legislation, and then working to erode the rights of Africans who might compete against white farmers. In 1892, he introduced what became the Franchise and Ballot Act which raised income and education qualifications for the all-male electorate. This was calculated to exclude African men from the ballot at a time when increasing numbers of African peasants had successfully improved their economic status through selling produce to the expanding Cape markets. In some Cape districts, African peasant voters had even become the majority, and this threatened the white farmers against whom they competed. Rhodes also sought to manipulate land tenure which was the foundation of potentially independent African producers. In 1894 he passed the Glen Grey Act. The aim of the Act was to force African workers off the land and into jobs with a heavy tax while also limiting to ten acres the amount of land Africans could claim. This was intended to prevent Africans from getting sufficient land for voting qualifications. The act was not very effective, and it was limited to just a few districts in the Cape. It did, however, set the foundation for what emerged later as a countrywide system of representative councils for Africans which worked to exclude them from the white-controlled government. Rhodes combined these political maneuvers with unabashed claims about the supposed superiority of the British "race" and civilization and the belief that it had to be extended to the white Afrikaner republics, though not to African people.

Rhodes' ambitions turned again to the Transvaal, where the gold mines, including his own Consolidated Gold Fields, continued to show profits. He found in the *uitlander* community and fellow mine owners what appeared to him as a likely cause upon which build his machinations. As much as the Transvaal Afrikaners resented the British interference which frustrated their independence, the *uitlanders* resented Afrikaner authority even more. Within just a few years of the discovery of the reef, the *uitlanders* had started to agitate against the Afrikaner government. They cried foul at advantages given to Afrikaner farmers, the privileges of monopolies given to Afrikaners businesses, and their effective exclusion from Transvaal politics. Similarly, the mine owners complained of exorbitant costs, an inept Afrikaner bureaucracy, and the inability of the government to provide sufficient cheap labor to satisfy their demands. Rhodes saw these complaints as the foundation for a scheme to instigate an *uitlander* uprising against the Transvaal government. He gained initial approval from his powerful allies in the British imperial government, including his close friend and an investor in Rhodes companies, Hercules Robinson, who was high commissioner for South Africa. His scheme gained momentum when the ardent imperialist, Joseph Chamberlain, took over as secretary of state for the Colonies under a new conservative government in Britain.

Rhodes concocted an elaborate and risky plan known as the Jameson raid. First, he would have his associate, Dr. Leander Jameson, muster a force of British South African police along the border between British Bechuanaland and the Transvaal, claiming the threat of hostile Tswana as the ruse for justifying the assembly of troops. Then, he would arrange for the *uitlanders* to rise in rebellion with the arms which he had smuggled in for them. Rhodes then had a false letter prepared which contained a call from the "women and children" of the *Rand* to the British to come to their rescue during the rising. He planned to leak the letter to the sympathetic Cape press in time to justify the invasion. Finally, none other then the high commissioner, Robinson, was poised to board a train to Johannesburg. He was to arrive just in time to keep the peace by calling for an election of a new assembly by all adult males, which would naturally favor the majority *uitlander* population.

Rhodes' plot ended in miserable failure. The *uitlanders* and mine owners balked and asked for the plan to be postponed. Jameson, however, was determined to go forward and his column advanced into the Transvaal in December 1895 to be met not by cheering supporters, but by Afrikaner troops who surrounded them and, after some killing, forced their surrender. The *uitlanders* had formed a committee for reform, but it was unarmed and could only negotiate with Kruger's government. Rhodes and especially the British imperial government were totally embarrassed, and severely weakened politically. Robinson was forced to travel to Johannesburg, hat in hand, to apologize and plead for leniency for Jameson's troops and the reform rebels. While Chamberlain denounced Rhodes and denied all complicity in the poorly executed plot, Rhodes was forced to resign as prime minister of the Cape. Nevertheless, Rhodes had his day. In the wake of the foiled rising, Kruger's government, which had shown remarkable mercy to the raiders and rebels, was riding high on its success at foiling the rising. Kruger happily received congratulations from the German Kaiser. This appeared to many as evidence of an Afrikaner-German alliance, and it served to swing British and Cape popular opinion positively back to Rhodes as the hero of imperialism. Rhodes saved his public reputation and his charter for the BSA by riding the wave of British patriotism and imperial jingoism and by threatening to reveal Chamberlain's role in the plot. The overall effect of Jameson's raid was simply to sharpen tensions between the Transvaal and the British as both sides now had apparent cause to assert their own nationalist interests in the face of the other's obvious hostility.

THE SOUTH AFRICAN WAR OR THE SECOND ANGLO-BOER WAR

Buoyed by the failure of the Jameson raid, the Transvaal Afrikaners declared war in October 1899 in response to escalating pressure from the British. Just as the Afrikaners were as determined as ever to assert their independence, the British imperialists were committed to subduing the Transvaal government. The new high commissioner for South Africa, Alfred Milner, arrived in 1897 with considerable imperial experience and a resolute dedication to furthering the political and economic interests of what he and others referred to as the "British race" over the Afrikaner and African "races" (his theory of race types was gaining momentum in imperial circles in South Africa at this time, but of course this racist ideology flies in the face of what we now know are the inconsequentially small genetic differences which are manifest in the range of appearances of our one human race).

Milner took it upon himself to pre-empt any peaceful resolution of tensions. In the same way that arch local imperialists such as Frere and Shepstone had provoked war with the Zulu, Milner whipped up propaganda to convince the imperial government that war was essential. He used renewed *uitlander* agitation for political rights in the Transvaal, and the growing concerns of the mine owners over the needs of the gold industry, to force President Kruger

AFRIKANERS DURING THE SOUTH AFRICAN WAR   Afrikaner republicans posed a challenge to British imperial designs. *Source: National Archives of South Africa.*

into negotiations. Although Kruger made some significant concessions by allowing for an extension of the franchise to the *uitlanders,* he would not accept British supremacy over the Transvaal. The latter proved to be the issue on which Milner would not compromise. Milner had also ensured imperial support for his plan by relaying inflammatory petitions from the *uitlanders* back to London. He and Chamberlain then prepared to issue an ultimatum to Kruger as they called for British troops to start massing in South Africa. Paradoxically, this South African war simultaneously set the stage for the shaping of a white-dominated state and the rise of the conquered and embittered Afrikaner nationalists.

The Afrikaners sought to take quick advantage of their momentary military advantage, but the war soon bogged down into a bloody and vicious affair. Until the bulk of the imperial army arrived, the Afrikaners had a larger force than the standing British compliment of about 20,000 and it was well-armed, thanks to imports from Germany. The Afrikaner forces took the early offensive and struck into Natal and the Cape, but to the frustration of one of their leading generals (and later prime minister of the country), Jan Smuts, they did not press this advantage. Nevertheless, the Afrikaners gained momentum as fellow Afrikaners in the British territories rose to join the cause. The British forces were stalled at Ladysmith, Kimberley, and Mafeking, where Lord Baden-Powell, founder of the Scouting movement, was lionized for a heroic defense despite his apparent lack of confidence.

In early 1900, Generals Roberts and Kitchener arrived with massive numbers of imperial reinforcements, including troops from Canada, New Zealand, and Australia, to join the South African colonist forces—the total imperial compliment reached nearly 500,000 over the two and a half years of the war—and they started the push into the Transvaal. Substantial numbers of Africans were involved on both sides. While the Afrikaners enforced a policy of not arming Africans, many African women and men were employed to help with collecting and transporting materials and food and in building defenses. On the British side, there may have been up to 30,000 African fighting men. Many of them joined the imperial forces in the hopes of ensuring a fair dispensation if they won since the British had often claimed Afrikaner ill treatment of Africans as one justification for the war.

Early on, the Afrikaner forces collapsed and withdrew in the face of the British war machine, but they quickly re-emerged to draw out the war. The Afrikaners undertook a different strategy of guerrilla warfare, using the hit-and-run tactics of the commando even though this ultimately provoked brutal British reprisals. Afrikaner women also played an important role in combat and intelligence networks, as they had done previously in countless frontier battles. The commandos were very effective against the more formal European style of British engagement in battle. They struck at railroads and trains, and as the British pursued them, they would lead them far away from the former's reinforcements, only to turn back and strike the British again. Frustrated in their inability to capture or contain the commandos, the British reacted with a severe scorched earth policy and a new range of dirty tactics. Everywhere the commandos went, British troops burned Afrikaner farms, destroying not only supplies but also the livelihoods of noncombatants. Afrikaner civilians claimed that the British committed horrendous atrocities of rape and other brutalities, which fueled a woman's protest movement. The British, moreover, dragged civilians into the melee by forcing hostages to ride the trains as a deterrent to Afrikaner attacks. The harshest British tactic, and the one that perhaps deepened the Afrikaners' bitterness and sense of injustice the most, was the use of concentration camps.

The British forced both Africans and Afrikaners into segregated camps where conditions were appalling, even more so for Africans who received fewer rations. The prisoners suffered horrendous rates of mortality from harsh treatment, (especially Afrikaner prisoners who had relatives who were still fighting) poor rations, and spiraling rates of disease. Nearly 28,000 Afrikaners, mostly women and children, and more than 14,000 Africans lost their lives in the camps from measles and dysentery. Understandably, after the British humanitarian agitator Emily Hobhouse and others exposed them, the camps became a major scandal for the imperial forces who had claimed, but clearly lost, the moral high ground in the war. While the Afrikaners' commandos managed to hold out until early 1902, they did so at a considerable cost. They lost the war to attrition not just in battle, but also among their families who struggled to survive famine. Overall, the war exacted a terrible toll in life, material goods, and relations between British and Afrikaners. In many respects, the war was the high water mark of direct British imperial intervention and following its conclusion, the British retreated from the scene, leaving the state in the hands of white settlerdom. Although the Africans had participated in and suffered from the war, they gained little in the end. The war was fought to settle white concerns about power, and the overall effect on the Africans was their increasing subordination to the imperatives of white supremacy and capitalism.

PEACE, RECONSTRUCTION, AND THE BUILDING OF THE WHITE STATE

The peace, established in the Treaty of Vereeniging in May 1902, set the stage for conciliation with the Afrikaners, an imperial retreat from their internal affairs, and for creating the conditions favorable to the mining industry. Significantly, it also meant the abandonment of African political rights and an intensification of controls for African workers by a unified white state. The peace treaty stipulated that the franchise for African men—there was still no sign in any world democracy of extending the vote to women—would be dependent upon the consent of the local governing body once responsible government was restored. This amounted to a betrayal of African interests, since for the whites-only governments of the Orange River Free State and the Transvaal as well as in British Natal, the refusal to extend the African vote was a foregone conclusion. Milner addressed the issue of a policy for Africans by appointing the South African Native Affairs Commission (SANAC) in 1903.

The SANAC made recommendations for a more overt and rigid separation of African and whites both in terms of land ownership and politics; these recommendations had far-reaching implications for the development of later segregation policy. Moreover, the process of reconstruction after the war supported the integration of the state and the mines. Milner, who remained in South Africa until 1905, tried to ensure that the British victory brought with it the ability to shape a British-dominated country which would attract more British settlers and support the growth of mining and industry. He and his Oxford University-trained advisors, who were referred to as a "kindergarten" because of their youth and enthusiastic support of the mine owners, tried to delay the restoration of responsible government to the Afrikaners and to undermine their power with plans to overwhelm them with British immigrants. They failed on both counts. First, British immigration, while increasing somewhat to the Cape and Natal, never reached the levels needed to swamp the Transvaal Afrikaners. Second, imperial authorities came to believe that responsible government was essential for ensuring white colonial support for unification.

White politicians in South Africa soon realized that political unification was vital for their respective interests, all of which centered on supporting mining and controlling African labor. Indeed, increasing challenges from below, especially the Bambatha rebellion in Natal in 1906 (see the discussion in "African Resistance and African Labor"), and many miners' strikes made it clear to British and Afrikaners alike that they needed to create a united white front against potential African challenges. By 1907, a new liberal administration in London provided for the Orange Free State and the Transvaal to have responsible governments. In the Transvaal, Louis Botha and Jan Smuts, both distinguished generals in the war, rose to prominence as leaders of the *Het Volk* ("The People") party. They played upon Afrikaner nationalist sentiments of anti-imperialism to win the election, but they soon realized there was much to be gained by cooperating with the mining interests. They saw cooperation as a means of ensuring Transvaal prosperity through taxation, which could help their chief supporters, the Afrikaner farmers. Indeed, *Het Volk* supported the mine owners to the extent of calling in imperial forces to suppress a white miners' strike in 1907. Similarly, J. B. Hertzog, a shrewd Afrikaner ideologue, formed the *Orangia Unie* (United Orange) party and led it to power in the Free State's responsible government.

In the Cape, an anti-imperialist, J. X. Merriman, inherited the Afrikaner Bond support and won the Cape for his South Africa party, which relied on a local British and Afrikaner alliance, while F. R. Moor, who supported unification with the other colonies, won a crucial election in Natal in 1906. By 1908, these leaders were discussing the best ways to overcome the problems of competing rail and customs tariffs, which drove costs up and inhibited development, as well as how to follow through on the recommendations of the SANAC for limiting African access to land and political power. In the interim, Milner and the transitional imperial government had set about ensuring that the mining industry would prevail. After the war, they provided for the increased integration of transport networks, limited taxation, and the reduction of customs duties, which would smooth the flow of goods and improve mining.

These politicians believed that a union was the most expedient way to deal with ensuring that the whites would rule and profit from the South African economy as they controlled the African labor within it. Delegates from each colony met at a constitutional convention in Durban to hammer out the necessary compromises which would ensure white political unity and safeguard the mining industry. They provided for a unitary state along parliamentary lines, over the objections of Natal, which hoped for some sort of federal relationship to preserve its unique British flavor, and for the acceptance of Dutch (later Afrikaans) as well as English as the official languages. The most contentious issue to be resolved was the non-racial Cape franchise. The Cape delegates argued passionately that its franchise, which allowed any man, white or black, to vote if he was literate and had at least £50 a year income, must be preserved and extended to the whole country. In a shoddy compromise that was a severe blow to African voters, the convention allowed the Cape to keep its color-blind franchise and protected it from alteration without a two-thirds majority in parliament, but prohibited blacks from being elected to the central parliament. To achieve a check against potential domination by urban centers and industry, the electoral divisions and process favored dispersed white rural voters, and this would be important for future elections. The convention finally agreed on the terms of the South Africa Act of 1909 and sent delegates to London for the official ratification of the constitution, but they were not alone.

AFRICAN RESISTANCE AND AFRICAN LABOR

By this time, a group of influential, Western-educated elite Africans organized the Native National Convention to protest the limits on the Cape franchise. This set the stage for new and wider ranges of protest and resistance from Africans, who were simultaneously excluded from political power as they were more forcibly incorporated into subordinated positions in white south Africa. From the mid-1880s, African opposition political and social movements started to spring up, including a whole host of African separatist independent churches such as N. Tile's Thembu Church, new African education associations and, more importantly, African language newspapers such as John Jabavu's Xhosa *Imvo Zabantsundu* ("Voice of the People"). Moreover, Africans such as the Western-educated Sol Plaatje, who wrote a moving account of African suffering during the war, argued that Africans should be recognized for their contributions and be granted rights accordingly The Native National Convention sent John Jabavu and W. Rubusana as delegates to London to press for the extension of the African vote. Jabavu and Rubusana were joined by Dr. A. Abdurahman of the African People's Organization (APO), which represented Coloured people, and this marked the beginning of new forms of African protest politics. Their protests fell on deaf ears, however, and despite considerable support from liberal politicians, the British parliament abandoned any attempt to further a non-racial political system in South Africa. In May 1910, the new Union of South Africa was formed with Loius Botha as the first prime minister of the white state. As we shall see in Chapter 8, "From Union to Apartheid: The Consolidation of a White State and the Rise of African Opposition, 1910–1948," as the Union shut out and stonewalled even conservative-minded elite Africans from most of the avenues of meaningful political participation, the many African opposition movements gained momentum.

As white politicians worked to ensure their supremacy, the mines were busy enhancing their power. The critical factor of production for the mines was labor. Following the war, the Chamber of Mines tightened and stream- lined its recruitment and control of African labor. Yet it first had to counter the movement for a white labor policy which threatened to drive up costs. In the aftermath of the war, many poor whites in the Transvaal lost access to land altogether and became *bywoners* or poor tenants. They struggled, often ineffec- tively, to compete against African peasants and tenants whom the white land- lords found easier to exploit than landless whites with the vote. As a result, some government officials and F. Creswell, a mine owner, recommended that African mine workers be replaced by poor whites and not surprisingly, the idea was very popular among white workers. The Chamber, however, rejected the ideas because it knew the white workers could not be controlled or exploited as easily as the African migrant workers.

The whites demanded higher wages on the basis of being skilled and hav- ing to maintain an entire family in a "civilized" lifestyle. In contrast, the African migrant workers were expected to subsidize their earnings by relying on what extra money they could derive from their families' agricultural and pastoral production in the rural areas. Moreover, Africans had no political rights and were subjected to pass laws and other discriminatory legislation in a rigorous labor discipline which clearly could not be imposed on whites. In the end, the Chamber argued effectively to keep strict limits on the number of whites engaged in mining, in part by later establishing a stringent color-bar which preserved select categories of higher paid "skilled work" for whites only. While whites were employed for these special jobs above ground, increasing numbers of Africans were employed for arduous underground work.

Despite state support and white political power, the mines struggled to se- cure adequate sources of labor. In the short term, the tightening of pass law en- forcement, which helped bind the Africans in the country to a fixed white employer, and increasing taxation did not produce the desired results. This was in part because many Africans still had access to sufficient land to allow them to meet cash and tax needs through their own peasant agricultural production. It was also in part because the rural whites siphoned off much of the available African labor before it could reach the mines. Since African workers were not coming forth from within South Africa, the mines looked elsewhere. In 1901, Milner renegotiated an agreement with the Portuguese Mozambique govern- ment to allow the mines to recruit migrant workers there in exchange for di- rect fees paid in gold and preferential rates for the Delagoa Bay-Johannesburg rail line.

The Chamber of Mines created the centralized monopoly of the Witwa- tersrand Native Labor Association, which had complete control over recruiting outside the country. It had considerable success, providing up to 60 percent of the mines' total black labor force, with an annual average entry of 50,000 Mozambican migrant workers. Still, the harsh working conditions, the increasing length of time which the workers had to spend fulfilling contracts, and especially the low wages served to discourage black South Africans from working in the mines. Indeed, following the war, the Chamber instituted an across-the-board wage cut for Africans. Later in 1912, it instituted an industry-wide limit to African wages with the creation of the maximum average wage per shift, and it extended its control of recruitment with the creation of the Native Recruiting Corporation, which pulled in workers from all of the British colonies of southern Africa.

Over time, the mine owners found more coercive means of forcing Africans to work for them, including support for segregation legislation (see Chapter 8), and the payment of advances on wages to recruits from the rural areas where impoverishment hit hard. The advances had the effect of creating debt bondage since the payments were made to the worker's family, often in cattle for bridewealth, and the employee was then expected to work this off at wage rates far below what could sustain him and his family. Finally, until a durable, uniform policy for recruiting and controlling African workers in South Africa could be hammered out, the mine owners turned to another outside source of labor. Just as the Natal government had earlier imported indentured Indians, the Chamber started to import Chinese workers. As with African migrant workers, the Chinese were viewed in racist terms as easily exploitable unskilled labor. The mine owners had learned another racist lesson from Natal and its frustration over Indian migrants settling in the country, so the Chamber of Mines prevented the nearly 60,000 imported Chinese workers from gaining rights to stay in the country after their contracts ended. The Chinese workers were very unpopular with both the white workers who resented the potential competition, and the British humanitarian lobby which protested against their conditions of employment. Still, the Chinese provided the labor necessary to get the mines back on their feet after the war until the state and Chamber could implement the more comprehensive means of economic and legislative coercion which was the hallmark of the segregation era. Yet, the consolidation of white rule under the control of the settler-dominated local states served to provoke opposition and even outright rebellion.

The most explosive force to respond to increasing pressure from the settler-dominated political block came in the form of the 1906 Bambatha rebellion in Natal and Zululand. Once the British granted to Natal a responsible government (which provided for an locally elected legislative assembly and prime minister in control of local affairs and finances, but which kept colonial matters in the hands of the imperial government) in 1893, the colony intensified its efforts to force Africans off the land and into working for whites. Land companies started to evict increasing numbers of African tenants from their holdings, which they turned to commercial purposes, especially sugar cane. Moreover, the Natal government managed to get imperial agreement to carve up and throw open to white settlers a large part of the recently conquered Zulu territory.

Although it took some time for Africans to be pushed off these lands, the anticipation of the loss served to heighten African resentment. This measure was part of the rather paranoid Natal settler agenda to undermine any possible recrudescence of Zulu royal power which they had feared. These fears had grown since the return of the Zulu king, Dinuzulu, whom the British had placed in exile following the civil war (see Chapter 6) and who might serve as a rallying point for African opposition. Natal officials also deposed legitimate chiefs within the Shepstone system for even minor infractions, thereby creating resentment. The final straw for Africans came in the form of a poll tax on all African men who were not already paying a hut tax. It was designed to force even more men out to work, but Africans saw it as overly burdensome since it aimed to end their economic independence. By early 1906, many rural Africans in Natal and Zululand were refusing to pay the tax. A heavy-handed Natal response led to some disturbances where protestors killed two white policemen. Soon rumors circulated on both sides. Whites were convinced that Africans were about to embark on a mass uprising. Africans looked to a reluctant Dinuzulu as a symbol of unity and powerful resistance as they embraced millenarian visions of revival through the purging of white settler-introduced tools and animals such as pigs. Whites were unnecessarily terrified when Africans started the mass slaughter of pigs in part because they believed that lard could be used to draw lightening to strike tax collectors.

It was the brutal response from Natal authorities to these otherwise minor protests which actually provoked a wider rebellion. Officials sent a large force of police after Chief Bambatha when he refused to heed a summons for his arrest due to his inability to get all his followers to pay the tax. After taking a short refuge with Dinuzulu, he returned to his chiefdom only to find he had been deposed. He rose in open rebellion and again retreated to the deep forests of Zululand, where a large number of followers joined him. Many of his fellow rebels were younger men who may have sought to use the rebellion as a means of challenging the patriarchal authority of fathers and chiefs who cooperated with colonial officials in order to retain their control over the youth. After a few minor skirmishes, the Natal forces moved in to crush the rebels in Zululand. Thereafter, the Natal government not only mopped up the few remaining rebel groups in other areas, it also engaged in a wholesale repression of African society.

Natal forces seized thousands of African cattle, torched entire villages and fields, and killed more than three thousand Africans. In stark contrast, fewer than thirty whites—soldiers and civilians—had died in the fighting. The

DINUZULU, KING OF THE ZULUS The Zulu kings struggled to balance resistance to colonial rule with dependence on colonial power. *Source: National Arcives of South Africa.*

effects of the rebellion were significant. In one way, the rebels achieved an indirect success because they forced the whites to recognize that there were limits to how far the Africans could be pushed. In other ways, however, the rebellion failed and served only white interests. Although Dinuzulu had made a concerted effort to avoid supporting the rebels and had even offered assistance in rooting out the rebels, he was still condemned as a symbol of dangerous African resistance. He was imprisoned and then later released by his childhood friend, Louis Botha, the first prime minister. Dinuzulu died in exile in the Transvaal in 1913. Following the brutal suppression of the uprising, more Africans were turned off the land and the Natal government enforced tax and pass laws even more rigorously. This achieved the desired effect of increasing the number of African workers going to the Transvaal from the region by nearly 60 percent. By the time of Union, as much as 80 percent of adult African men from Natal and Zululand were engaged in migrant labor.

Conclusion

Gold mining shifted the spatial focus of political and economic activity in South Africa to the city of Johannesburg and the Rand. Mining capitalists required new forms of investment and production including the development of a cheap, easily controlled African work force to offset the high costs of white labor and machinery. The old imperial imperatives for unification re-emerged as industrial capitalists sought to ensure their control over the phenomenally profitable gold industry. What emerged was a powerful block of mining capitalists in the form of the Chamber of Mines which was eventually able to secure the cooperation of the state to ensure its profitability. Yet there were significant obstacles in the way. Not least of these was the apparent resistance of fellow whites in the Transvaal, the Afrikaners. Clearly, industrial capitalism was more concerned with profits than it was with racial solidarity.

Both the British and the Afrikaners then couched their agendas in a new form of ethnic "racial" consciousness which pitted the two against each other and led to the South African war. The driving force behind this war was the combination of imperial strategists who saw the independent Transvaal as a threat to British interests, and local industrialists, led by Rhodes, who saw the Afrikaners as a threat to the continued success of gold mining. The war was particularly nasty and probably an unnecessary affair, with atrocities committed on both sides. It was the Afrikaners, however, who ended up harboring a justified sense of bitterness and resentment of the British after the war, and this would have particular importance for the course of white politics thereafter. Ultimately, the war achieved sufficient agreement on the conditions of white unity and control to provide for the domination of Africans. The last vestiges of imperial humanitarian safeguards for African rights and interests were abandoned in favor of white settler control of the unified country. Africans, however, would not sit passively by as they were increasingly subordinated to the demands of white settlers and the mining industry. There were indications of growing African opposition and resistance to white rule but there was as yet no united front. The Bambatha rebellion did not draw together the wide range of African interests, such as chiefs and rural peasants, migrant workers, and Western-educated African elite, which might have made it a more effective movement. Nevertheless, Africans had started to respond in new ways to the increasing pressure and reactionary tactics of the white state and capital.

QUESTIONS TO CONSIDER

1. How did gold mining accelerate the processes of change that were underway in South Africa and what ambitions did Rhodes see being helped by these processes?
2. What impact did gold mining have on African migrant labor?
3. How did the expansion of industrial capitalism in mining change the relations between the British and the Afrikaner and African states of the interior?
4. Why did the British precipitate the Anglo-Boer war and what effect did it have on white politics in the country?

5. How did Africans respond to the consolidation of white rule following the end of the Anglo-Boer war and what were the different ways they could resist the demands of the mine owners and the white state?

FURTHER READINGS

BEINART, W., and BUNDY, C., *Hidden Struggles in Rural South Africa: Politics and Popular Movements in the Transkei and Eastern Cape, 1890–1930* (London, 1987). A detailed collection of essays analyzing the range of forms of resistance to white expansion and the dispossession of Africans in the rural areas by the two leading historians of African rural societies.

CARTON, B., *Blood From Your Children: The Colonial Origins of Generational Conflict in South Africa* (Charlottesville and London, 2000). Carton provides a fresh look at the tensions and issues surrounding the Bambatha rebellion. He considers generational tension as a key factor in the uprising, and he shows how lines were drawn between those who supported and those who opposed the resistance to colonial pressure in Natal.

CRUSH, J., JEEVES, A., and YUDELMAN, D., *South Africa's Labor Empire: A History of Black Migrancy to the Gold Mines* (Montreal, 1991). A comprehensive analysis of the nature of gold mining and how it drew in black labor from the entire southern African region. It provides political, economic, and geographic analysis in a well-researched book.

JEEVES, A., *Migrant Labor in South Africa's Mining Economy: The Struggle for the Gold Mines' Labour Supply, 1890–1920* (Kingston, 1985). An authoritative analysis of the motives and means of migrant labor in the mining industry. Jeeves provides great insights into the entire nexus of mine labor recruitment in the region and why it persisted as a labor regimen.

MARKS, S., *Reluctant Rebellion* (London, 1970). This groundbreaking work by a leading scholar on Natal-Zululand and South African history is an analysis of the patterns of pressure and resistance which led to the 1906 African uprising known as the Bambatha rebellion in Natal. Marks has provided an insightful explanation of the events and an excellent analysis of black-white relations in the region.

MARKS, S., and RATHBONE, R., *Industrialization and Social Change in South Africa, 1870–1930* (London, 1982). This is an excellent collection of essays covering everything from the nature of mining to African society and culture to gender issues. It is still essential reading for the period in question.

MAYLAM, P., *Rhodes, the Tswana, and the British* (London 1980). A well-crafted analysis of Rhodes policies and the impact on the Tswana. Maylam writes clearly and concisely, and his work brings out the importance of the African initiative in the story of unfolding imperialism.

NASSON, W., *Abraham Esau's War: A Black South African War in the Cape, 1899–1902* (Cape Town, 1991). A fascinating study of another dimension to the impact of the war on people not directly involved in the imperial dimension. Nasson provides great insights into the implications of the war for the status of blacks.

NASSON, W., *The South African War, 1899–1902* (New York, 1999). A new look at the war and its importance for world history. It does an excellent job of deconstructing identities for both Boers and British in the conflict and explaining how each side changed tactics and policies as the war unfolded. It is a concise and readable new analysis.

ODENDAAL, A., *Vukani Bantu! The Beginnings of Black Protest Politics in South Africa to 1912* (London, 1984). A comprehensive look at the rise of black opposition and the various strands of protest politics in the country. It captures both the complexity and passion of African and Coloured ideals and their early struggle for equality.

PAKENHAM, T., *The Boer War* (London, 1979). One of the best overall accounts of the war and its implications. It is particularly sensitive to Afrikaner ideals and the impact of the camps on them, but it does not give as much coverage to Africans as it should.

PLAATJE, S., *Boer War Diary*, edited by J. Commaroff (Chicago, 1973). A black man's perspective on the war and the impact it had on blacks. Plaatje wrote movingly of black concerns and experiences in this and other works.

ROTBERG, R., *The Founder: Cecil Rhodes and the Pursuit of Power* (New York, 1988). A comprehensive and well-researched biography. Rotberg not only encapsulates and builds upon other biographies of Rhodes, he also provides a clear sense of the context in which he emerged.

WARWICK, P., *Black People and the South African War, 1899–1902* (Cambridge, 1983). A good guide to the roles which blacks played in the war, and the impact it had on them. It covers a range of people and their relationship to the politics and economics of imperialism at the time.

CHAPTER VIII

From Union to Apartheid: The Consolidation of a White State and the Rise of African Opposition, 1910–1948

In the first four decades of the twentieth century, the compromises and accommodations made by the whites provided a unified front for dealing with the Africans. The new settler-dominated government created comprehensive legislation to address the changed social and economic circumstances in South Africa. Within the context of the expanding capitalist economy of mining and commercial farming, race and a perceived racial hierarchy became increasingly important. The state developed a broad set of policies based on the intersection of race and class in which, increasingly, dark skin would be associated with manual work and lower status. This came to be known as segregation. Segregation policies were derived from a range of mutually supporting ideas about race, many of which were in vogue in other parts of the world, including in America and in colonies in India, Asia, and elsewhere in Africa. These included whites' economic demands for a cheap black ("black" is a term which came to include African, Coloured, and Indian South Africans as a term of solidarity for all those who suffered racial oppression) labor force, racist "scientific" notions about the perceived differences between whites, Africans, Coloureds, and Indians, and the reworking of ideas about "white supremacy" and ethnic identities.

Although there were contradictions inherent in segregation policies, the state worked to reconcile these. The state, for example, believed that it was imperative to maintain the profits from industrial capitalism in order to fund the development of the country. Yet, at the same time, class differences among whites were suppressed to a certain extent as the government continued to privilege whites. The state used mining profits to help support rural white farmers, many of whom grew maize (corn) and who represented the most powerful political block in the country. This was referred to as the "alliance between maize and gold." Tensions and conflicts in white politics came to reflect the cultural differences between the English- and Afrikaans-speaking groups. Overall, however, white society set aside these differences for the sake of a united front against the greater numbers of black people. This enabled the white minority, which numbered some 1.25 million people in 1910, to dominate the African majority of about four million people, as well as half a million Coloured and 150,000 Indian people. Thus, "white power" settled like a blanket over the country, suffocating independent African producers and aspiring elite African political leaders as well as Indian professionals and market gardeners and Coloured workers and farmers.

Segregation also meant strict limits on the place of Africans in the Union. Most British South Africans abandoned the ideals of the civilizing mission or became less convinced of their efficacy. Instead, they clung to the imperatives of the white-dominated state and the economy just as the Afrikaners used political power as the vehicle for their own upliftment. In contrast, the trend for increasing numbers of Africans was to be torn from the land and forced into various forms of migrant wage labor. Despite the very real success of many Africans in coming to terms with the colonial world, they remained frustrated in their aspirations. Those Africans who had embraced Christianity and then had used it as a means to gain Western education, improve their farming, and engage in professional work were to be barred from upward mobility.

Similarly, those Africans who sought to retain their economic independence in the rural areas found themselves squeezed off their land and forced into burdensome tenancy arrangements on white farms, or into poorly paid migrant wage labor. In both cases, segregation required them to retain certain features of their traditional way of life with a stake in the rural areas reserved for them. Yet, while Africans were expected to persist with a traditional way of life under their chiefs, everything else had changed and strongly conspired against those traditions. As Africans were incorporated into the white-dominated capitalist economy, they had to work for wages to buy goods and pay taxes, thereby reducing the labor they could apply to their own homesteads. Their chiefs no longer represented African interests; they had to serve the white state. The central feature of the state plan to reconfigure African lives was the perpetuation of the migrant labor system through the reduction of the amount of land available for exclusive African use. This contributed to the process of proletarianization (the creation of a wage worker who can only sell his or her labor and has no means of producing an independent income) and over the years it would lead to millions of African workers going to the cities of

South Africa in search of work and a place to live. Yet Africans, Coloureds, and Indians sought to shape and resist these processes of subordination with multiple and sometimes overlapping strategies.

White Politics and the State

The first Union government, led by the former Afrikaner generals, Botha and Smuts (as his deputy), struggled with white political unity. They worked to accommodate a wide range of white political interests in their South African National party, including white farmers and professionals, but they were opposed in the white parliament (the legacy of the British imperial system) by the industrialist-supporting Unionist party and the small Labor party, which represented the white workers. Botha and Smuts worked perhaps too hard at reconciling English- and Afrikaans-speaking interests, and so they faced dissent from within. J. B Hertzog, the staunch Afrikaner republican from the Free State, joined Botha and Smuts as the new Minister of Justice. He resented the conciliatory gestures which Botha and Smuts had made to the English-speakers and also what appeared to him as efforts to keep close links with imperial Britain. His concerns coincided with the increasing immigration of predominately British English-speakers. Hertzog and his supporters feared that the Afrikaners would be swamped by the English language and culture. The political reality in South Africa, however, was that Afrikaners made up more than 55 percent of the total white electorate (although in Natal, British men made up the electoral majority), and so the Afrikaners dominated parliamentary politics just as the British dominated industry.

Eventually, Hertzog undermined Botha's bid to win re-election by arguing that South Africa should be run only by true Afrikaners. Hertzog precipitated a split in the party, and in 1914, he formed the National Party, while Botha and Smuts simplified their party name to the South Africa Party (SAP). Hertzog's National party gave voice and a national political platform to the rising Afrikaner nationalism. The Afrikaner ideologues set about forging a political and social identity based upon their common language, their shared bitterness over British atrocities during the war, the loss of their independence, and an invented mythology derived from their memories of the Great Trek and a covenant with God. The National Party's message appealed to a wide range of Afrikaners, including professionals who resented British control over the economy and especially farmers who wanted state support in getting control of more African labor. The National Party appeal soon proved successful, not least because the electoral system disproportionately favored rural Afrikaners.

The government of Botha and Smuts steadily lost Afrikaner support as it faced new challenges both locally and internationally. The first challenges came from white miners who sought to safeguard and extend their positions of privilege in the face of economic downturns and a hostile state. As we have seen, in 1907, before the South African war, the Transvaal government suppressed a strike by white miners who wanted to ensure that certain categories of skilled work, such as blasting and the supervision of drilling teams, remained open to whites exclusively. Many white miners had pressed for the extension of this color bar after they had successfully applied it to imported Chinese labor (see Chapter 7, "The Second Phase of South African Industrialization: Gold Mining and the Creation of a Unified Write State").

The state provided for the extension of the color bar indirectly in the 1911 Mines and Works Act, which required certification for certain jobs. Certification was, in practice, provided only to whites because of the formal education qualifications. In contrast, the 1911 act also inhibited African workers from organizing unions or striking. In 1913, white miners began to organize unions to represent their interests in negotiations with mine management. While some workers' organizations and unions did stretch across the racial divide, allowing African, Indian, Coloured and white workers to organize and even strike together, the actions of the state and the mine owners, as well as other events, conspired against this kind of non-racial working-class solidarity. In the case of the 1913 action, the white workers demanded recognition for their unions, but they did not extend this demand to their fellow African workers. When some mine owners rejected the demand, the white miners went on a strike which quickly spread and then exploded into open riots. The Botha-Smut's government's use of imperial troops to quell the strike, combined with too few concessions to the strikers, provoked further action. In early 1914, even more white workers, from the coal mines in Natal to the Cape railways to the gold mines, went out on a national strike. This time, Smuts invoked martial law, which allowed him to suspend people's rights in order to crush the strike. Smuts later argued that his actions were necessary to restore order and security; this led to the later Riotous Assemblies Act (1930) which would be used against African strikers.

Afrikaners viewed Smuts and Botha with even greater suspicion during the outbreak of World War I. In 1914, the British imperial government called upon South Africa, as a self-governing member of the empire, to side with it against the Germans. Botha and Smuts not only agreed to support the empire, they also acceded to British requests to lead South African troops against the Germans in their adjacent colony of South West Africa. Many Afrikaners, recalling the South African war, were sympathetic to the German cause, and certainly were anti-British. They called for at least South African neutrality if not outright support of the Germans, and they rose in rebellion as Smuts started to invade South West Africa. With imperial support, Smuts took the German colony and brutally crushed the Afrikaner rebellion. Largely because of Smuts' international statesmanship and his role in formulating the postwar League of Nations, South Africa took over South West Africa (which became independent Namibia in 1990) as a League mandate territory following World War I. South Africa then drew African people of the territory into the ambit of its political economy and applied the same discriminatory policies.

Afrikaners resented Smuts' role in supporting the British cause and especially for crushing the rebellion, and this fueled even greater Afrikaner nationalist aspirations. By the end of the war, the SAP was fast losing ground to Afrikaner nationalists. Many Afrikaners became increasingly concerned not only with what appeared to them to be government favoritism for the British at home and abroad, but also with the plight of poor Afrikaners who suffered in comparison with well-off English-speaking capitalists. They felt it was the state's duty to support whites as a special social group over blacks and to save them from poverty. In 1918, leading Afrikaner professionals and academics formed a secret organization, the *Broederbond* ("Brotherhood"), or *Bond,* aimed at protecting Afrikaners, their language, and culture. As we have seen, however, they shared these social features as well as a common genetic heritage with the Coloured people of the Cape, although they were not prepared to extend their cause to include them.

Afrikaners also worked to extend and enhance their cause and support for each other. Wealthy Afrikaners founded a nationalist Afrikaans language newspaper, *Die Burger* ("the Citizen"), as well as insurance and investment companies aimed specifically at poor Afrikaners' needs. The continued problems of white labor unrest and government repression led to greater Afrikaner opposition. Over the war years, as wealthy white farmers sought to make more productive use of their land, they turned off increasing numbers of poor whites as well as Africans. These landless people flocked to the cities in search of work, especially in the mines where wages were high. During the war, many white workers were absorbed into the armed forces, and so the skilled jobs they held in the mines were taken over by African workers. By 1918, the white workers had pressured the mine owners to agree that no African should take a white man's job. At the end of the war, however, the mine owners faced rising costs and a drop in the fixed price of gold. Since one of the largest costs to the mines was white wages—on average, whites were paid twelve times more than Africans—the mine owners decided to allow more Africans who could be paid less into skilled jobs, thus contravening the 1918 agreement.

In 1922, Afrikaner workers responded to threats to their employment status by staging a massive strike. The strike expanded into the "Rand Revolt" as the striking workers took over the entire mining area and Johannesburg. They flew a banner which, borrowing from but misrepresenting non-racial communist traditions, called for "workers of the world to unite and for a white South Africa." Although the Communist Party of South Africa (CPSA was disbanded in 1950 and reformed as the South African Communist Party SACP), formed in 1921, had a white leadership and membership, it was already shifting to a non-racial and primarily African worker focus. Since the strike threatened to overwhelm the city and the mines, Smuts (Botha died in 1919) once again sent in the troops in clear support of the mines. Determined to smash the strike, Smuts ordered artillery and even tanks into the streets. The strikers were forced to accept the mine owners' terms, and their unions were curtailed by further legislation. Yet, in time, white workers regained their status and the number of their positions in the mines while also achieving a more rigid form of segregation in the mines. The effect of Smuts' state repression of the revolt was to drive the white workers' Labor party to seek new political allies. They found that they had many causes in common with Afrikaner farmers who also wanted to keep African workers "in their place" which, as far as they were concerned, was working for them on their farms and not competing for "white" jobs in the mines. Hertzog's Afrikaner-dominated National Party allied with the working class Labor Party to win the 1924 election. This set the stage for more intensive segregation legislation and a more vigorous Afrikaner nationalism.

Through the 1920s and into the 1930s, Afrikaners rallied to the nationalist cause and the state supported them as whites at the expense of other groups. Prior to the blow of the Great Depression in the 1930s, Hertzog's party gained a lot of ground with its Afrikaner base. Afrikaners promoted their culture and language with state help. Afrikaans joined Dutch, along with English, as an equal official language in 1925. Afrikaans was seen and heard in greater amounts through Afrikaans translations of books, including the Bible and the adoption of *Die Stem van Suid Afrika* ("The voice or call of South Africa") as the national anthem. Hertzog won the 1929 election largely on the basis of his rhetoric against Smuts and the "Black peril." He claimed that Smuts' proposal for a South African-led British confederation of African states would overwhelm the white population in the country with black Africans. Yet, Hertzog still did not as yet have sufficient political support to remove the Cape color-blind franchise, though he wished to. Instead, to increase his potential constituency, in 1930 he extended the vote to all white men without qualification as was required for blacks, and to white women. By this time, women in the suffrage movement had been fighting for the vote in democracies around the world. In South Africa, they stopped short of demanding the vote for black women as well, apparently because their white privilege was more important.

During the Depression, Hertzog stumbled with his initial refusal to take South Africa off the gold standard as other countries had done. This policy made South African exports too expensive and cost the economy dearly until he relented in 1932. However, his government did boost the economy in other ways. Significantly, the government privileged whites—predominantly working class Afrikaners and farmers—with state support to offset the depression. The state invested huge sums of money in white farming through land bank and equipment loans, irrigation schemes, erosion control, livestock support, and, as we shall see, keeping black labor cheap and available. Increased profits from the rebounding gold industry allowed for greater state investment in other industries as well. The government-controlled South African Railways became the largest employer of Afrikaners, many in sinecure positions, and the state-run electricity (ESCOM) and steel (ISCOR) companies also became protected havens for white workers. Despite Hertzog's nationalist politics, he could not win over sufficient support from English capitalists, and so in 1933, he was forced to form a "Fusion" coalition with Smuts in the new United party in order to stay in power as prime minister. Smuts and Hertzog worked well together, despite their ideological differences, and they managed to generate an economic recovery.

By the end of the 1930s, Afrikaner nationalist determination and the looming Second World War forced white politics away from compromise. In 1934, D. F. Malan, a member of Hertzog's cabinet, founded the breakaway *Gesuiwerdes* (purified) National party (GNP, which was later reformed as a re-unified National Party in 1940) in protest over Hertzog's compromises with Smuts. Malan, an Afrikaner ideologue and editor of *Die Burger,* had the support of the growing *Broederbond* and he attracted many disillusioned Afrikaners to his more openly ethnic nationalist party. Malan nurtured an increasingly inward-looking and insular Afrikaner politics of white domination. It relied upon cultural icons of language and mythologized history. This cultural politics was particularly evident when, in 1938, the *Bond* staged a massive celebration of the Great Trek centenary. The event drew thousands of Afrikaners to see a recreation of the highly mythologized trek at the site of what would become the imposing *Voortrekker* Monument. Both English and Afrikaners, influenced by anthropologists and scientists who tried to categorize people as "white," "yellow," and "black," each group with its own biologically determined characteristics and abilities, began thinking increasingly along the lines of essential biological racial types. This meant that South African society would become obsessed with race as a defining feature of people and their social and economic relations.

Within this racist context, Afrikaners sought to define their own race type, and they called on the state to protect their "white purity." They thought of themselves as a special group, the pure *volk* or people. Malan also championed Afrikaner political and economic power as opposed to the broader international capitalism which the British dominated. Hertzog, discredited for his alliance with Smuts, resigned from the United Party, leaving Smuts in control. When Smuts once again supported the British empire by leading South Africa into World War II as an ally, many prominent Afrikaners, including two future

THE AFRIKANER VOORTREKKER MONUMENT   Afrikaner nationalists interpreted their past to justify the racist laws and ideology of apartheid. *Source: National Archives of South Africa.*

prime ministers, B. J. Vorster and P. W. Botha, openly supported Hitler's fascist cause or called for neutrality. Such was Afrikaner hostility to "Smuts' war" and the imperial cause that the *Ossewabrandwag* ("Ox-wagon brigade"), an Afrikaner cultural movement which emerged in 1939, turned to acts of terror and sabotage against South African Army installations. Although Smuts managed to retain power in the 1943 election, increasing numbers of whites perceived him to be too moderate in dealing with Africans. By the time of the next election in 1948, rising African opposition would push even more whites into the reactionary National Party fold (see Map 8–1 on page 191).

SEGREGATION LEGISLATION AND AFRICAN COMMUNITIES

From 1900, black South Africans faced an increasingly powerful and cohesive white settler state bent on dominating them through control of the economy and the policies of segregation. This control quickly spread across the land and permeated every aspect of black people's lives, from where they lived, whom they married and associated with, to where and how they worked. Although they fought to hold their ground, Africans found that there were fewer and fewer havens and niches where they could escape the grasp of the white state or remain independent of the white-dominated capitalist economy. The state's discriminatory legislation grew with and reflected its growing power and self-assurance. Similarly, the mines and the rapidly growing urban industry enhanced their ability to control and exploit African labor. The movement of Africans within the country was a major concern for the state. In part because of the potential for resistance, but mostly to control labor flows, the state and

Map 8–1 The Union of South Africa and Railways. *Adapted from Omer-Cooper, History of Southern Africa, 2/e. 1994.*

the white employers had developed a patchwork of pass laws governing African movements.

The Union government worked out a more efficient and uniform system of pass laws. Originally, pass laws required that all African men must report to a white official upon entering a town or mining area and get permission to seek work for a specified number of days. Over time, these laws were tightened or relaxed, depending upon the labor demands of the white employers. After 1910, the government streamlined the pass laws and prevented Africans from leaving their rural reserves or the white farms they resided on without the permission of their chief, if from a reserve, or a pass signed by the farmer or a white official. The settler state also subjected Africans to a comprehensive range of taxes, from hut taxes levied on every dwelling a man owned for all his children and wives to poll taxes levied on unmarried men eighteen and older. These were designed to ensure that no African male—for the system was based upon patriarchy which sought to keep all women and youths under the authority of a male elder—escaped a tax liability which forced him into wage labor.

Once within the web of migrant labor, Africans came under even greater controls. First, nearly of half the mine workers came from outside the country, principally Mozambique, and were on a very tenuous footing since their homes were so far away. Indeed, all the black workers in the mines were migrants, and the state prevented them from gaining a legitimate standing in the urban industrial areas, as we shall see below. Second, from the point of recruitment in the rural areas by the recruiting agencies (see Chapter 7) to the time they reached the hot, narrow passages leading to the rock face, African miners were subjected to rigorous controls. They faced harsh, dangerous working conditions and their lives were strictly regimented in a military-style environment where white managers commanded workers through African "boss boys" in the common parlance of *Fanakalo,* a simplified Zulu-based language of work orders. Although their wages and food rations were better than for most African workers, over the years, tens of thousands died of mine accidents and even more suffered from mining-related diseases such as tuberculosis. The migrant labor environment was also hard on family lives. The male-only compounds separated husbands from wives and family and disposed the men to seek other liaisons, which often resulted in the contraction of venereal disease. Many established homosexual relations or "mine marriages." These allowed experienced men to take coerced "wives" from the new male recruits. Workers had few rights. The 1911 Mines and Wage Act and the 1922 Apprenticeship Act forced their pay down, prevented them from going on strikes, and relegated them to positions of unskilled work. The 1924 Industrial Conciliation Act excluded them from status as "employees" entitled to unionize or settle labor disputes. Despite the obvious limitations on their lives, Africans flocked to the cities in search of work. From the early 1930s, they were spurred on by drought and depression, which undermined the viability of the rural reserves, which were already too congested to support any more people in any event.

African urbanization was the major force shaping the country by the later 1930s. Previously, there was an exodus of Africans from white farms, and then depression and congestion in the rural reserves had driven increasing numbers of Africans into the white cities. The state rightly identified the collapse of the reserves as a contributing factor to urbanization. The 1936 Natives Trust and Land Act recommended that additional land be added to the reserves to provide for African needs, as opposed to seeking to accommodate them in the cities. By the later 1930s, the Africans faced tighter state controls as they sought jobs in the growing urban industries. World War II provided a further stimulus to industrial growth, and this drew in even more people into the new and vibrant urban African culture. As the whites went off to war, their employers replaced them with African workers who increasingly took on skilled work and forced the state to relax the pass laws. Smuts' wartime government turned a kind eye to liberal arguments for reform and instituted a number of investigative councils and commissions aimed at improving conditions for Africans, such as a non-racial national health service and investments for the African reserves, although nothing meaningful came of these.

Although most migrants tried to maintain at least some links with their rural homes, events often conspired against this. The result was continued African migration to the cities where they had only a tenuous footing. While living conditions in the African urban slums were deplorable, Africans worked to create whatever social networks and distractions they could. Women rose to the forefront of many urban families, often as single mothers or as principal breadwinners through the sale of home-brewed beer. Young men built new urban associations to provide them with a sense of identity and community. These associations took many forms, from sports organizations to male dance groups (*Ngoma* dance competitions were an aspect of Zulu rural culture which translated well into the urban work environment) to street gangs. Many of these groups were of colorful character and drew upon violent gangster images from American popular culture. There were, moreover, overtly criminal gangs which preyed upon workers for their wages. In the otherwise highly controlled world of the white cities, Africans sought to empower themselves as best they could. Similarly, they sought distractions in the lively culture of the *shebeens* (an Irish term for an illicit drinking establishment) and the syncretic township *Marabi* music, which blended African rhythms with Western instruments.

Ideas about segregation predated the formation of the union. As we have seen, early frontier relations often led to attempts to separate people on the basis of culture and livelihood, but these were not overtly racial. By the turn of the twentieth century, the intermingling of whites and blacks, especially in urban areas, caused concern for the increasingly race-conscious state. As more Africans flocked to the towns and cities in search of work, white residents became increasingly nervous about "race mixing." When the plague struck Cape Town in 1902, the city authorities used public health laws to push the Africans out of the central white urban areas. Thereafter, similar sanitation measures were applied more comprehensively to segregate Africans and whites in urban areas, especially when communicable diseases appeared to threaten white health. In 1918, the worldwide influenza pandemic hit South Africa, killing thousands. The death toll was particularly heavy among Africans in the urban areas. In response, the government passed the Native (Urban) Areas Act of 1923, which stated that the cities and towns of the country were to be the privileged domain of whites. Africans would be allowed in only to work for whites; they were to have no permanent rights there. They were mostly relegated to urban "locations" or later, to nearby formal townships created by the state. Without support for the creation of an adequate infrastructure of facilities, these areas quickly became wretched and whites perceived them as places of crime, filth, and disease. Yet, despite state efforts to reduce mingling, Africans continued to be a major part of urban society, where they remained in close contact with whites as domestic servants living in white homes and in intimate personal relationships.

Perhaps the most far-reaching and pernicious of segregation legislation was the 1913 Natives Land Act. This act segregated Africans and whites by demarcating areas reserved for each group, and it prevented Africans from purchasing land from whites outside the reserves. It was intended to extinguish an independent African peasantry and to make more labor available to white farmers and industry by strictly limiting the amount of land available to African farmers. It identified about seven percent of the land as "African," with recommendations for the addition of substantially more land for African areas. Settlers in each of the provinces vociferously protested the proposed additions, and it was not until the 1936 Natives Trust and Land Act that the government made a later reckoning which provided for African ownership of about 13 percent of the land and whites with the remaining 87 percent. The Act, moreover, prohibited the very large numbers of Africans who still lived on white-owned farms from remaining on them unless they rendered at least ninety days of labor service to the owner. This prevented successful African farmers from sharecropping or paying a rent, and it allowed whites to turn thousands of Africans into labor tenants or to force them to leave their homes on white-owned farms. Their plight was taken up with great passion by Sol Plaatje, who condemned the Act for making Africans outcasts in the land of their birth. Thus, the state squeezed Africans from their rural areas and shunted them along to work as labor tenants on white farms or within the rigidly controlled mining industry in white-dominated urban areas.

In 1927, the government sought to further limit black-white relations both socially and politically. In that year, it passed the Immorality and Native Administration Acts. The former made it illegal for Africans and whites to have sexual relations outside marriage (although marriages across "races" were not explicitly prohibited until 1950, largely because the state believed the social stigma would be sufficient to prevent it). The latter removed Africans (except the few remaining Cape qualified black voters) from direct participation in government and provided for the state to have authority over them without having to consult the parliament. A central feature of this segregation legislation was that Africans would be excluded from the central government, and instead be forced into their "natural" or "traditional" state of communal living under their chiefs. Africans were left without recourse to democratic parliamentary politics, save the mute protests of their paternalist white liberal representatives. Instead, the government encouraged Africans, as well as Indians and Coloureds, to think and act along their own separate racial and ethnic lines. The intention was to deflect any mass opposition from Africans which could unify workers from around the country along socialist lines. By the mid-1930s, Hertzog's government expanded and intensified the segregation legislation aimed at uplifting whites at the expense of Africans. In 1936, the government passed the Native Representation Act which removed more than 10,000 qualified African and Coloured voters from the common role. They were instead allowed to vote for three largely powerless white representative members of Parliament as part of the countrywide but hollow sham of the Native Representatives Council (NRC), which was designed to sideline African politicians and opposition. The NRC consisted of elected and nominated African representatives who had a merely advisory role in reporting to the Secretary for Native Affairs, the sole government official in charge of all Africans in the country. Although Africans' white parliamentary representatives continued to press for reforms, they made little progress, and African opposition politics was left to extra-governmental actions.

OPPOSITION MOVEMENTS AND THE ROOTS OF AFRICAN NATIONALISM

Despite the intensification of measures designed to stifle African mobility and prosperity, Africans developed a range of remarkably creative adaptations and challenges to the system, demonstrating their strength and resilience. Since before the turn of the century and the consolidation of the white state, Africans had resisted white conquest, the imposition of colonial rule, and their unequal status in the country. Yet Africans also engaged this new world through one of the unintended effects of colonial rule and its attendant features, the civilizing mission and a capitalist economy. They soon developed a range of new strategies to combat the inequities in the system, drawing upon established tradition and modern roles. From all over the country, the cities, the mines, the country towns, and the rural areas, Africans sought to challenge and shape the new state. Some brought more conservative liberal ideas about working within the system while others sought to confront it head on. In the rural areas, Africans fought to retain their rights to the land and their independence.

In all events, however, the white state conspired to manipulate, undermine, or crush African opposition. Whether it was by co-opting Africans into the powerless ghettos of the government, controlling their chiefs in the rural areas, or suppressing striking workers and radical political organizations, the government worked to subordinate blacks. In classic colonial fashion, the state also played upon perceived and real ethnic tensions and divisions through divide-and-rule tactics. Thus, while the broad assault on black opposition movements helped to unify Africans, Coloured, and Indians in opposition to the state, black opposition remained divided and largely ineffective in the short term. The more moderate African political leaders emerged from the mission experience. They had embraced and mastered the English-speaking world of enlightened liberal politics and "civilized Christian" culture including dress, Western education and literacy, and the political ideals of equal rights espoused by missionaries and imperial politicians alike.

In the 1880s, fledgling African opposition movements emerged to debate the political inequities in the country. As we have seen in Chapter 7, opposition rose from independent African churches, many of which had become overtly political in nature, from highly educated and sophisticated African newspaper editors, and from a growing African elite who sought to ensure their rights in what they had hoped would be a non-racial state. African leaders also rose from Western missionary-founded schools such as Adams College in Natal, Lovedale in the Cape, and especially the university-level College of Fort Hare in the Ciskei where later opposition leaders would be trained. In addition to Jabavu's eastern Cape *Imvo Zabantusundu, Sol Plaatje published a Setswana* (the Tswana language) and English paper, *The Bechuana Gazette,* and The Rev. John Dube, who had established a meaningful connection with African-American political leaders in the United States, published *ILanga Lase Natal* ("The Sun of Natal"). These well educated and sophisticated men, influenced especially by liberal overseas mission societies, embraced education as a means of self-improvement. Indeed, Dube modeled his own Ohlange Institute on Booker T. Washington's Tuskegee Institute in the United States. They were also concerned with the need for political action to assert their interests as "civilized" men, according to the rhetoric of the British imperial humanitarian mission. They had no initial desire for revolution or to overthrow the white state, merely to be recognized as civilized men within it and to have the right to vote in a color-blind, but not class-blind, democracy. As an African elite, however, their political interests and protests reflected their class interests. They tended to chart a relatively conservative course by seeking to work with the state for reform, but they had not yet connected with broader movements.

Indian South Africans shared the experience of economic subordination and state repression. By the 1890s, they too started to organize protests against discriminatory laws on the basis of the struggle for their own rights and interests. Many Indian indentured workers still suffered under the hash work regime and poor living conditions on the Natal sugar cane estates, but others had moved near and into the urban areas in Natal and the Transvaal as market-gardeners, traders, and aspirant professionals. Whites felt threatened by their facility with Western English education and finance and so sought to undermine their potential political and economic strength. Natal worked to exclude Indians from the vote and the Cape prevented Indian traders from gaining access to the Transkei, but their plight was worse in the Afrikaner-dominated areas. The Free State barred Indians from entry altogether. The Transvaal excluded Indians from citizenship, prevented them from owning land, and forced them to pay a steep £3 fee and be fingerprinted and registered as aliens.

Although the British imperial government had protested these harsh measures, it allowed them to stand and be tightened after the South African war. In the Union, Indians were subjected to the Asiatic Law Amendment Ordinance and were required to carry their registration certificates with them at all times upon penalty of imprisonment. The Indian elite who protested these laws had among them a newly British-trained lawyer, Mohandas (later Mahatma, the Indian honorific title for "great soul") Gandhi, who lived in South Africa from 1893–1814 before returning to India to help his country win independence from Britain. Gandhi claimed that his bitter personal experience of being put off a train just outside Pietermaritzburg (where a statue commemorating the event shows Gandhi with his back to the offending station) for traveling first class sparked his drive to resist the racist laws; his reaction also revealed his elite interests.

Initially, Gandhi worked for elite Indians with a strategy of passive resistance which spread and later became a model for oppressed people's struggles around the world. Along with local merchants and leaders, he formed the Natal Indian Congress and helped Indian property owners in the Transvaal form the British Indian Association, which fought for their bourgeois rights. He professed a clear loyalty to the British empire, and he came out solidly for it in the South African War and against African rebels during the Bambatha uprising, partly in the hopes that this would improve the Indian position. Nevertheless, Gandhi mobilized an impressive resistance movement based upon *Satyagraha* or soul force which aimed to win over the oppressor with a demonstration of a higher moral authority based on "truth and love." He refined his ideals and shifted his focus to be more inclusive of poor Indians while he built his model community at Phoenix. Phoenix was near to John Dube's Ohlange Institute, and Gandhi established a political dialogue with Dube as well as with religious leaders as he formulated his strategies. His *Satyagraha* campaigns employed passive resistance or non-cooperation in order to frustrate the authorities. This was similar to the African forms of "go slow" work resistance whereby subtle forms of non-cooperation could frustrate white employers without provoking a violent response from the state. In 1908, Gandhi and about one hundred followers openly defied the registration laws as unjust and were imprisoned.

These actions, which drew upon Hindu as well as Western traditions of non-violent resistance, helped to develop a common Indian identity in the country as they gained international publicity. Yet Gandhi did not seek to broaden his movement with links to similarly oppressed Africans. After Union in 1912, the state invalidated Indian marriages, rendering all married Indians adulterers and their children illegitimate. This provoked a widespread working class Indian reaction, and in 1913 the Indian coal miners and sugar cane cutters in Natal walked out on strike. Over five thousand strikers marched into the Transvaal, courting arrest in a move designed to flood the jails and provoke a reaction. Although Gandhi did not lead these strike actions, he was able to take advantage of the working class leverage which they provided. This may have been in part because the fledgling South African state had yet to build its all-white defense force to the level where it could cope with mass resistance. Gandhi managed to get an audience with Smuts on the basis of potential mass Indian resistance, and he negotiated a removal of a tax on Indians and the restoration of their marriage rights.

Satisfied, Gandhi left for India, where he applied the tactics of mass movements and non-violent resistance to even greater effect. He had highlighted the plight of the oppressed in South Africa, and his methods helped inspire African nationalist leaders. He had not worked to gain African support because the black communities were still deeply divided along ethnic lines in South Africa at this time, but he did provide a sound model for later opposition by mass movements. By the 1940s, Indian success and relative affluence in Natal enabled many of them to acquire residential property in "white" areas. The Natal provincial government, responding to white outcries over the prospect of having to live next to Indians, severely restricted Indian land purchases in the white city with the 1943 Pegging Act. Despite a considerable uproar from the Natal Indian Congress, a passive resistance campaign which led to hundreds of arrests, and the denunciation of the Act by the Indian government, Smuts' government did little. As a sop to the Indians, the government passed the Asiatic Land Tenure and Indian Representation Act, which maintained the restrictions on Indian property purchases and provided for largely powerless Indian representatives in the white parliament along the lines of the NRC. The Indian government withdrew its diplomatic mission and enforced an economic boycott of South Africa in protest, and the Indian community made further overtures to the growing black resistance movement.

By the end of the South African War and the rise of the white settler state, African politicians had organized to protest the loss of their political rights. In 1901, Dube and other Natal leaders who worked to realize African aspirations through their own efforts, rather than with white aid, founded the Natal Native Congress and in 1902 the South African Native Congress and the Native Vigilance Association emerged in the Cape to fight for franchise rights. Other similar African organizations rose in the Transvaal and Free State as well as among the Pedi and the Sotho. In 1909, these groups met in Bloemfontein in the South African Native Convention to plan a protest over the planned loss of their voting rights. The convention sent John Jabavu, W. Rubusana (the only black man ever elected to the Cape provincial council in 1910 from a predominantly black constituency), and Dr. A. Abdurahman of the APO (the Coloured organization) on a failed mission to London to press for the extension of the vote. By 1912, these frustrated men and organizations heeded a call from the American- and British-trained African lawyer, Pixley Seme, to meet again in Bloemfontein to form a national African political organization. There, John Dube (the first president), Sol Plaatje (the secretary), Seme, and other elite leaders drafted the constitution for the new South African Native National Conference, renamed the African National Congress (ANC) in 1923.

The ANC leaders asserted a clearly African nationalist message in opposition to the increasingly racist policy of segregation. They reasoned that if whites championed their race cause, then they too should work to fulfill black aspirations. They sought to be inclusive of a broad range of African political movements, and the constitution provided for a nominated upper house of chiefs even though there were tensions between the political philosophy of the Western-educated elite and the traditions of chieftainship. The ANC and other democratic leaders had an ambiguous relationship with the chiefs. They tried to draw upon the powerful ethnic symbolism of the African chiefs and the royal families, which could attract large numbers of followers who harkened back to the perceived glories of pre-conquest African kingdoms. For their part, the chiefs were wary of the Western-influenced and democratic tendencies of the ANC and other black leaders who owed no direct allegiance to the chiefs and their ancestors. Still, many influential Zulu chiefs were involved, as was the Swazi royal family. The ANC leaders included themselves in Cecil Rhodes' earlier slogan of "equal rights for all civilized men" without seeking to extend the vote to other Africans. They remained cautious about mass movements which appeared to challenge the hierarchy perhaps too strongly.

In its formative years, the ANC pursued the *Hamba Kahle* ("to go safely") politics of working within accepted government channels with petitions and deputations, appealing in vain to the vestiges of a liberal humanitarian group of whites. Indeed, Jabavu and other conservative members of the ANC argued along liberal lines that the 1913 Natives Land Act could actually serve to safeguard some land for Africans since it prescribed reserved areas for Africans which no white could purchase even if it provided the lion's share for whites. They agreed that the Act was unfair, but they also pointed out that few Africans could actually afford to buy any land even if the whole country were thrown open for sale. Sol Plaatje, however, pointed out the great hardship it caused to thousands of African tenants as well as the limits it placed on aspirant African landowners. As the government and whites in the country became increasingly racist and exclusionary, ANC leaders saw that they had much in common with the racially oppressed majority. Although the various African, Coloured, and Indian peoples all had very different histories and experiences, they did share the common experience of racial oppression. It was some time before mass nationalist organizations such as the ANC could weld together the disparate groups who remained divided by regional and ethnic differences and which were fueled by state segregation policy. Nevertheless, black people were increasingly transformed by the changing economy and society. Urbanization and proletarianization began to have a significant impact. Once the franchise was eroded and the Africans lost their rights to the land through evictions and other discriminatory legislation which curtailed African rights in the urban areas, the ANC made some tentative links to the broader mass protest movements.

Although African opposition movements remained comparatively restrained in their policies, they had to contend with a groundswell of mass discontent. In 1913, Charlotte Maxeke, who later founded the ANC women's contingent, gained some limited support from a wary ANC for her leadership of a women's anti-pass campaign in the Free State city of Bloemfontein. She and some five thousand fellow women signatories employed the standard ANC tactic of sending a deputation with a petition protesting passes to the parliamentary authorities in Cape Town. When they were rebuffed, they tore up their passes in front of police at a passive resistance demonstration, which invited arrest. Their efforts highlighted the plight of a growing number of African women who were moving to the cities in search of work and probably independence. In Bloemfontein, many of them took work as domestic servants and washerwomen, jobs which were held by men in other cities until later in the century. As their numbers increased, white authorities extended the pernicious pass laws to the women. Thus women joined the ranks of the urban oppressed, and so they too rose up in opposition.

For many Africans, of necessity, the focus remained on their day-to-day material concerns. As living costs rose but wages did not, African miners went on strike. Initially, African mine workers had tried to ally themselves with white miners in strike action, but state and Chamber of Mines intervention served to undermine any attempts at non-racial class solidarity. African workers had even less chance of success against the allied forces of the state and mining capital than the white strikers who faced the army in 1913–1914. Many workers resorted to other tactics. In 1918, Mozambican migrant workers undertook a successful boycott of the mine stores, which were the only ones readily available to them in the closed compounds and where prices were greatly inflated during World War I. After a successful white municipal workers strike which cut power in Johannesburg and won the strikers a substantial raise, African city workers followed suit. Typical of the place and times, these African municipal workers were employed in sanitation services because the city had yet to develop a complete sewage system. The some six thousand men known as "bucket boys," who were responsible for collecting human effluent,

AFRICA WASHER WOMEN'S PROTEST   African women often led protests and resistance movements against the white state. *Source: National Archives of South Africa.*

struck for a modest increase in wages. They faced harsh reprisals from the city authorities who broke the strike and arrested more than a hundred men.

Following the strikers' lead, the ANC was drawn into the more radical politics of working Africans. In June 1918, the Transvaal ANC called for mass worker action to demand an increase in wages for all Africans, and they threatened a general strike if the demand was not met. At one meeting, protestors took to the streets and in a violent action destroyed the British flag, symbol of liberal aid, and stoned cars and busses in an effort to bring traffic to a halt. They called off the strike when Prime Minister Botha agreed to meet with them and to appoint a commission of inquiry. Although the commission made did not recommend a raise, the ANC declined to pursue further support of strike action. The ANC then turned to the related problem of passes. They argued that the pass laws undermined workers' ability to seek work and to strike for better wages and conditions. In 1919, the ANC called for a mass passive resistance campaign against the passes, and they organized gatherings where workers demanded higher wages and handed their passes in to the authorities. While the mine owners, with the aid of chiefs brought in from the workers' rural areas, were able to contain the meetings within the compounds, outside, the demonstrations exploded. Across the city, African workers met in massive groups of up to two thousand and challenged the police. In some cases, reactionary whites formed gangs which moved in to break up the ANC meetings, and this provoked violent riots. The workers, who started to sing *Nkosi Sikelele y-Afrika* (God bless Africa), which later became the ANC anthem and is now the national anthem of South Africa, tried to hold their ground but were pushed back by mounted police and so the workers' effort collapsed.

By 1920, African workers felt acute economic pressure since their wages had remained stagnant during the war years while costs soared and white wages had risen by about 40 percent. They took up the cause which the ANC had abandoned and demonstrated their capacity protest with a massive strike. In February 1920 over 71,000 workers (about one-third of the total) at twenty-one mines laid down their tools and walked off the job in a highly disciplined action. Such an organized and well-coordinated strike scared the mine owners, who now realized the potential of a peaceful African working class action to bring a halt to production. The fearful state acted in typical fashion by sending in the troops, arresting leaders, and breaking up the strikes. Workers were told to return to the shafts or be imprisoned and at the Village Deep mine, resisters were shot and killed. Such violent protests and repression were too much for the ANC moderates, and the organization retreated from the tactics of worker protests and strikes, preferring to continue to work through petitions and deputations. This left a vacuum in opposition politics which would be filled by more radical elements.

The Industrial and Commercial Workers Union (ICU) and the Communist Party of South Africa (CPSA) breathed new life into the African struggle. Although it was beset by internal rankling which eventually led to its collapse, the ICU managed to bridge the divides between major opposition forces, radical and conservative as well as urban and rural, in an attempt to create a national movement. Clements Kadalie, a mission-educated migrant worker from Nyasaland (Malawi), founded the ICU in 1919 among African dockworkers in Cape Town. The movement drew support away from the ANC because it was prepared to organize strike activity in areas where the ANC demurred. It soon spread among workers in the coastal towns of Port Elizabeth and East London, and then to the *Rand* and eventually to the rural areas. The ICU promised to initiate collective action against the pass laws, to fight for higher wages, and even to acquire land for its members, although this was practically impossible. After some initial success with strike action, however, internal tensions surfaced. In 1923, the ambitious and charismatic A. W. G. Champion, a leading African mine workers organizer from Natal, joined and vied with Kadalie for the leadership. The movement was, moreover, deeply divided between more moderate elements and a radical group of Communist Party members who called for militant action. Kadalie felt threatened by the Communists because they questioned his commitment to mass action and accused him of corrupt control of ICU finances. Champion managed to convince the membership that Communism was incompatible with ICU aims, and so the ICU expelled the party members. The CPSA then sought other allies, principally in a competing union movement. Nevertheless, by 1928, Kadalie had attracted more than 100,000 members and the organization was far larger than the ANC.

Eventually, the movement stalled and fragmented due to inactivity and corruption. Kadalie led the breakaway independent ICU after a British trade unionist, W. G. Ballinger, challenged his leadership, and Champion led what became the strongest branch in Natal, the *ICU Yase* (of) *Natal*. Before its demise in the early 1930s, the ICU had considerable success. Kadalie's ICU staged a long-term general strike despite his arrest. In the rural areas, the ICU's radical message appealed to the mass of evicted tenants and struggling peasants who paid their subscriptions in the hopes of gaining some land. Most of the money disappeared, though, and subscribers became disillusioned. The ICU also gained notoriety for its decidedly anti-white rhetoric. Champion's Natal ICU was particularly successful, in part because it sought to build a bridge to more traditional forms of rural authority, the chiefs, and the Zulu royal house. The radicalism of the ICU, however, served as a caution to the Zulu king, Solomon kaDinuzulu. He preferred to ally himself with more conservative African politicians such as John Dube. Together, with state support, they developed *Inkatha* (literally, a "grass coil," symbolic of Zulu unity under the king) under the auspices of a segregationist movement which would support conservative Zulu royal authority and thwart radicalism.

Meanwhile, the ANC was infused with a new radical spirit from its young members. In 1927, James Gumede, a young radical who favored an alliance with the Communists, was elected as president of the ANC. By this time, the Soviet Union supported an international Communist movement which embraced the idea of independent socialist revolutions in each country. It called for African states to fight for their own black socialist "Native republics," which appealed to the radical youth. These radical ideas, however, were too threatening to the ANC moderates, and Gumede was replaced by the more conservative anti-Communist, Pixley Seme.

The ANC returned to its moderate politics for a time, but the radical element in opposition politics had stirred it to broader action. During the 1930s, the ANC linked up with the Communists, the Cape Native Voters' Association, the Coloured people's APO, the remnants of the ICU, and the Indian Congress to press for black voting rights. They came together at the All African Convention (AAC) to consider how to respond to Hertzog's segregationist land and franchise legislation, which would remove Africans from the common voters' role and sideline them into a separate representative council. The AAC declined to follow up on proposed protest rallies and chose instead to rely on the standard ANC tactics of appeals to the government. Although the AAC members rejected the segregationist principles of Hertzog's legislation, they nevertheless agreed to work with the white government. The AAC members accepted racially separate political institutions and they competed for and won six of the twelve seats in the separate Natives Representative Council. By the end of the 1930s, both the AAC and the ANC were in decline as other more radical groups such as the unions rose.

RURAL AFRICAN OPPOSITION

By the 1930s, rural Africans also presented a broad but unorganized front of opposition to state policy and intervention in their lives. Since Africans were excluded from the urban areas (under the 1923 act), the reserves were their last refuge. As drought and depression struck rural South Africa, those Africans living on the land were particularly hard-hit. Fearing the total collapse of the reserves, which made cheap migrant labor possible and diverted African political agitation away from the cities, the government finally started to address rural problems. The state implemented a series of half-measures for the improvement of reserve farming in a vain attempt to shore up the crumbling reserve economy, which faced a range of pressures including the loss of land, overcrowding from the influx of refugees, environmental degradation from the intense use of grazing and farm land, and the rising power of white commercial farmers. African farmers and herders therefore had resisted state-sponsored improvement schemes for containing erosion or for preventing disease in cattle because they perceived them to serve only the interests of the rural whites. In the rural areas, opposition was complicated by the role of the chiefs who had to navigate an ambiguous path between representing their people's interests and following the demands of the white state lest they be removed from power. As we have seen above, the Zulu royal family provided a rallying point for some leaders with the *Inkatha* movement. Yet *Inkatha* fell under the sway of white state segregationists who sought to adapt it to contain rural opposition from spreading with the likes of the ICU. Solomon, the Zulu king who relied upon state support, refused to take up the popular call for opposition to the government, preferring instead to bolster his own ethnic nationalist movement. As in other areas, many Zulu chiefs blended their conservatism with state segregation, and increasing numbers of dissatisfied rural reserve residents there resorted to other more radical grassroots forms of opposition.

Rural Africans drew upon a wide range of ideas and actions to confront the economic and state pressures which they faced. In many cases, rural protest was shaped by African Christianity derived from adaptations of missionary messages and the new Zionist independent African church movement. In the Free State, rural women drew upon the example of mine workers in the compounds and staged a boycott of white-owned stores and mission schools, both of which they associated with government repression. These women then embraced a message of religious and political renewal under their own chosen chief in a nationalist cause. The charismatic mission-educated Wellington Buthelezi developed a similar popular movement in the Cape and Natal. Buthelezi combined his roles as traveling merchant and healer with a call to evangelical politics in order to attract a large following. His message was based upon an African-American-inspired ideal of self-help and black nationalism which promised purification and salvation. He drew upon a widespread belief that African-Americans, who were believed to have access to guns and planes, would come to liberate Africans in a millenarian prophecy. While his movement had significant appeal, it did not go beyond the host of rural schools and churches devoted to his ideals.

During the early 1940s, the focus of opposition politics shifted again to the ANC and the urban areas as it became more radical and more national in its outlook. After Gumede was ousted from the leadership, the ANC retreated to conservative politics for a time. Meanwhile, World War II stimulated new industry in South Africa, and African workers were drawn into the cities to replace those whites who had enlisted. This industrial growth also meant that employers needed more skilled workers. They started to accept the arguments made by those liberal whites who supported the Institute for Race Relations and by Africans that a more stable, skilled African work force would be more efficient and productive than the costly white skilled work force. Their pressure on the government resulted in a relaxation of the pass laws, which enabled tens of thousands of Africans to find work in the cities. As they did so, they began to organize unions and fight for better wages and working conditions.

By the end of the war, there were over a hundred new unions with 150,000 members in the umbrella organization of Non-European Trade Unions. These unions initiated anti-pass protests and demands for better wages. Moreover, since urban segregation laws forced Africans to live well outside the white urban areas, they had to rely upon bus and train transport to their places of work. As white bus companies with state support pushed African bus owners out of competition, the former raised prices to excessive levels. African workers responded by boycotting the buses and walking to work—up to twenty miles round trip in some cases. Africans also began settling illegally as squatters (those without rights to own the land) on land outside the white urban areas. When the white municipal authorities attempted to exact rents and control the settlements, the squatters rose up in an open riot. These sorts of movements prompted the moribund ANC to revive its activities and to begin to connect again with mass political action.

The revived ANC emerged under the leadership of Dr. A. B. Xuma and the new radicalized Youth League. The Youth League was led by gifted young men such as the lawyer Anton Lembede and Fort Hare graduates Nelson Mandela and Oliver Tambo. These men were inspired by the new postwar global ideals of non-racial democracy and civil rights, but they embraced an African nationalist political plan. They criticized the older leadership for inaction and for working with the structures set by the segregationist government. They called for mass action with a passive resistance campaign which would directly confront the state. The more militant ANC then began mass protests and marches in an anti-pass campaign in 1944. Fearing state reprisals, however, the ANC then retreated to the old tactics of a petition; they gathered more than 850,000 signatures in protest against the pass laws. As the ANC revived, the Coloured people in the Cape were faced with the challenge of the state's creation of yet another segregated institution, the Coloured Affairs Department (CAD). In 1944, concerned Coloured people formed the Anti-CAD Movement and joined forces with the AAC in the broad Non-European Unity Movement which rivaled the ANC in the Cape. Then, in 1946, African mineworkers who were influenced by Communist Party organizers staged a massive strike. The African Mineworkers Union, noting recommendations made by a government commission, demanded a living wage and that the mines pay for the boots and equipment which they were forced to buy. When the Chamber of Mines refused and claimed the Union had no legal standing, more than 70,000 men went on a sustained strike. The police violently put down the strike, killing several workers in the process and then arresting the Communist party leaders who had been involved. Nevertheless, the strike demonstrated the strength of the African trade union movement. By the end of the 1940s, the ANC and the rising trade unions were poised to engage in sustained and effective mass action against the state.

CONCLUSION

In the first decades of the twentieth-century, white South Africans began to consolidate their hold over the country. They developed a new range of ideas for controlling the black population; these were referred to as segregation. New segregation policies emerged over the next few decades, drawing upon the political and economic aspirations of both whites and blacks. The critical feature of the application of segregation policies was the grotesquely uneven nature of the share of wealth and representation which was provided for blacks. On the purely white side of the racial divide, large numbers of whites continued to wrestle with the ethnic nationalist identities of British and Afrikaner. Many Afrikaners still bitterly resented what they perceived as the horrific treatment of their people during the Boer war, as well as their exclusion from power in the economy. J. B. Hertzog took advantage of these sentiments and the transition from imperial (British) to local (Afrikaner) rule to whip up support for an Afrikaner nationalist political movement. The two main thrusts of this movement were, first, to define the Afrikaner's identity on the basis of a mythologized past and, second, to ensure their supremacy as whites over blacks in South Africa. The Afrikaner nationalist cause drew considerable support and the Afrikaners grew rapidly in political and economic power.

In order to ensure white supremacy in South Africa, the all-white government developed a comprehensive series of policies and legislation meant to undermine blacks and subordinate them to white rule and the demands of the industrial capitalist economy. Segregation legislation aimed to divide the country and relegate all blacks to the status of servile workers for the whites. White farms and industries reaped their profits by relying on cheap, controlled African migrant workers. Segregation served this need for profit by providing the best land, resources, and state support for whites, especially Afrikaners, while dispossessing blacks of their land and their economic independence. Thus the state supported the extension of the migrant labor system. It also sought to strictly limit the number of Africans who could gain a foothold in the so-called "white" urban areas. Between 1910 and 1948, the white state sought to prevent blacks getting access to land which they could farm independently, thus forcing them to work for whites. They did this through a series of pernicious pass laws and land laws such as the 1913 Land Act. The white state also sought to divert African political aspirations away from the national government, and toward their traditional chiefly authorities. Despite these severe limitations, blacks still managed to carve out niches in the urban areas and to develop a vibrant life with rich musical and cultural diversions.

Blacks soon rose to oppose white supremacy and segregation. Initially, a range of sophisticated and Western-educated black men took up the leadership of opposition. They petitioned for equality and for greater inclusion in government because of the extremely limited avenues for political expression available to them. These elite men did not necessarily represent the interests of all oppressed blacks. Indians, such as Gandhi, and rural Africans too had cause to be distressed over the state's policies, but they remained separated from the mainstream of urban black opposition at the time. The opposition movements remained divided by class and ethnicity for a long time, although there were signs of an emerging wider solidarity. The South African Native Congress (ANC) began to make overtures to other groups and organizations such as the Coloured APO, and they all held national conventions in order to consider new forms of protest and action. The leaders remained comparatively conservative in their outlook and actions until they were prompted by other opposition groups. The ANC then turned to more radical and direct activities after black workers and women led the way with strike actions and public protests. Workers' opposition then came to the fore as the ICU and Communists sought to organize strikes and protests. By the later 1920s, the radical elements of black protest were infused into the ANC for a time, but the leaders remained cautious, holding back from developing a broader mass movement. It was not until in the later 1940s that all these elements converged to help create a popular organization that could challenge the white state.

QUESTIONS TO CONSIDER

1. What was segregation like in South Africa? How did it serve white interests politically, economially, and socially?
2. What was the relationship of Afrikaner nationalism to the white state and how did the Afrikaners perceive themselves?
3. Consider the various dimensions of segregation legislation. What were the most obvious features of segregation and how were they justified?
4. What were the different strands of opposition politics and action in South Africa at this time? What role did Indians such as Gandhi play in developing black protest politics?
5. Discuss the early formation and policies of the ANC. How did the ANC policy and tactics change between 1912 and the 1940s and why?

FURTHER READINGS

BEINART, W., and BUNDY, C., *Hidden Struggles in Rural South Africa: Politics and Popular Movements in the Transkei and Eastern Cape, 1890–1930* (London, 1987). A detailed collection of essays analyzing the different forms of resistance to white expansion and the dispossession of Africans in the rural areas by the two leading historians of African rural societies.

BEINART, W., and DUBOW, S. (editors), *Segregation and Apartheid in Twentieth-Century South Africa* (London, 1995). A collection of seminal articles and essays which have shaped historians' views of this period. The editors provide good, brief outlines of the important features of the pieces, and thus, the collection is an ideal teaching text.

BONNER, P., DELIUS, P., and POSEL, D. (editors), *Apartheid's Genesis* (Johannesburg, 1993). Another excellent collection of essays, most dealing with the antecedents to formal apartheid. This collection covers both the rural and urban dimensions of segregation and it too can be a useful teaching tool.

BRADFORD, H., *A Taste of Freedom: The ICU in Rural South Africa, 1929–1930* (Johannesburg, 1987). A detailed and well-written account of the ICU campaigns among rural Africans during a critical period in the political economy of the reserves and the rural areas.

DUBOW, S., *Racial Segregation and the Origins of Apartheid in South Africa, 1910–1936* (London, 1989). A carefully argued analysis of the nature of segregation and how apartheid both followed, and yet differed, from it. Dubow has shown how the political economy was mobilized to subordinate the blacks in a range of ways.

HARRIES, P., *Work, Culture, and Identity: Migrant Laborers in Mozambique and South Africa, c. 1860–1910* (Portsmouth, 1994). A very detailed account of the nature of migrant labor to South Africa from its principal foreign source in the region. Harries does an excellent job of placing unique African experiences in the broader capitalist context.

KARIS, T., and CARTER, G., *From Protest to Challenge: Documents of African Politics in South Africa, 1882–90,* five volumes (Johannesburg and London, 1972–1997). A well-organized and very useable collection of primary sources for African political movements and ideas ranging from early elite leaders' editorials in newspapers to ANC policy documents. It may be difficult to find all the volumes now.

MARKS, S., and TRAPIDO, S. (editors), *The Politics of Race Class and Nationalism in Twentieth-Century South Africa* (London, 1987). Another collection of well-researched and well-written essays dealing with a political economic approach to the issues prior to the transition to democracy. It is particularly good on issues of culture and class, and it has an excellent introductory essay by the editors.

MEER, F., *The South African Gandhi, 1893–1914,* Second edition (Johannesburg, 1996). A well-edited collection of Gandhi's writing and speeches while he was in South Africa. It is particularly useful when compared with some of the ANC documents.

MOODIE, T., *The Rise of Afrikanerdom: Power, Apartheid, and the Afrikaner Civil Religion* (Los Angeles, 1975). A still-excellent account of the nature of Afrikaner nationalism and how it was articulated through a religious lens. Moodie has shown the links between state rule and political ideology.

O'MEARA, D., *Volkskapitalisme* (Cambridge, 1983). A well-argued and cogently written analysis of the economic roots and dimensions of Afrikaner nationalism. This is an important work for understanding the ways in which the state drew Afrikaners in, and how ethnic nationalism was used for political domination in South Africa.

SWAN, M., *Gandhi, the South African Experience* (London, 1985). Swan is the leading biographer of Gandhi in South Africa and this is the best single-volume analysis of his life and work in the country. It is particularly useful for its analysis of his philosophy on passive resistance.

THOMPSON, L., *The Political Mythology of Apartheid* (London, 1985). A well-argued analysis of the later development of Afrikaner political ideology.

CHAPTER IX

Apartheid and South African Society

In the wake of World War II, the expansion of South African manufacturing and industrialization created the conditions to accommodate rising African urbanization. As increasing numbers of Africans made their ways to the cities and towns, they became an essential part of the urban economy and society. They moved to the cities to take advantage of new work opportunities and to make their homes in the new, vibrant, and diverse urban world they had created. Whites felt threatened by this trend on two fronts. First, the white farmers, many of whom were Afrikaners, lost control of their labor force. Africans in increasing numbers left the harsh working conditions of the farms and drifted to the towns and cities. Relaxed enforcement of the pass laws by a more liberal-minded United Party (UP) government under Smuts allowed them to find new but still tenuous niches. Second, African workers were gaining rapidly on whites in terms of experience and skills. This made them more attractive to employers who could take advantage of their enforced lower-paid and politically weak status.

In a context where racial supremacy was already established for whites, these perceived threats combined with a sense that the Smuts government had grown soft, which then drove whites to the National Party. Indeed, Smuts had lost much prestige in the eyes of white South Africans when he was confronted by opposition groups in an international arena. Following the war in 1946, Smuts went to the new United Nations to make the case for full South African control over its South West African mandate territory. In a charged atmosphere where post-war ideals of democracy and nationhood for European colonies reigned, delegates from India and Dr. Xuma, the ANC president, spoke passionately against the South African state and its racist policies. The Indian representatives condemned the ill-treatment of its people, and Xuma criticized the government for turning its back on Africans. As a result, the

United Nations rejected Smuts' request and humiliated South Africa as a pariah nation. Whites back in South Africa denounced the UP as inept. They also condemned the UP leaders for being on the side of the blacks, despite their role in developing segregation. At the same time, the National Party was bolstering its appeal by advocating a purified white state as well as a revival of a nationalistic Dutch Reformed Christian, Afrikaner culture.

THE NATIONALISTS AND APARTHEID

The National party attracted Afrikaners with its simple message of white supremacy and security for whites in a world that appeared to be moving toward a too liberal, non-racial position. The National Party and its allies won a slender victory in the election of 1948 and set about experimenting with their policy of *apartheid*. Although Afrikaner intellectuals had first mooted the principles of apartheid or "separateness" back in the 1930s, it was not until 1948 that Afrikaner nationalists won a sufficient number of seats in the all-white parliament to push through their agenda. By then, the National Party, in alliance with the *Broederbond*, had gained a stranglehold on white politics. In conjunction with white supremacist ideologues within the Dutch Reformed Church (DRC), they whipped up a fervor of white paranoia regarding race relations. They reckoned that, on the basis of demographics in the country, the approximately eight million blacks would soon overwhelm the two million whites. They warned of the *swart gevaar* or "black peril," and they referred to the rising numbers of Africans in the city as *oorstrooming* or a "swamping" of the whites. They pointed to the increased numbers of Coloureds and Africans now working alongside whites in the Cape garment industry, for example, as a threat to the status of white workers. While the Nationalists gained little ground in some industries, they did succeed in getting significant support for enforcing the jobs color bar from Afrikaners in the mineworkers and railway unions. The Nationalists' cause was, moreover, supported by Afrikaner workers who felt the sting of discrimination and heard the derogatory remarks by English-speaking workers. The Nationalists also relied upon the DRC's theological justification for preventing racial mixing and promoting Afrikaner supremacy as part of the apartheid plan.

Apartheid drew upon segregation and Afrikaner nationalist ideologies to create a landscape of social and economic dislocation. Blacks (African, Indian, and Coloured people) were exiled within their own country and forced to live in a twilight world which intersected with the white-dominated nation only through subordination and oppression. Apartheid, moreover, rendered the people visible only through roles based on race and class. It emerged from the minds of men such as the new prime minister, D. F. Malan (1948–1954), and his minister of native affairs (and later prime minister from 1958–1966), H. F. Verwoerd, the "architect of apartheid." H. F. Verwoerd was a Dutch-born academic trained with a doctorate in psychology who later served as professor at the University of Stellenbosch, the leading Afrikaner institution. He developed the sophisticated concepts of separate development for African "nations" to justify a domination of blacks in ways that the earlier, crude ideas of segregation could not. In 1966, Verwoerd, who had survived an earlier attempt on his life, was assassinated as he sat in the parliament by a white clerk. His successor, from 1966–1978, was B. J. Vorster, previously the minister of justice and a staunch Afrikaner republican. Together, these men honed new ideas about race domination, social engineering, and the protection of the white republic. They constructed the ideology of apartheid to further their ideals politically and economically. However, its racial exclusivity flew in the face of post-war views of the world as an open society where all people had the same basic rights regardless of race, origin, and gender.

The Nationalists aimed to further white and especially Afrikaner interests at the expense of blacks in a more systematic and comprehensive manner than previously possible, but they did not have a complete plan for implementing apartheid. State policy was shaped by local developments and exigencies. While the primary focus of apartheid was the consolidation and economic advancement of white Afrikaner society, its concomitant goal was racial exclusivity. According to apartheid theory, each race had its own biologically determined identity and concomitant abilities as laid down by God. The Afrikaner ideologues argued that in order for each race to fulfill its destiny, it must be allowed to develop on its own. They contended that contact, especially sexual relations and the creation of mixed-race offspring, would lead to the degeneration of both races. These arguments were put forward most vehemently by theologians, academics, and pseudo-scientists of the *Federasie van Afrikaanse Kultuurverenigings* (FAK), the Federation of Afrikaans Cultural Organizations, who claimed to have scientific evidence that race-mixing led to degeneration and that this was against God's will. They claimed that theoretically, rather than just a means for white supremacy, apartheid was also meant to free blacks to pursue their own cultural and political destiny away from the world of the whites.

South African society was then more rigorously divided between "whites" and "non-whites," who were further defined according to rigid categories which did not reflect the real historical fluidity of South African society. Thus, the stated defined "Coloured," "Indian," and "Native" (later *Bantu*—an African term which simple meant "people," but which was corrupted and used in a derogatory manner to refer to the African majority) groups and then further reduced Africans to a series of separate "tribal" minorities such as the Zulu or Xhosa (eventually the state identified ten separate African "nations"). By this means, whites became the majority and, therefore, according to the logic of apartheid, were entitled to rule the country. The African people were then to be allocated their own separate "homeland" (later called Bantustans) where they were to develop along their "own" lines based upon traditional chiefly forms of government. Significantly, however, black political self-determination would be severely curtailed by the white state, which oversaw the reserves and demanded their full compliance with white needs. The two key features of apartheid which undermined the freedom of blacks were strict limitations on their movements and rights to land and their exclusion from political participation. Blacks would be completely removed from participation in the state's central government.

There were other forces shaping South Africa as well. Industrial capitalism continued to expand and manufacturing became a growth industry. Moreover, Africans, despite the limits imposed on them by the state, increased significantly in population size. South African society also moved towards urbanization. These historical processes were shaped by apartheid policies, but they could not be contained or stopped. African urbanization meant that many blacks lost their direct links to older patterns of life in the rural areas and instead engaged in the modern city life. Moreover, the South African economy became more complex, diversified, and linked to the world. From the mid-1940s, more black and white workers were employed in skilled manufacturing and service work than in agricultural and heavy industrial work. Yet whites also came to dominate agriculture and they took over more than 70 percent of the land in the country during those years. White agriculture dominated the countryside and, with substantial state support for tractors and irrigation, white farmers expanded their farming considerably as they displaced the traditional African crop production and herding. The country was opened up internally with the expansion of road, rail, and air networks, and overall both the economy and the population grew rapidly.

Once in power, the National Party consolidated its hold on political power. It promoted the advancement of Afrikanerdom and the primacy of Afrikaners in politics and the economy. First, the party deftly gained further parliamentary leverage by passing legislation which provided for the addition of six new seats in the House of Assembly and four new seats in the Senate to represent whites in the mandate territory of South West Africa. The Nationalists won these seats and then absorbed allies and political competitors alike from within Afrikaner society. The party then presided over a policy for the unprecedented promotion of Afrikaner ethnic nationalism in both the state and private sectors. Afrikaners, especially well-placed members of the *Broederbond* and National Party supporters, were promoted in all parts of the government bureaucracy from the civil service and defense forces to state-controlled industries such as ISCOR (for steel) and ESCOM (for electricity) and the railways and harbors. The government supported the expansion of organizations which promoted Afrikaner nationalist economic and political advancement. Santam and Sanlam, for example, originated in the *Helpmekaar* (Afrikaans for "help each other") movement which aided Afrikaners who rebelled against the state during World War I. Santam was the first Afrikaner ethnic financial investment company and Santam was developed to serve Afrikaners' insurance needs. Along with the *Volksbank* (The People's Bank for Afrikaners), they came into their own once the Nationalists were in power, and they acted as a counterbalance for Afrikaners to the English-dominated financial networks. The Nationalists also made South Africa a republic in 1960 despite considerable opposition from English-speakers.

With state patronage, other Afrikaner cultural, religious, and educational movements and organizations flourished. Universities such as Stellenbosch, Afrikaans language newspapers such as Verwoerd's *Die Transvaler,* and the Dutch Reformed Church all benefited from their alliance with the Nationalists in power. The overlapping membership and leadership of these government, political, cultural, and business organizations allowed Afrikaner ideologues to look increasingly within the confines of their own insular society for support. Soon the Afrikaner elite was able to attract large numbers of Afrikaner supporters through patronage couched in explicitly racial and ethnic terms. They gained the loyalty of poor Afrikaners, who had an advantage in the political system, which was biased in favor of rural whites. They moreover sought to safeguard Afrikaner culture through the system of education. First, Africans were to be educated separately and in accordance with their subordinated position so as not to "contaminate" whites. Second, English and Afrikaner children were to be educated in different schools according to their home language and culture.

Thus "Afrikanerdom"—the South African society of and for the Afrikaners, where they reigned supreme—was clearly defined and the Nationalists were the coordinating body for this increasingly close-knit society. While it was intended that all whites who accepted the principles of apartheid would benefit—which meant that English-speakers too shared in the world of racial privilege—it is true that apartheid served Afrikaner nationalist interests first and so tended to exclude the English-speaking white industrial and manufacturing capitalists from direct access to political power and patronage. This inhibited the development of open capitalist market forces and the liberalizing effects of economic development. Nevertheless, the Nationalists well understood the value of the mining and manufacturing sectors for generating wealth which they could use, and so apartheid accommodated their needs and benefited them as well. It was this contradiction between economics and ethnic politics which created tensions that the African opposition could exploit.

BLACKS AND APARTHEID POLICIES

The Nationalists developed apartheid as a means of social engineering which, in their words, was intended to "keep the black man in his place, and that place was working for the white man." It laid out bold plans for managing and manipulating people based on a patriarchal system which went beyond the basics of existing segregation. It was as concerned with Afrikaner race purity and supremacy in social relations as it was the bedrock race-based system of black migrant labor exploitation. In practice, apartheid was built upon myths and hypocrisy and it never functioned as an effective uniform state policy. Instead it divided the people and raised the whites to a privileged status above all others. At the heart of apartheid lay the Nationalist program to secure its political base by providing for Afrikaners' material interests and economic power gained through political action. It was more comprehensive, invasive, had more nuance, and was therefore a more dangerous system for blacks than segregation. Over the next twenty-five years, the state developed a vast array of legislation aimed at preventing the intermingling of the "races," enhancing the power and prestige of the whites, and ensuring that the blacks continued to provide cheap, exploitable labor.

The government grudgingly conceded that Africans, Indians, and Coloureds would continue to remain an integral part of South African society. It nevertheless sought to separate and push them out, away from whites. In all areas where whites and blacks continued to intermingle, the state sought to make race and ethnicity highly visible so that strict limits could be placed on interaction. The Afrikaners' race consciousness manifested itself in a drive to prevent miscegenation (reproduction by parents of different races). In 1949, the government passed the Prohibition of Mixed Marriages Act which prevented people perceived by officialdom to be of different races from marrying. Within a year, the Immorality Act (1950), which punished common sexual relations between unmarried people, was bolstered to include harsh penalties for illicit sex across the color lines. Its expressed purpose was to punish both white men who strayed from the ideal of race purity and the black women they dominated in these sexual relations.

In order to implement this race-based legislation in a society where racial lines and relations were so obviously blurred (and had been so since the earliest times), the state passed the Population Registration Act in 1949 to identify and categorize race types. This empowered the state to classify every person into a racial group supposedly based upon scientific principles (which have since been shown to have no validity) and then require them to carry documentation to this effect. Of course, classifying people solely on the basis of perceived race, especially in the white and Coloured communities where intermingling had been considerable over the centuries, proved impossible. Thus, the government had to rely on interpretations of social and cultural aspects of people's lives to judge. In many cases, the classification could have gone either way and some whites were reclassified as Coloured. The absurdity of the system was revealed when, in some cases, people from within the same family were classified differently as white or Coloured, and some people were reclassified a number of times. This would become a particular hardship for some Coloured families when members of the same family were cut off from each other by the state. Moreover, some in the Coloured community suffered crises of identity as they sought to pass for white, which entailed moving to a white neighborhood and establishing a new social identity while leaving other family members behind.

Coloured people also suffered the last great blow to black political participation in the central government. This was also a final blow to the remaining vestiges of liberal safeguards for a non-racial government. In 1951, the Nationalists passed the Separate Representation of Voters Act to finally extinguish any direct black voters' rights in the Cape. Under the Act, all Coloureds were to elect four white representatives to parliament rather than to participate in general election procedures on the common voters' roll. Intriguingly, whites and blacks alike protested the passage of the Act. White supporters of the United Party (UP) argued that the Act violated the constitution which had entrenched Coloured voters' rights at Union and therefore would have required a two-thirds majority of parliament rather than just the bare majority which the Nationalists had gained.

These whites in opposition were joined by the Black Sash, a white women's movement which stood solemn vigil at public gatherings and outside parliament to mourn the demise of the South African constitution and the Torch Commando, a group of war veterans who had fought for the principles of democracy in World War II. The Black Sash protested what they saw as the end of justice and the rule of law in South Africa as the Nationalists overrode the constitution. The Torch Commando, likewise, organized mass rallies and torch-light processions to protest the Afrikaner government's summary exclusion of Coloured voters without recourse to due constitutional process. They remained aloof, however, from the ANC and Communist party-organized Franchise Action Committee as well as the Cape Unity Movement, both of which also took up the Coloured voters' cause. Nevertheless, Coloured voters did manage to successfully challenge the legislation in the Appellate Court. This forced the Nationalists to resort to parliamentary manipulation in order to restore the Act. It was the wily prime minister, Strydom, who managed to get the law re-instated. He packed the Senate with his supporters and in turn, they appointed sympathetic Afrikaner judges to the Appellate Court and they upheld the Act in 1956. By the 1960s, Coloured people were further removed from a parliamentary voice with the creation of the Coloured Council, a separate talking shop along the same lines as the African Natives Representative Council which was abolished in 1951.

The notion of inequality in the spatial division of the racial hierarchy was clearly put forward in legislation which affected the use and quality of public amenities and places. Public facilities such as park benches, post offices, and municipal train stations (as we saw in Chapter 8, "From Union to Apartheid: The Consolidation of White State and the Rise of African Opposition, 1910–1948," Gandhi's experience showed there was already a racial exclusivity to first-class rail travel) had, in many places, provided equal access and amenities for whites and blacks. Under apartheid, the state required blacks to use separate, and in most cases, decidedly inferior facilities from whites. When the ANC coordinated challenges to the exclusion of blacks from the main train station facilities in Johannesburg and Cape Town, the Appellate Court ruled in their favor that facilities could be separate, but not unequal. In response, the Nationalists passed the Reservation of Separate Amenities Act (1953) which allowed for separate and inferior facilities for blacks. Soon, the entire country was marked by signs which reserved facilities such as swimming pools, beaches, park benches, service counters, buses, toilets, and virtually all common public spaces for either "*blankes alleen*/whites only" or "*nie-blankes*/non-Europeans." These "petty" apartheid measures reorganized all public movement and activity along racial lines. They were a constant and visible reminder of the indignities visited upon every black South African by white supremacy.

Apartheid was also concerned with protecting white workers' (who were also voters) rights by managing the flow of Africans into the areas where they could compete for jobs. To prevent the further uncontrolled influx of Africans into the cities, the government refined and tightened the system of passes under the 1952 Abolition of Passes and Consolidation of Documents Act. This provided for the creation of a single document book, the *dompas* which all Africans had to carry. Africans had to present their pass books to state officials upon arrival in the city, and they were allowed up to three days to find work or be "endorsed out" of the area. If they failed to comply, they could be charged and fined or jailed or both. This was rigorously enforced with massive numbers of police raids and "flying squads" devoted entirely to controlling Africans in the towns and cities. Over the next twenty years, literally millions of African men and women were convicted of pass law violations. The police used the law to harass and intimidate Africans, descending upon sleeping men and women in the middle of the night to check documents, or confronting people in the streets.

The law was enforced somewhat selectively over time. The government intensified pass raids when political opposition increased. Enforcement was relaxed when employers demanded more workers, or tightened when rural farmers complained of the loss of their labor to the cities. These fluctuations, however, were not conducive to increasing productivity or providing larger local markets. Manufacturing and light industry companies wanted to establish a stable, skilled, and cheap African work force which would work more efficiently, experience less turnover, and provide more consumers. The state responded to their demands by allowing some Africans special rights in the urban areas. Contrary to the theory of apartheid, Section 10 of the new Urban Areas Act of 1952 provided for some Africans to gain special rights in the cities. Section 10 people could stay and work freely in town if they had been born there, lived there for at least fifteen years, or worked for the same employer for at least ten years. They could get preferential access to housing and employment opportunities. This was done also, in part, in the hopes of creating a stable family-based community to act as a counter to the volatile single male society which was a product of the migrant labor system and which was prone to gangs, crime, and violence. For most Africans, however, tighter restrictions on movement and the reservation of jobs for whites meant that they had only a tenuous niche in the urban areas.

The Nationalists also had to ensure they served the needs of white industrialists, manufacturers, and commercial farmers, since the capitalist economy was still the engine of the the apartheid state. As we have seen, the state differentiated the urban labor supply between Section 10 blacks who served as a stable, skilled work force from the burgeoning manufacturing sector and those migrant workers who served the mines. Indeed, the mines remained (and still remain) committed to migrant labor, employing approximately 350,000 migrant African workers by 1960 (the number rose to over 450,000 by 1990, then it started to decline). Over 60 percent of these men came from outside South Africa proper (most of these were from central Africa and Mozambique, and others were from the enclave states of Lesotho and Swaziland). Another 150,000 or so came from the African reserves of rural South Africa and so, as we shall see, the reserve system remained an essential feature of the apartheid economy. Influx control also ensured that white farmers could still tie workers to their farms. Increasingly, however, they could recruit only inexperienced foreign migrants, the young or old and the inform, for agricultural work remained the least attractive and harshest form of employment for Africans.

The overall circumstances for African workers declined significantly under apartheid. In all sectors, Africans were prevented from organizing proper unions, their labor disputes were handled separately from whites, and they were banned from strike action. By the 1970s, their real wages—the value and purchasing power of the money they earned—had actually dropped to below what they had been fifty years earlier. Moreover, there was a marked wage gap between whites and Africans. Africans earned between four and five times less than whites in manufacturing and over twenty times less than white mine workers, and there was little improvement until the 1980s. A more telling problem was rising African unemployment. Although the economy was growing at a steady pace and there was increased employment for Africans, many remained jobless. During the first twenty years of apartheid, African unemployment doubled to about 2.3 million and nearly 25 percent of the African population lacked formal employment.

AFRICAN SOCIETY AND THE IMPACT OF APARTHEID

The combined effects of apartheid policies and rapid, unplanned urbanization without adequate services had a profoundly negative impact on black South Africans. In addition to the increased levels of unemployment and falling wage levels, Africans also suffered from the effects of both rural poverty and urban squalor. In contrast, most whites enjoyed secure and prosperous lives. They had state-supported access to good, high-paying jobs. They lived in fine homes, often with African servants, and in far more affluent neighborhoods than blacks, and their overall level of material wealth was high. Their segregated schools, hospitals, and public amenities and facilities were of a high standard. Overall, their health and life expectancy were much higher than for blacks. Whites did, however, suffer a very high rate of heart disease, which was consistent with the lifestyles of the wealthy in industrial countries. Moreover, they were conditioned through government education and propaganda to accept the inequities of apartheid and the privileges they had as their racial right. Most whites were not fully aware of the plight of Africans. State control of the media, and "national security" tended to obscure the miseries suffered by blacks. The ideologues of apartheid argued that Africans were happy in their "traditional" homelands despite the fact that their impoverished state was created by modern racism and industrial capitalism.

Blacks had different experiences in the urban and rural areas, but they shared the common problems of poverty, inadequate facilities, poor health, and racial oppression. In the urban areas, they were forced into overcrowded, squalid settlements without safe water, electricity, or other services on the fringes of the towns and cites. In the rural homelands, the combined effects of a continued reliance on migrant wage labor with its inadequate wages and collapsing homestead agriculture took a heavy toll on African lives. Despite the government's Tomlinson Commission (1956) recommendations for the economic upliftment of the homeland reserves (to sustain the increased number of residents created by forced removals), the state made little investment in them compared to the white areas. Overcrowding put great pressure on the land and social relations. Few could feed themselves from agriculture, let alone make a living from it. There were few roads and no electricity or running water. Hospitals were too few and underfunded.

Migrant labor not only provided insufficient wages, it broke up families and contributed to ill health. Urban, industrial diseases such as tuberculosis and venereal diseases were brought back to wives and families by workers who had endured the crowded single-sex compounds and unhealthy conditions of the mines. This had a devastating effect on African health as well as a profoundly negative psychological impact on family relations and mental health. Mental stress and aggressive state oppression created a culture of violence in South Africa which contributed to extremely high rates of violent crimes such as murder and rape. The pervasive problems of inadequate nutrition and unsafe water supplies predisposed Africans to a greater susceptibility to other health problems. Mothers and children were particularly hard hit. Rural Africans especially suffered very high rates of infant and child mortality, and perhaps as many as fifty percent of children were undernourished. There were few and woefully inadequate public health facilities for Africans compared with those provided for whites. These conditions, combined with poverty and state neglect, meant that Africans also suffered from preventable diseases and health problems such as gastroenteritis, typhus, and cholera. Moreover, they were hit disproportionately hard by epidemics of malaria, polio, and even plague.

Africans also suffered from lack of opportunities for advancement. The state sought to condition Africans into a subordinate status through education. The Nationalists' Bantu Education Act (1953) took control of African education away from the long-established mission societies' schools, where many Africans had succeeded in gaining decent Western educations, and placed it under state control. The government felt that the predominantly English-speaking mission schools fostered liberal ideals which were subversive of white, Afrikaner supremacy. Instead, the Bantu Education Act segregated African children from whites, yet it required the use of Afrikaans as well as English for instruction. In keeping with the apartheid notion of separate development for Africans, the schools were also forced to use the various African languages in order to emphasize "tribal" identities. Over the years, the curriculum was revised to reflect the dominant racist views of the government. The express purpose of the Bantu Education Act was to control African learning in such a way as to ensure that Africans had no false assumptions about having equal rights, and that they would never rise above the inferior status of laborer for whites.

As a striking example of the differential treatment of Africans and whites, the Bantu Education Act's system was grossly underfunded; the government spent over ten times more per student on whites than on Africans. School facilities for Africans were inferior and African teachers were paid much less than their white colleagues. This system was extended in 1959 to the segregation of universities. Blacks could only attend a "white" university with ministerial approval. Instead, the state created separate education systems for Coloureds and Indians (though with slightly better facilities than for Africans) and separate colleges for each "race." The government took over the premier Native College at Fort Hare, restricted its enrollment to Xhosa students and subjected it to the Bantu Education Act policies. These included a curriculum devoted to an Afrikaner-centric view of the world. African student enrollment, nevertheless, mushroomed from well under a million in the old mission schools (which probably could not have accommodated the rising numbers of students in any event) prior to 1950 to nearly three and one half million students by 1980. Africans made the most they could of the poor education system. Despite state-imposed constraints, African literacy rose significantly, and new generations of students learned a great deal as they waded through the state propaganda and finally obtained some meaningful knowledge.

Despite these severe constraints, Africans were remarkably successful at taking advantage of limited opportunities and creating for themselves vibrant communities in the interstices of the apartheid state. Some Africans who gained formal education struggled up into the ranks of urban professional employment. They became teachers and, notably, African women became nurses, although these professions accounted for only a small fraction of the black work force. Nursing was virtually the only professional avenue open to African women. African entrepreneurs such as traders and small businessmen also thrived in the cities. Others joined the lower ranks of government service as clerks, police and messengers, although the well-salaried positions were to be found in the elite ranks of the homeland ministers and administrators.

Many of the comparatively better-off Africans came from the ranks of Western-educated mission society. They sought material goods such as cars, clothes, cigarettes and store-bought (as opposed to home-brewed) liquor, as well as their own homes, which distinguished them from their fellow township residents. These successes, however, do not suggest easy or expanding opportunities for Africans to advance economically but rather they reflect the remarkable inventiveness and resilience of Africans. The majority of Africans, who remained locked into poorly paid wage labor, fell into two broad social categories: migrants and township residents. On the one hand, black township residents had managed to establish long-term places in the urban areas. They shared the common experiences of the city, and they tended to see themselves as part of a broader social group. Migrants, on the other hand, retained significant ties with their rural areas and traditions, which reinforced an ethnic dimension to their identities in the cities where they were separated from other Africans in migrant workers' compounds. As we will see, these different experiences contributed to increasing tensions between migrants and residents, especially as the migrants embraced the ethnic nationalist identities which were grounded in the homeland system.

Africans sought refuge in their own communities and in the changing contours of urban and rural culture. In the rural areas, some of the chiefs still provided a rallying point for reworked ethnic identities. They maintained and adapted traditions such as agricultural festivals, weddings, and beer-drinks to bind communities together. They also interpreted and applied customary law in the new context and organized community settlement. In the cities, Africans turned to a wide-range of cultural forms which drew upon both rural traditions and new urban experiences. Soccer ("football", in South African parlance) became a hugely popular spectator sport. It also attracted African players because it required little in the way of equipment and could be played virtually any where. It became the most popular sport by far as township teams such as the Orlando Pirates became celebrity icons with large fan followings. By 1977, the state allowed the formation of a multiracial soccer league. Most sports, especially those favored mostly by whites such as cricket and rugby (the British import which became almost the "national" sport of the Afrikaners), remained segregated. Once the state allowed the sale of manufactured beer and liquor to Africans after 1962 (largely at the behest of the white-owned liquor companies), they displaced African home-brew. This caused vehement objection and resistance from African women who were the producers of home-brew. Nevertheless, *shebeens* (illicit drinking establishments) in the urban areas were run predominantly by African women, the *"shebeen* queens." These remained the focus of African socializing and drinking despite frequent police raids. They were also the venues for listening to the vibrant musical styles of township jazz and the new *mbaqanga,* which blended African rhythms with American influences.

Urban youth gangs, sometimes styled on images of American popular culture from gangster films, also emerged as social organizations which provided empowering identities in the cities. Gang violence rose as they vied for control of neighborhoods and they made the townships dangerous places. Others, especially women, sought solace in the growing number of urban independent Zionist churches. Groups such as Isaiah Shembe's Nazarite Church in Natal and the Zion Christian Church in Soweto attracted vast followings with their combination of redemptive messages, healing, baptism, and African music and ceremonial traditions. These social and cultural forms were a creative and eclectic blend of African, American, and other Western European styles, yet they operated in the undeniably new and predominantly African urban context of South Africa.

The apartheid state developed a massive bureaucracy and a wide range of mechanisms for the enforcement of apartheid laws and the repression of those in opposition. Opposition to the state, especially by radical African worker and political organizations, was prevented by the Suppression of Communism Act (1950). The Act, born in the context of racist post-war South Africa, employed the paranoid rhetoric of the cold war as a means to suppress opposition. Typically, it was used in a catch-all manner. The state labeled virtually all opposition groups and individuals, regardless of actual political affiliation or outlook, as subversive "communists" and subjected them to summary judgements and harsh treatment. The tools of enforcement were developed through the rapid growth of the security establishment, including a large national police force. These were focused primarily on containing and suppressing militant worker and political resistance to the state. South African security legislation reflected an increasingly fearful state.

In response to rising political opposition and mass action between 1950 and 1960, the state passed the Riotous Assemblies Act (1956), the Unlawful Organizations Act (1960), the Sabotage Act (1962), and the Terrorism Act. By the 1970s, repressive measures became common and the security establishment permeated every part of South African society. This thinking would eventually fuel the building of the African continent's most lethal army as the state sought to combat "enemies" both internal and external. Police engendered fear and loathing among blacks as they ruthlessly enforced the pass laws, broke up demonstrations, and removed people from the urban areas. The state developed the power to suppress all forms of opposition, including mere statements of criticism, by "banning." Banning meant that a person or group was prevented from making public statements, they could not organize or meet to discuss their ideas, and they were subject to summary imprisonment for breaking the banning order. The government's increasingly frequent application of the Public Safety Act (1953), which provided for the declaration of a state of emergency and the Internal Security Act (1976), turned South Africa into a virtual police state. These acts allowed the government to suspend the rule of law and due process. People could be detained for ninety days (or more later on) without cause, and the government could prevent them from receiving legal counsel. Moreover, the government's powers of censorship allowed it to muzzle the press and prevent the reporting of "sensitive" material and of areas under a state of emergency. This could include any militant black resistance and peaceful demonstrations.

It was the spatial organization of people along racial lines which was perhaps the most striking feature of apartheid. African access to and rights in white South Africa (which constituted the vast majority of the country and all the major towns, cities, and economic zones) were strictly limited or abolished. Africans were allowed to remain in the white cities only on sufferance, and only where they served white needs as proclaimed by the state. As we have seen, the policies of segregation, particularly the Natives Land Act (1913) and the Natives Trust and Land Act (1936) had already laid the groundwork for the territorial separation of Africans from whites, and Indians in Natal had been similarly limited to designated areas. Now, Coloureds too were physically separated from white society. In practice, the government could not physically seal the white areas from blacks, nor did it want to. First, African urbanization was a continent-wide force which could not be reversed even by the likes of such a repressive and powerful state as South Africa. Second, as previously noted, the economy required a larger and increasingly stable skilled African work force. Nevertheless, the Nationalists inscribed on the land vast areas where blacks would be excluded from having any rights.

While Africans had previously been excluded from most urban areas, they retained substantial freehold footholds in places such as Sophiatown in Johannesburg where they had bought land prior to the prohibitions of the 1923 Urban Areas Act (see Chapter 8). Similarly, Coloured and Indian communities thrived, respectively, in Cape Town's District Six and Durban's Cato Manor (which also had a substantial African community). The government invoked the rhetoric of the black peril in the white cities to justify the 1950 Group Areas Act. The Act provided for a new racist dimension to urban planning by defining areas for people to live and work in on the basis of race. Not surprisingly, whites enjoyed rights to both the economic hearts of the city centers and the secure and serene suburbs. The Act allowed the state to remove and relocate black urban communities. These were perceived to threaten whites' "race purity" as well as to be dangerous, diseased slums which harbored subversive "communists" and prevented urban development. With the addition of the Prevention of Illegal Squatting Act (1951), the state had enormous powers to expropriate property and move people about. During the peak period of the 1950s alone, over 600,000 Coloured and Indian people were removed from the cities. Following the tragic forced removal of its residents (which began in 1966 and was completed in early 1980 after residents protracted the process), District Six was leveled, and yet it remained undeveloped for decades. Ironically, one street in the new all-white area was renamed Justice Street. Similarly, Sophiatown, haven for and symbol of a vibrant independent African community of creative African writers and musicians, gangs, and *shebeens,* was brutally crushed. It was replaced by a sanitized and orderly white suburb named *Triomf,* the Afrikaans term for "triumph," symbolizing the power of the state to eradicate the black presence.

To compensate for the removal of urban Africans, the government provided for the establishment of formal "townships" within "commuting distance" (which could be up to three or four hours each way) of the white cities. This tactic displaced African urbanization from the white areas to "more acceptable" segregated locations and homelands. Many of these, like Soweto (for South West Township), which reached over half a million residents by 1970, had their origins earlier during the period of segregation, but they mushroomed with the manufacturing boom from the later 1940s. Some were newer planned townships with rudimentary facilities, but most were informal shack settlements where appalling conditions prevailed. The "newspeak" of apartheid provided some townships with bitterly ironic names such as *Jabulani,* which

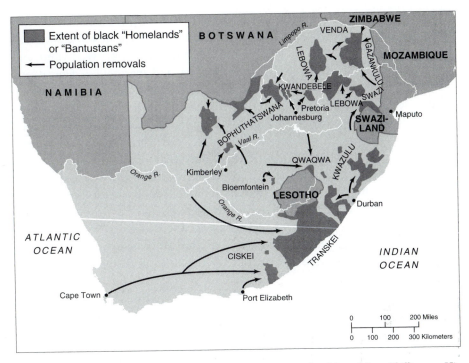

Map 9–1   South Africa: Bantustans and Population Removals. *Adapted from Shillington, History of Southern Africa. 1997.*

means "happiness" in Zulu. They became the wretched dumping grounds for the labor pools of apartheid. Inadequate and slow public transportation along with a thriving private taxi industry served to cycle impoverished workers to and from jobs in the white cities (see Map 9–1).

The Homelands

A major pillar of apartheid was the development of an institutional political framework for the segregated African areas. In 1951, the state passed the Bantu Authorities Act which paved the way for a more comprehensive system of segregation based on the apartheid logic of providing a separate trajectory of "development" for Africans. It gave the force of "legal" identity to the spatial separation of people along racial and ethnic lines. Under this Act, and a myriad of associated legislation including the Group Areas Act, Africans were excluded from political rights in the white areas and in national government. The Act abolished the Native Representative Council, the only remaining formal representative political institution for Africans in the white government. Instead as Africans were forced out of white areas, they were given rights in their own *Bantustans* or "tribal homelands." This empowered the state to subordinate Africans completely when they were in the white areas. The government now had the means to prohibit Africans from residing in white areas and to remove them to distant areas, thus creating buffer zones between white and African residential areas. A key principle of the act, and apartheid in general, was an attempt to stall or reverse the emergence of a common African identity which the state feared would contribute to rising African nationalism and radicalism.

Paradoxically, as we will see, historical forces such as the increasing need for settled, skilled African labor and rising African urbanization had already undermined separate ethnic identities in the urban areas, and they would eventually outpace the state's efforts to prevent a united front of opposition. The Bantu Authorities Act, nevertheless, aimed to institutionalize "tribal groups" in separate nations. While the whites, who came from diverse European backgrounds, were to form a single group, the Africans were divided into territories based on language and perceived ethnicity. There would eventually be ten separate "homelands" or nations for the Zulu in Natal and Zululand, for the Xhosa in the Transkei and parts of the Ciskei, and for the Tswana, Ndebele, Venda, Pedi, and other smaller groups in the Transvaal and Free State. Although these areas, outlined in the earlier land acts, contained some useful features, they were mostly fragmented, distant from the towns and cities, and without decent transport links.

The development of the homeland policy required two major changes. First, the state recognized the need for at least some improvements in the material viability of the homeland reserves. Earlier government commissions, especially the 1930–1932 Natives Economic Commission (NEC), had identified the severe decline in economic circumstances in the reserves. By the 1950s, it was clear that the homeland economies were on the verge of collapse. In 1956, the Tomlinson Commission made sweeping recommendations for the economic upliftment of the reserves. It supported the continuation of "betterment" policies that were aimed at combating soil erosion (which was, ironically, blamed on large and growing African cattle herds), livestock improvement, and agricultural rehabilitation. Stemming from the recommendations of the Commission, the government began to boost the economic framework of the homelands. First, it began acquiring the additional land which the earlier land commissions had recommended as necessary for the support of the reserves. The government purchased thousands of white farms adjacent to the reserves' at a fair market price, and included them in the homeland system. This additional land, however, was woefully insufficient for the massive numbers of Africans who were being forced out of white areas and into the reserves, as we shall see.

One of the harshest and most tragic features of the homeland policy was the forced removal of millions of Africans from white areas. In addition to the earlier relocation of blacks from the white urban areas under the provisions of the Group Areas Act, Africans who were deemed to be superfluous to the needs of white employers were forced to leave their homes in areas not designated as their homeland. This included the elderly, widows, children, wives or husbands, the ill or unfit, or anyone not employed in the cities. It also included African peasants who were still trying to make an independent living on "black spots" (land which they had acquired prior to apartheid but which now fell into a white area), on mission stations, or as rent tenants on white farms. Some of these African communities had owned their lands for generations. Nevertheless, the government claimed that Africans willingly accepted the removals.

In reality, the victims of the forced removals were intimidated into moving. After official notification, the police forced people to collect what belongings they could on short notice, abandon their soon-to-be bulldozed homes, and endure an arduous trip often to a barren location, where, if they were lucky, they were provided with only rudimentary site services such as water. In some cases, people who resisted or delayed their removal were forced at gunpoint and then suffered the added hardship—and insult—of having to pay for the rental of private trucks which were readily offered by neighboring white farmers. By the 1980s, more than a million Africans had been forced from their farms. Increasing protests by Africans often led to violent confrontation with the police and some farm protest leaders were killed. Although the government then allowed some long-standing African farming communities scheduled for removal in the Cape to remain, most "black spots" were removed and the former owners were forced to relocate to their respective homelands or to the areas of settlement and townships provided for them outside the white cities.

According to the state, it was only in the homelands that Africans were to fulfil their own separate destiny. This homeland policy required the "retribalization" of Africans. Retribalization was an attempt to force all Africans, regardless of their experiences or lifestyle (as we have seen, many Africans lived in urban areas, had Western educations, and were Christians) into revived and enhanced "traditional" communities. It was based upon certain features of African customs and traditions, such as communal rights to land, African forms of customary law, and rule by chiefs. Yet it was the white "experts" who identified which features of African societies would be legitimate and acceptable to the apartheid state. In the process, many important African traditions were corrupted and manipulated or re-invented to serve modern needs that were quite different from the ones originally intended. Under the administration of this system, white officials oversaw the African leaders or chiefs. The chiefs were to govern people in their designated areas according to African customs and laws, but only if they were acceptable to the white state. The lynchpin of the Bantu Authorities Act was the resuscitation of the institution of chieftaincy. The state, often with painstaking though skewed anthropological research, identified and installed appropriate and acceptable men who would act as compliant chiefs by working within the apartheid framework. The new chiefs were to be the vanguard of a reworked "traditional" African leadership class.

Despite the impact of conquest and colonial rule, the African chiefs still retained significant influence in the rural areas, and the state sought to harness their legitimacy to its own ends. Many chiefs, whether traditional or appointed, stepped up to take advantage of the new powers, especially if money was offered by the government. The idea of a restoration of their traditional powers and the integrity of even a part of their pre-conquest society was clearly very appealing. Yet, this placed them in a deeply ambiguous position because they were caught between the government requirements for compliance with apartheid rule and the demands of their people to have their interests represented.

Another significant tension associated with chieftaincy was its deeply patriarchal nature. The chiefs sought to contain the growing independence of women. Increasing numbers of women had fled to the cities to escape the authority of fathers and husbands, and others had established their own homesteads in the absence of men engaged in migrant labor. This self-reliant lifestyle threatened what was seen as their essential traditional role in child-rearing and maintaining the homestead. The Bantu Authorities Act enhanced the ability of chiefs to enforce the customary law which provided for the subordination of women as legal minors. In this way, the chiefs' interests converged with those of state officials who also wanted to prevent women from undermining the traditional authority which underpinned the homeland system. As many chiefs more openly supported the government, they were increasingly discredited in the eyes of their followers. Yet, chieftaincy remained (as we will see in Chapter 11, "The New South Africa, 1994-Present") a central feature of rural politics although it was contested by the state and people alike. Some chiefs managed to walk a tightrope of compliance and resistance while they struggled to support popular causes. Some openly embraced state support which provided them with power and the means to extend patronage to win over supporters. Others engaged in outright defiance, as we shall see.

The government further extended and enhanced African authority in the homelands through the granting, or in some cases the forcing, of self-government and eventually "independence" to homeland leaders in the puppet states. This was apartheid, South Africa's hollow attempt at decolonization. It was supported by the Bantu Homelands Citizenship Act (1970), which assigned all Africans citizenship in their various homelands. In effect, this made foreign citizens of Africans in the land of their birth if they were born in white South Africa! The Bantu Homelands Constitution Act (1971) provided for the state to grant independence. The Transkei was the first to be made "self-governing" in 1963 and then independent in 1976. Bophuthatswana, Venda, and The Ciskei followed with independence in 1977, 1979, and 1981, respectively. KwaZulu (the "Place of the Zulu," comprising parts of Natal and what remained of Zululand after the delimitation of large tracts of white land) accepted self-government in 1972 but did not agree to a later offer of "full independence." Independence was an ironic term, for none of the homelands had a sufficiently strong economic infrastructure to survive without South African state support and a continued reliance on migrant labor earnings. Nor could their leaders exercise effective independent political authority. Not surprisingly, the rest of the world did not recognize these puppet states.

The two most prominent homeland leaders to play the government's game of dependence politics were Chief Kaiser Matanzima of the Transkei and Chief Mangosuthu Buthelezi of KwaZulu. In the Transkei, as in the other homelands, the apartheid state had guaranteed the chiefs *ex officio* status in the local government. This ensured that the conservative tendencies of state-supporting chiefs, a legacy of the segregation era, would continue to influence homeland politics. With the support of the apartheid state and through deft manipulation, Matanzima easily managed to persuade the chiefs in the Transkei to side with him against the far more popular paramount chiefs, Victor Poto (who won 38 of 45 electoral seats) and Sabata Dalindyebo. Mantanzima, who clearly supported "separate development," took over as prime minister in 1963 and moved quickly to consolidate his power against Poto and Dalindyebo, both strongly opposed to the apartheid state and its policies for the Transkei. Matanzima worked well with the white state to mold Transkei into a model independent homeland. He did win some popular support for insisting that English be the medium of instruction for Transkeians rather than Xhosa, which was seen as a "tribal" language at the time. He also successfully lobbied for the expansion of his territory in the Republic of Transkei. Kaiser and his brother George ruled with iron fists, effectively closing the region to meaningful opposition political activity until they fell from power in 1987 (see more information in Chapter 10, "The African Transformation of South Africa, 1976–1994").

Mangosuthu Buthelezi charted a more ambiguous course in KwaZulu. In the 1950s, Buthelezi retreated from radical opposition politics after he briefly dabbled with the ANC while he was a student at Fort Hare College. Instead, he took up the strands of traditional Zulu chiefly politics in the KwaZulu homeland. With remarkable cunning he manipulated the system to sideline the hereditary king, Goodwill Zwelethini Bhekuzulu, and to promote himself into the key power position as the king's chief minister. Buthelezi had (and still has, as we will see) a keen sense of the power and influence of Zulu ethnic politics derived from the ongoing development of a fictionalized history dating

CHIEF KAISER MATANZIMA AND WHITE OFFICIALS   Some compliant African leaders embraced the limited powers and independence that the white state offered. *Source: National Archives of South Africa.*

back to early colonial perceptions of Shaka. He wielded this largely invented history to great effect, winning mass popular support for his criticism of some aspects of apartheid policy. Yet he also emphasized a vibrant Zulu ethnic nationalism in the development of a revived *Inkatha* (the Zulu cultural-political organization which was first developed in the 1920s and '30s; see Chapter 8).

Eventually, *Inkatha* acted as a vehicle for his political aspirations. It also appealed to many, but certainly not all, Zulu-speaking Africans who sought to revitalize their own black nationalism in opposition to the state. Buthelezi's strategy was to manipulate and challenge apartheid from within by embracing the powers which the state offered through the Bantu Authorities Act. He had some leverage with the government because he emphasized the ethnic dimension of homeland rule, which was the foundation of the apartheid system. Shrewdly, however, Buthelezi refused to take full independence. This gave him a significant bargaining chip with state officials who wanted to fulfill the plan for separate nation status for all the homelands. Instead of accepting independence for the very fragmented areas of KwaZulu, Buthelezi worked for the consolidation of the territory. Moreover, in the 1970s, he tried to draw together the other homeland leaders into a "federation of homelands" which could work together to assert their demands for a better dispensation from the white government. This effort was part of a broader front of opposition to the white government and apartheid policies.

In the long term, the self-governing homelands proved to be untenable. First, the territories they comprised were greatly reduced fragments of the areas that the early African states had used and occupied. Despite the rhetoric of re-tribalization, Africans, even if they wanted to, could no longer sustain themselves according to traditional methods of farming and herding. The reserves were becoming far too overcrowded to support their inhabitants, in part through natural increase but mostly from the forced removal of Africans from the white areas. Moreover, there were no alternative forms of making a living in the rural areas, so the homelands served to reinforce the system of migrant labor since the residents had to find work in the white cities and towns just to survive. Without the right to stay, however, Africans were forced to return regularly to the reserves. This tended to reinforce rural attachments which relied upon working with the chiefs and finding ways to use the ethnic dimensions of homeland politics. Indeed, as state support for the "separate development" of the homelands grew, Africans used their ethnic identities in a defensive manner in order to carve out a niche for themselves and to protect their interests. They had little choice when the state manipulated and made African "tribal" identities so significant to the apartheid system. Nevertheless, the processes of urbanization and proletarianization made a profound impact on black South Africans. Even as Africans drew upon rural traditions to aid them in their daily lives, they also looked to new social relations and the broader forms of opposition which they could support.

The state also eventually sought to expand economic opportunities by situating industry and manufacturing businesses nearby the homelands. This provided for the displacement of African urbanization to the rural areas and also allowed employers to take advantage of the adjacent pools of labor in the homelands. Initially, the government disallowed direct white investment in the homelands. It was not until the 1970s that industry and tourist development occurred in places such as Bophuthatswana's "Sun City," an "international" (an apartheid euphemism for a place where blacks and whites could socialize) casino resort which served a largely white clientele. Under the Bantu Authorities system, the state also funneled large sums of money into the homeland government bureaucracies. This money supported the new African leaders and their systems of patronage. While some benefited from these infusions of cash which represented the bulk of the homelands budgets, most Africans relied on migrant labor and remained poor. Overall, for the majority of the residents, the homelands remained an economic backwater.

OPPOSITION POLITICS: STRATEGY AND TACTICS

Mass opposition, which represented the interests of the majority of black South Africans, rose as the burdens of apartheid legislation and the capitalist economy mounted. The black majority had rising expectations for improvements in their country. Some men had fought for freedom and democracy with the Allies during World War II, and they expected to see these principles applied at home. Their political consciousness and organization were sharpened by the increasingly racist and intransigent apartheid state. Beginning in 1949, opposition leaders took the first steps toward a broad-based national form of resistance, even though there would remain significant tensions and rifts among the opposition movements. As we have seen, the ANC had already changed its makeup and outlook with the infusion of more radical militant politics from the Youth League. Dr. J. S. Moroka replaced the more cautious Dr. A. B. Xuma. Young radicals, such as Neslon Mandela and Oliver Tambo, Fort Hare–trained lawyers, were elected to the National Executive. They were joined by Walter Sisulu, a gifted trade union leader, who took over as secretary general. The prominent black communists, J. B. Marks and Moses Kotane, also rose in the ranks. Together, they met to re-invigorate the ANC with new strategies and tactics for peaceful mass defiance. They devised "Program of Action" to challenge the state and its repressive laws with mass action such as boycotts, strikes, and civil disobedience.

Before the ANC could implement its program, it had to overcome tensions in the black community, which had been plunged into violent conflict because of apartheid's racial policies. In Durban, segregation and apartheid laws had exacerbated tensions between Africans and Indians. Indians dominated the local segregated trading and market sectors and they sought to make considerable profits from their African clientele. In this context, the government also applied its apartheid rhetoric to a supposed racial differentiation between Indians and Africans, heightening tensions between the people in these communities. In some cases, the state provided Indians with preferential access to land and business licenses in order to foster a sense of racial hierarchy. When an Indian shopkeeper beat and injured—at a busy public bus terminal—an African youth for having struck his shop assistant, riots broke out. That evening and the following day, Africans who resented Indians with economic advantages attacked and damaged Indian homes and businesses across the city, killing 142 people and injuring hundreds more. Black leaders moved quickly to quell the violence and heal the rift of racial tension. Two ANC leaders, Dr. Xuma and A. W. G. Champion, formerly of the Natal ICU, met with Natal Indian Congress leader Dr. Yusuf Dadoo and they agreed on a plan to address racial intolerance. They immediately recognized that both their communities suffered from apartheid and that they therefore had a common interest in opposing the state in a united front. Further talks between the ANC and the South African Indian Congress (SAIC) led to a partnership. They planned a broad-based, non-racial movement of non-violent non-cooperation (along the lines which Gandhi and other leaders of civil disobedience had developed) to challenge the government, which emerged as the Defiance Campaign.

Prior to the launch of the Defiance Campaign in June 1952, there emerged other persistent, internal tensions within the opposition movement. Some African nationalists in the ANC were uneasy with the growing influence of the Communist Party, especially among trade union members. They were concerned that the Communist emphasis on class struggle would not serve their interests. Some Communists were likewise suspicious of ANC motives which appeared to favor a hierarchy of educated men and chiefs. In the face of state repression under the Suppression of Communism Act, however, the Communist Party dissolved itself, although the members continued to organize with other opposition movements (it re-formed in secrecy as the South African Communist Party, SACP). The Communists demonstrated their solidarity with broader movements such as the ANC by organizing a May Day protest for higher wages and better working conditions in 1950. When the police killed eighteen Africans for their part in the protest, it showed the common threats that all opponents of apartheid faced. Thereafter, African nationalists, Communists and socialists, Indian and Coloured people put aside their differences. African and Coloured workers further demonstrated their common, non-racial cause with a joint strike in 1951.

The Defiance Campaign of 1952 brought together African, Indian, and Coloured people in a mass resistance movement. The ANC took up organizational leadership and it teamed with SAIC. They planned a national campaign of peaceful non-cooperation and civil disobedience. All over the country, volunteers defied apartheid laws. They courted arrest by challenging the restrictions for segregated amenities. Beginning in Port Elizabeth and concentrated in the eastern Cape, the campaign spread to Bloemfontein, Durban, and other major cities. Protesters sat on benches, used entrances and facilities, and filled railway cars which were for "whites only." They also broke curfew laws and burned their passes. Police arrested over 8,000 people by the end of the campaign, swamping the jails and courts. The campaign started as a great success, raising black awareness of political protest and action, and drawing African, Indian, and Coloured people together. It moreover focused an international spotlight on South Africa, and the United Nations (UN) created a permanent committee to consider racism in South Africa.

The government sought to smash the campaign by raiding the homes and offices of campaign workers and arresting ANC and SAIC leaders. In response, the opposition grew violent. Although, overall, the protesters were very disciplined and people acted peacefully, some people in the segregated townships started to riot. In frustration, they stoned police and attacked government buildings. Rioters killed six whites, including a nun. The police killed some thirty Africans as they set up road blocks and opened fire with automatic weapons in a bid to contain the demonstrators. Although there was no clear link between the violent demonstrations and the campaign, the violence had a chilling effect. The government blamed the ANC for the violence and it became more determined to shut down opposition protests. Similarly, ANC leaders and many blacks were horrified at the rioters' violence and the brutal state response it provoked. The campaign fizzled out without achieving any concessions from the state, and blacks lost their enthusiasm for mass action protests. The Nationalist Party won a greater majority in the 1953 election by whipping up white fears of the rioters and preparing to get tough with the opposition movement.

After a brief period of decline, the mass opposition movement was reinvigorated by new alliances, the rising African women's movement, and widening resistance in the rural areas. Yet opposition politicians still struggled to achieve a united national front for action. Chief Albert Luthuli, an educated Christian Zulu-speaker who was awarded the Nobel Peace Prize in 1960 in recognition of his role in fighting apartheid, took over as ANC president. He organized a series of conferences with the SAIC, the reformed South African Coloured People's Organization, and the predominantly white radical Congress of Democrats. It was significant that workers also joined the movement and the non-racial South African Congress of Trade Unions (SACTU) took a leading role in representing their interests at meetings. The conferences culminated in the Congress of the People in 1955 at which more than three thousand delegates from all races and opposition groups met to create a political platform. They established the Congress Alliance and adopted the Freedom Charter, which set out a basic list of fundamental human rights and called for equal rights.

The Freedom Charter pronounced that South Africa belonged to all who lived there, regardless of race. It further called for the country to become a full non-racial democracy with all people free from restrictions on movement, religion, political beliefs, and expression. In addition to these liberal ideals which were current in parts of Europe and the United States, the Charter also outlined ideals for the economy, stating that all people should get equal pay for equal work and that there must be improved conditions of work and education. In specific reference to the mining industry, it called for the nationalization (ownership by the state for the benefit of all the people) of all the mineral wealth of the country as well as the nationalization of the banks and industry. It also called for an equitable redistribution of the land. The government perceived this declaration, and its socialist ideals for the redistribution of wealth, to be a major threat. The state argued that the Charter was a "communist" document and that the Congress of the People had conspired to overthrow the government by violence. The police arrested 156 Congress leaders and put them on trial for treason. The state dragged on the "Treason trials," which lasted from 1956 until early 1961, in a calculated effort to keep the opposition leaders out of circulation. Although the opposition leaders were frustrated by this tactic, all 156 were eventually acquitted in a major vindication. The trials had the unintended effect of drawing even more attention to the ANC and its allies and strengthening their resolve.

WOMEN'S RESISTANCE AND RURAL PROTESTS

Although men dominated opposition political leadership, African women also rose in defiance. The ANC inaugurated its Women's League in 1943, and its members played a prominent role in mass action. In 1956, Lilian Ngoyi, president of the Federation of South African Women (FSAW), and Helen Joseph, a white liberal (and later member of parliament) helped organize a mass women's protest against the extension of the pass laws to women. They began with a petition-signing campaign which gathered nearly 100,000 signatures. They then rallied more than 20,000 women to converge on the government in Pretoria to stand in a powerful yet passive silent protest. Although they won no concessions, the protest demonstrated the organizational abilities and importance of women in the opposition movement. Shortly thereafter, more than 2,000 women showed their courage by refusing to accept passes and they were arrested. Women were also at the forefront of township bus boycotts against rising fares. They joined fellow male workers in walking to work, up to twenty miles each day, for three months in early 1957. Women also led protests against the prohibition of home-brewed beer, which many relied on as an important source of income. In some cases, African women directed their hostility against men from their own communities who appeared ready to accept government-approved beer sales. Government beer sales undercut the women's income, and the proceeds were also used to fund state control of Africans, as had been the case in the Durban (municipal) system started in the 1920s. Then, in 1959, a police liquor raid on the African urban location of Cato Manor sparked serious rioting and nine police were killed leading to further state repression of African protesters.

Women and men alike shared in rising rural resistance to apartheid. By the later 1950s, African families in the countryside faced an increasingly interventionist state. They resisted government interference with agricultural and herding practices under the guise of "rehabilitation schemes" such as soil-erosion works, which limited their access to arable land, cattle-dipping for disease eradication, which was costly, and other "improvements" which people feared would undermine their independence. In cases where women appeared to be holding their ground, the government stepped in to support the chiefly patriarchy. The government replaced Chief Abram Moilwa with Chief Lucas Mangope as the Bantu Authority for Bophutatswana, for example, when Moilwa sided with women in the anti-pass campaign. The ANC also made some tentative links to rural resistance in the 1950s. In Sekhukhuneland (named for the earlier paramount ruler, soon to be renamed as the homeland of Lebowa), the migrant workers' movement *Sebatakgomo* drew on ANC philosophies and tactics to fight the Bantu Authorities Act and land rehabilitation. Women led the movement against local government-appointed chiefs in Natal and Zululand during 1959–1960. Instead, they favored popular claimants to chieftaincy who would better represent their interests and who might fend off state interference.

The most widespread and open rural resistance during this period was in Pondoland in the Transkei in 1960. It also began as opposition to the introduction of the Bantu Authorities Act in the territory which was to be the model for apartheid. African rebels had rejected the rule of the government-appointed chief, Botha Sigcau, in eastern Pondoland. They disputed his legitimacy and challenged his role in the implementation of rehabilitation measures which cut them off from the forests and important grazing lands. These men retreated to the surrounding hills to form "mountain committees" in order to plan their resistance. Under the leadership of Solomon Madikizela, a Christian peasant farmer, they attacked and intimidated those who allied with Sigcau and the government. They sought to form their own independent government and to control their own land. They managed to undermine the state's authority in the hills until the government sent in the army. In a powerful show of force and the will to use it, the army gunned down more than a dozen men after they had been tricked into a peaceful meeting to discuss a settlement of grievances. Nevertheless, the rebels had demonstrated their ability to organize and they had also, significantly, made contact with urban opposition leaders in the Congress movement. This showed the possibility for a broad-based national front of opposition which linked the countryside to the urban areas.

RISING TENSIONS, STATE REPRESSION, AND RADICALISM

State repression, which intensified in the 1960s, and the failure of resistance and protest widened internal divisions within the opposition movement. Africanists became increasingly uncomfortable with the form and direction opposition was taking. While the ANC embraced non-racialism and pursued left-leaning or socialist policies, Africanists felt that Africans should stand alone against the government since they suffered from its racist laws. The Africanists rejected foreign socialist ideologies, preferring to embrace their own culture and history of resistance to white invasion. The Africanists were suspicious of the growing radicalism of the ANC leaders such as Oliver Tambo and Nelson Mandela because they maintained contact with white Communists who had been forced underground. In 1959, Robert Sobukwe, a member of the ANC Youth League, broke away and formed the Pan Africanist Congress (PAC), splintering ANC unity. The PAC espoused a more militant Africanist platform than the ANC and this appealed especially to rural migrant workers whom the ANC had neglected. Within a year, PAC membership surpassed 25,000. The PAC then sought to upstage the ANC with its own campaign of mass action.

In what turned out to be a fateful event, the PAC planned to pre-empt ANC anti-pass demonstrations by organizing its own campaign. The PAC plan was to mobilize as many people as possible to march on police stations without their legally required pass books and so invite arrest. They sought to swamp the police with so many offenders that they could not arrest them all, thereby demonstrating that the pass system could not work if people refused to cooperate. Things did not go as planned. In March 1960, the first day of what was to be a sustained campaign, a large crowd of demonstrators and on-lookers approached the police station at Sharpeville, an African township outside Vereeniging, south of Johannesburg. As they pressed against the fence which surrounded the station, the nervous police inside opened fire on the unarmed people. The terrified crowd scattered and ran from the station, yet the police continued to shoot at the fleeing demonstrators. Sixty-nine people were killed—most of them were shot in the back—and perhaps two hundred more were wounded. The shocking massacre had a major impact on the country. On the one hand, it drew a resounding international condemnation of the apartheid government's actions and policies. On the other hand, it galvanized both black and white in South Africa. Africans rose in mass defiance.

The ANC president, Luthuli, joined the PAC protest and publically burned his pass in an act of solidarity. Large numbers of Africans then marched in protest in Durban and Cape Town and even appeared on the verge of storming the whites-only parliament. The whites became increasingly nervous as they prepared to confront and suppress the opposition. The police struck out against the protesters, arresting over 18,000 people within days. The government declared a state of emergency, which provided for even greater police powers of search and arrest. They sealed off townships, swept the country to arrest dissidents, and banned the PAC and ANC. At the same time, the Nationalists reaffirmed white supremacy and made South Africa a republic in 1961. The government also took South Africa out of the British Commonwealth (the association of former British colonies) despite considerable opposition from white English-speakers, thereby further isolating it from the international community. In the wake of the Sharpeville massacre, the government declined to apply for re-admission as a republic because of the anticipated opposition from a whole host of newly independent African member states of the Commonwealth and international disapproval of apartheid policies. Britain and the United States, however, blocked a UN effort to completely isolate South Africa through sanctions, in part because they still had significant investments in the country.

As the government became increasingly repressive and intransigent, Nelson Mandela was at the forefront of the ANC and PAC leadership which now felt they had no alternative but to resort to more militant action. Mandela, who was born the son of a chief in 1918, grew up in the rural Transkei. There he learned about African traditions and embraced what he saw as the virtues of African democracy for all men, although he admitted this did not extend to women. He was strongly influenced by his Christian education and the politics of rural chieftaincy. After attending Fort Hare, he left for the opportunities of Johannesburg in 1941. There he trained to be a lawyer and learned about radical politics. He rose rapidly in the ranks of the ANC Youth League where he made fast friends with Oliver Tambo, his law partner, and Walter Sisulu. He became First Deputy President of the ANC in 1952, and he furthered the party's commitment to non-racialism and an alliance with the Communist party. By 1960, he shared the younger radical leadership's bitterness over government repression. While they did not abandon the tactics of mass action, they felt there was a need for a more militant resistance to the apartheid state.

Mandela went underground and with Sisulu and Joe Slovo of SACP formed *Umkhonto we Sizwe* or simply MK ("The Spear of the Nation"), the new armed wing of the ANC. They argued that the state itself was illegitimate and that because it used violence to repress political opposition, they needed to begin an armed struggle. MK, however, sought to avoid attacks on people. It targeted government installations (including the offices of Bantu Authorities leaders), electricity pylons, railways, jails, and post offices for sabotage with explosives. The PAC established Poqo as a more militant armed force aimed at open guerilla warfare. Members of Poqo killed government informers and police and made attempts on the lives of various homeland leaders and chiefs. Both the ANC and the PAC suffered from the constraints of being banned, so they sent operatives out of the country to get assistance from supportive nations and to set up in exile. They traveled to other sympathetic independent African countries, and they also established ties with socialist and communist states such as the Soviet Union and East Germany. The government was determined to crush these organizations and it intensified its police activities with more brutal tactics.

The government arrested Mandela in 1962 after he returned from travels overseas. In 1963, the police managed to infiltrate the PAC and then arrested over 3,000 members, bringing the organization to its knees. Later that year, the police descended on a house at Rivonia, oustide Johannesburg. There they captured seventeen other leaders of MK and put them on trial for sabotage. Mandela was included as a defendant in the proceedings at which he made a moving speech (he could not otherwise speak in public because he had been banned) where he declared he was prepared to die for what he saw as the ANC's just cause. He and his fellow accused were found guilty and sentenced to life imprisonment (excepting one acquittal). Mandela and others were sent off to be incarcerated on Robben Island, just off of Cape Town. There, through surreptitious communications, they continued to plan and prepare to liberate the country. Although the loss of the leadership was a major blow to the ANC, the people continued to fight for change. As the leaders were taken away, the defiant crowd shouted a soon to be common refrain, *amandla ngawethu* ("Power to the people").

Despite the increasingly repressive tactics of the government and the set-backs for internal black political organizations, black South Africans from all walks of life were increasingly focused on resistance. By the later 1960s and early 1970s, two new forces emerged to join the "liberation struggle." First, the growing numbers of skilled African workers in the urban areas organized broader union movements. As more urban workers became politically conscious, they fused day-to-day workplace concerns with broader political demands. Fueled by poor wages and lousy accommodations and probably sparked by a fiery speech from the Zulu king, Goodwill, Durban workers went on a massive strike in 1973. While these strikes spread, they did so among non-unionized African workers. As more strikes erupted over the next few years, they set the stage for a broader framework of trade union organization and political activity.

Second, there emerged a reworked political philosophy of "black consciousness," which drew upon earlier Africanist ideas, and the wave of "Black Power" emanating from the American civil rights movement. Fostered in black colleges and politically active churches, it was articulated most eloquently by Steve Biko. In 1968, Biko had led the black South African Students' Organization (SASO) to break away from the multi-racial National Union of South African Students (NUSAS) in an effort to free it from what he argued was dependence on white liberals. Black consciousness was based on, among other things, a deep sense of pride and confidence in being black. Although it appeared to some as equally race-conscious as apartheid, black consciousness actually challenged the ethnic and racial divisions of the state because "black" specifically included Indian and Coloured people. The term was intended to be a positive assertion of a unified identity for all those oppressed by apartheid. By 1972, the broader Black People's Convention formed in order to bring together various black consciousness groups, including the Black Allied Work-ers Union, and black community health programs run by Mamphele Ram-phele, a personal friend of Biko's. It was school children, though, who were the driving force behind the next major demonstration against apartheid.

Infused with the ideology of black consciousness, school students started to protest the state's Bantu Education Act policies. By the mid-1970s, the number of African children attending schools had risen three-fold since the in-ception of apartheid to more than 3.5 million. Faced with the harsh realities of life under apartheid, these students developed a sophisticated understanding of mass action to protest against government policies. They organized under the South African Students' Movement (SASM) and began protesting the woefully inadequate facilities and resources which the state's Department of Bantu Edu-cation provided. While making links with the underground ANC and the black consciousness movement, the SASM leaders obtained a broader picture of the entire system of oppression in the country. They saw the connections between the state's racist policies, the pernicious effects of the migrant labor system and capitalism, and even the detrimental effects of alcohol abuse. Be-ginning in 1976, SASM leaders helped organize country-wide protest marches against broader economic problems such as the reduction of government sub-sidies on essential food items including bread, rising unemployment and rents, and urban overcrowding. Yet they were most concerned with the poor educa-tion system, and specifically the government's introduction of Afrikaans (which they termed the "language of the oppressor," even though it was also the first language of most of the million-plus Coloured people) as a mandatory medium of instruction.

SASM initiated a series of school boycotts and drew national attention when the police responded with force and shot a 13-year-old protester. The students then organized a large demonstration for the schools in Soweto in June 1976. Children from all the area schools converged in a protest march which took them to a nearby soccer stadium. The police, in notorious fashion, once again greatly overreacted and used massive force to disperse the students. The demonstrations then developed into confrontations with the police and riots which spread and boiled over the whole country, including Coloured and Indian students as well. The government's harsh reaction helped to provoke a year-long series of school boycotts and attacks on police and government buildings and state-run municipal beer halls. The protests escalated and the state retaliated with brutal violence. Police shot into crowds of unarmed demonstrators, killing hundreds. The police, moreover, made thousands of ar-rests and resorted to the particularly harsh tactic of killing people in detention, although these were officially reported as "suicides." The summer of 1976 was the period of the most widespread and sustained level of unrest and state vio-lence yet, and it reflected a growing sense of frustration and urgency for change among the blacks. These frustrations soon spread out among the oppressed majority, and the courage of the Soweto school children and the effect of police actions inspired more people to rise in mass defiance of the state.

SOUTH AFRICA IN THE GLOBAL CONTEXT

From the 1950s into the 1970s, the South African state was increasingly isolated and condemned. Its bloody repression of the initially peaceful African resistance in South Africa and the rise of the independent African states across the continent revealed the Nationalist government to be intransigent and reactionary. As African statesmen such as Kwame Nkrumah of Ghana were winning independence for their new countries, there was growing international pressure on South Africa to reform and recognize the rights of Africans. Indeed, in 1960, the British prime minister, Harold Macmillan, spoke to the white parliament in Cape Town about the "winds of change" blowing across the continent. The new African states, moreover, offered the best promise of new markets for South African exports. In response, Prime Minister Verwoerd sought to make apartheid appear more palatable to the world without undermining its protection for white privileges. Although his government made some lingering attempts at reform, including "decolonization" and the granting of independence to some homelands, the international community correctly viewed these actions as hollow propaganda. By the mid-1970s, the United Nations had called on South Africa to leave Namibia (South West Africa) and it sought to bring sanctions against the country, declaring apartheid to be a "crime against humanity."

There were additional pressures within the southern African region. Although it still supported South Africa through trade investment, Britain had refused to transfer Lesotho, Swaziland, or Botswana to South African control. These states achieved independence through the 1960s, even though they remained heavily dependent upon the South African economy. White-dominated regimes were toppling all around. The Portugese were also forced to rapidly relinquish their colonies in Angola and Mozambique after African opposition forces in these countries precipitated a coup in Portugal. Similarly, the intransigence of the white colonial government in Rhodesia to the north of South Africa, and its declaration of independence from Britain in a vain bid to preserve white rule, also led to an African nationalist war for liberation.

In Namibia, the South Africans faced another armed struggle from the South West African People's Organization (SWAPO). The South African regime lashed back. It stepped up its cold war rhetoric of anti-communism against the ANC and other opposition groups. Although the ANC had certainly made connections with the Soviets for aid and training, it remained an open and non-aligned movement. Still, the South African state was able to convince the United States and Britain that it was fighting against the spread of communism since the Soviets had supported Cuban troops in their bid to help the Popular Movement for the Liberation of Angola (MPLA). United States forces then joined the South Africans in what would be a protracted and brutal war in Angola, ostensibly pitting the West against the communists. This strategic alliance between South Africa and the United States helped to dull the blows of sanctions and growing international pressure for South Africa to change, but only for a time. South Africa could still bargain with the valuable strategic minerals such as manganese and platinum which it produced. Eventually, however, it had to work at self-sufficiency in oil and weapons because other nations refused to trade with the racist state. These international pressures had the effect of driving the Nationalist government into an even more inward-looking stance. For a time, the party was divided between the *verkramptes* (the cramped), those who opposed any reforms, and the *verligtes* (the enlightened), those who felt South Africa had to change in order to survive and try to preserve white rule.

CONCLUSION

Apartheid brought together the political agenda of the Nationalists with the demands of white-dominated industrial capitalism. Through its experimentation with apartheid policies, the government sought to promote the Afrikaners as the dominant ethnic nationalist power while also finding ways to update segregation to cope with rising African urbanization and political aspirations. In doing so, it created a far more comprehensive and complex landscape of racial difference. First, the Nationalists defined and promoted their own ethnic identity to the exclusion of all others except for those English-speaking whites who accepted their views. They provided for the advancement and privilege of white Afrikaners in government structures as they enlarged the bureaucracy and state-supported industry. Afrikaner cultural organizations then flourished with state patronage.

As the Nationalist government became increasingly race conscious, it sharpened its racist ideology to prevent "race-mixing" in all spheres of life. The state sought to render blacks more visible and hence more vulnerable through racial identification as Native/Bantu, Indian, and Coloured people. The state ensured that there was a hierarchy assigned to these perceived racial differences and "non-whites" were destined to serve "whites" in subordinate roles. Race classification was extended to define all Africans as members of "tribal" categories. These were only loosely based upon certain features of traditional, pre-conquest African societies and they disregarded the actual common experiences of Africans. This categorization further divided South African society, and the state used it to sideline Africans from national politics. Africans were then allowed to pursue only their "traditional" political and economic aspirations in their designated "homelands." As part of the exclusion of Africans from South African society, the state perpetrated the forced removal of millions of blacks from white areas. They were then forced to languish in overcrowded and economically unviable rural homelands and urban townships. Still, a small number of ambitious African leaders managed to carve out a niche for themselves in the homeland governments. Men such as Matanzima and Buthelezi represented a new group of African leaders who embraced state support for a reworked ethnic nationalism. They drew upon powerful and popular ideas grounded in their history, but they did not represent the common interests of large numbers of urban Africans. Neither these policies nor the considerable power of the dramatically increased state police apparatus could contain the forces of historical change contained in African urbanization. Africans continued to move to the cities and, despite state efforts to contain and control this influx, they became essential and permanent parts of the "white" cities.

Black opposition to the government rose to meet the challenges of the apartheid era. The ANC first had to work to overcome the tensions within the black society. Segregation and the tactics of the South African state had accentuated ethnic and racial differences to the point where it was hard to forge a united front. Over time, however, mass action and sophisticated leadership made alliances which overcame internal tensions. Women and rural Africans were also a major part of the opposition movement. They played significant roles in shaping the issues of protest and in making links between rural and urban opposition. State repression and intransigence provoked more militant and radical opposition movements. Communists and Africanists both contributed to the formulation of new opposition ideologies. While the ANC embraced an alliance with the Communists, the Africanists spawned the PAC and later the black consciousness movement. Together, these organizations put increasing pressure on the apartheid state, and they also drew international attention to the plight of all black South Africans. The state responded not with meaningful reform, but with intensifying repression. These rising tensions set the stage for broader mass opposition and more intense confrontations with the state.

Questions to Consider

1. How did the National party consolidate an Afrikaner government?
2. What were the key features of apartheid and how did the state apply apartheid laws? What were the homelands and how were they intended to function?

3. What impact did apartheid have on black society, and how did blacks find ways to cope with and overcome the repression?

4. How did blacks organize their mass opposition to apartheid? How did their policies and strategies change? What role did black women and rural Africans play in the opposition movements?

5. How did state repression infuse the opposition movements with new inspirations and approaches to the demand for change in South Africa?

FURTHER READINGS

ADAM, H., and GILIOMEE, H., *Ethnic Power Mobilized* (London, 1979). A critical analysis of Afrikaner ideology and its application to state rule. This work uses a sociological and political science framework and it is well-organized and clearly written.

CELL, J., *The Highest Stage of White Supremacy: The Origins of Segregation in South Africa and the American South* (New Haven, 1982). A useful but now dated comparative analysis which allows students to get a sense of the similarities and differences in segregation in both countries, and to understand why South Africa developed apartheid.

GERHART, G., *Black Power in South Africa: The Evolution of an Ideology* (Berkeley, 1979). A comprehensive analysis of black political thought and the socialist and Communist influences which shaped the approach of many radicals to mass action. It emphasizes the African initiative and it does a fine job of clearly explaining the origins of black nationalism and consciousness.

KARIS, T., and CARTER, G., *From Protest to Challenge: Documents of African Politics in South Africa, 1882–90,* five volumes [Volume 5 was co-edited by Karis and Gerhart] (Standford, Johannesburg and London, 1972–1997). A well-organized and very useable collection of primary sources for African political movements and ideas ranging from early elite leaders' editorials in newspapers to ANC policy documents. It may be difficult to find all the volumes now.

LUTHULI, A., *Let My People Go: An Autobiography* (London, 1962). A richly detailed account of the ANC struggle by the former president of the organization and Nobel Peace Prize recipient. Luthuli provides great insight into the tensions between the urban and rural elements of the opposition.

MANDELA, N., *Long Walk to Freedom* (London, 1995) and *No Easy Walk to Freedom* (London, 1965). Two revised editions of the autobiographies of the former first black president of South Africa. Mandela's words are as insightful as they are moving. He provides a vivid picture of his whole life, with an emphasis on his political work and his struggle for justice and freedom. These are essential reading.

MARKS, S., and TRAPIDO, S. (editors), *The Politics of Race Class and Nationalism in Twentieth-Century South Africa* (London, 1987). Another collection of well-researched and well-written essays using a political economic approach to the issues prior to the transition to democracy. It is particularly good for issues of culture and class and it has an excellent introductory essay by the editors.

MAYLAM, P., *A History of the African People of South Africa* (Johannesburg, 1986). An excellent general introduction to all of the African societies in the country. Maylam also takes his insightful analysis up to the modern period of black protest politics, and he provides sound insights into the emergence of opposition movements.

MELI, F., *South Africa Belongs to Us: A History of the A.N.C.* (London and Harare, 1988). An interesting interpretation of the ANC by a member of the organization. This does not take the standard scholarly approach to writing and analysis, nor is it unbiased, but it can be read both as a secondary work and as a primary source.

O'MEARA, D., *Forty Lost Years: The Apartheid State and the Politics of the National Party, 1948–94* (Randburg, 1996). An masterful analysis of the political economy of apartheid and the ethnic nationalism of the Afrikaner-dominated National party. It is at once a fine, scholarly work with sound research and a moving lament for the destruction of South African society during the apartheid years.

SAMPSON, A., *Mandela, The Authorized Biography* (New York, 1999). An updated and recent analysis of Mandela. Although it provides due praise, it is not uncritical of Mandela, and it does a fine job of outlining some of the internal controversies surrounding the formulation of ANC policies.

CHAPTER X

The African Transformation of South Africa, 1976–1994

By the mid-1970s, black South Africans were ready to force change and they began to push the apartheid state into a defensive stance. They made a major impact on the apartheid state in two ways. First, they showed, through urbanization and their role as the primary source of skilled and unskilled labor, that they were the most important part of the growing economy. Second, they showed their ability to organize a powerful front of protest and resistance to apartheid. In the wake of the massive strikes by African workers and the mass protests sparked by the Soweto uprising, the state used increasingly repressive tactics to fend off all internal challenges to white rule as well as to combat the increasing number of external challenges from the international community and the "frontline" states which bordered South Africa. The South African state provoked regional tensions as it sought to undermine other revolutionary insurgencies based in neighboring countries. It perceived these new "leftist" governments to be threatening to South African interests. These actions served to draw greater attention to South Africa and to fuel the international condemnation of its politics. Meanwhile, the blacks worked to create a united front of opposition within South Africa and to transform the new wave of international disapproval into an effective weapon in the struggle for liberation. As the South African economy grew, industrial capitalists realized that many features of apartheid were now dysfunctional. Racism, the repression of all opposition, and the migrant labor system had served effectively to undermine the full and unfettered participation of all blacks—who, we must recall, constituted the majority of the population—in the economy as workers and consumers. In the long run, however, it was the sustained mass action of black South Africans which would show the apartheid regime that it could not continue its racist and undemocratic form of government.

The South African Security State and Regional Politics

As the pressures for change mounted, there emerged new political alignments both within the white government in Pretoria and among the opposition factions. First, the Nationalist Party (NP) faced a growing split within its ranks and from other white liberal opposition groups. As the state grappled with attempted reforms to the apartheid system, increasing numbers of white conservative hardliners called for a return to the days of more rigid white supremacist apartheid. The NP had already faced a split when, in 1969, Hertzog broke away to form the even more conservative *Herstigte Nasionale Party* (Restored National party) to fight for the restoration of rigid apartheid. On the other side of the white political spectrum, the Progressive Federal Party, which pressed for liberal reforms and an opening of democratic institutions to blacks, lost ground as whites feared being swamped by the growing black majority. Then, by the 1980s, NP efforts to appease opponents and introduce reform measures—albeit very limited—drove out a core of hardliners who then joined up with the Afrikaner ideologue, Dr. Andries Treurnicht, in the Conservative Party. An even more far right white political faction, the *Afrikaner Weerstandsbeweging* (Afrikaner Resistance Movement, or AWB) emerged in 1978 under Eugene Terreblanche as an extra-parliamentary opponent to the NP. The AWB quickly assumed a white fascist racist stance and openly displayed stylized swastikas. As the NP worked to hold the majority of whites in the center, the white political spectrum was shifting to the right. The NP then faced a crisis as news of an internal scandal broke. The press revealed that the government had misappropriated public funds to be used in secret propaganda tactics. This led to the resignation of Prime Minister Vorster and the election of P. W. Botha in 1978. As minister of defense, Botha, had built the South African military into the continent's most formidable force. As prime minister, he remained prepared to use as much force as necessary to maintain white power, but he was also prepared to consider some reforms if these assured white domination of the country.

Beginning in the late 1970s, under Botha, the South African security establishment and army became increasingly powerful and influential in political matters. A United Nations embargo from 1977 prevented member states from trading arms to South Africa; in response, the South African state developed its own sophisticated arms manufacturing company, Armscor. White military strategists who were prone to a paranoid cold war mentality began referring to the mounting opposition to the apartheid state both internally and externally as a "total onslaught." The South African state's security apparatus was enhanced and extended to cope with the intensification of mass internal resistance and the broadening scope of military operations in the region. It also included dehumanizing black opponents as "communists"—who were perceived as undermining not only white supremacy, but the whole fabric of capitalist society as well—in order to justify destroying them.

The South African security establishment, which included a national police force, a clandestine internal secret police force in the Bureau of State Security (BOSS), and the South African Defense Force (which also had secret contingents for "black operations"), ratcheted up its activities. Under Botha, the government developed a "total strategy" of what it considered to be a counter-revolutionary plan to thwart its opponents. This was based upon the reactionary counter-insurgency tactics which colonial regimes such as the French and later the American military in Viet Nam, as well as the repressive regimes in Chile and El Salvador, had used to suppress opposition movements. This "total strategy" included police and military suppression of opponents as well as programs of political reform and "socio-economic upliftment" to "win the hearts and minds" of the blacks. The strategy was calculated to render the opposition ineffective. In any event, it failed on all counts.

The highly militarized South African government engaged in a series of counter-revolutionary wars in the frontline states. This was done in part to protect itself against infiltration, and in part to cultivate an alliance with the United States and Britain as part of a broader cold war strategy of fighting communism around the world. The South African government saw itself—and wanted to be seen by Western allies—as the last bastion against communism in Africa. Toward this end, it mounted increasingly involved and costly military operations against leftist liberation movements in Angola and Mozambique, and it continued to occupy South West Africa (Namibia). South African forces, including very effective co-opted African troops, supported the National Union for the Total Independence of Angola (UNITA) in its bid to oust the new revolutionary Angolan government. In the context of Cold War tensions, the United States also provided UNITA with arms and funds just as the Soviets supported the Cuban troops who fought on the side of the Angolan government. South Africa, moreover, provided arms and technical assistance to the counter-insurgents of the Mozambique National Resistance (RENAMO) who were fighting against the leftist post-colonial Mozambican government. In each of these cases, including the struggle of the South West African People's Organization (SWAPO) to oust the South Africans, the wars would prove increasingly costly for the South African state.

South Africa was also becoming isolated regionally. As the Portuguese left their colonies, the Rhodesians were losing their battle to the black Zimbabwean liberation movement. Despite South African assistance, the white settler regime lost control and Robert Mugabe's Zimbabwe African National Union (ZANU) government took over Zimbabwe in 1980. The South African government made some attempts to establish diplomatic relations with the black southern African states in an effort to counteract its negative image and isolation. Yet only Malawi (formerly Nyasaland), under the conservative independent leader, Hastings Banda, showed any interest, and then only in the economic benefits which the Pretoria government offered. Despite its propaganda and diplomacy, South Africa was increasingly isolated and vilified.

South African forces also sought to close off any external havens for opposition movements. Escalating conflicts with and in neighboring states had left open the way for the African National Congress (ANC) and other opposition movements to establish bases in those states from which they could infiltrate guerillas back into South Africa. So fierce was the fighting in Mozambique, however, that the Mozambicans agreed, in the Nkomati Accord of 1984, not to allow the ANC to operate from their territory in exchange for a South African promise not to support RENAMO. South Africa continued to support the rebels, but Mozambique could not afford to resist South African power. South Africa's economic dominance in the region proved to be the key leverage it needed to ensure that neighbor states did not provide assistance to the ANC and other opposition movements thereafter. Yet South Africa defied international opposition and censure as well as the law of sovereign states when it continued to make attacks on opposition bases in neighboring states such as Zimbabwe and Botswana during the later 1980s. Although the frontline states (Angola, Mozambique, Malawi, Swaziland, Lesotho, Tanzania, Zambia, and Zimbabwe) tried to break free of South African economic domination by organizing the Southern African Development Coordination Conference (SADCC), those countries remained heavily reliant on South African exports of oil, electricity, and goods as well as the migrant workers' earnings in South Africa. This dependence meant that there were definite limits to the extent to which these states could defy South Africa or lend support to opposition movements.

By the mid-1980s, the South African government faced international disapproval. Even its allies, Ronald Reagan and Margaret Thatcher, the right-wing conservative leaders of the United States and Britain, could not forestall the growing global effort to isolate South Africa. Both Reagan and Thatcher had initially condemned the ANC as a "terrorist, communist organization" and opposed economic sanctions against South Africa. They preferred to support "constructive engagement" (continued investment in the hopes this would lead to reform) until it was clear that public opinion in the United States and Britain was so strongly against apartheid that they were compelled to enforce broad sanctions to isolate South Africa and force change. By that time, in the mid-1980s, however, the situation in South Africa had deteriorated so badly that the country was ungovernable, and the forces for change were gaining the upper hand.

Resistance from Below and the Failure of "Reform"

Post-1976 black resistance forced the state to consider some attempt at reform. The growing forces of opposition, especially urban Africans, demanded improvements in their working and living conditions as well political change, even if the latter was an uncertainly defined factor. Following the demands of white business and industry, and the recommendations of a series of government commissions, P. W. Botha's government warned that the Afrikaners must "adapt or die" and others in the government pronounced the death of apartheid. The directors of major corporations, such as Harry Oppenheimer of Anglo-American, which dominated the South African financial world (Harry's father Ernest had engineered the takeover of Rhode's De Beer's diamond company and parlayed his holdings into a dominant share of the gold mines), became openly critical of the limits which apartheid imposed on the efficiency of African labor upon which they depended and on the "free market." These criticisms also resonated with the growing popularity of the Western world's "anticommunist" free market rhetoric, and the South African state wanted to align itself with these British and American policies. The government realized that extending limited separate powers to a handful of Africans in the isolated homelands was insufficient to contain opposition and provide for growth. They now believed they needed to co-opt more blacks as allies in the cities.

First, the state increased spending on African society. Soweto and other townships were electrified, and other services were slightly improved. The state also offered some blacks the possibility of purchasing property in the black townships in order to increase their stake in the system. The state significantly increased expenditure on black education, but there remained a gap between the amounts spent on white and black children. The government also promised a gradual erosion of the protection of jobs for whites only, as well as the possibility of participating in local black township government, which hitherto had been run by white bureaucrats. Over the next few years, other features of "petty apartheid" were also relaxed. The government allowed for more interracial sports activities and teams, certain hotels were opened to all who could afford them, and "Section 10" Africans were granted greater rights to move from town to town and to remain in the white urban areas. Some Africans were now allowed to bring their families with them into the urban areas and to establish some sort of permanent, stable existence there. The majority of Africans, however, would still be limited to rights in the homelands only. Urban blacks were then to be granted some greater degree of control over their own communities. In 1977, the government passed the Community Council Act which provided for elected local governments in the townships. The government's hope was that elected black councilors would defuse discontent and provide the aspirant black middle class some stake in the system. These councils, however, were in-effective and they failed to deflect opposition.

Not surprisingly given the recent state violence against them, the blacks remained deeply suspicious of government motives, and they continued to re-sist while pressing for change. First, banned and illegal African trade unions continued to work for labor improvements, but they also started to make links with broader grass-roots community organizations known as "civics." The Fed-eration of South African Trade Unions (FOSATU) and the Council of Unions of South Africa (CUSA) had deep roots among increasing numbers of workers on the shop floor, and they extended their activities to include more overtly political demands on behalf of blacks. While some unions remained non-racial, others such as the South African Allied Workers' Union (SAAWU) were more openly oriented toward black consciousness, and they represented mostly black workers' issues. SAAWU was moreover involved in community-level civics issues and it openly opposed the homeland government in the Ciskei, where there was strong union support. The unions grew substantially in mem-bership and power by the early 1980s. They also made significant links with the civics, often joining in mutually supportive action. Black Johannesburg consumers, for example, boycotted Colgate Palmolive brand products in 1981 in support of a workers' bid for union organization in the company. Workers also went on strike in Port Elizabeth in support of the work of the local black civic association. Over the next few years, protest politics would bridge trade unions, community organizations, and student movements.

Beginning in 1979, there was a massive new wave of protests sweeping South Africa. Students across the country engaged in widespread stayaways and destruction of schools as they called for the creation of a single, non-racial education system. They formed the new Congress of South African Students (COSAS) which reached out to the radical white students' National Union of South African Students (NUSAS) and also made links with unemployed youth who were not in the schools. Black consumers also held very effective boycotts of white-owned businesses, and there was little the police could do when peo-ple simply refused to purchase goods or use bus services. The state, however, grew increasingly frustrated with the resistance and it lashed out with riot po-lice and tougher security measures designed to intimidate and suppress opposi-tion. In response, the blacks banded together in the civics to work for change at the community level. They protested high rents and poor services as they raised awareness of government policies. New magazines and newspapers emerged to report on issues and educate people in the townships about resis-tance politics. There was also a growing militancy among many Africans in the wake of the brutal state repression of the Soweto protests. In 1977, the police announced the death in detention from "a hunger strike" of the black

AFRICAN WOMEN FACE THE POLICE   African women, who often bore the brunt of economic depression, sought to challenge state policies. Here they face the police after a demonstration at Cato Manor, Durban. *Source: Getty Images, Inc./Hulton Archive Photos.*

consciousness leader, Steve Biko. Almost no one believed this official version of his death, and it was later revealed he died as a result of a brutal police beating.

A new black consciousness movement, the Azanian (***Azania*** was the black consciousness name for South Africa) People's Organization (AZAPO) was formed in 1978. It took a hard African-socialist line in support of black workers, but failed to win wide support. The ANC remained the leading opposition movement even though it was banned and could not operate openly in the country. Unable to engage in political action in South Africa, thousands of young men and women left the country to learn about ANC and radical politics and to train in guerilla tactics with the ANC's military wing, MK. They went to secret bases in sympathetic nearby states such as the Solomon Mhlangu Freedom College in Tanzania (named after an ANC member who was killed in a shootout with police), or even overseas, where there was a growing community of opposition exiles. They planned to infiltrate South Africa in order to further the liberation struggles and to develop an opposition government in waiting. Some MK guerillas managed to return clandestinely to South Africa, where they sabotaged government installations.

POLICE DISPERSE WOMEN PROTESTERS   The white state was determined to break African resistance by any means. The police broke up a protest in the Cato Manor area in Durban. Three people were killed and 15 were injured. *Source: AP/Wide World Photos.*

The government responded to the growing discontent and the more effective political strategies of the opposition with a renewed but ultimately a hollow attempt at reform. First, the state sought to defuse workers' tensions in order to address the needs of capitalists for a stable and efficient work force. They allowed blacks to form legal trade unions that would have rights to negotiate with management and owners, and significantly the right to strike, but only if they registered with the government, and if they provided a list of all their members. While a few African unions rejected this offer, other powerful unions took advantage of this new political clout and then showed that they would not be controlled by the state. By the mid-1980s, the umbrella labor organizations of the Congress of South African Trade Unions (COSATU) and a revived National Union of Mineworkers (NUM) had emerged as a major political force which linked with broader popular opposition movements. Following the principles of the "total strategy" for political reform, Botha's government also embarked on a strategy of incorporation and co-option.

In 1983, Botha devised a new constitution which elevated him to an all-powerful executive presidency (similar to the United States model) and created a race-based "tricameral" (three houses) parliament. The new parliament, which came into effect in 1984 following approval in a whites-only referendum, consisted of a 178-member House of Assembly for whites, an 85-member House of Representatives for Coloureds, and the 45-member House of Delegates for Indians. It was an attempt to provide a political outlet for some blacks but in a racially divisive way. A significant feature of this system was that even in joint sessions, whites outnumbered Coloureds and Indians 178-130, ensuring that white supremacy could be maintained. More importantly, it still left the majority African population out of the country's formal political structures. As president, Botha held supreme power and he presided over a cabinet which dealt with general state matters, including all matters pertaining to the majority African population. Education, local government, and health issues were left to each group's racially defined "own affairs" department. Local administration for services across the country was to be governed by localized Regional Services Councils which included blacks, but only as government appointees.

By 1986, the government had relaxed some other features of the apartheid system. It allowed Africans greater freedom in the cities, freedom to rent apartments and to engage in small-scale trading. It also lifted bans on interracial sex and marriage. It recognized that the homelands could not sustain the populations assigned to them, and it allowed for an increase in African urbanization, in part to serve the needs of industry. The state repealed many of the myriad pass laws, but still sought to contain Africans in designated urban townships. Yet, because of the total lack of services in these zones, Africans preferred to take their chances by moving into what would become vast, informal shack settlements near to the city centers such as Khayelitsha ("new home") outside of Cape Town. These squatter settlements became sites of unrest as discontented and impoverished urban Africans squared off against the police who sought to contain the urban sprawl. Overall, the few reforms were outweighed by greater state repression of those who refused to be co-opted.

Through the early 1980s, a new culture of resistance emerged. It cut across lines of age, gender, and ethnicity as Indians, Coloureds, Africans, and a growing number of young whites joined forces to oppose the state and specifically its proposed reforms. Botha had underestimated the level of unity which the black opposition had achieved and he therefore miscalculated the degree to which the white state could co-opt parts of black society in a piecemeal fashion. Social-, worker- and community-based associations, some of which were new and others which had their roots back in the nineteenth century, took the place of the formal political organizations such as the ANC which could not operate in the country. The churches, moreover, became an important force in opposition politics since their leaders could still operate in public. Desmond Tutu, the Anglican Archbishop of Cape Town who won the Nobel Peace Prize in 1984 for his anti-apartheid work, was a prominent and vocal critic of the government. Similarly, Beyers Naude, a white former member of the Afrikaner Dutch Reformed Church, appeared to many Afrikaners to be a traitor when he led the World Alliance of Reformed Churches in opposition to apartheid policies. These men dealt strong blows to the government on moral grounds. In August 1983, they met with trade unions, women's groups, student organizations, and churches, among others, in order to form the United Democratic Front (UDF). Radical leaders still within South Africa such as Nelson Mandela's wife, Winnie, who suffered constant police harassment while her husband was in prison, and Anglican Bishop Desmond Tutu were prominent members of the new movement.

The UDF accepted the ANC's basic principles and the Freedom Charter as its platform, but it rejected the idea of armed struggle and other strategies, preferring instead to rely upon peaceful mass action. While the UDF's national leadership maintained links with the underground ANC, there were also local, grassroots organizations in the front which did not always agree or work with the ANC. Nevertheless, the UDF did weld together a broad range of disparate groups. Its chief aim was to oppose the new racially divided and exclusive parliament as well as the black township councils. It orchestrated a countrywide series of demonstrations including strikes at factories, student and consumer boycotts of schools and white businesses, township insurrections and rent boycotts, and general mass stayaways or general strikes. The UDF also relentlessly repeated calls for the unbanning of the ANC and other opposition parties and the release of Nelson Mandela. This was the rising tide of mass action which would force the apartheid state to consider changing its policy from reform to negotiation and outright change.

THE REJECTION OF "REFORM": UPRISINGS AND OPPOSITION TENSIONS

The UDF set in motion a series of popular struggles which would achieve its aim of rendering the country ungovernable using "the people's power." Black South Africans, especially in the urban areas, had rejected government reforms and were bursting to liberate themselves from the combined effects of apartheid and poverty. Thus, the geography of resistance reflected the concentration of people and activism in the major black settlements and townships surrounding Johannesburg, Cape Town, and Durban. A UDF-led campaign focused on opposition to elections for the tricameral parliament and the township councils. In the elections of 1983 and 1984, fewer than 15 percent of those eligible voted in council elections in the Johannesburg region, and about the same low number voted in the elections for the Indian and Coloured houses of parliament. The black councils, which tried to operate despite the lack of popular acceptance, became a target of opposition. African councilors were forced by the state to raise their own operating revenues. They faced the impossible task of having to provide for millions of new residents with limited resources. When the councils raised rents sharply, the township residents protested and condemned the system. They perceived the councilors, some of whom were corrupt and skimming off revenue into their own pockets, as government stooges and sellouts. Residents then engaged in rent boycotts and demonstrations, killing councilors in some cases. Other insurrections flared in townships across the Transvaal as people protested the new parliament and state attempts to enforce rents and to remove squatters. Strikes, bus boycotts, and stayaways left millions of people at home where they demonstrated and confronted the police. By 1985, the townships and urban settlements were boiling over.

The government precipitated an upward spiral of urban violence by declaring a national state of emergency in 1985 in response to the mass action. Although Botha's intention was to re-establish government control of the townships and to return to the reform process—he initially hoped to "cross the Rubicon" to negotiations with the ANC—he instead used the state of emergency as a means for further repression to safeguard white interests. By this time, the Nationalist government was facing increased opposition from the white right and the Conservative Party. In order to contend with this element and its expectation that black mass actions be shut down, Botha unleashed the security forces. This reflected the reactionary, somewhat desperate situation which the apartheid government found itself in as a result of mass opposition to its policies.

Under the state of emergency, the army was sent into the townships to support the state police in what was, in effect, a war against its own citizens. The police detained thousands of people without due process, tortured and abused hundreds during interrogations and killed dozens, although many of these deaths were attributed to "suicide." The funerals of those killed by state violence often became venues for political rallies where the flags of banned organizations such as the Pan Africanist Congress (PAC) and the Communist Party were flown and people spoke in defiance of the state as they referred to the dead as martyrs in the struggle. In response, the state increased its banning of people and political organizations, including the UDF. Moreover, it suspended the rule of law and placed severe restrictions on the media, thus preventing reporting on unrest and protests across the country. The government also relied upon increasingly militarized homeland government forces and African police as well as other secret vigilante forces of government-supported infiltrators who fought against the opposition forces. These forces were drawn from the ranks of those blacks who feared the radical politics of township youth and therefore allied with the white state to further their interests.

Far from stabilizing the country, the state of emergency had the opposite effect. First, the political and economic situation in the rural homelands was in crisis. In some rural areas, students and other youths engaged in political action and even revolt against the various parts of the apartheid regime. In Sekhukhuneland in the northern Transvaal, for example, the youths led a revolt against the local government-aligned chiefs and they conducted a brutal campaign of burning alleged witches—often those seen to be supporting or deriving benefit from the white state. Their mobilization also alienated the elders of Sekhukhuneland, and this reflected a generational tension between radical and often very violent youth and the more conservative older generation which feared this extreme radicalism. Growing numbers of Africans, moreover, were quitting the meager stakes they had under the chiefs and flocking to the cities in search of jobs. Once in the urban areas, they joined the ranks of the urban unemployed who boycotted rents and buses, challenged the authority of the councils, and protested against the white government. As they faced intensifying state repression, the townships became violent and chaotic.

Radicalized elements of the youth groups drew upon ideas derived from militant socialist insurgencies in Mozambique and elsewhere. They referred to themselves as "comrades" and they danced the *toyi-toyi* (a rhythmic high-stepping march) as they aligned themselves with radical ANC, AZAPO, and communist politics. ANC flags and symbols became common sights as the youths defied state laws prohibiting such displays. A culture of violence also grew as the youth groups and rogue elements took it upon themselves to attempt to govern the townships. They burned government buildings and terrorized anyone suspected of sympathizing with the government regime. They also set up "people's courts" and "popular committees" which applied summary justice to those accused of political as well as normal crimes. There certainly were police informers and black police in the townships, but the UDF leadership did not advocate making them targets of violence, in part because of fears of police retaliation.

The comrades, however, claiming vengeance in the name of "people's power" against black enemies in the townships, resorted to often gruesome violence. They employed the tactic of public "necklacing" where they hung a gasoline-filled tire around a victim's neck and set it on fire, allowing the flames to engulf the head while the rubber melted over the body. Such brutal spectacles revealed these youthful "comrades" spiraling out of control as they internalized the repression and violence of apartheid society within their own communities. These often macabre acts reflected both the psychology of living under state oppression and the growing sense of desperation and urgency for change among the young. Similarly, by the mid-1980s, black education was in crisis as many students boycotted "apartheid education" and called for "liberation before education." In 1986, however, the National Education Crisis

Committee and the UDF called for alternative education programs to encourage students to go back to school in preparation for a future liberated South Africa. By the later 1980s, therefore, the UDF and ANC were clearly starting to anticipate a time when they might be in power even if it was not clear how far into the future this would be.

There remained other elements in black politics which sought to make good their claims to power. They were suspicious of the ANC and its allies, the South African Communist Party (SACP) and the COSATU, who were fighting for a non-racial South African nationalist state including some elements of socialist politics. Members of the PAC and black consciousness movement rejected cooperation with whites and a non-racial platform. They preferred to promote their own African interests first to achieve liberation since the system of apartheid was race-based. In the urban areas, a range of vigilante groups emerged to challenge the youth comrades. They often represented older men or migrant workers' desire to control the townships. Yet the migrants, who lived in separate workers' hostel residences, were perceived to be outsiders who did not fully integrate into township society. When the youth started to assert their control over township life, the older men and migrants mounted open attacks on township residents. As we shall see, in this and other instances, the state security establishment started to provide arms and support for the migrant vigilante groups in order to foment instability in the townships to challenge the UDF and the comrades. Some of these vigilante groups were supported by homeland leaders who were trying to ensure that they too had a hold on the urban areas where migrant workers from their rural strongholds worked. Similarly, homeland leaders, who relied upon both state support and "traditional" chiefly rule to sustain their rurally-based ethnic politics, sought to remain outside the vanguard of UDF-ANC politics. In some cases, such as with Simon Skosana of KwaNdebele and Lucas Mangope of Bophuthatswana, the men who controlled the rural power bases managed to amass considerable means of force with their own warlords' armies. But it was Mangosuthu Buthelezi of the KwaZulu homeland administration who presented the most formidable and complex African challenge to the majority-supported, mainstream UDF-ANC movement.

Buthelezi charted his own course of opposition to the apartheid government with his ethnic-based *Inkatha* movement (see Chapter 9, "Apartheid and South African Society") Initially, Buthelezi had aligned himself with the broader black national liberation movement. His political machinations allowed for some degree of accommodation with the white government, and in 1975 he accepted the leadership of KwaZulu, the state-created Zulu ethnic territory. Members of the black consciousness movement vilified him for what they perceived to be his sell-out to the state. He then sought his own independent route to power based upon an appeal to rural "Zulu" tradition and patriarchal chiefly rule. He tried to manipulate the Zulu king, Zwelethini, as a popular symbol representing a fictionalized martial past, and this had significant popular appeal for many, but certainly not all, Zulu-speaking people. Buthelezi then distanced himself from the broader UDF-ANC movement. This was in part because of his political stance, which included trying to work for change within the structures of apartheid, and in part because he emphasized an exclusionary Zulu ethnic politics which ran counter to the ANC's non-racial and all-inclusive structures. He argued for a more moderate form of opposition to apartheid which rejected the armed struggle and socialism. Instead, he condemned the international economic sanctions on South Africa which he felt undermined the pressure for change, and he emphasized free market capitalism. His stance was acceptable, even appealing, to the government because he appeared prepared to support a negotiated federal political system which allowed for regional autonomy for different ethnic groups, including his Zulu-speaking supporters.

It was Buthelezi that the government, and conservative foreign leaders such as the U.S.'s Ronald Reagan and Britain's Margaret Thatcher, promoted

MANGOSUTHU BUTHELEZI AND KING GOODWILL   Mangosuthu Buthelezi, the Zulu nationalist politician, continued to try to use the Zulu monarchy in his maverick regional politics. *Source: Aran S. MacKinnon.*

as an alternative to the ANC. Yet Buthelezi took an increasingly belligerent approach to his regionally-based politics. He consolidated his power through his control of KwaZulu township services such as education, housing, and pensions, and through intimidation. He and his warlord deputies whipped up a fervor of support by calling upon a militarized view of the Zulu past and getting loyal followers to form *impis*—based on the idea of military regiments formed during the old Zulu kingdom (see Chapter 4, "The Making of New States"). The *Inkatha impis* were directed to attack UDF and ANC supporting comrades in the hotly contested townships outside Durban and Pietermaritzburg. By 1986, the KwaZulu-Natal townships were overwhelmed by pitched battles as *Inkatha* men tried to force residents to submit. Since the state tended to favor Buthelezi over the UDF, the police were less likely to harass them as they armed for battle. Both sides included Zulu people, but *Inkatha* claimed it had a monopoly on how to define Zulu qualities for its members. Contrary to government claims, these were not ethnic conflicts between "Zulu" and Xhosa (perceived to be ANC supporters), but rather political battles over turf and generational tension between younger township comrades and older rural men. It was these sorts of tensions and conflicts that the state sought to exploit as it was forced into a political corner and had no choice but to negotiate.

INKATHA FREEDOM PARTY Modern Zulu nationalist politics have often taken a violent direction. *Source: Aran S. MacKinnon.*

MOUNTING PRESSURES AND THE ROAD TO NEGOTIATIONS

By the later 1980s, the opposition forces of the internal UDF campaigns and the external ANC efforts to focus international pressure for change on South Africa had placed the white state in isolation. Botha's government was struggling to hold the country together. It was just barely managing to stay on the tightrope between reform impulses on the one hand and demands from reactionary conservative whites and the securocrats (police and army security officials) for an intensification of the "total strategy" on the other. At the same time, international condemnation of the country made South Africa a pariah state. In 1986, just as Commonwealth leaders were visiting South Africa and making recommendations aimed at facilitating a peaceful solution to the country's problems, South African forces bombed alleged ANC bases in three neighboring states. The Commonwealth leaders, recognizing the Botha regime's intransigence, immediately left the country and roundly condemned the South African government. The international community, including Britain and the United States, who had sympathized with the South African government, stepped up its calls for change. More significantly, popular opinion and calls for change from the Western leaders led to a widening and deepening of economic and political sanctions against South Africa. The United States finally passed the Anti-Apartheid Act in 1986, over President Reagan's veto, and the British parliament passed similar legislation limiting its formal links to South Africa. People, moreover, pressured businesses and investment companies to begin closing operations and disinvesting (withdrawing invested capital and loans) in South Africa. Consumers in the West also boycotted South African products such as fruit and wine. This pressure, combined with the growing political instability in South Africa, prompted a massive withdrawal of investments and severely curtailed any future investment plans.

As sanctions bit in, and internal destabilization undermined productivity, the South African economy rapidly declined. Foreign banks called in their short-term loans to the South African government and inflation rose to nearly 19 percent by 1987 as unemployment skyrocketed. This economic downturn added a heavy burden to the already beleaguered white population which was smarting from international boycotts of their popular rugby and cricket sports teams. Nevertheless, there appeared to be some initial cause for hope. Some in the West believed that Botha was making a good faith effort at reform, and they argued not to further isolate the country with punitive economic sanctions which might push the government to lash out at the black opposition. Moreover, Buthelezi had presented moderate whites with a viable, nonviolent, and capitalist-oriented alternative to the ANC approach. In South Africa, however, the Conservative Party was making further inroads against the National Party majority in the parliament. They and other white conservative

hardliners saw Botha's efforts at reform as an unacceptable sell-out of white interests. Their politics played upon the sentiments of many men in the security
establishment who also sought to contain the black opposition and to re-assert
their authority over the country. The government, therefore, appeared to be
working for peace, but also preparing for war.

It was pressure from the white right and the rising mass opposition's ability to make the country ungovernable which opened the way for elements
within the government to undertake an even more brutally violent campaign
against black opposition. A new state-sponsored element—which would later
be called the "third force"—set about to intimidate and disrupt the opposition. Hit squads, which were made up of security officers and former army
special operations personnel, operated clandestinely in the townships. They attacked homes and brutalized and killed blacks in an all-out effort to re-
establish control over the townships. Their activities were co-ordinated by the
Civil Cooperation Bureau (CCB), ostensibly a civilian vigilante group, but led
by members of the South African Defense Force. During the later 1980s and
into the 1990s, the CCB and the police also aided and abetted *Inkatha* forces
as they led migrant workers in the urban hostels to attack township residents.
The security forces, despite their involvement, claimed that these clashes were
clear evidence of irrational "tribal" or "black on black" violence and that only
the white state could ensure stability in the country. In effect, they both instigated violence and then justified intervention to quell it in order to disrupt the
black opposition. These violent developments made the situation in South
Africa very volatile and uncertain.

Despite the spiraling levels of violence and instability which appeared
ready to engulf the country, a momentum for positive change emerged in the
mid-1980s. First, Cold War tensions between the United States and the Soviet Union were beginning to ease. Both countries recognized the material
and political costs of maintaining a threatening stance and they started to
back off from areas of potential conflict. For the Soviets, this was part of
their broader forces of change from within. By the end of the 1980s, the Soviet Union opened up to Western influence, and the old regime collapsed. As
the Soviets declared their intention to withdraw from challenging Western
hegemony in Africa in 1986, the United States lost interest in maintaining
its support of South African intervention in Namibia and Angola. South
African actions in the region had become very unpopular in the eyes of
United Nations member states, especially since the UN had passed a resolution calling for South Africa to leave Namibia. South Africa had stepped up
its incursions into the frontline states, especially Angola, in a bid to prevent
opposition guerillas from infiltrating the country. When the Soviets decided
to withdraw support, Angolan and Cuban troops made a major offensive to
drive out the UNITA rebels and the South Africans. The South Africans

responded in kind leaving both sides quagmired. The United States and the Russians then brokered a UN peace settlement which set up a cease-fire and a planned withdrawal of troops. More significantly, the UN resolution led to a complete South African withdrawal from Namibia and provided for democratic elections. In March 1990, the opposition SWAPO forces formed a coalition government in a new multi-party democratic independent Namibia. Within South Africa, however, the transition to democracy was far less certain.

NEGOTIATIONS AND THE ROAD TO DEMOCRATIC ELECTIONS

By the mid-1980s, the South African government had started to seriously consider negotiations with the opposition only after it realized there were no other viable solutions to the escalating violence. Indeed, it appeared that Botha's reforms only seemed to provoke further resistance, which in turn led to more brutal state repressions. Africans roundly condemned and rejected the government's offer in 1988 of "power sharing" in a merely advisory joint National Council which provided for only very diluted popular democratic representation. Then, Africans staged a successful boycott of township council elections later that year. During the later 1980s, ANC-led saboteurs also set off a series of bombs in the cities, killing 32 people and injuring hundreds more, which unnerved the white population. Extremists on both the far left opposition and the white far right threatened to drag the country down into even greater turmoil. In the opposition, the PAC and the AZAPO evinced a more militaristic tone with some youth groups calling for "one settler, one bullet" as a remedy to white domination. On the white right, the AWB demanded that the government carve out a fortified white state. There was, moreover, the long-term problem of the unstable economy. African trade unions had been flexing their political muscles for some time, and when Cyril Ramaphosa, the charismatic and politically adept leader of the NUM, led a massive strike of some 250,000 mine workers in 1987, the shutdown of work had a sobering effect on industrial capitalists.

The impetus for whites agreeing to negotiations came from the business community. Many white business leaders had already seen the writing on the wall as a clear need for significant political change and not just reform. They recognized that blacks, as workers and consumers, were essential for economic prosperity and that only political change which accommodated their interests could ensure a stable country and economy. Thus, white business leaders finally made a move to reach out to blacks. The ANC, which had been calling for open dialogue since its inception, presented itself as the opposition group which had the most popular support and was the best organized. In 1985, Gavin Relly, who had taken over the powerful Anglo-American corporation, led a group of South African businessmen to meet with the ANC president, Oliver Tambo, who was in exile in Zambia. In 1986, the new *verligte* (enlightened) leader of the newly reformed Afrikaner *Broederbond,* Pieter de Lange, met with ANC representatives in New York. Key among the ANC members was Thabo Mbeki, the organization's director of international affairs who had also gone into exile in 1962. He had a strong ANC pedigree as the son of Govan Mbeki, a key ANC and Communist Party leader from the Cape, and he brought considerable diplomatic skills and patience to the informal meetings with whites. These white business leaders had considerable influence on the government, and they managed to encourage President Botha to go beyond the cycle of limited reforms, resistance, and repression which had deadlocked the country.

In 1985, Botha, who was unleashing the forces of repression in a state of emergency, had also started to make overtures to the ANC as the only viable opposition movement. He claimed, however, that there were two major obstacles to further negotiations with the ANC: the armed struggle and the demand for majority rule in a true democracy. Botha, had moreover, made public statements that he was not even considering the possibility of a black majority government. Yet, by this time, the government had recognized Nelson Mandela as the leading member of the ANC prisoners in South Africa and accepted that he had become the focus of popular support both in the country and internationally. Botha reasoned that if he could get Mandela to negotiate, it would carry significant weight with the black majority. He offered to release Mandela and other political prisoners if they renounced the use of violence and their "revolutionary" ideals.

Mandela was already understood not to be openly a communist, but the socialist ideals of his allies in the Communist Party appeared threatening to the government. Mandela rejected Botha's offer in an impassioned written speech which was his first public statement allowed by the government since his incarceration. Nevertheless, it seemed to Mandela that political pragmatism required that the ANC and the government move ahead with discussions, and so he sought out Botha. For its part, the government kept the channels of communication with Mandela open and transferred him to the more accessible Pollsmoor prison on the mainland. There, he was allowed to meet with visitors, including foreign leaders, to make contact with the ANC leadership in exile, and even to make short trips outside, where no one recognized the aging man who had not been seen in public for years. In 1988, the government further courted a better relationship with Mandela by moving him to a comfortable house on prison grounds near Cape Town.

By the end of the 1980s, further progress toward open negotiations was made. Mandela, recognizing what was perhaps a softening in the government's stance, continued to refuse accepting his release while it was conditioned by government demands. Instead, in early 1989, he said that the government would first need to un-ban the ANC, release all political prisoners, and end the state of emergency. He also called on both the government and the ANC to enter negotiations for a political settlement as a matter of urgency. Although Mandela was conducting his discussions with the government without the full knowledge of the rest of the ANC leadership, he felt this was necessary to build the momentum for negotiations. He professed himself to be a loyal and disciplined member of the ANC. The ANC leaders in exile were more cautious about their meetings with white South Africans. They did, however, suggest that apartheid could be ended through peaceful negotiations when they made the Harare Declaration from neighboring Zimbabwe, but only if the government ended the state of emergency, removed troops from the townships, legalized opposition political activity, and released political prisoners. It was significant that, in 1989, P. W. Botha, who seemed unwilling to go any further with reform, suffered a stroke and lost his grip on power. He was replaced by the more flexible and younger Frederick Willem (F. W.) de Klerk. De Klerk's National Party roots reached back to his grandfather, and he appeared deeply committed to the Afrikaner cause, yet he also realized that the need for meaningful change was urgent. He and his supporters were prepared to concede that black political dominance was inevitable, but they still hoped to safeguard white interests through a negotiated settlement.

After meeting with Mandela in 1989, de Klerk set the stage for momentous change by un-banning the ANC, the PAC, and the South African Communist Party (SACP), removing restrictions on other opposition parties, and freeing political prisoners. He also removed hateful petty apartheid legislation such as separate amenities as well as the Group Areas and Land Acts. On 11 February 1990, in an historic event, the government unconditionally released Nelson Mandela, after 27 years in prison. Mandela, whose stature at home and abroad had risen to heroic dimensions, emerged as a triumphant leader of the ANC, ready to take the liberation struggle to a hopefully peaceful conclusion. He met with thousands of jubilant supporters in Cape Town, and, speaking to the whole nation, he called for discipline and restraint. There was a wave of excitement and optimism as blacks for the first time felt that they could reclaim their country. Members of the opposition movements could now suddenly speak and organize in public. Blacks continued to maintain pressure on the state with school and consumer boycotts and by shutting down more township councils. Many felt that an inevitable change, leading to an ANC-led black majority government, had been set in motion. Yet, there was nothing inevitable about this. The ANC now faced the challenge of trying to transform itself from an opposition liberation movement, divided by contending views and the different experiences of those returning from exile compared with those who had remained in South Africa, into a political party ready to run the country. There also remained many pitfalls ahead in the negotiations with the government, and challenges from other forces opposed to the ANC.

When the ANC leaders emerged from exile and prison, they forged a more unified political front to engage in negotiations with the government. This was no simple task since the ANC national hierarchy now had to connect with a broad range of grassroots opposition groups such as the civics, unions, churches, and the UDF. There were differences of opinion on everything from whether there should even be negotiations, to negotiating strategy, to plans for a democratic election, to what type of state an ANC government would preside over. A critical test was the ANC's relationship with the more radical SACP. Many members on the far left of the ANC were also members of the SACP or shared their views about the need for a guided transition to a socialist state and economy. Others took a more moderate line, but remained highly suspicious of the white government. Nevertheless, most agreed that South Africa should become a full, non-racial democracy. In 1991, at its first full convention since its banning, the ANC reached an understanding with its allies and formed the Tripartite Alliance with COSATU and the newly relaunched SACP under the pragmatic leadership of Joe Slovo. Mandela, who was elected president of the ANC, Chris Hani, the gifted and diplomatic leader of the ANC's military wing, MK, and Cyril Ramaphosa of COSATU, who was elected secretary-general, helped steer the alliance toward negotiations. Mandela remained the voice of calm and reason amid the rising black expectations for rapid change and the gathering storm of violence which threatened to plunge the country into chaos. His efforts were nothing short of remarkable given his long years in jail and the disturbing news that his wife, Winnie, who had remained loyal throughout his incarceration, had become a challenging, maverick political force of her own. Mandela was deeply disturbed by Winnie's increasingly outrageous behavior and her involvement in the murder of an ANC youth activist. He and Winnie separated not long after his release. Chris Hani also managed to quell MK opposition to the ANC's suspension of the armed struggle in 1990, which was a government precondition for negotiations.

In the prelude to formal negotiations, the ANC also softened its socialist line. Many non-communist members were mindful that they did not want to "kill the goose which laid the golden eggs," referring to the capitalist engine of the economy. The NP had already started to privatize many state-run corporations such as ISCOR (Iron and Steel) and the railways in order to make later nationalization by a black government more difficult. Despite a deep-rooted sense of commitment to socialist ideals, many in the opposition did not see a collectivized economy as a viable alternative in the short term. The ANC recognized that the country desperately needed foreign investment after decades of tough sanctions. Nationalizing the economy and thus risking economic destabilization would not be attractive to investors in the context of post-Soviet Union world politics, where communism had been discredited. New thinkers, especially Thabo Mbeki, warned that a new black government would not want to be burdened with running such industries as mining with its complicated operations and substantial migrant labor headaches. Instead, they recommended a plan for "growth through redistribution" which emphasized higher taxation of industry, greater government spending on education and training, and welfare and housing for blacks. The planned entrenchment of private property also served to assuage whites in government as did the arch Communist, Slovo's, recommendation for "sunset clauses" which would allow standing officials to retain their jobs and pensions through retirement. The stage appeared set for meaningful negotiations.

Before all interested parties could meet, and during the negotiations from 1990–1994, there remained the specter of violence which kept the country on the verge of open civil war. The two main forces at play in attempts to derail the negotiations were Buthelezi's *Inkatha* and elements of the security establishment within the Nationalist government itself. For its part, the white government's suspicions of the ANC were apparently well-founded because, after peace talks had begun, it discovered documents pertaining to Operation Vula (opening), a secret plan to overthrow the state by force. Although the ANC and its allies were somewhat discredited for this, they had suffered far greater violence at government hands than anything they had planned. A secret "third force" directed by state security officers was at work in a vicious, "dirty tricks" campaign. This force instigated widespread violence and intimidation through the townships. As it aided and abetted reactionary forces and directly engaged in acts of political violence, it left more than 14,000 people dead. Buthelezi and *Inkatha* would become an increasingly dangerous and unpredictable element.

The security forces believed that it was to their advantage to delay and disrupt the negotiations since it could weaken and split the opposition. It would eventually become clear that the dirty tricks campaign could be traced through the highest echelons of the government, including to F. W. de Klerk. The state also lent significant support to Buthelezi and his *Inkatha* warlords as they terrorized ANC supporters in the townships. Buthelezi then launched a competing political party, the *Inkatha* Freedom Party (IFP), based on his ethnic nationalist political base. In a bid to win national leverage, the IFP set out to overwhelm the ANC youth comrades in Natal. They invoked a conservative traditional message as they went to war against the ANC in Natal, killing hundreds and displacing thousands from their homes. These acts, along with continued vigilante actions, inflamed violence across the country and especially in the townships, where poor squatters clashed with migrant workers in hostels. Other far right groups also sought to disrupt progress toward a peaceful settlement. Far right reactionaries assassinated Chris Hani in 1993 and this drew widespread shock from opposition groups. Radical elements in the *Azanian* People's Organization threatened to step up violence against whites.

Despite the threats to peace, Mandela and de Klerk managed to keep cool heads. They forged ahead with formal negotiations which began under the Convention for a Democratic South Africa (CODESA) at the end of 1991. A wide range of political groups and homeland leaders met in Johannesburg to begin discussing how a new government could be created. Extremists such as the Conservative party on the white right, and the AZAPO and the PAC in the opposition declined to participate. De Klerk and the NP sought to find a way to entrench white minority rights in a new South Africa. To this end, they rejected the idea of a unitary state (favored by the ANC) and preferred a federal system which would preserve decentralized power to dilute a forecast ANC majority government. Homeland leaders, who had strong regional bases but no really national appeal, also favored a decentralized form of government.

CODESA did achieve some success with agreements on a number of important constitutional principles. Significantly, the Women's National Coalition, spearheaded by the ANC women's league but formed from a range of political parties in 1991, rose to prominence in the negotiations, thus ensuring that gender issues were addressed. All parties agreed to full democracy with universal suffrage, a bill of rights for all people, a unified country which reincorporated the homelands, a separation of powers in the government, including an independent judiciary, and protection for private property. No agreement could be reached on an amending formula because the NP insisted on an unreasonably high majority requirement. Then CODESA was halted by violent flare-ups. The "third force" attacked ANC supporters south of Johannesburg, and the ANC withdrew from talks but kept an informal channel of communication open to the NP. Violence erupted in various places, including the homelands where NP-supported leaders resisted the negotiations which were to lead to a dismantling of their puppet states. The ANC, however, was determined to force the homelands to re-incorporate. Their bold efforts drew a backlash, and important ANC leaders such as Hani and Ramaphosa were fired upon when they marched in protest against the homeland leader of the Ciskei. The Transkeian leader, Bantu Holomisa, however, favored re-integration and he welcomed the ANC ascendency in national politics.

Exercising great restraint and guided by Mandela's unswerving statesmanship, the ANC returned to the peace talks. The ANC and the NP realized that

there was too much at stake to allow the considerable violence to derail the negotiations. Indeed, it was perhaps because of the high level of violence that
there was even greater urgency to find a peaceful solution. Mandela demanded
and got a commitment from the government, the "Record of Understanding,"
to prevent further violence between the *Inkatha* hostel dwellers and the ANC
township residents. *Inkatha* members were prevented from carrying what they
deemed "traditional" weapons such as spears and axes which they had used in
violent acts. The ANC also persuaded the government to share power as a prelude to a full democratic election, and the NP agreed to a transitional executive
council which would include ANC counterparts in executive offices of state. In
1993, open negotiations resumed with the Multi-Party Negotiating Forum. At
the Forum, a broad range of parties and interest groups, including traditional
chiefs and homeland leaders, agreed to develop an interim power-sharing constitution. At the end of 1993, both Mandela and de Klerk shared the Nobel
Peace Prize for their work in negotiating an end to apartheid (see Map 10–1).

The interim constitution was closely followed by the permanent constitution, which was hammered out and ratified by 1999. It provided for a

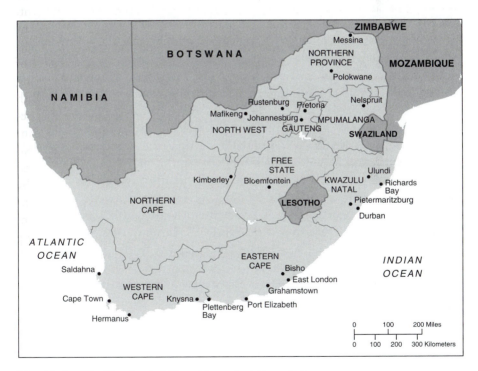

Map 10–1   The New South Africa with provincial boundaries.
Adapted from http://www.travelsouthafrica.com/maps.

two-house parliament, nine provinces with local governments, a bill of rights, a two-thirds majority amending formula, and a constitutional court. The bill of rights outlined some significant new features of intent, including planned land restitution for blacks and economic rights to basic health care and nutrition, but these would be difficult for a new government to guarantee. Other important features of the interim constitution included specific guarantees for women's rights and provisions for eleven official languages, nine of which were African. In some cases, these protections created inherent paradoxes which would need to be resolved later. A clause entrenching the role of traditional chiefs, for example, ran counter to both the spirit of democracy (since chiefs are not elected to their position) and women's rights (although there had been some women chiefs, it was still a deeply patriarchal institution). The forum also fixed the date for South Africa's first non-racial democratic election for April 1994. Then, in 1993, the ANC and NP agreed to share power during a transitional period until 1999 by forming a "Government of National Unity" to steer the country through the transition.

There remained some major holdouts to this negotiated settlement, and they still threatened to destabilize the process of transition. In the run-up to the elections, *Inkatha* and the white right continued to try to undermine stability in the hopes of gaining more leverage for their minority interests. They refused to register to contest the democratic elections unless their demands for regional autonomy were met. Leaders from the far right, the Conservative Party, and the army generals had formed the *Volksfront* coalition under the leadership of Gen. Constand Viljoen. The *Volksfront* (later the Freedom Front) made a curious alliance with the reactionary homeland leaders of the Ciskei, Buthelezi and the IFP in KwaZulu, and Lucas Mangope of Bophuthatswana. Together the generals and the homeland leaders posed a considerable threat to a peaceful transition because of their military training and their willingness to use it. They demanded a different constitutional dispensation which would provide for greater local power in a loose federal system of autonomous states based on the old apartheid ideas of the homelands and a separate, albeit smaller, white state. They argued that this was the only way their minority rights could be safeguarded against an ANC majority in the planned unitary, centralized state.

Eugene Terreblanche's Afrikaner Resistance Movement (AWB) also got into the act. The group had gained widespread media coverage in 1993 for a theatrical stunt in which they drove an armored truck through the glass doors and into the lobby of the World Trade Center in Johannesburg where the Multi-Party Negotiating Forum was meeting. Although there was no other violence, and the negotiators were able to quickly resume their work, it was clear that the AWB, which rejected a democratic settlement, wanted to be the spoiler. Then, in a more bizarre event, Lucas Mangope openly rejected the re-incorporation of Bophuthatswana into South Africa and the upcoming election. He called upon his *Volksfront* allies to enter and secure his homeland against ANC supporters who were the majority in the homeland and who demanded re-integration. Instead, the AWB took the opportunity to unleash its ragtag "army" and it entered Bophuthatswana to defend Mangope against mass opposition. Armed AWB men drove through the capital, Mmabatho, shooting wildly at people. Bophuthatswana police and army forces then deserted Mangope and turned to drive out the AWB. In a dramatic incident that was televised across the country, the police caught up with and shot dead three AWB men. This lessened fears that the white far right would mount a successful military action to stop the transformation of the country. After the event, Viljoen and the Conservative Party accepted a political solution to differences, and they registered to participate in the elections.

Buthelezi and the IFP, however, were not so easily dealt with. Buthelezi had significant widespread support from the Zulu-speakers in Natal and Johannesburg as well as from conservative whites who accepted the notion of a loose federal state which provided for separate power bases. He refused to sign accords which paved the way for a settlement, and he threatened to boycott the elections. IFP members were still on the rampage in the Johannesburg region and in Natal. They attacked ANC comrades in the townships and unsettled the country. In March 1994, just weeks before the election, the IFP staged an intimidating march through central Johannesburg to Shell House, the ANC headquarters. ANC security officials, frustrated by IFP tactics which still included members brandishing "traditional" weapons, opened fire on the marchers, killing more than fifty. The reckless shooting inflamed Buthelezi and he claimed that the incident was part of the ongoing ANC intimidation of political competitors. He withdrew from the talks and refused to participate in the election. Mandela and de Klerk feared that if the IFP did not participate, it could undermine the entire process, fracture KwaZulu-Natal, and lead to even more intense violence. They extended the deadline for electoral registration and made some major concessions to Buthelezi, including constitutional allowances for greater powers at the provincial level and a recognition of the Zulu king, Zwelethini, as the reigning monarch within KwaZulu-Natal. Buthelezi still refused to cooperate. It was only in the eleventh hour, after an international delegation of mediators had persuaded Buthelezi that if he did not participate he would become isolated, lose foreign investment for his region, and probably be brought down by force, that he finally agreed to register and contest the election only a week before voting started.

South Africa's first truly democratic election began on 26 April 1994. Although there were irregularities, the election process went smoothly. IFP supporters used intimidation and violence to hamper other parties from campaigning in their stronghold and to discourage people from voting for the

ANC. Some ANC supporters used similar tactics in the areas they controlled. Overall, however, the parties' election campaigns were open and fair. The "new" NP sought to re-invent itself for the elections. It courted non-ANC black voters as the guarantor of private property and a capitalist economy, and interestingly, a protector of Afrikaans, the language of most Coloured people as well as the Afrikaners. The ANC developed a very sophisticated campaign based on a well-organized party structure and many widely publicized position documents. The ANC and especially its heroic leader, Mandela, had obvious African majority support as the most popular party. Yet it also campaigned hard among Coloured and Indian voters, and Mandela made reassuring comments to soothe even the white voters. In its campaign, the ANC promised to deliver a reconstruction and development program for the future which included very ambitious plans for improving Africans' lives with jobs, clean water, housing, land, education, and electricity. Such offers, and the understandable excitement at the prospect of having a majority-supported black government, created very high expectations among the African electorate. It was an historic and euphoric occasion to have blacks and whites lined up together for the first time to vote, and the world watched with great excitement.

Voting was extended for three days to accommodate all the people in the limited facilities. International observers and the South African Independent Electoral Commission (IEC) declared the results free and fair. Voting seemed to reflect regional and racial lines of support. The IFP won KwaZulu-Natal (KZN), and the NP won support in the Afrikaans-speaking Western Cape, where it convinced many Coloured people that the ANC would be hostile to non-Africans. Overall, the ANC won the day. It gained 62 percent of the vote and won 252 seats in the new National Assembly, the NP gained 21 percent and won 82 seats, and the IFP gained 11 percent for 43 seats. The leading parties then formed the new Government of National Unity (GNU). This had been agreed to by all parties as a power-sharing mechanism which would delay an African domination of national politics and therefore assuage white concerns about being "swamped." In the GNU, Mandela was elected president and, under the interim constitution, Thabo Mbeki became the first deputy president while F. W. de Klerk was elected the second deputy president. A new South Africa was born, based on a negotiated political transition to democracy, not a revolution.

CONCLUSION

After the Soweto uprising, black resistance in South Africa spread wider and deeper. Mass action placed the white government on the defensive and forced it to consider more sophisticated strategies for co-opting blacks and containing their resistance. The NP concocted a "total strategy" to combat what it perceived as a "total onslaught" from within and outside the country. The state then enhanced its powers by building a formidable security state which combined an advanced arms industry with internal police, secret security officials, and a massive army. Rising opposition pressure also caused a fracture within the NP. White politics started to diverge as reform-minded politicians considered ways to reduce tensions with black South Africans and reactionary hardliners prepared for a violent military solution to black insurgency. President P. W. Botha led South Africa into increased isolation as he sought to combat African communism both within the country and in the frontline states. His intransigence and military operations against the liberation movements and governments in Namibia, Angola, Mozambique, and Zimbabwe only served to heighten the international disapproval of apartheid and the NP government. Moreover, as global politics shifted, and the Cold War ended, South Africa's role as a last bastion of capitalism in Africa was no longer appropriate or appealing to the West. Botha's attempts at internal reform, and particularly the new constitution for a tricameral parliament for whites, Coloureds, and Indians was not only woefully inadequate, it was based upon a fundamental miscalculation about the strength and unity of black resistance. As Botha's reforms failed, he engaged in greater efforts to repress the black majority through the security apparatus. In the end, the government had to choose between continued violence and tension, possibly leading to civil war, and a political solution.

Black resistance forced the government to consider alternatives to continued repression. As the South African economy changed and developed, it became apparent that the majority African population was essential to the economy. Manufacturing required stable, skilled labor, and this necessity forced new patterns of urban settlement which the government had to accommodate. Moreover, as Africans acquired more skills and became more urbanized, they were able to create a more unified front of opposition based on their common experiences. Even though the state had banned and driven underground several formal African opposition political movements such as the ANC, it could not extinguish the resistance movement. Even the state of emergency served to inflame the resistance. From all over the country, and all parts of black society, unions, civics, and church groups banded together in a new mass movement; the United Democratic Front (UDF).

The UDF reflected the mushrooming nature of mass opposition and it operated as an effective umbrella for organization. It allied itself with many features of the now-banned ANC policy, but it represented a broader range of views. Yet even the UDF could not contain the growing splits within the black opposition. The pressure-cooker environment of South Africa created the conditions for violence among blacks. ANC-supporting youth "comrades" sought to make the country ungovernable by the white state, and to assert their own authority. In the context of mounting state brutality, the comrades developed a culture of violence to match the times. On the other side of the conflict, conservative homeland leaders, such as Mangosuthu Buthelezi, sought to extend their regionally-based power over the rural and urban areas. In order to achieve this goal, they shared the government's desire to contain the ANC and the UDF. The spiral of violence between Buthelezi's IFP and the comrades was aided and abetted by the government. As the country teetered on the brink of outright civil war, the government realized that there was more to be gained from negotiations with the opposition than from continued state-sponsored repression.

As South Africa became increasingly isolated by the international community, the costs of maintaining white domination became too great. As the South African business community grew more frustrated with the constraints of the apartheid system, it demanded change. These demands coincided with widespread black trade union pressures for change. Faced with international pressures, the bite of economic sanctions, and the financial downturn from political instability, the government finally decided to open talks with the ANC. Yet the NP would not relinquish power easily. It continued to try to undermine the opposition with a "dirty tricks" campaign and the "third force." It took the ousting of Botha and the arrival of de Klerk to shift NP thinking far enough for talks to begin. By this time, Nelson Mandela had emerged as the leading figure in ANC politics. His charisma and calm statesmanship made constructive negotiations amid great suspicion and violence possible.

Both Mandela and de Klerk realized the importance of persevering to create a peaceful democratic solution to the country's problems. There remained, however, those within the white and black communities who remained bent on asserting their own interests. Yet the newly formed white right wing, *Volksfront,* did not have sufficient power to derail the peace process. The AWB perhaps came closer to disrupting negotiations with its brazen assault on the World Trade Center. In the end, they were revealed to be rather inept thugs in their attack on the people of Bophuthatswana, and they retreated to lick their wounds. Buthelezi and the IFP, however, remained (and still are) a potent force for destabilization. Had it not been for the considerable diplomatic pressure brought to bear on Buthelezi, and his recognition that the costs of holding out were too great, he could well have plunged the country into a protracted civil war. Despite these challenges, all South Africans emerged in 1994 as the winners in the first non-racial democratic elections. Thereafter, the ANC government would have to contend with equally thorny issues related to healing the nation's psychological wounds, providing good governance, meeting rising black expectations for an economic peace dividend, and the continued problems associated with the health and welfare of South African society.

Questions to Consider

1. What was the Nationalist government's "total strategy" and how did it seek to combat the opposition?
2. What effect did the changing South African economy have on the impetus for a negotiated settlement between the government and the ANC?
3. What role did the UDF play in filling in the vacuum of political opposition after the banning of formal opposition parties?
4. Why did Buthelezi and the IFP threaten to undermine the peace process?
5. Why was Mandela essential for the negotiations?

Further Readings

ALDEN, C., *Apartheid's Last Stand: The Rise and Fall of the South African Security State* (London, 1996). A very thorough analysis of the Nationalist government's security strategy. This work considers the influence of various counter-insurgency strategies and how the South African state applied them to their "total strategy." It is particularly useful for understanding the nature of the security establishment and its thinking.

DUBOW, S., *The African National Congress* (Gloucester, 2000). A concise and readable history of the ANC with an emphasis on the establishment of democracy. This is a useful revision and synopsis of previous histories of the ANC.

ELLIS, S., and SECHABA, T., *Comrades Against Apartheid: The ANC and the South African Communist Party in Exile* (London, 1992). A very well-researched and well-written consideration of the opposition movement in exile and the struggles it faced. It is perhaps not as critical as later events suggested it could have been, but it provides a balanced and sympathetic account.

GERHARD, M., and HAMILTON, G., *An Appetite for Power: Buthelezi's Inkatha and South Africa* (Johannesburg, 1987). A balanced assessment of the homeland leader and his ethnic politics. It reveals the extent to which regionally-based ethnic political movements have grown and the power they wield in the rural areas.

HALISI, C., *Black Political Thought in the Making of South African Democracy* (Bloomington, 2000). An insightful and scholarly account of the strands of black politics prior to and through the transition. This is a fresh look at black political philosophy and it sheds new light on various political traditions in South Africa.

LODGE, T., *Black Politics in South Africa Since 1945* (Johannesburg, 1983). A definitive analysis of opposition politics prior to the transition to democracy. It stops short of dealing with the problems associated with the state of emergency and beyond, but it is still essential reading.

MANDELA, N., *Long Walk to Freedom* (London, 1995) and *No Easy Walk to Freedom* (London, 1965). Two revised editions of the autobiographies of the former first black president of South Africa. Mandela's words are as insightful as they are moving. He provides a vivid picture of his whole life, with an emphasis on his political work and the struggle. These are essential reading.

MELI, F., *South Africa Belongs to Us: A History of the A.N.C.* (London and Harare, 1988). An interesting interpretation of the ANC by a member of the organization. This does not take the standard scholarly approach to writing and analysis, nor is it unbiased, but it can be read as both a secondary work and as a primary source.

MZALA, *Gatsha Buthelezi: Chief with a Double Agenda* (London 1988). A strong critique of Mangosuthu Buthelezi, the IFP leader, and his politics. The author, an ANC member who wished to remain anonymous and so used a pseudonym, provides a biased but open analysis of the KwaZulu leader and his ethnic politics.

O'MEARA, D., *Forty Lost Years: The Apartheid State and the Politics of the National Party, 1948–1994* (Randburg, 1996). A masterful analysis of the political economy of apartheid and the ethnic nationalism of the Afrikaner-dominated National party. It is at once a fine, scholarly work with sound research and a moving lament for the destruction of South African society during the apartheid years.

SEEKINGS, J., *The UDF: A History of the United Democratic Front in South Africa, 1983–1991* (Cape Town, 2000). An excellent study of the organizational structures of the UDF and its approach to mass action. It emphasizes the ways in which the UDF sought to create a mass movement by linking up regional players in a national organization which took up the struggle after the ANC was banned.

VAN KESSEL, I., *"Beyond Our Wildest Dreams": The United Democratic Front and the Transformation of South Africa* (Charlottesville, 2000). A very detailed and richly textured account of the rise of the UDF and the politics of grassroots mass protest. This work is based on sound research and oral interviews and it considers a broad range of opposition strategies.

Chapter XI

The New South Africa, 1994–Present

Many observers, both within and outside South Africa, have commented that the relatively peaceful transition to democracy was nothing short of a miracle. It should not be forgotten, though, that there was considerable violence during the transition. What is perhaps more remarkable was that there was not more violence and that the people pulled the country back from the brink of civil war. This was the miracle. The question for post-apartheid South Africa is whether the people can sustain the miracle. After the euphoria of the elections in 1994, Mandela and the ANC government faced the more mundane task of governing the new "rainbow nation," as South Africa was now called. First, the ANC had to deal with the business of government. It had to continue to forge a new constitution in cooperation with the other members of the Government of National Unity (GNU), the nationalist party (NP), and the IFP. It also had to resolve differences and tensions within the folds of the opposition movement.

The ANC was still in an alliance with the powerful South African trade union movement, COSATU, and the Communists of the SACP, but there were new tensions emerging within the alliance. As the new government had to make some tough decisions, it was bound to offend some while winning over others. Moreover, with the opening of democracy, many different voices from the opposition emerged to take their own place in South African politics and, as we have seen from the past, they did not necessarily share all or most of the ANC views or strategies. It is difficult to speculate on the historical impact of the transition since many aspects of the profound political and economic changes are still in process. Historians tend to shy away from making definitive judgments about recent events, preferring to let the passage of time provide a clearer perspective so that meaning can be inscribed from a suitably objective distance. This text shares this reluctance, and therefore much of what follows is tentative. Nevertheless, there are some important indicators of how the transition has unfolded which may provide a sound basis from which to make some rough projections about developments in the near future.

Although the vast majority of blacks and whites managed to overcome their mutual suspicions and mistrust, and there has been little open hostility between the two groups, there remain substantial tensions and resentments from some whites which could threaten to destabilize the country. The IFP and some former homeland leaders, moreover, continue to press for a political geography of separation, where regional interests are more important than national unity. By far the greatest threat to political stability, however, comes from the persistence of economic inequities in the country. Nevertheless, the transition has been the first step in the national effort to achieve the political and spatial re-integration of all the people of the country. Suddenly, the old geography of the apartheid maps disappeared and a unitary state appeared. The removal of the lines did not erase the economic, regional, and ethnic differences which persist. It appears, however, that the seeds of a solid system of democracy have taken root in a re-united South Africa. A series of further elections, including another national election in 1999, has shown that most South Africans are willing to represent their political ideals through a democratic process and to resolve their differences through the power of the ballot box. The new government, despite allegations of spreading corruption between white and black alike, has been far more open, inclusive, and transparent in its work.

The ANC leaders have demonstrated a sincere commitment to ethical governance and accountability, and these principles are entrenched in the constitution. There are significant exceptions to these trends. Mangosuthu Buthelezi and the IFP continue to employ the political tactics of regional ethnic nationalism which have their origins in the old homelands. In addition to the fragmented geography of apartheid, the ANC government also inherited some significant and challenging legacies from the past. Not the least of these was a shattered economy, a country torn apart by violence, political tensions, and the impending disaster of major health problems, including the modern world's most devastating epidemic, AIDS. These will be all the harder to control because of heightened expectations from the black majority who believe they were promised, and who now demand, a substantial material peace dividend.

For the people of South Africa, particularly the black majority, it is hard to capture the enormous sense of joy and dignity which they won through their creation of and participation in a democratic government. South Africa has become an "African" country once again, and the cultures which were so long suppressed are emergent. The new flag incorporates the African nationalist colors—green, black and gold—and the new national anthem begins with the ANC anthem, *Nkosi Sikelel' iAfrika* (God bless Africa) but it contains verses from the old Afrikaners' anthem, "The Call of South Africa" in Afrikaans and English. South Africans took great pride because their sports teams could once again compete internationally, and the country hosted both the Rugby World Cup in 1995 and the soccer World Cup in 1998.

Yet these are clearly only the first steps in a more protracted struggle to overcome the structural, economic, and social inequities caused by hundreds of years of white domination. The country still suffers from the legacy of the fragmented nature of regional politics based on the "balkanized" homeland system. Africans suffer disproportionately from the problems of poverty, poor education, lack of proper housing and health care, and especially a culture of violence which makes South Africa one of the most crime-ridden countries in the world. Although the economy has great potential with a rich resource base and substantial manufacturing possibilities, it remains inefficient and skewed. Whites still dominate most of the business world and particularly the best-paid upper levels of management and ownership. The ANC government has addressed this problem with legislation aimed at placing more Africans in these positions. It plans to have blacks prepare for these posts through skills transfer programs where whites with knowledge and experience are asked to pass these on to Africans on the job. Still, the vast gap in wealth between the rich and the poor remains. Although there is an increasing number of affluent blacks, the wealth gap follows along primarily racial lines, with a small number of whites owning most of the wealth while the vast majority of Africans remain very poor.

THE NEW GOVERNMENT AND THE ASCENDANCY OF THE ANC

The ANC government faced a double burden of having to live with the white-dominated bureaucracy of the past and of having to rebuild the country as it forged ahead with consolidating its own position. The interim constitution had guaranteed the continued presence of whites in government and the courts through the "sunset clause." Although in some cases, their experience and expertise were essential to the transition, their presence had a negative effect on the eager new blacks who aspired to these posts. The old system, moreover, was vast and inefficient. The ANC government, for example, inherited 19 separate departments of education which had been created for each different racial or homeland group. The ANC set about to improve the state bureaucracy by streamlining departments and re-assigning whites to more essential posts. It also planned to make the civil service reflect the new democratic politics of the country through the affirmative action hiring of blacks. Yet, because of the inadequacies of the old education system, it proved to be very difficult to find qualified blacks to fill the positions. Nevertheless, the new

THABO MBEKI AND NELSON MANDELA The transition to full multiparty democracy and majority rule under African leadership has been a qualified success as Thabo Mbeki (left) and Nelson Mandela (right) pledge an oath of allegiance before their inaugurations as president and vice president respectively. *Source: AP/Wide World Photos.*

ANC government has created a solid base of leadership which has survived the tumult of change. As older members of the ANC retire, dissidents set out to find new vehicles for their political expression and a new generation will take over.

The internationally acclaimed statesman, Nelson Mandela, stayed on as president from 1994–1999. He appointed Thabo Mbeki as his first deputy president and heir apparent. This decision displaced the able trade union leader, Cyril Ramaphosa, and he soon left the ANC to take up a lucrative position in the private sector. Mbeki has become a capable and relatively popular leader, notwithstanding some controversial views. He has heightened South Africa's continental profile and has championed the idea of an "African renaissance" for all African states for the next century. Important factors influencing the new non-racial government are the members from the various ANC allied organizations. Prominent members of COSATU and the SACP were given important posts, such as Alec Irwin who became minister of finance and Tito Mboweni who became minister of labor and later the head of the South African Reserve Bank. The new state was guided by a strong ANC, which was riding the crest of its popularity with a large electoral majority (252 of 400 seats). During the final negotiations for the new constitution (which was put in place in 1999), the ANC fended off demands from the NP and IFP for a decentralized federal state which could accommodate regional power bases.

The government did agree, however, to create nine provinces with local powers over factors such as education and social services, but significantly, without much power to raise revenue. The nine provinces then could send representatives to the National Council of Provinces (NCOP), which replaced the previous upper chamber of the parliament. The ANC government dominated the NCOP and the provincial administrations. This was because the local leaders did not have the capacity and experience needed to run provincial affairs and also because corruption threatened to bankrupt some provincial administrations. The ANC then accrued more power to the central government as its members turned up increasingly frequently in appointed provincial posts. The government did recognize the importance of traditional authority in the rural areas and understood that this was a force which the IFP could use to its own ends. It therefore made space for traditional leaders as a concession to Buthelezi and the IFP. In a further gesture of conciliation, Mandela appointed Buthelezi as minister of home affairs, although this was also a clear move to co-opt the maverick IFP leader. By 1997, de Klerk, frustrated in his efforts to win minority protections for whites in a federal system, called on the NP to withdraw from the transitional government and he resigned from politics. The NP then disintegrated, losing many members to the Democratic Party, which took over as the official opposition in the 1999 elections. Since then, white opposition politics appears to have fragmented even further, and the whites seem to have neither the will nor the ability to create a united political front.

There were some significant ambiguities in the new government. Some critics have noted that there has not been as great a peace dividend and redistribution of wealth as expected and there are other troublesome legacies from the apartheid past. For example, the ANC chose to accommodate the country's massive armed forces in a new combined South African National Defense Force (SANDF). This could be considered as compromise politics, for the ANC did not want to demobilize the old armed forces and leave the soldiers, many of whom were veterans of wars against the liberation movement, without jobs. Instead, it melded together the old force with the members of the ANC military, MK, and the Azanian People's Liberation Army, and the soldiers of the old homeland governments. The new armed forces were problematic for three reasons. First, they consumed a substantial part of the government budget—at least ten percent more than under the old NP government—and many questioned if this large, costly force was justified given that the country was no longer at war either internally or with the frontline states. Second, the army contained a large number of whites who did not share the new government's vision, and they posed a potentially destabilizing threat to the peace. Finally, many former guerillas resented being folded into the hated army of the apartheid state and they did not care for the treatment they received. Still, the creation of the new force satisfied certain needs, not the least of which was to ensure that the former soldiers did not again become an armed threat. The new government also maintained the very lucrative and sophisticated state-controlled arms industry which it inherited from the old regime. Critics questioned whether it was ethical to continue to reap profits from a business which had been central to the previous state oppression and which still manufactured the tools of violence. The new national police force was also beset with problems. Whites dominated the higher ranks and between the whites and the blacks there remained racial tensions. The police were poorly paid and they faced skyrocketing levels of crime. They faced increasingly dangerous work conditions, and many turned to corruption and violence themselves.

Overall, the new constitution was perceived as a very progressive liberal democratic document, but containing some major contradictions, mostly born of political compromise. In its favor, the new constitution specifically enumerated human rights and gender equality and aspired to deliver on constitutional rights to health, welfare, housing, and education, among other important goals. Many of these expensive items would, however, be hard to deliver in the near future. Despite gaining their rights for gender equality, women still occupied a deeply ambiguous place in the new South Africa. On the one hand women did rise to significant posts of power, including as members of parliament (more than one quarter of the ANC MPs are women) and ministerial cabinet positions. The new government also recognized the Women's National Coalition and appointed one of its key members, Frene Ginwala, as the first speaker of the new parliament. On the other hand, women continued to suffer disproportionately from poverty and especially crime.

There was also controversy over the place of traditional chiefs in the new government. As the ANC moved ahead with consolidating its own power, it did not want other power bases to flourish outside of the parliamentary politics which it dominated. This meant that it had to either incorporate the older, rurally based forms of political authority, or risk allowing them to forge their own trajectory which could lead to further fragmentation. The new constitution expressly recognized the role and importance of chiefs, but it sought to constrain them since chieftaincy was a non-democratic institution. Chiefs would be allowed to continue to allocate land and to preside over customary law courts as long as they did not infringe upon the new constitutional rights. In 1987, many rural chiefs, including Zulu speakers from KwaZulu-Natal, formed the Congress of Traditional Leaders of South Africa (CONTRALESA). This organization aligned itself with the ANC in the run-up to the elections, but the ANC government was cautious about this relationship. Buthelezi and the IFP had sought to entice the chiefs into their fold, and for a time they had a powerful rallying point for them in the image of the Zulu king, Zwelethini. The IFP challenged the ANC's attempt to exert central authority over the chiefs, and it even sought to pay their stipends, but the ANC government fended off this tactic.

While many chiefs remain loyal to the ANC, and King Zwelethini has distanced himself from Buthelezi and the IFP (largely over personal conflicts and because Buthelezi sought to manipulate the king), others became increasingly uncomfortable with ANC policy. Patekile Holomisa, the leader of CONTRALESA and a former ANC MP, has declared that his organization will seek its own political path, separate from the ANC. The new revised constitution provided for a House of Traditional Leaders, so that the chiefs continue to be part of the formal government structure. While most representatives of government at the local level are elected officials, the hereditary chiefs still have power. Although more than 60 percent of South Africans are now urbanized and the numbers are growing, the chiefs and their forms of "tribal authority" left over from the apartheid period still hold considerable sway over people in some rural areas. For the time being, the chiefs remain a potentially powerful rallying point for traditional forms of African opposition to the ANC government. Similarly, other groups are seeking to reclaim cultural and ethnic identities such as the Griqua, Khoe, and the San groups, and these are reflected in an upsurge in cultural institutions such as museums for community heritage or social associations. Nevertheless, the ANC's powerful hold on both national politics and the popular imagination have tended to work against the resurgence of regional or ethnic "tribalism."

The ANC was very successful at consolidating and extending its power, but at the expense of maintaining some alliances. In the second national elections in 1999, the ANC increased its share of the vote to 66 percent. The NP collapsed. In its place, the new Democratic Party (DP) became the official parliamentary opposition (the party with the next highest number of seats) and it absorbed the old NP into a new party, the Democratic Alliance. The new president, Mbeki, is able and very intelligent even if he has not enjoyed the same levels of popularity as Mandela. Mbeki's presidency (he is still president) has been criticized for the "Africanization" of the state (the right-wing critic's euphemism for incorporating Africans into the upper echelons of state and business) and it has even been accused of favoring only Xhosa members of the party over others, although this appears not to have been the case. The government has remained largely open and transparent, accommodating all blacks, Indians, and Coloureds, as well as a significant number of whites.

The ANC has also charted an independent course in foreign policy. Soon after his release, Mandela traveled around the world, courting international aid, especially from the United States, for South African development. Yet he and the ANC government have made no apologies for keeping ties with non-aligned states and even with some nations such as Cuba and Libya, which the West has shunned. There have emerged, however, tensions within the Tripartite Alliance. COSATU has sought to flex its own political muscle independent of the ANC even though there are still close ties between the two. Yet COSATU has lost much of its influence over economic and broader political policies. It has been forced, by the more powerful ANC, to retreat into its more traditional realm of union activity. Significantly, COSATU objections to ANC economic policy have led the union movement to call for a number of major strikes, including a 1999 walkout by thousands of public sector workers and teachers. The alliance with the SACP has likewise been strained over what the Communists see as an ANC abandonment of socialist economic ideals.

Although the ANC has been careful to incorporate important SACP members into the government, there are growing tensions. Both Mandela and Mbeki have rebuked the SACP for its criticism of the government and its apparently close relationship with South African business and industry. But it is not only the SACP and the unionists who have criticized the new black government. Some elements in the media have also accused the ascendent members of the ANC of conspicuous consumption and corruption. These accusations do not sit well with a political party which had strong ties to socialist ideals, yet which seems comfortable enjoying the substantial material rewards which have come with winning power. Still, the ANC has used the state and its vast bureaucracy to its advantage. It has wielded government patronage to great effect, bringing former opponents into its tent and extending its power in an increasingly centralized system. The ANC now dominates South African politics, and it is very unlikely that it will be displaced or even seriously challenged by opposition groups in the next elections in 2004. The question which remains, then, is how the minority opposition can seek to hold the ANC accountable and prevent the fragile South African democracy from dissolving into a one-party rule as exists in many other African states.

THE ECONOMY

The new government's economic policies, which drew criticism from many quarters, were a compromise between addressing the country's substantial needs for reconstruction and development and ensuring that the economy continues to grow. Toward these ends, the ANC abandoned many of its socialist plans for massive state spending and welfare support. Instead, it has pursued a fairly orthodox conservative economic policy to keep inflation in check. Protections and tariffs for many sectors of the economy, such as agriculture, were dropped and South Africans now face the challenges of competing in the global marketplace. Critics, especially the unions, complained that the government has embraced an economic policy which favors protections for the capitalist system at the expense of government expenditure and the workers. The ANC created the overly ambitious Reconstruction and Development Program (RDP) as its first official policy. The RDP envisaged harnessing a robust economy with significant rates of growth to fuel public works such as universal health care for children under the age of six, the extension of clean water and electricity to black homes, and the construction of at least 300,000 new homes. The RDP met with limited success. Economic growth hovered at an anemic one percent per year and formal unemployment rose to more than 30 percent. While there are probably many people working in the informal sector unaccounted for, the unemployment problem still appears staggering. To some limited extent, the success of the African trade union movement in the 1980s has created a mixed result in the post-apartheid economy.

The black work force had fought and won for itself some improvements in conditions of work, and especially higher wages. The high wages which black South African workers now receive make them comparatively expensive by world standards. Coupled with other inefficiencies, they have led the South African manufacturing sector to be uncompetitive in world markets. Moreover, the unions have won significant labor protections in ANC legislation, and these have appeared too costly to appeal to the profit-minded multinationals which have since declined to invest in South Africa. Although the ANC did create new approaches to development by bringing together the private and public sectors, it still fell far short of most of its targets. Problems with corruption and disorganization meant that many of the limited funds were squandered. Nevertheless, hundreds of thousands of homes were electrified, although when consumers boycotted paying their rates, the electricity company, Eskom, installed pay-as-you-use meters. The government also did eventually meet some home-building targets, but demand still vastly outpaces supply. Still, cash flows to the poor and needy were definitely enhanced. The national old-age security pensions, which were extended to Africans by the white government as part of its reforms, were maintained. These remain important infusions of money for recipients and their families, the majority of whom are Africans. Moreover, government spending on vital sectors such as education, health, and welfare has increased significantly, even if it has not met the vastly inflated expectations of many blacks.

By 1996, it was clear that the RDP was not a success, and the government replaced it with an even more stringent policy, the Growth, Employment, and

Redistribution program or GEAR. This policy kept South Africa in line with the accepted global capitalist practices of the 1990s, including keeping a tight leash on expenditures and constraining inflation through proper debt-servicing. This meant that there were very real limits to the redistribution of wealth which the ANC and its socialist allies had aspired to before taking power. Many laudable goals for education, welfare, and health have remained clauses of intent and hope in the constitution rather than implemented public policy. Moreover, instead of reversing the outgoing NP's privatization of important government-controlled industry as was expected, the ANC continued to bring the rigors of the private ownership and market forces to bear on the country. This did produce a welcome increase in growth of about three percent in 1996, but it was short-lived.

As the workers became increasingly disenchanted with progress, the tensions with the ANC's main political ally, COSATU, began to intensify. COSATU staged a series of mass actions aimed at safeguarding workers' rights in the new constitution and legislation, culminating in a major strike in 1999. Nevertheless, the government remained committed to improving employment opportunities. It passed the Employment Equity Act in 1999 which aimed to create quotas for black employment in the private sector. The act improved the rate of black hiring, but in some cases, predominantly white firms sidestepped the intent of the act by creating subsidiaries and positions for blacks which act as a front to satisfy affirmative action quotas. Still, there were new policies put in place for skills transfers whereby experienced white employees prepared blacks to take over their professional posts. Toward the end of the 1990s, however, the South African economy suffered as the global economy stalled and gold prices plunged. High crime and instability in the country scared off investors and South Africa faced staggering unemployment, perhaps as high as 40 percent in some sectors.

The fragile South African economy did see some recent cause for optimism, although there remain profound problems. First, there has been an opening of the economy to blacks. A new black middle class has risen within the ranks of the government and the private sectors. Although they remain a minority in the ranks of the country's wealthy elite, affluent blacks engaged in conspicuous consumption have become a more common sight. Critics of the ANC have pointed to what are perceived as the bourgeois and decadent lifestyles of many in the government as a sell-out to the people. Moreover, former trade unionists, such as Cyril Ramaphosa, and even ex-Communists have taken high-ranking and very well-remunerated posts in private firms. It would seem that these wealthy and ascendent types are part of a broad range of blacks who had earlier embraced the struggle for success in the capitalist sector, but who were largely ignored and invisible during apartheid, as opposed to the "snatch-and-grab" class of latecomers they are now portrayed as. Nevertheless, blacks remain a disproportionately small minority (perhaps less than 20 percent of company executives) of the business elite, although their numbers are rising.

There are also recent promising signs of extended economic benefits as more blacks receive electricity and water supplies, and new consumer cultures emerge around purchasing televisions and cell phones. These are offset, however, by the dramatic insufficiencies of the private sector role in delivering municipal services. The privatization of water services and the attendant poor maintenance of the delivery system in Natal, for example, may have been a key cause of a recent devastating outbreak of cholera. These problems are unlikely to disappear in the foreseeable future. The South African population is growing at a fast rate and the economy still attracts a significant number of immigrants from the continent. As these people settle in burgeoning informal settlements on the fringes of the cities, they place even greater demands on the infrastructure. Finally, there is a significant growth industry in the country: tourism, a weak *Rand* (the South African currency named for the wealth derived from the Witwaters*rand* gold "reef"), combined with the post-apartheid dividend made South Africa a popular destination for overseas tourists once again. The natural beauty, the internationally famous game parks, such as Kruger National Park, and the more recent allure of people and places of the liberation struggle draws increasing numbers of tourists to the country. This gain may be offset by the high rates of crime which deter many from the country and also contribute to the loss of skilled professionals who can afford to emigrate. Still, the country has significant resources and the infrastructure and capacity to rebuild and extend the economy in the future.

LOOKING BACK, HEALING, AND MOVING FORWARD: THE TRC AND THE LAND QUESTION

The negotiations between the NP government and the ANC and other parties which led to a peaceful transition were grounded in the politics of compromise. As we have seen, there had been significant violence in the country during the transition, and the white government, as well as the reactionary white right, still wielded considerable military power. In order to prevent provoking the army or paramilitary forces, the ANC reassured whites that they and their property would be safe in the new South Africa. At the same time, the ANC was dedicated to healing the country and finding a way to reconcile the crimes and hatred of the past. A central feature of these safeguards was an ANC agreement to create a mechanism for granting amnesty to those people who had committed politically motivated acts of violence and human rights abuses during apartheid. Initially these people were understood to be predominantly members of the white state and their associates, whether secret or official, who had perpetrated politically motivated crimes, but members of the ANC and other opposition organizations were also expected to participate.

In 1995 the government established the Truth and Reconciliation Commission (TRC) under the Promotion of National Unity and Reconciliation Act of 1994. The commission comprised three committees: one on reparations, one on amnesty, and one on human rights violations. It was similar to other such commissions which existed in Latin America and eastern Europe in that it sought to aid in the transition from an oppressive authoritarian regime into a peaceful democracy. Yet the TRC was also different. Its purpose was to facilitate healing through acts of confession by the perpetrators of violence. It held open public hearings—during which the perpetrators confessed their crimes, often revealing for the first time the truth about murders and disappearances which previously could only be guessed at. Moreover, victims of past violence and abuse could directly confront the tormentors. Significantly, the people of South Africa were at center stage. Blacks went from being hunted "enemies of the state" as "terrorists" and "communists" to being praised as the long-suffering heros of the struggle. They could finally speak the unspeakable. They could tell of the horrors and inhumanities they had suffered, and hopefully gain peace and closure.

The TRC set an ambitious agenda, but its exact remit was not clear, and its process and findings have left many dissatisfied. It was informed by a religious morality brought by the leading members of the commission. The archbishop of Cape Town, Desmond Tutu, presided as chairman and Dr. Alex

ARCHBISHOP DESMOND TUTU   Tutu and the TRC sought to expose and heal the wounds of the past but they may have left an ambiguous legacy, leaving some South Africans dissatisfied. *Source: AP/Wide World Photos.*

Boraine, president of the Methodist Church of Southern Africa, was his deputy. These men guided the commission to seek an understanding of the violence for the purpose of healing and forgiveness, not for revenge or retribution. Seventeen commissioners, mostly anti-apartheid activists, gathered evidence from around the country over the next three years, and finally published a controversial but comprehensive report in 1998. The commission considered evidence only for the period from 1960 (the time of the Sharpeville massacre) until 1994 (the end date was extended at the last minute to include acts committed by the AWB and the white right in the Bophuthatswana as well as by the IFP in Johannesburg and by the ANC in the Ciskei in the run-up to the elections). This left all the acts of injustice and violence against blacks prior to that time out of consideration.

The commission was supposed to assess the evidence and pay reparations to the victims, but this process has been less than satisfactory, and many of the TRC's recommendations for financial compensation have not yet been fulfilled. The TRC granted amnesty to those who willingly gave evidence of their crimes and these perpetrators avoided any civil or criminal prosecution as individuals. In a few cases, however, court proceedings were already under way, and the murderers of Steve Biko and Chris Hani were not granted amnesty after they were found guilty in court. Those who did not confess could face criminal proceedings. The process did not require acts or statements of contrition, only the truth. Nevertheless, the hearings were very dramatic, and much new information came out about past victims.

In the short term, many South Africans were decidedly disappointed in the TRC process and its findings and there were also those who resisted. The NP initially demanded a blanket amnesty because it was the former governing party, but the TRC denied the application. The former NP president, P. W. Botha, refused to comply with a summons to appear, claiming that all of his acts as head of state were legitimate. He was eventually prosecuted for failing to appear, but he avoided jail time on the basis of a technicality. F. W. de Klerk appeared before the Commission twice. As he apologized on behalf of the NP for apartheid, he distanced himself from any knowledge of or responsibility for the "dirty tricks" campaign, although the evidence suggests the contrary. Mangosuthu Buthelezi appeared, but he blamed the ANC for instigating violence and he claimed that the IFP acts of violence were justifiable defense.

The TRC declared that both Botha and Buthelezi had committed gross violations of human rights, and that de Klerk had been an accessory to gross violations. The TRC also expected the ANC to make disclosures about its acts of violence and alleged human rights abuses in its training camps and prisons. In what was a controversial move, the ANC and many members resisted. The leadership declared that the ANC had fought a "just war" for liberation, and that its methods were therefore justified. The TRC also denied the ANC a blanket amnesty and declared in its report that the ANC had perpetrated gross violations. The commissioners stated that there was a difference between a justifiable war and unjustifiable means and they criticized the ANC for the latter. The ANC roundly criticized the findings and stated that its acts in the liberation struggle should in no way be seen as the same as the former government's unjust acts. In other ways, the report and the process were highly criticized. Many blacks felt that mere confession and contrition were insufficient and they called for a strong justice which would provide punishment, retribution, and greater compensation. Nevertheless, the TRC's massive records and findings constitute a major historical resource for the country, and the process did provide meaningful closure for many acts of apartheid violence. The longer-term test of the TRC's effectiveness will be to what extent it succeeds in creating a permanently transformed consciousness among the whites. Will the legacy of the TRC be to bring most, if not all, whites to a full acknowledgment that they benefited from apartheid, even if they did not necessarily agree with it? It also remains to be seen whether the TRC will prompt a more open effort to compensate the many victims of apartheid in a meaningful material way.

Another—in this case, more material—feature of the new government's efforts to redress the wrongs of the past is land reform. Significantly, the TRC did not factor in the land rights question in its proceedings, and some critics have condemned the TRC for failing to address this major wrong. Ironically, it was the former NP government under de Klerk which enacted legislation aimed at redressing the land issue. In 1991, it provided for the repeal of all previous discriminatory land laws dating back to the 1913 Natives Land Act in the Abolition of Racially Based Land Measures Act. It was not until 1993, however, after considerable criticism from the ANC negotiators, that the NP government amended the act to provide for the acquisition and redistribution of land to Africans. It is, moreover, worth noting that the apartheid state actually purchased more land on behalf of the Africans as part of the process of consolidating the reserves than the ANC government plans to set aside for redistribution.

Nevertheless, in 1994, the ANC government passed the Restitution of Land Rights Act. It was also aimed at resolving claims to land from blacks displaced since 1913 when the Natives Land Act defined land allocations for whites and blacks. Significantly, land lost by entire communities through conquest and white settlement prior to 1913 was not to be considered. Some communities, including the Khoe and the Xhosa people, understandably object to these limits since it precludes them from making claims to land lost to whites earlier. Nevertheless, land redistribution is a highly emotional topic for blacks who, as we have seen, were forcibly displaced from their homes. Their rights to the land are bound up with important issues of place, identity, and economy, since many blacks were driven from what was agriculturally productive land. The land redistribution policy is, therefore, a very important piece of legislation.

Despite the government's efforts, many have seen the process of land restitution as inadequate. The initial plan was for the state to provide funding for Africans to purchase land, but it could not always find suitable plots or willing sellers. Moreover, there was not sufficient money or resources available to redress all the claims of all the individuals and all the communities who were forced from their land. Given the enormous pressure to provide land for residential purposes in the urban areas, the government does not feel it can afford to provide farms as well to all those who lost them. In many cases in urban areas, land restitution cannot take place because there are other people or buildings on the plot. This was the case with one of the most infamous acts of apartheid's forced removals in District Six. In 1996, the Land Claims Court convened in Cape Town and provided for the restitution of the land to former landlords and tenants of District Six. Current plans provide for the compensation and return of up to 20,000 residents to this once vibrant, multi-ethnic neighborhood, but the large Cape Technikon School sits on a large tract of land in the area. Instead, residents explored other ways to restore the sense of community and identity which was once bound up in that land, and to that end they have created new heritage sites and a museum. In other cases, communities had to be satisfied with the exchanges of land for parcels lost, such as communities which had held land in national parks. In another similar case, a community which claimed land in Kruger Park accepted payments and development projects in exchange for the land lost in the park.

The new government has also made provision for other Africans to gain access to land. Labor tenants (those people who lived on white-owned farms and provided labor service in lieu of a cash rent as provided by the 1913 Natives Land Act) would gain some security in land rights under the Labor Tenants Act of 1996. It protects labor tenants from eviction and also enables those tenants who have lived on a farm for at least five years to purchase the land to which they have access. This has unsettled many rural white farmers who feared they would be forced to sell their land under the willing seller, willing buyer rules. This became less a concern than was the rising number of attacks on and murders of white farmers by Africans seeking vengeance. Given that neighboring Zimbabwe currently faces massive upheavals as African squatters invade white farms, the specter of similar rural violence in South Africa remains real. As with other parts of the economy, informal approaches to land acquisition have proved more efficient, if unorganized. Now, most rural poor favor establishing squatters' rights in the urban areas, and informal shack settlements have mushroomed on the edges of Durban, Cape Town, and Johannesburg, as well as other towns. In response, the government has given legal form to land claims made on state land by these squatters. Many hundreds of

A SQUATTER SETTLEMENT OUTSIDE DURBAN   The problems of unemployment, poor health-care, lack of affordable housing, and poverty contribute to the economic inequality that continues to plague South Africa. *Source: Aran S. MacKinnon.*

thousands may now claim rights to small plots in the urban areas. These rights, however, do not guarantee access to services or water. Consequently, the thousands who daily make their way to these informal settlements face the daunting prospect of poor sanitation, no clean water supplies, and the likelihood of suffering from a host of concomitant diseases.

CURRENT CHALLENGES: HIV/AIDS AND CRIME

The greatest challenges for the new South Africa remain the health and welfare of the people. Ill health and crime stalk the country. The ANC government has made many important strides forward, especially given the monumental challenges it faced. The development of education and the expansion of primary health care have been impressive, as have been projects for electrification and the delivery of water, although the recent trend in privatizing the latter has led to problems. The new government has de-racialized schools and universities, it has built new health clinics, and it has worked to make basic drugs more affordable. Despite these efforts and the relative power of the economy, the vast majority of blacks still suffer from poor living conditions, nutrition, and health care. These problems have contributed to widespread and persistent health problems.

In addition to problems associated with under-nutrition and sanitation, and unclean water supplies, South Africans face a massive and devastating problem with infectious diseases, particularly HIV/AIDS (Human Immuno-deficiency Virus/Acquired Immune Deficiency Syndrome), which is transmitted primarily through heterosexual relations. There are significant incidences of "tropical diseases," especially malaria, which looks ready to burst once again into epidemic proportions in the northeastern parts of the country as in the past. Predominantly black South Africans, moreover, have suffered high rates of sexually transmitted diseases (STDs) and tuberculosis alongside a host of other diseases associated with the effects of poverty and modern industrialization. While these diseases remain a major problem for the country, they are overshadowed by the vast problems associated with AIDS.

HIV/AIDS, which has caused major epidemics in other parts of Africa, looks set to lead to a crisis in South Africa. AIDS was first diagnosed in the country in 1982. Since then, it has spread along with truckers, migrant workers, and sex workers along the major transport routes of the region into the urban and industrial centers. From there, as with STDs and TB, it has circulated into the rural areas. Paradoxically, South Africa's relatively vibrant economy and successful transition to democracy have facilitated the opening of the country to ever-increasing sources of infection. Public health efforts to contain the disease, however, were slow and rates of infection have rapidly climbed to alarming levels. More than 30 percent of pregnant women are estimated to be infected, and the rates among sex workers and migrants may be over 40 percent. More than a quarter of the adult South African population is probably HIV-positive, and more children will be infected with the virus in a few days than in all of the United States in an entire year. Poverty, social dislocation, risky sexual behaviors, infrequent use of condoms, and people's mobility have all contributed to its rapid spread. Many people do not fully understand the disease or how it is transmitted. Young women in their teen years are particularly susceptible to infection because they are often targeted by men who perceive them to be uninfected or, in some cases, to be the source of a cure as virgins. Many men still want unprotected sex, and others prefer "dry" sex where the risk of infection through lesions is greater.

These problems are difficult for the government to cope with since they suggest a critique of African male sexual activity which would be unpopular. There is, moreover, as in other parts of the world, a marked stigma attached to those with the disease, so many live in denial, preferring a fatalistic acceptance that they will die along with so many others. The impact has been devastating, and it appears from all projections that it will only get worse. Without proper treatment, the rates of death from AIDS alone are set to decimate entire

generations, and they have already contributed to a reduction in official esti-
mates of life expectancy. Community resources, which in the past have been
mobilized to help with such problems, are taxed to the limit, leaving those with
AIDS without support. AIDS orphans, for example, are now having to run
their own households as they care for infant siblings who were infected *in utero.*

The AIDS epidemic has created great challenges and led to controversy for
the new government. Initially, the ANC government planned to tackle health
issues, and AIDS in particular, head on. In addition to new clinics, the government sought to make cheap generic drug equivalents widely available and to
provide treatment. Yet, when the Department of Public Health sought to have
AIDS labelled as a "notifiable" disease requiring that cases be recorded and
reported, the trade union group, COSATU, strenuously objected on the
grounds that this would lead to discrimination against the victims. Then the
government health department appeared to lose direction. It wasted millions
of rands on a play aimed to increase AIDS awareness but which failed miser-
ably. Government health officials were, moreover, at odds with each other over
what courses of treatments and drugs should be used. These issues were only a
prelude, however, to the much greater controversy surrounding President
Mbeki's views, and the government's manifest refusal to extend treatment to
those in need.

Mbeki intervened in health policy issues and, on the basis of claims made
by a small number of unorthodox Western scientists, he started to raise questions about the nature of AIDS and the intentions of Western drug companies
in delivering treatment. He offered the questionable view that HIV does not
necessarily cause AIDS (this was immediately and convincingly countered by
the vast majority of scientists working in the field) and that the drug companies were racist for seeking to use Africans in drug trials for AIDS instead of
whites in the West. Mbeki's position seemed odd, but given the context of the
South African crisis, it is perhaps somewhat understandable. First, as noted,
South Africa faces many health and economic challenges, and a government
admission that AIDS was the priority may have been seen to undermine
other efforts. Second, Mbeki raised widely held concerns about Western drug
companies.

The high cost of the AIDS treatments put them out of reach of all but a
very few Africans, and the drug companies have resisted allowing the African
countries to change agreements which prevent the production of less costly
generic equivalents for the treatments. Finally, AIDS is an international problem, and Mbeki rightly pointed to the impact of poverty and deprivation in
the globalizing world as root causes of this and other health problems. The
government has since made a good faith effort to deal with the AIDS crisis.
Government spending on HIV/AIDS has tripled since Mbeki became president and Durban hosted an international conference on the issue in July of

2000. Both Mandela and Mbeki have spoken in public about the crisis and how people can take measures to reduce the risks of transmission. While these efforts have helped raise AIDS awareness, much remains to be done, and the government has not been forthcoming with any new programs or financial support for the victims.

A new host of grass roots organizations has arisen to demand that the government provide better care and universal access to free or low-cost drugs to AIDS victims. The National Economic Development and Labor Council (NEDLAC) reached a tentative agreement with the government to provide drugs to prevent the spread of the virus, but these have been slow in coming and they were made available at only eighteen pilot sites. Then, in response to government intransigence, the Treatment Action Campaign (TAC) was formed. Using tactics which harken back to the mass action campaigns of the anti-apartheid movement, the TAC has staged a number of demonstrations. Most significantly, in December 2001, the TAC convinced the Pretoria High Court to issue an order forcing the government to provide the drug Viramune (brand name: Nevirapine), which helps prevent the transmission of the virus, to all pregnant women. Then, in July 2002, the Constitutional Court upheld the ruling and denied the government leave to appeal the decision. The court stated that the government's policy of limiting access to this and other anti-retroviral drugs was an infringement on citizens' constitutional right to life.

The government, citing concerns about how extensive treatment campaigns could cripple the country financially (a concern shared by many governments in the developing world faced with the AIDS epidemic), reluctantly agreed to extend the provision of the drug to pregnant women. It also laid out plans for better AIDS training of health care workers and the creation of AIDS-specific treatment centers. Most recently, in February 2003, however, the TAC staged a "Treat the People March" on the parliament buildings in Cape Town. The more than 10,000 protestors demanded that the government abide by its agreement with NEDLAC to extend treatment to all South Africans afflicted with AIDS. Invoking the major icon of the past liberation struggle, many of the marchers donned shirts which had pictures of Nelson Mandela wearing an "HIV positive" shirt in solidarity with the sufferers, although Mandela did not authorize this. Clearly, grass roots movements and mass demonstrations are still a force in South African politics. Yet the massive problems posed by the epidemic will not easily be dealt with. The recent failure of a trial vaccine for AIDS in 2003, while providing some useful hints at how to further investigate treatments, does not show much promise for combating the epidemic in the near future.

There is, moreover, an insidious culture of crime and violence which has become entrenched in South Africa. In addition to the creeping culture of corruption in the ranks of business and government, the far more widespread problem of violent crime haunts the country. Despite government efforts to improve education at all levels and a significant increase in school and university enrollment, much of the African youth remains uneducated, unemployed, and frustrated. Indeed, many black youth deliberately eschewed education, demanding liberation first. They have, moreover, grown up in a culture of violence, both within and between their communities and from the former white state. They have suffered the indirect violence of poverty and racism. In response, many developed the tactics of street justice and defiance of authority. They turned to gangs and crime in order to survive and to combat the abject sense of powerlessness which accompanied living under apartheid.

Yet the past does not explain all about the dramatic increase in violent crime in the country. There are the forces of rapid urbanization, rampant poverty, social dislocation, and the lack of government structures in the vast and expanding informal settlements. The new South Africa also has seen a significant rise in drug use and the criminal activity associated with it as the country becomes more open to international criminal cartels. There has also been a spate of thefts from and murders of white farmers in the rural areas; crimes which have their roots in political vengeance as much as in economic needs. It does not as yet appear that these will escalate as they have in neighboring Zimbabwe, but it is possible. Perhaps the most pernicious aspect of rising crime has been family violence, and violent crimes against women especially have risen to horrific levels since 1994. This would appear to be a definite and disturbing trend in male behavior which seeks to forcibly subordinate women.

Crime in South Africa has taken on frightening proportions and dimensions. South Africa has the world's highest rates of rape and murder. Rape has become a central feature of gang criminal activity and initiation, and the police appear indifferent to this gendered crime. Armed robbery and carjackings are also commonplace, and people are particularly cautious about free movement in urban areas. Gang violence and crime have also spawned a range of vigilante movements in the townships, which have also contributed to a vicious cycle of violence. These problems have overwhelmed the police who do not have the numbers or capacity to combat all levels of crime, especially outside the urban areas. Moreover, the hazards of police work, including many killings of officers and poor pay, have led to problems of corruption. In response, the government has created the new "scorpions" task force to police the police, but the results are not yet clear. There now appears to be a continuing trend of wealthier South Africans, mostly whites, relying upon private security. The security industry has long been a fixture in the wealthier suburbs as people installed home alarms, gates, and razor wire, and employed rapid armed response units to defend them from criminals.

Private security has now become even more common, but it is available only to those who can afford it. Now South African businesses have also changed their operations, and many have relocated to new suburban centers such as Sandton just north of Johannesburg, and Umhlanga Ridge outside Durban. Here, corporations and their wealthier employees can live, work, and shop in secure venues controlled by private security firms, while the majority are held at bay by fences and access fees. Thus it would seem that the spatial division of South African society persists, but that it is more clearly grounded along the lines of class than race. Unless and until a more stable economy and a more even distribution of wealth and services are provided, the problems of crime and the wealth gap will continue to undermine and divide South African society.

CONCLUSION

On the basis of developments since 1994, it would appear that the new South Africa holds great promise despite a number of difficult challenges. The country has seen the rise of an able, ethical, and popularly elected leadership. This is significant for the relatively smooth and peaceful transition to full democracy in the country. Although there had been widespread political violence during the run-up to the first nonracial elections, South Africans managed to avoid having the situation deteriorate into all-out civil war. This is quite remarkable given the previous tensions in the country, and the very difficult legacy of apartheid which the new government faced. Significantly, though, the ANC has accepted certain features of the old state. These included vestiges of the old army and police which have been revamped to reflect current politics, and the old arms industry which generates substantial revenues. So far, the institutions and traditions of democracy seem to have taken root. Recent local and national elections have been conducted in a more or less "free and fair" atmosphere, and multiparty electioneering is still in place for the next elections in 2004.

Perhaps the most significant change in the government's institutional culture has been the crafting of a progressive new constitution and a system of checks and balances which safeguards its operation. Women, notably, are more visible and more important in government than previously. There have also been significant adaptations and concessions to African institutions. Chiefs and traditional authority have been ensconced in the constitution just as they remain in place in the rural areas. To what extent this powerful force, which draws upon aspects of cultural heritage and which plays to regional ethnic nationalism, may influence future political developments is hard to say, but it is likely to remain a factor. White opposition has retreated and fragmented in the face of ANC inclusiveness, and it is unlikely that purely race-based minority parties will be a major factor in the future. There would also appear, however, to be a trend toward the increased domination of the ANC in the structures of state. While there remains a fairly robust multiparty democratic system, which is moreover safeguarded by strong civic, grass roots, and media organizations which are critical of the current government, it is not clear whether these can restrain the ANC. In some ways, the ANC appears to be less comfortable with consultation and power-sharing with its allies, the SACP and the COSATU, than it once was. This has been most evident in the government's approach to economic policy.

The South African economy has, by most accounts, weathered the storms of the recent global financial crises, but the government has not yet been able to harness it to fulfill its original goals of growth and redistribution. Early on, the ANC government abandoned many of its socialist ideals in the hopes of creating a robust capitalist economy which would generate the substantial profits needed for the promised public spending on health, education, housing, and welfare. The ANC's RDP policy, however, failed to create either the conditions for significant growth or the funds and resources needed to address the heightened expectations of the majority of South Africans for a peace dividend. Instead, the government opted for the even more controversial GEAR program. GEAR relied on conservative fiscal policies for coping with the country's debt and attracting investment for private sector growth.

While GEAR delivered some improvement in economic growth, it has not enabled the planned spending policies to alleviate rampant unemployment and poverty. Still, there has been some upliftment for blacks. A new and vibrant, albeit relatively small, upwardly mobile African middle class has emerged. They have enjoyed the fruits of government patronage and new opportunities, but they have been severely criticized for their decadent lifestyles and conspicuous consumption in the face of widespread poverty. ANC allies, especially the COSATU and the SACP, have become increasingly concerned with the apparent persistence of the wealth gap which has left most of the black population still impoverished. It appears as if these allies, which have challenged ANC policy and their abandonment of socialist ideals with mass actions and strikes, will continue to demand a more equitable distribution of the country's wealth. There have, however, been some marked improvements in government spending and assistance programs. Housing, education, and health have all been prioritized and have received greater amounts of money for the majority under the ANC than ever before.

The new government has also worked to redress the wrongs of the apartheid past. As part of the negotiated settlement with the former NP government, the ANC agreed to grant amnesty to perpetrators of past political crimes and violence in exchange for learning the truth about these crimes. This process was facilitated by the ambitious TRC which was led by members of the black opposition and religious leaders such as Desmond Tutu. The purported purpose of the TRC was to facilitate healing by getting to the truth of past hatred and violence. While the TRC unearthed a monumental amount of information, and it placed former victims at center stage in the process, it did not satisfy all. First, it did not require any profession of contrition on the part of the perpetrators, and it provided no form of punishment as a form of justice, and this left many victims unsatisfied. Second, the planned payment of compensation to victims is still not completed. Third, the ANC resented the implications of the TRC report which criticized it for its own abuses. The ANC felt that it was not fair to equate the mistakes it made with violations of human rights (which they argued were coincidental to its "just war") with the systematic and planned policies of abuse and murder which the apartheid state perpetrated. Still, the TRC has been hailed as a successful practical approach to allowing a country to heal in the aftermath of a violent and unjust past. There has, moreover, been a good faith effort to compensate and accommodate those blacks who lost land during the apartheid period. The Restitution of Land Act and the Land Claims Court have gone a long way in assuaging people's feelings of loss from the past by allocating land to or compensating those who were forced off their land since 1913. Although this process does not address the much greater losses sustained prior to 1913 during the process of white conquest, it is perceived to be providing some justice in a material form.

Finally, South Africa faces some daunting challenges with health problems and pervasive crime. The HIV/AIDS epidemic poses the greatest current threat to the country. It appears set to decimate an entire generation, thereby further undermining the work force and the economy for years to come. Initially, the ANC government approaches to the problem were wholly inadequate, although these were partly a function of the limited resources available, and the challenges from other problems of health and poverty such as lack of nutrition, unclean water, and tuberculosis. Although the government has increased health spending and has targeted AIDS as a major concern, its response has been found wanting by the people of the country. New mass opposition groups, such as the TAC in conjunction with the COSATU, have risen to demand a greater response. They and the courts have pointed to the human rights listed in the ANC-drafted constitution as the justification for a better effort. The liberalizing of the political culture in the new South Africa may also have contributed to the current problems of persistent and widespread crime. Crime, both in terms of corruption in the ranks of government and business and in terms of social violence, has contributed to instability and a general lack of confidence in the country's financial future. Women, moreover, represent a disproportionate number of the victims of crime, especially rape, and this suggests a disturbing trend in the continuing oppression of women in the country.

Despite the very real challenges which all South Africans face, there are good prospects for the country to develop a strong democratic state with the potential to continue redressing and overcoming the problems of the past. Most South Africans remain resolute in their love of their country and their hopes for its future. While a professional "brain drain" may mean that the country will lose valuable skills in the short term, in the long term, there is every probability that equally capable blacks will emerge to fill the gaps. Although the ANC appears to dominate the current government, it operates in a far more open and fair manner than the previous regime, and it still appears prepared to accept a strong civil society and robust democracy which can check the accretion of power in its hands. Although difficult questions remain regarding economic development and the redistribution of wealth, these are challenges faced by many developing states, and South Africa is better poised than most to tackle them. The real challenge will be to what extent the government can meet the rising expectations of its people before they lose confidence in its ability to do so. It remains to be seen whether the people can hold the ANC government responsible for the plans and ideals it professed as a liberation movement. In the final analysis, the achievements and current status of South Africa are nothing short of remarkable, and it is a country which is sure to have just as rich and fascinating a future as its past.

QUESTIONS TO CONSIDER

1. How and why did the ANC government change its economic policies?
2. What were some of the compromises the new government had to make to ensure a peaceful transition to democracy?
3. How successful do you think the TRC was? How was it viewed by various South Africans? How else has the ANC sought to redress past wrongs?
4. How has the ANC consolidated its hold over the government, and what implications does this have for its alliances and democracy in South Africa?
5. What challenges do South Africans and the government face with crime and HIV/AIDS?

FURTHER READINGS

ANDREWS, P., and ELLEMAN, S. (editors), *The Post-Apartheid Constitutions* (Johannesburg, 2001). A useful legal analysis of the new constitutions and the implications they have for human rights and welfare for all South Africans.

The essays are concerned with the making of the new constitution and the various political traditions which were involved. They emphasize the very progressive role that ANC members played in the reworking of the state and the creation of an ethical government subject to real checks and balances.

BEINART, W., *Twentieth-Century South Africa* (Oxford, 2001). A very well-written text on the social and economic history of the country in the twentieth century. Beinart, who is the leading social historian of South Africa, has provided a wealth of information in a concise narrative. It is short on maps and illustrations, but remains essential reading.

DAVENPORT, T., *The Birth of a New South Africa/The Transfer of Power in South Africa.* (London, 1998). A helpful and insightful overview of the transition process with particular attention to the politics of compromise and the character of the politicians involved. Davenport has a keen eye for the implications the process has for future developments.

DE KLERK, F., *The Last Trek: a New Beginning* (Johannesburg, 1998). An autobiographical account of the transition by the last white president of South Africa. De Klerk remains unapologetic in this book, and even lashes out at the ANC from behind the cover of the pages, but it is still interesting reading.

JAMES, W., and LINDA VAN DE VIJVER, *After the TRC: Reflections on Truth and Reconciliation in South Africa* (Athens, Ohio, 2000). An important collection of essays about the TRC and the impact it has had on South Africa. It is perhaps too uncritical and many of the contributors were members of the TRC. Still, it is a useful account and it provides a wide range of views on the healing process.

LODGE, T., *South African Politics Since 1994* (Cape Town 1999). A brief summary of important recent events by one of the most insightful political commentators of the country. Lodge makes some interesting projections for the future, and he gives a fair assessment of ANC politics since it was elected.

MANDELA, N., *Long Walk to Freedom* (London, 1995) and *No Easy Walk to Freedom* (London, 1965). Two revised editions of the autobiographies of the former first black president of South Africa. Mandela's words are as insightful as they are moving. He provides a vivid picture of his whole life, with an emphasis on his political work and the struggle. These are essential reading.

MARAIS, H., *South Africa. Limits to Change. The Political Economy of Transition.* (New York, 2001). This revised edition of Marais' insightful work is essential for understanding the complexities and challenges of the new South Africa. It considers all the problems that the ANC government faces and suggests the historical roots for many.

REYNOLDS, A., *Election '99 South Africa.* (New York, 1999). A topical contemporary series of essays on the elections which saw the end of Mandela's reign and the arrival of Mbeki. It covers everything from provincial government to the various major parties in a concise and readable volume, and it suggests some important trends for the future elections.

SHELL, R., *HIV/AIDS: A Threat to the African Renaissance* (Johannesburg, 2000). An insightful, well-researched analysis of the problems of AIDS in South Africa and the challenges it poses for the government. It is highly critical of ANC policies for the AIDS epidemic.

VILLA-VICENCIO, C., and VERWOERD, W. (editors), *Looking Back, Reaching Forward. Reflections on the Truth and Reconciliation Commission of South Africa* (Cape Town, 2000). Another collection of fine essays, co-edited by a grandson of Hendrick Verwoerd, the so-called "architect of apartheid" who became an ANC member of parliament. It contains more openly critical essays on the TRC and the limits of the healing process. It provides fresh insights into the entire process and its implications for peace in the country.

Glossary

The following is a list of glossary terms that are standard and common in South African history and which are used frequently in the text, but are otherwise unique and therefore require some explanation.

African: These are defined for the purposes of this book as those people who were of the Khoesan, Nguni, and Sotho-Tswana language groups which are part of the continent-based Bantu language family as well as some others such as the Venda and Lemba languages as opposed to people of European and Asian descent.

Afrikaner: People of mixed ethnic descent, including Dutch-Boer and French who sought to define themselves as a unified group with a heritage based on a particular sense of social, religious, and economic practices including farming, Dutch Reformed Church Calvinism, and the Afrikaans language.

Azania: An Arabic term for the south eastern coastal parts of Africa. Black nationalists and the Black Consciousness Movement adopted this term for the country instead of "South Africa," but it was not used to rename the country after the 1994 election.

Boer: A farmer. A person of Dutch descent who farmed and herded in the interior. The term was later used in a derogatory way by the British, especially during the Anglo-Boer War.

Black: A term referring to those people perceived to be outside European or white society including Malay, Khoesan, and mixed race people. It was later used to collectively identify all those who were oppressed because of the color of their skin including Indians, "Coloureds" and Africans.

Chiefdom: A chiefdom is a political unit in many African societies. It consists of a number of clans which are subordinate to an established, dominant, chiefly clan and the leader or chief. Chiefdoms claim control over defined territories although these can be expanded by settlement or conquest. Clan members are related through kinship, real or fictive, and their basic social organization is based on family relations within homesteads. This contrasts with the chief who controls the political relations for all the clans.

Ciskei/Transkei: The Xhosa region of the Cape side of the Kei river, hence cis-near side- kei and trans -across- kei.

Commando: A term referring to the mounted cavalry of frontier whites and blacks who raided or skirmished against African and black societies in the interior. The tactic was later used to great effect by the Afrikaners during the Anglo-Boer War.

Compradores: A term denoting an indigenous people who cooperated and collaborated with colonizers. It has some negative connotations since these people have been perceived to be traitors to their societies. It is not used here in this sense but rather to capture the inventive strategies which some Khoe people used to take best advantage of the colonial context.

Induna: A term which initially refers to a military official in Shaka's amabutho regimental system, but later means an African official with either real or invented claims to legitimate authority who served in the segregated colonial administration of indirect rule.

Mfecane: A term with no definite origins which has been interpreted to mean variously the time of troubles, the crushing, those who crush others, wandering hordes, wars, the weak and famished Difaqane "wandering horde".

Peasant: A peasant is a producer of an agricultural commodity or food who has one foot in the capitalist market economy, and one foot in a customary, African or "traditional" economy.

Trekboer: An independent-minded frontier wandering farmer who sought access to open grazing land and trade in the interior, beyond the control of VOC or British colonial officials.

White: A term used to denote people who perceived themselves to be "white" and of exclusive European heritage.

Witwatersrand: The white waters ridge or rand. This refers to the area of gold-bearing ores along the "reef" near Johannesburg.

References

The following bibliographical list of books and materials is intended as a general guide for readers who want to pursue further reading on the broad range of historical and contemporary topics covered in the text. The list is intended to be a starting point of the best, most useful, and recent texts and Internet resources available. These resources also reflect some of the materials that were consulted in the preparation of the text.

Recommended General Texts

Beinart, W., *Twentieth-Century South Africa,* (Oxford, 2001).

Davenport, T. and Saunders, C., *South Africa: A Modern History*, Fifth Edition (New York, 2000).

Omer-Cooper, J., *History of Southern Africa*, Second Edition (Portsmouth, 1994).

Readers Digest Illustrated History of South Africa, C. Saunders, Ed., (London and New York, 1994).

Ross, R., *A Concise History of South Africa,* (Cambridge, 1999).

Shillington, K., *History of Southern Africa,* (Edinburgh, 1997).

Thompson, L., *A History of South Africa*, Third Edition (New Haven, 2001).

Wilson, M. and Thompson, L., *The Oxford History of South Africa*, Two Volumes (Oxford, 1969, 1971). Note that a new version of this work is due out in 2004.

Worden, N., *The Making of Modern South Africa,* (Oxford, 1994).

Recommended Further Reading

Acocks, J., *Veld Types of South Africa*, Second Edition (Cape Town, 1975).

Adam, H. and Giliomee, H., *Ethnic Power Mobilized,* (London, 1979).

Alden, C., *Apartheid's Last Stand. The Rise and Fall of the South African Security State,* (London, 1996).

Andrews, P. and Elleman, S., (Eds.). *The Post Apartheid Constitutions,* (Johannesburg, 2001).

Beinart, W., *Settlers, Livestock and the Cape Environment, c. 1770-1950,* (forthcoming).

Beinart, W., *The Political Economy of Pondoland,* (Cambridge, 1982).

Beinart, W. and Bundy, C., *Hidden Struggles in Rural South Africa: Politics and Popular Movements in the Transkei and Eastern Cape, 1890-1930,* (London, 1987).

Beinart, W., Delius, P., and Trapido, S., (Eds.), *Putting a Plough to the Ground: Accumulation and Dispossession in Rural South Africa,* (Johannesburg, 1986).

Beinart, W. and Dubow, S., (Eds.), *Segregation and Apartheid in Twentieth-Century South Africa,* (London, 1995).

Bonner, P., Delius, P., and Posel, D., (Eds), *Apartheid's Genesis,* (Johannesburg, 1993).

Boonzaier, E., Malherbe, C., Berens, P., and Smith, A., *The Cape Herders,* (Cape Town and Johannesburg, 1989).

Bradford, H., *A Taste of Freedom: The ICU in Rural South Africa, 1929–30,* (Johannesburg, 1987).

Bundy, C., *The Rise and Fall of the South African Peasantry,* (London, 1979).

Carton, B., *Blood From Your Children. The Colonial Origins of Generational Conflict in South Africa,* (Charlottesville and London, 2000).

Cell, J., *The Highest Stage of White Supremacy: The Origins of Segregation in South Africa and the American South,* (New Haven, 1982).

Cobbing, J., "The Mfecane as Alibi: Thoughts on Dithakong and Mbolompo", *Journal of African History,* 29, 1988.

Cope, R., *The Ploughshare of War. The Origins of the Anglo-Zulu War of 1879,* (Scottsville, 1999).

Crais, C., *White Supremacy and Black Resistance in Pre-Industrial South Africa: The Making of the Colonial Order in the Eastern Cape, 1770-1865* (Cambridge, 1992).

Crush, J., Jeeves, A., and Yudelman, D., *South Africa's Labour Empire: A History of Black Migrancy to the Gold Mines,* (Montreal, 1991).

Davenport, T., *The Birth of a New South Africa, The Transfer of Power in South Africa,* (London, 1998).

Deacon, J., *Human Beings in South Africa: The Secrets of the Stone Age,* (Cape Town, 1999).

De Klerk, F., *The Last Trek: A New Beginning,* (Johannesburg, 1998).

Delius, P., *The Land Belongs to Us. The Pedi Polity, the Boers and the British in the Nineteenth-Century Transvaal,* (London, 1984).

Dubow, S., *The African National Congress,* (Gloucester, 2000).

Dubow, S., *Racial Segregation and the Origins of Apartheid in South Africa, 1910-1936,* (London, 1989).

Duminy, A. and Guest, B., (Eds.), *Natal and Zululand. From Earliest Times to 1910,* (Pietermaritzburg, 1989).

Elphick, R., *KhoiKhoi and the Founding of White South Africa,* (Johannesburg, 1985).

Elphick, R. and Davenport, T., (Eds.), *Christianity in South Africa: A Political, Social and Cultural History* (Berkeley, 1997).

Elphick, R. and Giliomee, H., (Eds.), *The Shaping of South African Society, 1652-1840,* (Cape Town, 1989).

Eldredge, E., *A South African Kingdom. The Pursuit of Security in 19th-Century Lesotho,* (Cambridge, 1993).

Eldridge, E., and Morton, F., (Eds.), *Slavery in South Africa: Captive Labour on the Dutch Frontier,* (Pietermaritzburg, 1994).

Ellis, S. and Sechaba, T., *Comrades Against Apartheid: The ANC and the South African Communist Party in Exile,* (London, 1992).

Etherington, N., *The Great Treks. The Transformation of Southern Africa,* 1815-1854, (London, 2001).

Etherington, N., *Preachers, Peasants and Politics in Southeast Africa,* (London, 1978).

Gerhard, M. and Hamilton, G., *An Appetite for Power: Buthelezi's Inkatha and South Africa,* (Johannesburg, 1987).

Gerhart, G., *Black Power in South Africa: The Evolution of an Ideology,* (Berkeley, 1979).

Giliomee, H., *Afrikaner Political Thought* (Cape Town, 1983).

Guy, J., *The Destruction of the Zulu Kingdom. The Civil War in Zululand, 1879-1884,* (London, 1983).

Guy, J., "Gender Oppression in Southern Africa's Precapitalist Societies' in Walker, C., ed., *Women and Gender in Southern Africa to 1945,* (London, 1990).

Halisi, C., *Black Political Thought in the Making of South African Democracy,* (Bloomington, 2000).

Hall, M., *The Changing Past. Farmers, Kings and Traders. The People of Southern Africa, 200-1860,* (Chicago, 1990).

Hamilton, C., *Terrific Majesty, the Powers of Shaka Zulu and the Limits of Historical Invention,* (Cape Town, 1998).

Hamilton, C., *The Mfecane Aftermath. Reconstructive Debates in Southern African History,* (London, 1995).

Hammond-Tooke, W., *The Bantu-Speaking Peoples of Southern Africa,* (London, 1974).

Harries, P., *Work, Culture and Identity: Migrant Labourers in Mozambique and South Africa, c. 1860-1910,* (Portsmouth, 1994).

Inskeep, R., *The Peopling of Southern Africa,* (London, 1978).

James, W. and Van De Vijver., *After the TRC. Reflections on Truth and Reconciliation in South Africa,* (Athens, Ohio, 2000).

Jeeves, A., *Migrant Labour in South Africa's Mining Economy: The Struggle for the Gold Mines Labour Supply, 1890-1920,* (Kingston, 1985).

Karis, T. and Carter, G., *From Protest to Challenge: Documents of African Politics in South Africa, 1882-90,* five volumes, (Johannesburg and London, 1972–1997).

Keegan, T., *Colonial South Africa and the Origins of the Racial Order,* (Charlottesville, 1996).

Klein, R., (editor), *Southern African Prehistory and Paleoenvironments,* Balkema Press (Rotterdam, 1984).

Laband, J., *Rope of Sand: The Rise and Fall of the Zulu Kingdom in the 19th Century,* (Pietermaritzburg, 1996).

Lamar, H. and Thompson, L., *The Frontier in History: North America and Southern Africa Compared,* (New Haven, 1981).

Lodge, T., *South African Politics Since 1994,* (Cape Town, 1999).

Lodge, T., *Black Politics in South Africa Since 1945,* (Johannesburg, 1983).

Luthuli, A., *Let My People Go: An Autobiography,* (London, 1962).

Mandela, N., *Long Walk to Freedom,* (London, 1995).

Mandela, N., *No Easy Walk to Freedom,* (London, 1965).

Marais, H., *South Africa. Limits to Change. The Political Economy of Transition,* (New York, 2001).

Marks, S., *Reluctant Rebellion,* (London, 1970).

Marks, S., "Khoisan Resistance to the Dutch in the Seventeenth and Eighteenth Centuries," *Journal of African History,* Vol. 13, (1972).

Marks, S. and Atmore, A., (Eds.), *Economy and Society in Pre-Industrial South Africa,* (London, 1980).

Marks, S. and Rathbone, R., *Industrialization and Social Change in South Africa, 1870-1930,* (London, 1982).

Marks S. and Trapido, S., (Eds.), *The Politics of Race Class and Nationalism in Twentieth-Century South Africa,* (London, 1987).

Maylam, P., *A History of the African People of South Africa,* (Johannesburg, 1986).

Maylam, P., *Rhodes, the Tswana and the British,* (London, 1980).

Meer, F., *The South African Gandhi, 1893-1914,* Second edition, (Johannesburg, 1996).

Meli, F., *South Africa Belongs to Us: A History of the A.N.C.,* (London and Harare, 1988).

Moodie, T., *The Rise of Afrikanerdom: Power, Apartheid and the Afrikaner Civil Religion,* (Los Angeles, 1975).

Mostert, N., *Frontiers, the Epic of South Africa's Creation and the Tragedy of the Xhosa People,* (London, 1992).

Mzala, *Gatsha Buthelezi: Chief With a Double Agenda,* (London, 1988).

Nasson, W., *The South African War, 1899-1902,* (New York, 1999).

Nasson, W., *Abraham Esau's War: A Black South African War in the Cape, 1899-1902,* (Cape Town, 1991).

Newton-King, S., *Masters and Servants on the Cape Eastern Frontier, 1760-1803,* (Cambridge, 1999).

Odendaal, A., *Vukani Bantu! The Beginnings of Black Protest Politics in South Africa to 1912,* (London, 1984).

O'Meara, D., *Forty Lost Years: The Apartheid State and the Politics of the National Party, 1948-94,* (Randburg, 1996).

O'Meara, D., *Volkskapitalisme,* (Cambridge, 1983).

Omer-Cooper, J., *The Zulu Aftermath: A Nineteenth-Century Revolution in Bantu Africa,* (London, 1966).

Pachai, B., *A Documentary History of Indian South Africans,* (Johannesburg, 1985).

Pakenham, T., *The Boer War,* (London, 1979).

Peires, J., *The Dead Will Arise. Nongqawuse and the Great Xhosa Cattle-killing Movement of 1856-1857,* (Johannesburg, 1989).

Peires, J., *The House of Phalo. A History of the Xhosa People in the Days of Their Independence,* (Johannesburg, 1981).

Peires, J., (Ed.), *Before and After Shaka. Papers in Nguni History,* (Grahamstown, 1981).

Plaatje, S., *Boer War Diary,* Edited by J. Commaroff, (Chicago, 1973).

Reynolds, A., *Election '99 South Africa,* (New York, 1999).

Ross, R., *Beyond the Pale: Essays on the History of Colonial South Africa,* (Johannesburg, 1994).

Ross, R., *Cape of Torments: Slavery and Resistance in South Africa,* (London, 1983).

Ross, R., *Adam Kok's Griqua: A Study in the Development of Stratification in South Africa,* (Cambridge, 1976).

Rotberg, R., *The Founder: Cecil Rhodes and the Pursuit of Power,* (New York, 1988).

Sampson, A., *Mandela, The Authorized Biography,* (New York, 1999).

Schreuder, D., *The Scramble for Southern Africa, 1877-95,* (London, 1980).

Seekings, J., *The UDF: A History of the United Democratic Front in South Africa, 1983-1991,* (Cape Town, 2000).

Shell, R., *HIV/AIDS: A Threat to the African Renaissance,* (Johannesburg, 2000).

Shell, R., *Children of Bondage: A Social History of the Slave Society at the Cape of Good Hope, 1652-1838,* (Hanover, 1994).

Shillington, K., *The Colonization of the Southern Tswana,* (Johannesburg, 1985).

Swan, M., *Gandhi, The South African Experience,* (London, 1985).

Switzer, L., *Power and Resistance in an African Society. The Ciskei Xhosa and the Making of South Africa,* (London, 1993).

Thompson, L., *The Political Mythology of Apartheid,* (London, 1985).

van Kessel, I., *"Beyond Our Wildest Dreams," The United Democratic Front and the Transformation of South Africa,* (Charlottesville, 2000).

Villa-Vicencio, C. and Verwoerd, W., (Eds.), *Looking Back, Reaching Forward. Reflections on the Truth and Reconciliation Commission of South Africa,* (Cape Town, 2000).

Warwick, P., *Black People and the South African War, 1899-1902*, (Cambridge, 1983).

Webb, C., De B. and Wright, J., (Eds.), *The James Stuart Archive of Recorded Oral Evidence Relating to the History of the Zulu and Neighbouring Peoples*, Five Volumes, (Pietermaritzburg, 1976-2001).

Welsh, D., *The Roots of Segregation: Native Policy in Natal, 1845-1910*, (London, 1971).

Worden, N., *Slavery in Dutch South Africa*, (Cambridge, 1985).

Worden, N. and Crais, C. (Eds.), *Breaking the Chains: Slavery and Its Legacy in the Nineteenth-century Cape Colony*, (Johannesburg, 1994).

Worger, W., *South Africa's City of Diamonds: Mine Workers and Monopoly Capitalism in Kimberley, 1867-95*, (Johannesburg, 1987).

Web Sites

The following list of recommended Internet resources identifies sites which the author has reviewed and considers to be the best available for both general information on South African and its history. It also includes sites of general interest on South Africa, as well as sites for contemporary South African political and cultural issues.

General Gateway Portals:

Africa, general gateway site: *http://africafocus.library.wisc.edu/.* Has a search engine and links for the "sights and sounds of Africa"

African Studies Center University of Pennsylvania: *http://www.sas.upenn.edu/African_Studies/AS.html.* This is a good, scholarly site with many links and resources.

An A-Z of African Studies on the Internet, by Peter Limb at Michigan State University: *http://www.lib.msu.edu/limb/a-z/az.html.* This is an excellent gateway to a vast range of sites listed by country and topic.

Columbia University's gateway: *http://www.columbia.edu/cu/lweb/indiv/africa/cuvl/.* Another excellent site for the whole continent of Africa.

Mail and Guardian newspaper online: *http://www.mg.co.za/default.asp.* The leading source for a critical analysis of South African events with an excellent online archive.

NGO Information Site: *http://www.africapulse.org/.* Has a very good search engine and links to various nongovernmental organizations.

Sagonet: *http://www.sn.apc.org/.* A directory of web sites for a range of organizations in and related to South Africa.

South African Government Site for Links to Various Government Ministries, Policy Documents and Bills: *http://www.polity.org.za/.*

South African politics site from Dr. Alison Drew of York University: *http://www-users.york.ac.uk/~ad15/SApolitics-contents.* A good gateway to all the political parties.

Stanford University African Studies: *http://www-sul.stanford.edu/depts/ssrg/africa/guide.html.* An excellent gateway for African studies.

York University's gateway: *http://www-users.york.ac.uk/~ad15/SAInternetResources.htm.* An excellent gateway site to contemporary and historical web sites.

Sites by Topic:

African National Congress Web site: *http://wwwanc.org.za/index.*

African-American Historical Linkages with South Africa: *http://www.founders.howard.edu/reference/bob_edgar_site/.*

AIDS Information for South Africa: *http://www.safaids.org.zw/safaidsweb/* and
  http://www.apc/sahivaids/.
Center for the study of Violence and Reconciliation: *http://www.csvr.org.za/.*
Cape Flats Community Web site: *http://www.faranani.org.za/capeflats/.*
Congress of South African Trade Unions (COSATU): *http://cosatu.org.za/.*
District Six Museum: *http://www.districtsix.co.za/.*
Inkatha Freedom Party: *http://www.ifp.org.za/.*
Language ethnographic maps of South Africa: *http://www.ethnologue.com/*
  country_index.asp.
Pan African Congress: *http://paca.org.za/.*
Photographs of Resistance in South Africa: *http://www.axisgallery.com/*
  exhibitions/photo/index.html.
Robben Island Museum: *http://www.robben-island.org.za/home.php.*
South African Communist Party site: *http://www.sacp.org.za/.*
South African Council of Churchs: *http://sacc.org.za/.*
South African Review of Books: *http://www.uni-ulm.de/~rturrell/.*
South African History Online: *http://sahistory.org.za/.*
South African Museums gateway site: *http://www.museums.org.za/.*
South African National Archives: *http://www.national.archives.gov.za/.*
South Africa, A Social History and Cape Town, Iziko, Museums of Cape
  Town: *http://www.museums.org.za/iziko/social.htm.*
The Truth and Reconciliation Commission site and report: *http://www.doj*
  .gov.za/trc/index.html.
University of Cape Town poetry: *http://web.uct.ac.za/projects/poetry/poetry.htm.*
University of Natal Digital Imaging Project: *http://disa.nu.ac.za/.* Has a range
  of excellent photographs.
University Natal Campbell Library: *http://khozi2.nu.ac.za/.*
University of the Witwatersrand Historical Papers Collection: *http://sunsite*
  .wits.ac.za/histp/.
University of the Witwatersrand History Archives: *http://sunsite.wits.ac*
  .za/saha/.
U.S. Library of Congress Country Report for South Africa: *http://lcweb2*
  .loc.gov/frd/cs/zatoc.html.

INDEX

313

The Making of South Africa

CULTURE AND POLITICS

ARAN S. MACKINNON

The Making of South Africa: Culture and Politics synthesizes the author's insights with the latest scholarship on South African history in a highly readable and comprehensive text, ideal as the foundation for undergraduate and graduate courses on South African and African history. The book features detailed maps, photographs, and teaching supplements such as questions for students to consider, and an annotated list of recommended readings for each chapter. It also provides an up-to-date list of reviewed Internet sites that students and faculty can explore. The book covers South African history from the earliest foundations of human communities, through the era of segregation and apartheid to the most recent developments in post-apartheid politics and the HIV/AIDS crisis.

Praise for *The Making of South Africa*

"Aran MacKinnon has achieved a major work of synthesis. *The Making of South Africa* succeeds in drawing upon a wide variety of sources and perspectives to provide a deeply textured narrative that nicely balances economic, cultural, and political issues. Clearly written and engaging, this text will provide students with an excellent introduction to the history and historiography of this important African state. Further, Africanists who specialize in other regions of the continent, as well as historians of other world regions, will find it a valuable resource."

—*Jonathan Reynolds, Northern Kentucky University*

"The format and organization of the book are quite good and all of the major topics are covered thoroughly. *The Making of South Africa* will help American students better understand this important country."

—*Anthony Q. Cheeseboro, Southern Illinois University*

About the Author

Aran S. MacKinnon is associate professor of history at the University of West Georgia. He has lived and researched in South Africa and the United Kingdom, and has been published in the *Journal of Southern African Studies, Radical History Review,* and *The Canadian Journal of African Studies,* as well as in various edited collections on South African history.

Prentice Hall's new **Research Navigator**™ helps students make the most of their research time. From finding the right articles and journals, to citing sources, drafting and writing effective papers, and completing research assignments, **Research Navigator**™ simplifies and streamlines the entire research process. **Research Navigator**™ is free when packaged with any Prentice Hall textbook. Contact your sales representative for details, or take a tour at www.researchnavigator.com

StudentAid.ed.gov
FUNDING YOUR FUTURE.

PEARSON
Prentice Hall

Upper Saddle River, NJ 07458
www.prenhall.com

ISBN 0-13-040681-3

9 780130 406811

90000